Sinclair

PELICAN BOOKS   *1973*

GREEK LITERATURE IN TRANSLATION

Michael Grant has been successively Chancellor's medallist and
Fellow of Trinity College, Cambridge, Professor of Humanity
at Edinburgh University, first Vice-Chancellor of Khartoum
University, and President and Vice-Chancellor of the Queen's
University of Belfast. He has also been President of the Virgil
Society. He has also translated Cicero's *Selected Works*, *Selected
Political Speeches* and his philosophical essays (*On the Good Life*),
as well as Tacitus' *The Annals of Imperial Rome*, for the Penguin
Classics; his other books include *The World of Rome* (1960),
Myths of the Greeks and Romans (1962), *The Civilizations of
Europe* (1965), *Gladiators* (1967), *Roman Literature* (the last two
available in Pelicans), *The Climax of Rome* (1968), *The Ancient
Mediterranean*, *Julius Caesar* (both 1969), *The Ancient Historians*,
The Roman Forum and *Nero* (1970), *Cities of Vesuvius*, *Herod
the Great* and *Roman Myths* (1971).

He has also compiled a Pelican anthology of Latin literature
in translation, *Roman Readings* (revised edition 1967), of which
the present book thus constitutes a sister volume.

GREEK LITERATURE
IN TRANSLATION

*Translations from Greek Prose
and Poetry*

*Chosen by
Michael Grant*

PENGUIN BOOKS

Penguin Books Ltd, Harmondsworth, Middlesex, England
Penguin Books Inc., 7110 Ambassador Road, Baltimore, Maryland 21207, U.S.A.
Penguin Books Australia Ltd, Ringwood, Victoria, Australia

—

First published 1973
Copyright © Michael Grant Publications Ltd, 1973

—

Made and printed in Great Britain by
Cox & Wyman Ltd, London, Reading and Fakenham
Set in Monotype Bembo

CONTENTS

CONTENTS

INTRODUCTION

'WHAT should they know of England who only England know?'[1]
Or America? Or our whole modern civilization? If we want to see
ourselves in perspective, to understand our predicaments and possibilities, we must be able to make comparisons with some other
society altogether, preferably of quite a different time and place.
Only then shall we be armed with sufficient detachment to grapple
with our own problems and with the demands our own world makes
upon us.

The ancient Greeks are ideal targets for such comparisons; and
there is the additional advantage that what they wrote is thoroughly
entertaining. It is a dreadful thought that an enormous proportion
of their literature has vanished. Only forty-five plays have survived
out of thousands, only six epics out of scores. But the accidents of
survival have not been entirely accidental after all, for so much that
has come down to us is excellent. Indeed, even this small proportion
of all that was written adds up to the greatest quantity of varied
excellence that any literature in the world has ever produced.

These writings by the Greeks have a peculiarly large contribution
to offer to this second half of the twentieth century A.D. The inter-
vention of two and a half millennia has done nothing to hinder the
effectiveness of that contribution. Indeed, readers of Greek literature
have a lot in common with the Quechua Indians of Bolivia, who
speak of the past not as behind them but ahead of them, since it can
be grasped with the intelligence and consequently stands before their
eyes.[2] Similarly, the interval that has elapsed since the days of ancient
Greece strengthens rather than weakens the impact its writers make
upon our own minds.

For one thing, it is always pleasant to be encouraged and stimulated
and heartened. And that is above all what one gets from the Greeks.
True, facile optimism is not what they provide. On the contrary,

1. Rudyard Kipling, 'The English Flag', *Barrack-Room Ballads*, Methuen,
London, 1892.

2. E. A. Nida, *On Translation*, edited by R. A. Brower, Oxford University
Press, New York (Galaxy edition, 1966), p. 12.

the message is that nothing will come right unless the appropriate laborious steps are taken to make sure that it does. But from a great deal of Greek literature (though not all) floods forth the additional message that these steps *can* be taken. Human beings are capable of taking them. And, above all, Greeks were capable of taking them, and knew it. Certainly they were as liable to failures and faults as the next man, for Hellenic perfection was a noble but anxious ideal, never approaching realization. But the Greeks exceeded other people in the conviction that man or woman *can* be great enough to rise to any occasion and deal with any situation splendidly and successfully.

> Many marvels walk through the world,
> Terrible, wonderful,
> But none more than humanity.

And Sophocles adds, in this hymn to the potentialities of mankind, another and exceedingly Greek point: that the exclusive power and quality of the human race, which makes it superior to animals, is language and speech.

> The breath of his life
> He has taught to be language,
> The spirit of thought.[1]

This emphasis is just, for the Greeks were uniquely articulate: overwhelmingly so, it seemed to less quick-witted foreigners visiting Athens. Yet it was also this gift which led their words, first spoken and then both spoken and written, to the very heart of a subject, and did it justice with incomparable precision, candid courage and a relentless desire for the truth.

In this respect their literature is unique. It is also unique, as far as the western world is concerned, because it came first. The Greeks, it is true, borrowed and adapted ancient Near Eastern civilizations. But when they embarked on literature they were doing something new. Practically all its different species that later Europe has known were their inventions; and to trace the connecting threads that link them with medieval and modern times is one of the most enlightening of experiences. But if this historical aspect were all we had to consider,

1. Sophocles, *Antigone*, lines 332ff., translated by R. E. Braun, *Arion*, I, 3, 1963, p. 19; see also below, p. 135.

there would be nothing, apart from mere curiosity, to prevent us from accepting this literary legacy and forgetting who left it to us, just as we can also forget, for example, that we owe the Greeks the political institutions that are visible in Europe (western and eastern) and America today, democratic and autocratic alike. However, such an attitude would entirely leave out of account the direct, immediate, contemporary appeal that Greek literature still exercises in the 1970s. Even if we choose to pay no attention whatever to the historian's testimony that every intermediate century has borne witness to our overwhelming debt to Greece, even if we wish to regard history as making only a minimal contribution to our own daily preoccupations, it will still be a very strange thing if we can remain completely unaffected by the utterances and attitudes of these extraordinarily perceptive, talented men produced by ancient Greece. Some of the ancient Greeks, obviously, were shattering bores. But an astonishing number were not. Why such an extraordinarily high proportion of non-bores emerged at one and the same time and place – the fifth century B.C., which forms the hub of Greek literature and history – is a fascinating problem that I have discussed elsewhere.[1] The salient fact for our purpose is that they did emerge. And the aim of this book is to communicate part of what they had to say.

Obviously one single volume can only give a small selection from what has come down to us. But even so I hope it can catch them in some characteristic and entertaining and enlightening moments. Given the wealth of the material, it would be a poor book indeed if it could not. It presents the Greeks in English. A translation inevitably loses something of the original; the whole question is to decide what losses one ought to cut. I have tried to choose the versions that lose least – while slipping in occasionally one that loses a lot, but includes a stroke of genius all the same. I have also included just a few pieces which are hardly close enough to the originals to be described as translations; I have labelled these imitations or adaptations. Never have these problems of translation been more widely discussed than they are today. Never have the advantages and disadvantages of this and that method of dealing with them been so vigorously and actively

1. Michael Grant, *The Ancient Mediterranean*, Weidenfeld & Nicolson, London: Scribners, New York, 1969, pp. 315ff.

canvassed and disputed. We might almost be back in the days of the Elizabethans – translators are so powerfully aware of the job they have to do. For as in that time, though to meet another set of circumstances, people have once again become inspired with the same longing: the passion to transcend the boundaries set by their own language. And, once again, this has led not to any special proficiency in other tongues, but to the desire to convert what has been written in other tongues, ancient and modern, into their own.

This has meant that there are new waves of translators, some of them probably as good, or almost as good, as any there have ever been. The first wave consists of people who are now in their fifties and sixties. The second wave is formed of translators in their twenties and thirties. And they have their own vigorous contributions to make to what is now recognized as a distinct, worthy art.

So far, translations from Greek literature have played a vigorous part in this boom. But that happy situation will probably not last. Indeed it is almost certain not to last, because the next generation – and every generation has to have its own translators – will not be able to find enough people with a sufficiently good knowledge of Greek to do the job really well. Plans for getting Greekless writers to undertake it, with the few surviving Hellenists to advise them – the practice sometimes followed in attempting Chinese and Japanese translations – cannot produce the same good results.[1]

But meanwhile, there are translations; and they give out a breath of fresh and not un-Greek air. In 1922 a Mr Alfred R. Orage expressed the opinion that the period for perfect translation had not yet come, but that he expected it in about 1970.[2] Perfect, of course, was not the right word, because the very most that one can hope for is near-perfection, comparable to the approach of an infinite decimal number to infinity.[3] However, Mr Orage was not too far wrong. True, the translations of the Elizabethan age helped to found a whole culture and to form the English language, and those are tasks that

1. *Delos* (National Translation Center, Austin, Texas), II, 1968, pp. 29ff., gives the answers to an inquiry on this subject circulated to translators (question 9).

2. Alfred R. Orage, *Readers and Writers*, New York, 1922, pp. 48ff.

3. cf. J. Urzidil in *Life and Letters Today*, XLV, 1945, pp. 22f.

cannot be done a second time. But what modern translators can do once again, and are doing, is to relate their work and their art to the living literary interests and central cultural activities of the epoch to which they belong. That is what has been so lacking in recent generations; translation has not been in the swim, has not been the sort of thing that the best critics talk and bandy about when formulations of taste are at stake. But now translation is taking its place as an integral part of the literary scene once more.

In this book I have included excerpts from a number of writers who are making themselves responsible for this admirable development today. I have also included the work of earlier, sometimes much earlier, epochs, partly because it is good and partly because it is also valuable to look at the ancient originals from more than one point of view. Sir Philip Sidney (1554–86) managed to claim that translators 'were almost as good in reputation as the Mountibanks of Venice'. But when Jacques Amyot had translated Plutarch (1559), the grateful French king François I (let modern governments note) presented him with an abbey. After all, as Goethe declared in 1827 – and he was neither the first nor the last person to utter this truth – translation 'remains one of the most important and worthiest concerns in the totality of world affairs'.[1]

Where so many translations, old and new, exist – there are more than fifty of Aeschylus' *Agamemnon* alone – no one will agree completely with the selection that I have made here. I have left out two or three well-known translations that I might have wanted to include, because the copyright fees requested by their publishers seemed to me exorbitant. But otherwise I hope the choice is not too totally unrepresentative; or at least that it offers a symbolical picture both of the ancient originals and of the great diversity of translators.

For the reasons I indicated in *Roman Readings*,[2] I have taken the view that poetry can only be translated by poetry; though controversy on this subject still rages, it seems to me that the translator who attempts prose is starting off with too great a handicap altogether. But I should not wish people to think that poetry is the only part of

1. *Goethe-Briefe*, Berlin, 1902–5: letter to Thomas Carlyle, 20 July 1827.
2. *Roman Readings*, chosen by Michael Grant, Penguin Books, Harmondsworth, 1967, p. viii; cf. B. Raffel, *Delos*, v, 1970, pp. 50, 60.

literature that sets the translator lively problems, theoretical and practical alike. For the problems that beset the translators of Greek and Latin prose are also both severe and absorbing, though far less widely recognized and discussed.[1] Most of the prose translations in the present volume are taken from the Penguin Classics. This series has been recently criticized on the grounds that some of its contributors tend to iron out roughnesses and abruptnesses in the interests of an even equability that had not always been noticeable in the originals.[2] Personally I believe that this criticism is largely misplaced, since if you are writing something in modern English you have got to make it readable. I do not apologize for using this controversial term, because, failing readability, a version ceases to be English in any useful sense of the word. Certainly ancient roughnesses and abruptnesses have to be rendered by some means or other. But this can only be done by the employment of *other* devices for heightening the emotions, not by comparable verbal abruptnesses in English, since attempts in 1972 to be Carlylean or Tacitean merely mean that one is ceasing to write in a (readable) form of the English language. However, these are matters for argument;[3] and the more argument that arises about how translators ought to proceed, the better it will be.

I am very grateful to Mr Dieter Pevsner of Penguin Books Ltd for his help and encouragement with this volume, to Miss Fiona Mee and Miss Alexandra MacCormick for carrying out the complicated arrangements involved, and to Mr Peter Ford for preparing the book for the press. I also want to thank Mr Michael Haslam, Mr Peter Jay, Mr John Oates, Professor Sir Denys Page, the Right Reverend Bishop William Philbin and Mr Ian Scott-Kilvert for their assistance and advice, and my wife for help of very many kinds.

Gattaiola   MICHAEL GRANT
1972

1. cf. Cicero, *Selected Works*, translated by Michael Grant, Penguin Books (Penguin Classics), Harmondsworth, 1969, p. 22.
2. e.g. G. Morgan in *Arion*, VII, 3, 1969, pp. 474ff.
3. cf. *Ariel* (University of Calgary), II, 1971, pp. 7ff.

EDITORIAL NOTE

In rendering Greek names, I have not generally attempted uniformity of spelling. It seems right that translators should be allowed to choose their own.

M.G.

PART I

HOMER AND HESIOD

HOMER

Chios, Smyrna and other cities of the eastern Aegean claimed to be the birthplace of Homer, the author of the *Iliad* and *Odyssey* – if they were not the work of different men, as has often been argued (and contradicted). These epic poems, which, in more or less their final form, were written down before 700 B.C., brought a long oral tradition to its climax. All subsequent Greek literature, culture and education depended upon them.

*

THE ILIAD

KING PRIAM OF TROY APPEALS TO ACHILLES FOR THE BODY OF HIS SON HECTOR

'Achilles, fear the gods,
Pity an old man like thy sire – different in only this,
That I am wretcheder, and bear that weight of miseries
That never man did, my curst lips enforced to kiss that hand
That slew my children.' This moved tears; his father's
    name did stand
(Mentioned by Priam) in much help to his compassion,
And moved Aeacides[1] so much he could not look upon
The weeping father. With his hand, he gently put away
His grave face; calm remission now did mutually display
His power in either's heaviness. Old Priam, to record
His son's death and his deathsman see, his tears and
    bosom poured
Before Achilles. At his feet he laid his revered head.
Achilles' thoughts now with his sire, now with his friend, were fed.
Betwixt both sorrow filled the tent. But now Aeacides

1. i.e. Achilles, the grandson of Aeacus.

(Satiate at all parts with the ruth of their calamities)
Start up, and up he raised the king. His milk-white head
    and beard
With pity he beheld, and said: 'Poor man, thy mind is scared
With much affliction. How durst thy person thus alone
Venture on his sight that hath slain so many a
    worthy son,
And so dear to thee? Thy old heart is made of iron. Sit
And settle we our woes, though huge, for nothing profits it.
Cold mourning wastes but our lives' heats. The gods have
    destinate
That wretched mortals must live sad. Tis the immortal
    state
Of Deity that lives secure . . .

GEORGE CHAPMAN (1616)

THE SPLENDOUR OF ACHILLES

The Hero rose;

Her aegis[1] Pallas o'er his shoulders throws;
Around his brows a golden cloud she spread;
A stream of glory flamed above his head.
As when from some beleaguered town arise
The smokes high-curling to the shaded skies
(seen from some island, o'er the main afar,
When men distressed hang out the sign of war),
Soon as the Sun in ocean hides his rays,
Thick on the hills the flaming beacons ablaze;
With long-projected beams the seas are bright,
And heaven's high arch reflects the ruddy light;
So from Achilles' head the splendours rise,
Reflecting blaze on blaze against the skies.
Forth marched the chief, and, distant from the crowd,

1. The *aegis* was a goatskin worn by Pallas Athene, later shown in art with a border of snakes and a head of the Gorgon Medusa in the centre.

High on the rampart raised his voice aloud;
With her own shout Minerva[1] swells the sound;
Troy starts astonished, and the shores rebound.
As the loud trumpet's brazen mouth from far
With shrilling clangor sounds the alarm of war,
Struck from the walls, the echoes float on high,
And the round bulwarks and thick towers reply:
So high his brazen voice the Hero reared:
Hosts dropped their arms, and trembled as they heard;
And back the chariots roll, and coursers bound,
And steeds and men lie mingled on the ground.
Aghast they see the living lightnings play,
And turn their eyeballs from the flashing ray.
Thrice from the trench his dreadful voice he raised;
And thrice they fled, confounded and amazed.

ALEXANDER POPE (1715)

THE SHIELD FASHIONED FOR ACHILLES BY THE GOD HEPHAESTUS

Then first he formed the immense and solid shield;
Rich various artifice emblazed the field;
Its utmost verge a threefold circle bound;
A silver chain suspends the massy round;
Five ample plates the broad expanse compose,
And godlike labours on the surface rose.
There shone the image of the master-mind:
There earth, there heaven, there ocean he designed;
The unwearied sun, the moon completely round;
The starry lights that heaven's high convex crowned;
The Pleiads, Hyads, with the northern team;
And great Orion's more refulgent beam;
To which, around the axle of the sky,
The Bear, revolving, points his golden eye,
Still shines exalted on the ethereal plain,

1. Pallas Athene.

Nor bathes his blazing forehead in the main.
   Two cities radiant on the shield appear,
The image one of peace, and one of war.
Here sacred pomp and genial feast delight,
And solemn dance and hymeneal rite;
Along the street the new-made brides are led,
With torches flaming, to the nuptial bed:
The youthful dancers in a circle bound
To the soft flute and cithern's silver sound:
Through the fair streets the matrons in a row
Stand in their porches, and enjoy the show ...
Another part (a prospect differing far)
Glowed with refulgent arms, and horrid war.
Two mighty hosts a leaguered town embrace,
And one would pillage, one would burn, the place.
Meantime the townsmen, armed with silent care,
A secret ambush on the foe prepare:
Their wives, their children, and the watchful band
Of trembling parents, on the turrets stand.
They march, by Pallas and by Mars[1] made bold;
Gold were the gods, their radiant garments gold,
And gold their armour; these the squadron led,
August, divine, superior by the head! ...
Next, ripe in yellow gold, a vineyard shines,
Bent with the ponderous harvest of its vines;
A deeper dye the dangling clusters show,
And, curled on silver props, in order glow:
A darker metal, mixed, intrenched the place;
And pales of glittering tin the enclosure grace.
To this, one pathway gently winding leads,
Where march a train with baskets on their heads,
(Fair maids and blooming youths) that smiling bear
The purple product of the autumnal year.
To these a youth awakes the warbling strings,
Whose tender lay the fate of Linus[2] sings;

1. Ares.
2. A mythical figure whose death was lamented; also the name of the dirge itself.

In measured dance behind him move the train,
Tune soft the voice, and answer to the strain.

Here, herds of oxen march, erect and bold,
Rear high their horns, and seem to low in gold,
And speed to meadows on whose sounding shores
A rapid torrent through the rushes roars:
Four golden herdsmen as their guardians stand,
And nine sour dogs complete the rustic band.
Two lions rushing from the wood appeared;
And seized a bull, the master of the herd;
He roared: in vain the dogs, the men, withstood;
They tore his flesh, and drank the sable blood.
The dogs (oft cheered in vain) desert the prey,
Dread the grim terrors, and at distance bay.

Next this, the eye the art of Vulcan[1] leads
Deep through fair forests, and a length of meads,
And stalls, and folds, and scattered cots between;
And fleecy flocks, that whiten all the scene.

A figured dance succeeds: such once was seen
In lofty Gnossus, for the Cretan queen,[2]
Formed by Daedalean art; a comely band
Of youths and maidens, bounding hand in hand;
The maids in soft cymars of linen dressed;
The youths all graceful in the glossy vest;
Of those the locks with flowery wreaths inrolled,
Of these the sides adorned with swords of gold,
That, glittering gay, from silver belts depend.
Now all at once they rise, at once descend,
With well-taught feet: now shape, in oblique ways,
Confusedly regular, the moving maze:
Now forth at once, too swift for sight, they spring,
And undistinguished blend the flying ring:
So whirls a wheel, in giddy circle tossed,
And, rapid as it runs, the single spokes are lost.
The gazing multitudes admire around;
Two active tumblers in the centre bound;

1. Hephaestus.   2. Ariadne.

Now high, now low, their pliant limbs they bend:
And general songs the sprightly revel end.
  Thus the broad shield complete the artist crowned
With his last hand, and poured the ocean round:
In living silver seemed the waves to roll,
And beat the buckler's verge, and bound the whole.

ALEXANDER POPE (1715)

HEPHAESTUS (VULCAN) SERVES THE GODS WITH WINE

He said, and to her hands the goblet heaved
Which, with a smile, the white-armed Queen[1] received.
Then to the rest he filled; and in his turn
Each to his lips applied the nectared urn.
Vulcan with awkward grace his office plies
And unextinguished laughter shakes the skies.
  Thus the blest gods the genial day prolong,
In feasts ambrosial, and celestial song.
Apollo tuned the lyre; the Muses round
With voice alternate aid the silver sound.
Meantime the radiant Sun, to mortal sight
Descending swift, rolled down the rapid light.
Then to their starry domes the gods depart,
The shining monuments of Vulcan's art:
Jove on his couch reclined his awful head
And Juno slumbered on the golden bed.

ALEXANDER POPE (1715)

1. Hera (Juno).

ANTENOR TELLS THE TROJANS ABOUT MENELAUS AND ODYSSEUS

Then answer thus Antenor sage returned:
'Princess thou hast described him: hither once
The noble Ithacan,[1] on thy behalf
Embassador with Menelaus, came,
And at my board I entertained them both.
The person and the intellect of each
I noted; and remarked, that when they stood
Surrounded by the Senators of Troy,
Atrides[2] by the shoulders overtopped
The prince of Ithaca; but when they sat,
Ulysses had the more majestic air.
In his address to our assembled chiefs,
Sweet to the ear, but brief, was the harangue
Of Menelaus, neither loosely vague,
Nor wordy, though he were the younger man.
But when Ulysses rose, his downcast eyes
He riveted so fast, his sceptre held
So still, as if a stranger to its use,
That had'st thou seen him, thou had'st thought him, sure,
Some chafed and angry idiot, passion-fixt.
Yet, when at length, the clear and mellow bass
Of his deep voice brake forth, and he let fall
His chosen words like flakes of feathered snow,
None then might match Ulysses; leisure, then,
Found none, to wonder at his noble form.'

WILLIAM COWPER (1791)

1. Odysseus (Ulysses).   2. Menelaus, the son of Atreus.

THE GREEK AND TROJAN ARMIES

As when the billow gathers fast
   With slow and sullen roar
Beneath the keen north-western blast
   Against the sounding shore:
First far at sea it rears its crest,
   Then bursts upon the beach,
Or with proud arch and swelling breast,
   Where headlands outward reach,
It smites their strength, and bellowing flings
Its silver from afar;
So, stern and thick the Danaän[1] kings
   And soldiers marched to war.
Each leader gave his men the word,
Each warrior deep in silence heard;
So mute they marched, thou could'st not ken
They were a mass of speaking men;
And as they strode, in martial might,
Their flickering arms shot back the light.

But, as at even the folded sheep
   Of some rich master stand,
Ten thousand thick their place they keep,
   And bide the milkman's hand,
And more and more they bleat, the more
   They hear their lamblings cry;
So from the Trojan host, uproar
   And din rose loud and high.
They were a many-voiced throng;
   Discordant accents there,
That sound from many a differing tongue,
   Their differing race declare.
These, Mars had kindled for the fight;
Those, starry-eyed Athene's might,

1. Greek.

And savage Terror, and Affright,
And Strife, insatiate of wars,
The sister and the mate of Mars;
Strife that, a pigmy at her birth,
   By gathering rumour fed,
Soon plants her feet upon the earth
   And in the heaven her head.

W. E. GLADSTONE (1861)

THE TROJAN CAMP-FIRES

And these all night upon the bridge of war
Sat glorying; many a fire before them blazed:
As when in heaven the stars about the moon
Look beautiful, when all the winds are laid,
And every height comes out, and jutting peak
And valley, and the immeasurable heavens
Break open to their highest, and all the stars
Shine, and the shepherd gladdens in his heart:
So many a fire between the ships and stream
Of Xanthus blazed before the towers of Troy,
A thousand on the plain; and close by each
Sat fifty in the blaze of burning fire;
And eating hoary grain and pulse the steeds,
Fixt by their cars, waited the golden dawn.

ALFRED TENNYSON (1863)

ODYSSEUS DEALS WITH THERSITES AT THE ASSEMBLY OF WARRIORS

Then when he saw, or heard uplift his voice,
One of the people: with his sceptre he
Would thrust at him, and shout that he might hear.

31

'Sirrah! sit down, and stir not, but obey
Thy betters. Helpless and unwarlike thou,
Of none account in council or in strife.
We may not, look you, all be monarchs here.
The multitude of rulers bodes but ill.
Be one our lord, our king; to whom the son
Of wily Cronos[1] gave it: sceptre gave
And sovereignty, that he should reign o'er us.'

Ev'n thus he dealt his mandates through the hosts;
And councilward they rushed from tent and ship.
The noise was as the noise of boisterous seas,
That break on some broad beach, and ocean howls.

So all sate down, and halted each in his place.
Still one – Thersites of ungoverned tongue –
Brawled on. Much store had he of scurrilous words,
Idle and scurrilous words, to hurl at kings:
Aught that he deemed the Greeks would hear and laugh.
To Troy's gates none had come so base as he.
Bow-legged he was, and halted on one foot:
His shoulders, hunched, encroached upon his chest;
And bore a peaked head – scant hairs grew thereon.
Achilles and Odysseus most he loathed;
At them railed aye: but Agamemnon now
He taunted in shrill treble. All the Greeks
Were angered sore, and vexed within their soul.
At Agamemnon did he rail and cry.

'What lack'st thou? Why complainest, Atreus' son?
With brass thy tents abound: and in them wait
Many and peerless maidens; whom we Greeks,
Whene'er we take a town, choose first for thee.
Ask'st thou yet gold; which one mayhap shall bring –
A tamer of the steed – from Ilion,[2]

1. Zeus   2. Troy.

To buy his son? whom peradventure I,
Or some Greek else hath bound and made his prize?
Or yet a damsel to ascend thy bed,
Kept for thine own self? Nay, unkingly 'tis
To bring this mischief on Achaia's sons.
Oh cowards! oh base and mean – not men, but maids!
Home fare we with our ships: and leave him here,
To gorge him with his honours – here in Troy:
And see if we will fight for him or no.
For him, who scorned one better far than he;
For his hand took, he hath, Achilles' gift.
Yet naught Achilles frets, good easy man.
Else, son of Atreus, thou hadst bragged thy last.'

So chode Thersites him who led the host.
But straightway was Odysseus at his side,
And, scowling, with hard words encountered him.

'Thou word-entangler! Clear thy voice and shrill:
Yet think not singly to contend with kings.
I say no mortal, out of all that came
With Atreus' sons to Troy, is base as thou.
Wherefore thou should'st not lift thy voice and roar
And rail at kings, thy watchword still "Return."
We know not yet the end: whether for weal
Or woe we shall return, we sons of Greece.'

C. S. CALVERLEY (1866)

THE GREEKS BEFORE THE WALLS OF TROY

As on the mountain peaks destroying flame
Fires a great forest; far is seen the glare:–
From off the glorious steel the full-orbed light
Went skyward on through ether as they marched.

And even as great hosts of wingèd birds,

Storks, cranes, or long-necked swans, flit here and there
In Asian meadow round Caÿster's stream[1]
On jubilant wing: and, making van-ward each,
Scream, that the whole mead rings: – so poured their hosts
From tent and ship into Scamander's plain.
Earth underfoot rang fiercely, to the tramp
Of warriors and of horses. There they stood
Upon Scamander's richly-blossomed plain,
Innumerable, as flowers and leaves in spring.

And as great hosts of swarming flies that flit
In springtime, when the milk is in the cans,
About the herdsman's hut: so numerous stood
Before Troy's ranks the Greeks upon the plain,
And thirsted to destroy them utterly.

And as the goatherds sunder easily
Broad droves, as one flock feeding: even so
Their captains marshalled each his company
For war; amidst them Atreus' royal son,
In eye and front like Zeus, Ares in bulk,
In chest Poseidon. As among the herd
The bull ranks noblest, o'er the gathered kine
Pre-eminent: such glory in that hour
Gave Zeus to Agamemnon, to be first
And chiefest among hosts of mighty men.

C. S. CALVERLEY (1866)

HECTOR AND HIS SON ASTYANAX

'But may I be dead and the piled earth hide me
    under before I
hear you crying and know by this that they drag
    you captive.'

1. A river of western Asia Minor (the Küçük Menderes).

34

So speaking glorious Hector held out his
    arms to his baby,
who shrank back to his fair-girdled nurse's
    bosom
screaming, and frightened at the aspect of his own
    father,
terrified as he saw the bronze and the crest with
    its horsehair,
nodding dreadfully, as he thought, from the peak
    of the helmet.
Then his beloved father laughed out, and his
    honoured mother,
and at once glorious Hector lifted from his head
    the helmet,
and laid it in all its shining upon the ground. Then
    taking
up his dear son he tossed him about in his arms, and
    kissed him,
and lifted his voice in prayer to Zeus and the other
    immortals:
'Zeus, and you other immortals, grant that this boy,
    who is my son,
may be as I am, pre-eminent among the
    Trojans,
great in strength, as am I, and rule strongly over
    Ilion;
and some day let them say of him: "He is better by
    far than his father,"
as he comes in from the fighting; and let him kill
    his enemy
and bring home the blooded spoils, and delight the
    heart of his mother.'

RICHMOND LATTIMORE (1951)

THE PROPHET CALCHAS HAS ORDERED
AGAMEMNON TO HAND THE GIRL CHRYSEIS
BACK TO HER FATHER

... So saying, Calchas sat down, and after him the noble
Son of Atreus rose, wide-ruling Agamemnon,
Choked black with rage, his eyes glinting like points of fire.
First he turned to Calchas, face eloquent with hatred:
'You long-faced quack, have you ever prophesied good?
Doom's your delight, disaster your stock-in-trade –
Never a cheerful omen declared, much less fulfilled!
And now you stand up here with your miserable cantrips
And swear this plague from Apollo is all *my* doing –
Because I turned down rich ransom, and kept the girl Chryseis!
Why shouldn't I? I want her. I'd rather have her than my wife,
Yes, rather than Clytemnestra. She's better all round –
Prettier, nicer figure, more sense, and a damned sight handier
About the house. Still, even so I'm willing
To hand her back, if the public good demands it.
I have a responsibility for my men, I can't stand by
And see Achaeans slaughtered. But if I release the girl,
You'll have to find me another prize to replace her. How
Would it look if I was the only Argive[1] chief among you
Without a share in the booty? Think of it this way,
All of you: it means that I kiss my prize good-bye.'
   Then Achilles, the godlike, the swift of foot, replied:
'Most noble Agamemnon, high prince of covetousness,
How shall we, the Achaean warriors, find you a prize?
We are no tradesmen with a hoard of public funds;
Whatever we took when we sacked those towns has already
Been shared out. We cannot decently beg it
Back from its owners now. But if you are willing
To surrender this girl to the god, then we Achaeans
Will pay you back triple, no, fourfold, if Zeus grants us

---

1. Used generally in Homer to refer to the Greek army. Argos was a dependency of Agamemnon's Mycenae.

To storm the giant walls and citadel of Troy.'
  Then the lord Agamemnon answered him in these words:
'Fine soldier you may be, Achilles, and like a god,
But don't try your tricks on me. It's a waste of time.
You'll neither outwit nor persuade me. What are you after?
It's all right for you to say, "Give up the girl"
While your own prize is in no danger. Am I to agree to that?
No, I say. Either you get me a prize of equal value
To the one I'm losing, something well to my taste,
Or else, if you refuse, I shall help myself
To one of yours – your own, perhaps, Achilles, or yours,
Odysseus, or, Ajax, yours. We shall see how well you react
In the same position. But this can wait till later.
Our first concern is to fit out a ship, and take
Chryseis home. That means collecting a crew, to begin with,
And freighting cattle aboard for sacrifice, and choosing
A captain. One of our senior princes, naturally –
Ajax, Idomeneus, perhaps our good friend Odysseus,
Or even yourself, Achilles, with your unrivalled
Military reputation – to offer up sacrifices
And appease the Sky-Archer.'[1]

PETER GREEN (1961)

THE GODDESS HERA AT HER DRESSING-TABLE

So off she went to the private room her son Hephaistos had built
  her
With a properly fitting door and a secret bolt,
And once inside, with the door shut safely behind her,
First with suave ambrosia washed off the slightest stain
From her brilliant skin; then richly sweetened herself
With a swift and vividly scented oil of Olympos.
If that oil were shaken in the bronze dominion of Zeus
An erotic odour would be rained over Heaven and Earth.

1. Apollo.

37

She fondled this into her flesh and then softly combed
And plaited the intense fall of hair with her hands.
Then gently drew on a glinting dress that Athene
Had carefully designed for her, hatched with a hundred patterns,
And pinned it across her breasts with a golden clasp,
Rounding her waist with a belt flaring out in a hundred tassels.
She hung ear-rings with three clustering drops
Like mulberry berries in the pierced
Lobes of her ears, and O, how liquidly they glistened!
Then lastly the goddess secreted herself in a slender
Fresh veil that smiled as sweetly as sunlight
And bound finical sandals round her dazzling feet,
And all this finished, her finery fluent about her,
Left the boudoir, and beckoned her step-daughter, Aphrodite,
Apart from the other gods, and Hera said this to her . . .

IAN FLETCHER (1961)

PATROCLUS BEGS ACHILLES TO LEAVE HIS TENT AND FIGHT[1]

While they fought around the ship from Thessaly,
    Patroclus came crying to the Greek . . .

   'Why tears, Patroclus?' Achilles said.
'Why hang around my ankles like a child
Pestering mother, wanting to be picked up,
Expecting her to stop what she is doing, and,
In the end, getting its way through snivels?
   You have bad news from home?
Is someone dead, Patroclus? Your father? Mine?
But news like that is never confidential.
If it was true, you, me, and all the Myrmidons
Would cry together.

     1. This is an adaptation rather than a translation.

It's the Greeks, Patroclus, isn't it?
You weep because some Greeks are beaten dead beside their
    ships!
But did you weep when those same Greeks condoned my wrongs?
If I remember rightly you said nothing ... Yes?'

    And Patroclus:
'Save your hate, Achilles. It will keep.
Our cause is sick enough without your grudging it my tears.
You know Odysseus and Diomede are wounded?
Eurypylus, too – his thigh – and even Agamemnon.
And you still ask "*Why tears?*" Ach,
    Is there no end to your obdurate grudge?
No. Don't shrug me off. Remember who is asking.
Not Agamemnon. Not the smart Ithacan. No one save me –
And God forbid I share the niceness of a man who,
When his friends go down, sits tight
And claims their punishment as just amends
For the wrongs they did him.
    They are dying, Achilles. Dying like flies.
If you can't think of them, think for a moment
Of those who will come after them, what they will say:
"*Achilles The Grudgebearer*" – can't you hear it? – or,
"*Achilles The Strong*" – and just as well for that,
Because his sense of wrong was heavy – or,
"*Some people say Lord Peleus and Thetis,*
Lovely among the loveliest of women,
Were his folk. But if you want the truth,
His mother was a long bleak rock
That after centuries was moved
By the even bleaker, always disconsolate
Pestering of the Sea, until she had a son,
Achilles."
    Why make me talk to you this way?'

CHRISTOPHER LOGUE (1962)

THE DUEL BETWEEN ACHILLES AND HECTOR[1]

So saying, he poised his long-shadowing spear and hurled it,
But shining Hector, looking straight at him, escaped,
For he saw it coming and crouched, so that the bronze point
Flew over his head and embedded itself in the earth.
But Pallas Athena snatched it up, without
Hector's knowledge, and gave it back to Achilles. And Hector,
His people's commander, spoke thus to the great son of Peleus:
'You missed, O godlike Achilles. It seems that Zeus
Has not yet informed you concerning the day of my doom,
Though surely you thought that he had. You thought by your
        glibness
And cunning of speech to fill me with terror of you
And completely deprive me of courage and strength. But you'll not
Plant your spear in my back as I flee, but as I
Charge down straight upon you, drive it clean through my chest
If God has granted you that. Look out now and avoid,
If you can, my keen-cutting bronze. Here's hoping you take
The whole shaft into your hard flesh! Surely this war
Would be lighter for Trojans, if you, their greatest scourge,
Were dead.'
      Then poising his shade-making spear, he cast,
Nor did he miss, but struck full upon the shield
Of Achilles, from which a long way it rebounded, enraging
Hector, since his swift shaft had flown from his hand
In vain. And now, since he had no second ash spear,
He stood in deep consternation, then shouted to him
Of the dazzling white shield, Deïphobus, asking a long spear
Of him. But he was nowhere around, and Hector,
Aware now of just what had happened, spoke thus:
     'So be it.
Surely the gods have summoned me deathward. For I
Thought sure that the hero Deïphobus stood right behind me,
Whereas he is safe on the other side of the wall,
And Athena has tricked me. Now evil death is at hand

1. cf. above, p. 23.

For me, not far off at all, nor is there any
Way out. Such, I believe, has always been
Zeus's pleasure, and that of his far-shooting son Apollo,
Who have in the past been willing and eager to help me.
Now, though, my doom is surely upon me. But let me
Not die without a huge effort, nor let me dishonourably
Die, but in the brave doing of some great deed
Let me go, that men yet to be may hear of what happened.'
     So saying, he drew the keen blade that hung by his side,
A sword both heavy and long. Then bracing himself
He charged at Achilles, plunging upon him like some
Huge high-flying eagle that dives through dark clouds to seize
On the plain a tender lamb or cowering hare.
Even so, Hector plunged, his sharp sword held high. And Achilles,
Seething with savage wrath, met the advance
With one of his own, protecting his chest with his intricate,
Exquisite shield and tossing his head, so that all
The gold plumes that Hephaestus had thickly set in the crest
Of that four-horned helmet shook with a gorgeous glitter.
And from the bronze point of the spear that Achilles balanced
In his right hand there went forth a gleam like that
Which glints amid stars in the blackness of night from Hesperus,
Fairest of all the stars set in wide heaven.
Hefting that powerful spear, he scanned the form
Of his foe to find the spot where a spear was most likely
To pierce the firm flesh of Hector. He saw that his armour
Of bronze covered him all the way, the beautiful
Gear he had stripped from mighty Patroclus when he
Cut him down. But there where the collarbones separate neck
And shoulders, there at his throat, most fatal of targets,
Appeared a spot unprotected by bronze. So there,
As on him he charged, great Achilles drove in his spear,
And the point went through his soft neck and stuck out behind.
Even so, the ashen shaft, heavy with cleaving bronze,
Failed to sever the windpipe. Hence Hector could still say words
And answer his foe. Dying, he sprawled in the dust,
And shining Achilles exulted above him, vaunting

'Hector, I dare say you thought while stripping Patroclus
That you would be safe, nor did you have one thought of me,
Since I was not there and since you are a very great fool!
Behind at the hollow ships that man had a helper,
One mightier far than himself to avenge him – me,
The man who unstrung those knees of yours. Now dogs
And birds will ravin on your shredded corpse, defiling
You utterly. Meanwhile, Achaeans shall hold for Patroclus
A high and fitting funeral.'

      Then Hector, his bronze helmet
Gleaming, his small strength rapidly draining, answered:
'I beg you, Achilles, by your own knees and parents
And life, do not allow me thus to be eaten
By dogs at the ships of Achaeans. Instead, accept
What you want of our plentiful bronze and gold, a ransom
My father and queenly mother will gladly give you,
If only you'll give back my body, that Trojans and wives
Of Trojans may give me my due of funeral fire.'

      Then blackly scowling at him, fast-footed Achilles
Replied: 'Do not beg me by knees or by parents,
You dog! I only wish I were savagely wrathful
Enough to hack up your corpse and eat it raw –
In view of what you have done – but no man alive
Shall keep the dogs from your head, not even if here
They should bring and weigh out a ransom ten or twenty times
What you are worth and promise still more, not even
If Priam, descended of Dardanus, should tell them to pay
Your weight in gold – not even then should your
Queenly mother lay you on a bed and mourn you, the son
Whom she herself bore, but dogs and birds shall devour you,
Bones and all!'

      Then noble bright-helmeted Hector,
Rapidly dying, replied: 'I know you, Achilles,
All too well, and clearly forsee what you'll do,
Nor was there a chance of my changing your mind. The heart
In your breast is solid iron. But think what you're doing,
Or one day I may bring the gods' wrath on you, when Paris

And Phoebus Apollo destroy you there, great valour
And all, at the Scaean Gates.'
      As thus he spoke,
The final moment arrived, and his soul flew forth
From his body and quickly journeyed to Hades, bewailing
Her lot as one too soon bereft of youth
And manly vigour. And now to the corpse of his foe,
God-gifted Achilles spoke thus:
      'Die – and as
For my own fate, I'll accept that whenever Zeus wills
To fulfil it, Zeus and the other immortal gods.'
      He spoke, and drawing the bronze from Hector's throat,
He laid it aside and started to strip from his shoulders
The armour, sticky with blood. And the other sons
Of Achaeans ran up all around and gazed at the wondrously
Handsome body of Hector, nor did a man
Approach him without inflicting a wound in his flesh,
And many a one, with a glance at his neighbour, would say:
      'Aha! fierce Hector is not even nearly so hard
To handle now as when he hurled blazing fire
On the ships!'
      So saying, a man would step in and stab
Hector's body.

ENNIS REES (1963)

THE GREEKS RETREAT TO THE SHIPS

See now the two Greeks stumbling on with Patroclus
out from the fight, towards the shelter of the ships,
with the war pulsing about them wild as a fire
that leaps up unannounced in a busy city
and fastens blazing on houses which melt away
in ruinous flames, to the howling of the wind –
so, back they went, under a burden of clamour
raised by the clash of men and horses without break.

See them like mules exerting all their strength to draw
downhill some log or some great plank for a shipyard,
tugging it by a crazy track, till strain and sweat
have almost burst their hearts – so they went stumbling on.
Behind them the Ajaxes[1] held the enemy
as a wooded hogback of land bristling across
the open country will stem a flood, checking spates
of ruinous rivers, forcing them to turn back
down along the flatlands – impotently foaming
at that firm barrier. The Trojans still attacked,
the Ajaxes still defended the rear, but now
against two men who made the task hard: Aeneas
Anchises' son, Hector the dazzling. Imagine
a cloud of starlings or jackdaws clattering up
and crying out in panic at sight of a cruising hawk,
the sign of death to birds like them – so Greek with Greek
fled from Aeneas and Hector crying in fear,
careless of the fight. And the trench was littered round
with good Greek armour as they fled.

EDWIN MORGAN (1968)

1. Ajax the son of Telamon, king of Salamis, and Ajax the son of Oïleus, king of Locris.

THE ODYSSEY

ODYSSEUS SLAYS THE SUITORS OF HIS WIFE PENELOPE

Then, girding up his rags, Ulysses[1] sprang
With bow and full-charged quiver to the door;
Loose on the broad stone at his feet he poured
His arrows, and the suitors thus bespake.
   'This prize, though difficult, hath been achieved.
Now for another mark which never man
Struck yet, but I will strike it if I may,
And if Apollo make that glory mine.'
   He said, and at Antinous aimed direct
A bitter shaft; he, purposing to drink,
Both hands advanced towards the golden cup
Twin-eared, nor aught suspected death so nigh.
For who, at the full banquet, could suspect
That any single guest, however brave,
Should plan his death, and execute the blow!
Yet him Ulysses with an arrow pierced
Full in the throat, and through his neck behind
Started the glittering point. Aslant he drooped;
Down fell the goblet, through his nostrils flew
The spouted blood, and spurning with his foot
The board, he spread his viands in the dust.
Confusion, when they saw Antinous fallen,
Seized all the suitors; from the thrones they sprang,
Flew every way, and on all sides explored
The palace-walls, but neither sturdy lance
As erst, nor buckler could they there discern.
Then, furious, to Ulysses thus they spake.
   'Thy arrow, stranger, was ill-aimed; a man
Is no just mark. Thou never shalt dispute
Prize more. Inevitable death is thine.

1. Odysseus.

For thou hast slain a prince noblest of all
In Ithaca, and shalt be vultures' food.'
   Various their judgements were, but none believed
That he had slain him wittingly, nor saw
The infatuate men fate hovering o'er them all.
Then thus Ulysses, louring dark, replied.
   'O dogs! not fearing aught my safe return
From Ilium,[1] ye have shorn my substance close,
Lain with my women forcibly, and sought,
While yet I lived, to make my consort yours,
Heedless of the inhabitants of heaven
Alike, and of the just revenge of man.
But death is on the wing; death for you all.'
   He said; their cheeks all faded at the sound,
And each with sharpened eyes searched every nook
For an escape from his impending doom.

WILLIAM COWPER (1791)

ODYSSEUS ESCAPES FROM THE BLINDED POLYPHEMUS UNDER THE BELLY OF A RAM

But when the Mother of Morning, Rose-fingered Day-Dawn, shone,
Then all the rams of the cattle fared out to the field to begone,
While the ewes unmilked and bleating about the folds must go,
For their udders were swollen to bursting. But their King, all worn
    with woe,
With his hand was ever groping the backs of all the sheep
As they stood up there before him; but the fool no heed did keep
How under the breasts of the fleecy-fair sheep were bound the men.
But the last of the flock, the ram, came forth from the door of the den,
With his plenteous wool encumbered, and with me and my wily
    thought:
So to him spake the stark Polyphemus, as a hold of him he caught:
  'Dear ram, why then I prithee of the flock art thou the last

1. Troy.

46

To come forth from the den? aforetime ne'er left behind thou wast,
But first of all to be cropping the tender flower of the grass,
Still striding big; and foremost to the river wouldst thou pass.
And, first of all wert thou yearning in the eventide to hie
To the fold: but now art thou latest. Is it so that thou mournest the
    eye
Of thy Master, which he the losel[1] a while ago did blind
With his miserable fellows, when with wine he had vanquished my
    mind?
That No-man, who, I swear it, hath not yet 'scaped his bane.
Oh, if but as me thou wert minded, and a voice of speech mightest
    gain
To tell me where in the wide-world the man my might doth shun,
Then here and there o'er the rock-den his blood and brains should run
As against the ground I dashed him, and some solace should I have
For all the heap of evil which the nought-worth No-man gave.'

So saying, away without doors the ram from his hand he sent,
And a little way from the rock-den and the garth thereof we went;
And then first from the ram I loosed me, and my fellows presently.

WILLIAM MORRIS (1887)

THE SHIPWRECKED ODYSSEUS APPEARS BEFORE
NAUSICAA

    When the time had come
To go home, Nausicaa was about to yoke the mules
And fold the fine clothes, but bright-eyed Athena had plans
Of her own. She wanted Odysseus to wake up and see
The lovely girl, who soon would be his guide
Into the Phaeacian city.[2] So when next the Princess
Tossed the ball to one of her ladies, she threw it
Wide of her mark and into a deep swirl of the river.
At this they all gave a loud shriek, and the noble Odysseus

1. Scoundrel.
2. The Phaeacians were the people of Scheria, of which Alcinous,
Nausicaa's father, was the mythical ruler.

Awoke, sat up, and began to think things out:
    'O misery! among what manner of mortals can I
Be now? Are they cruel, unjust, and completely uncivilized,
Or god-fearing, hospitable men? Just now I thought
I heard the sound of maiden voices, the cry
Of nymphs, perhaps, ladies who haunt the high hills,
The springs where rivers rise, and the grassy fields.
Or can it be that I'm really close to men
With speech like mine? I'll go and see for myself.'
    So saying, the good Odysseus crept out from beneath
The bushes and with his great hand reached into the thicket
And broke off a leafy branch to hide his nakedness.
Then on he went like a bold lion of the mountains
Who goes through wind and rain with his eyes of fire
In search of cattle, sheep, or wild deer, and when
His belly bids him right into the close-barred fold
To attack the flocks therein. Even such was the need
Of Odysseus as he went in his nakedness to approach that party
Of girls with hair so beautifully braided. And to them
He appeared very terrible indeed, all encrusted with brine
As he was, and they scurried in all directions mid the jutting
Banks of sand. Only Alcinous' daughter
Remained. Made brave by Athena, who took the fear
From her limbs, she stood and faced him, while Odysseus tried
To decide whether he should embrace the lovely girl's knees
And so make his plea, or stay where he was and softly
Beseech her to give him some clothes and show him the city.
Thus pondering, he decided to stay where he was and speak softly
To her, since she might take offence at his embracing
Her knees. So without more delay he spoke these shrewd
And gentle words:
    'I implore you, O Queen – but are you
Goddess or woman? If you are a goddess, one
Of those who rule the wide sky, then surely in grace
Of face and figure you're most like Artemis, the daughter
Of almighty Zeus. But if you're a mortal, one
Of those who live here on earth, thrice-blessed are your father

48

And fortunate mother, and thrice-blessed your brothers are too.
I can well imagine the wonderful warmth and joy
You give them as they watch so lovely a flower taking part
In the dance. But happiest of all will be that man
Who wins you with the gifts of a wooer and takes you home
As his wife. For never before have I seen such a mortal
As you, whether man or woman. I gaze, completely
Astounded. Once indeed in Delos I saw something like you,
A lovely young palm shooting up by Apollo's altar –
In Delos, where I had gone with an army on a journey
Very rich in misfortunes for me – even so, when I saw
That tree, I marvelled long in my heart, for never
Has there been such another curving up from the earth. As I look
At you now I feel that same amazement, an awe
That keeps me from clasping your knees, though terrible
                     are the things
That have happened to me. Just yesterday I came out
Of the wine-dark sea after nineteen days of high wind
And waves that bore me from the island Ogygia. Now
Divine power has marooned me here to suffer I know not
What, for surely the gods have plenty of evils
In store for me yet. Have pity, O Queen, for you
Are the first to whom I have come after all my suffering
And toil, nor do I know any of the others who own
This land and this city. Give me some rag to put on –
An old wrapper from the laundry will do – and show me the city.
And as for yourself, may the gods grant all the desires
Of your heart – a husband and home and a wonderful oneness
Between you, for nothing is better or greater than a home
Where man and wife are living harmoniously together,
The envy of evil minds, but a very great joy
To men of good will, and greatest of all to themselves.'

   Then the white-armed maiden replied: 'Stranger,
     since it seems
That you're neither evil nor stupid, this misery of yours
Must be the will of Olympian Zeus himself,
Who gives happy fortune to men, whether good or bad,

To each as he sees fit. So you must, of course,
Endure it. But now that you've come to this land and city
Of ours, you shall not want for clothes or anything
Else that a wayworn castaway needs for his comfort.
I'll show you the city and tell you who we are.
This is the country and city of the Phaeacians,
And I am the daughter of great-hearted Alcinous, upon whom
The people depend for all the strength they have.'

   She spoke, and called to her ladies with the beautiful braids:
'Hold on! my friends. Since when do you run at the sight
Of a man? Surely you didn't think he would harm us.
That man doesn't live, nor shall he ever, who could come
Bearing malice to this land of Phaeacia, since the immortal gods
Love us too much for that. And besides, we live
Far out in the billowing sea, the remotest of men,
And no other mortals have any designs on us.
But this is some unlucky wanderer, and we must take care
Of him, for all strangers and beggars are surely from Zeus,
And a kindness that we think small is not so to them.
So come, my ladies, find food and drink for our guest
And bathe him in the river in a spot that's sheltered
     from the wind.'

ENNIS REES (1960)

ODYSSEUS BUILDS A RAFT AND LEAVES CALYPSO'S MAGIC ISLAND OGYGIA

So he spoke, and the sun went down and the darkness came over.
These two, withdrawn in the inner recess of the hollowed cavern,
enjoyed themselves in love and stayed all night by each other.
But when the young Dawn showed again with her rosy fingers,
Odysseus wrapped himself in an outer cloak and a tunic,
while she, the nymph, mantled herself in a gleaming white robe
fine-woven and delightful, and around her waist she fastened
a handsome belt of gold, and on her head was a wimple.
She set about planning the journey for great-hearted Odysseus.

She gave him a great axe that was fitted to his palms and headed
with bronze, with a double edge each way, and fitted inside it
a very beautiful handle of olive wood, well hafted;
then she gave him a well-finished adze, and led the way onward
to the far end of the island where there were trees, tall grown,
alder and black poplar and fir that towered to the heaven,
but all gone dry long ago and dead, so they would float lightly.
But when she had shown him where the tall trees grew, Kalypso,
shining among divinities, went back to her own house
while he turned to cutting his timbers and quickly had his work
    finished.
He threw down twenty in all, and trimmed them well with his
    bronze axe,
and planed them expertly, and trued them straight to a chalkline.
Kalypso, the shining goddess, at that time came back, bringing him
an auger, and he bored through them all and pinned them together
with dowels, and then with cords he lashed his raft together.
And as great as is the bottom of a broad cargo-carrying
ship, when a man well skilled in carpentry fashions it, such was
the size of the broad raft made for himself by Odysseus.
Next, setting up the deck boards and fitting them to close uprights
he worked them on, and closed in the ends with sweeping gunwales.
Then he fashioned the mast, with an upper deck fitted to it,
and made in addition a steering oar by which to direct her,
and fenced her in down the whole length with wattles of osier
to keep the water out, and expended much timber upon this.
Next Kalypso, the shining goddess, brought out the sail cloth
to make the sails with, and he carefully worked these also,
and attached the straps and halyards and sheets all in place aboard her,
and then with levers worked her down to the bright salt water.
    It was the fourth day and all his work was finished. Then on
the fifth day shining Kalypso saw him off from the island
when she had bathed him and put fragrant clothing upon him,
and the goddess put two skins aboard, one filled with dark wine
and the other, the big one, filled with water, and put on provisions,
in a bag, and stored there many good things to keep a man's
    strength up,

and sent a following wind to carry him, warm and easy.
Glorious Odysseus, happy with the wind, spread sails
and taking his seat artfully with the steering oar he held her
on her course, nor did sleep ever descend on his eyelids
as he kept his eye on the Pleiades and late-setting Boötes,
and the Bear, to whom men give also the name of the Wagon,
who turns about in a fixed place and looks at Orion,
and she alone is never plunged in the wash of the Ocean.
For so Kalypso, bright among goddesses, had told him
to make his way over the sea, keeping the Bear on his left hand.
Seventeen days he sailed, making his way over the water,
and on the eighteenth day there showed the shadowy mountains
of the Phaiakian land where it stood out nearest to him,
and it looked like a shield lying on the misty face of the water.

RICHMOND LATTIMORE (1965)

CIRCE'S ISLAND OF AEAEA

'In the forest glen they came on the house of Circe. It was
in an open place, and put together from stones, well polished,
and all about it there were lions, and wolves of the mountains,
whom the goddess had given evil drugs and enchanted,
and these made no attack on the men, but came up thronging
about them, waving their long tails and fawning, in the way
that dogs go fawning about their master, when he comes home
from dining out, for he always brings back something to please
    them;
so these wolves with great strong claws and lions came fawning
on my men, but they were afraid when they saw the terrible big
    beasts.
They stood there in the forecourt of the goddess with the glorious
hair, and heard Circe inside singing in a sweet voice
as she went up and down a great design on a loom, immortal
such as goddesses have, delicate and lovely and glorious
their work. Now Polites leader of men, who was
the best and dearest to me of my friends, began the discussion:

"Friends, someone inside going up and down a great piece
of weaving is singing sweetly, and the whole place murmurs to the
    echo
of it, whether she is woman or goddess. Come, let us call her."
  'So he spoke to them, and the rest gave voice, and called her,
and at once she opened the shining doors, and came out, and
    invited
them in, and all in their innocence entered; only
Eurylochos waited outside, for he suspected treachery.
She brought them inside and seated them on chairs and benches,
and mixed them a potion, with barley and cheese and pale honey
added to Pramneian wine, but put into the mixture
malignant drugs, to make them forgetful of their own country.
When she had given them this and they had drunk it down, next
    thing
she struck them with her wand and drove them into her pig pens,
and they took on the look of pigs, with the heads and voices
and bristles of pigs, but the minds within them stayed as they had
    been
before. So crying they went in, and before them Circe
threw down acorns for them to eat, and ilex and cornel
buds, such food as pigs who sleep on the ground always feed on.'

RICHMOND LATTIMORE (1965)

HESIOD

HESIOD was the son of a man who came from Cyme (Nemrutköy) in Aeolis, on the western coast of Asia Minor, and settled at Ascra in Boeotia. The poet lived *c.* 700 B.C. and wrote at least two epics: the *Theogony* and the *Works and Days* – if they are by the same man.

*

WORKS AND DAYS

PRUDENT ADVICE

Drink deep when the winejar's opened, or when 'tis running low;
In the middle, spare. Too late, when the dregs begin to show.
What to thy friend thou owest, pay it him full and fair.
When thy own brother borrows, smile – but have witness there.
By trust alike and *dis*trust has many a man sped ill.
Let no hip-wagging woman cajole thee to her will
(When 'tis thy barn she covets) with her flattering, fond deceit;
Who puts his trust in woman, trusts himself to a cheat!
Thou art wise if thou begettest but one son to sustain
Thy father's house – then the plenty within its walls shall gain.
And a second son thou mayest leave, if thou die old.
Nay, for still more, if He will, can God find wealth untold.

F. L. LUCAS (1951)

WINTER

But beware the month of Lenaion,[1] ill days of bitter frost,
Days that would flay an ox, when the wide seas are tossed
By Boreas,[2] blowing hard from the horse-pastures of Thrace,
And land and woodland bellow, as he wrenches from their place,
Amid the glens of the mountains, many an oak high-crowned,

1. Late January and early February.   2. The north wind.

Many a stalwart fir, and flings them to the ground,
Till the multitudinous forest shouts with a single cry.
Shivering under their bellies the tails of the wild beasts lie,
For all the fur that warms them – through the shaggiest breast it goes,
Through the hide of the ox himself that icy tempest blows,
And through the goat's lank hair – the fleece of the sheep alone
With its thick wool can baffle that blast from the northward blown.
It sets an old man running; and yet it cannot come
To the tender maiden sitting by her mother's side at home,
Of the golden Aphrodite as yet all unaware.
Ay, warm in an inner chamber – soft limbs new-bathed, and fair
With olive oil – she lays her down and slumbers sweet
Through the winter days, when No-bones must sit and gnaw his feet
Alone in his fireless house, and the depths of his dismal den;
For never forth to pasture the low sun lights him then . . .

But pass thou by the smithy and the warm seat in the sun,
In winter, when for the cold no work in the fields is done,
(E'en then a stirring fellow can still increase his store);
For fear the bleak December[1] bring misery to thy door
And thou press, with a vagrant's hand grown thin, a foot grown fat
    and sore.

F. L. LUCAS (1951)

STRIFE

It was never true that there was only one kind
    of strife. There have always
been two on earth. There is one
    you could like when you understand her.
The other is hateful. The two Strifes
    have separate natures.
There is one Strife who builds up evil war,
    and slaughter.

1. Hesiod says 'winter'.

She is harsh; no man loves her, but under compulsion
and by will of the immortals men
   promote this rough Strife.
But the other one was born
   the elder daughter of black Night.
The son of Kronos,[1] who sits on high and
   dwells in the bright air,
set her in the roots of the earth and among men;
   she is far kinder.
She pushes the shiftless man to work,
   for all his laziness.
A man looks at his neighbour, who is rich:
   then he too
wants work; for the rich man presses on with
   his ploughing and planting
and the ordering of his state.
   So the neighbour envies the neighbour
who presses on toward wealth. Such Strife
   is a good friend to mortals.

RICHMOND LATTIMORE (1959)

HESIOD TELLS HIS BROTHER TO WORK HARD

I mean you well, Perses, you great idiot,
   and I will tell you.
Look, badness is easy to have, you can take it
   by handfuls
without effort. The road that way is smooth
   and starts here beside you.
But between us and virtue the immortals have put
   what will make us
sweat. The road to virtue is long
   and goes steep up hill,
hard climbing at first, but the last of it,
   when you get to the summit
(if you get there) is easy going after the hard part.

1. Zeus.

That man is all-best who himself works out
   every problem
and solves it, seeing what will be best late
   and in the end.
That man, too, is admirable who follows one
   who speaks well.
He who cannot see the truth for himself, nor,
   hearing it from others,
store it away in his mind, that man
   is utterly useless.
As for you, remember what I keep telling you
   over and over:
work, O Perses, illustrious-born, work on,
   so that Famine
will avoid you, and august and garlanded Demeter[1]
will be your friend, and fill your barn
   with substance of living;
Famine is the unworking man's most constant
   companion.
Gods and men alike resent that man who, without work
himself, lives the life of the stingless drones,
who without working eat away the substance
   of the honeybees'
hard work; your desire, then, should be
   to put your works in order
so that your barns may be stocked with all
   livelihood in its season.
It is from work that men grow rich and own flocks
   and herds;
by work, too, they become much better friends
   of the immortals.

RICHMOND LATTIMORE (1959)

1. The goddess of the grain and of fertility.

THE THEOGONY

THE CREATION OF WOMAN

So Zeus, who knows imperishable counsels,
  spoke in his anger,
and ever remembering this deception
  thereafter, he would not
give the force of weariless fire
  to the ash-tree people,
not to people who inhabit the earth
  and are mortal,
no, but the strong son of Iapetos[1]
  outwitted him
and stole the far-seen glory
  of weariless fire, hiding it
in the hollow fennel stalk;
  this bit deep into the feeling
of Zeus who thunders on high,
  and it galled the heart inside him
when he saw the far-seen glory of fire
  among mortal people,
and next, for the price of the fire,
  he made an evil thing for mankind.
For the renowned smith of the strong arms[2]
  took earth, and moulded it,
through Zeus's plans, into the likeness
  of a modest young girl,
and the goddess grey-eyed Athene
  dressed her and decked her
in silverish clothing, and over her head
  she held, with her hands,
an intricately wrought veil in place,
  a wonder to look at,
and over this on her head

1. Prometheus.   2. Hephaestus.

she placed a wreath of gold, one
that the very renowned smith
  of the strong arms had fashioned
working it out with his hands,
  as a favour to Zeus the father.
On this had been done much intricate work,
  a wonder to look at:
wild animals, such as the mainland
  and the sea also produce
in numbers, and he put many on,
  the imitations of living
things, that have voices, wonderful,
  and it flashed in its beauty.

    But when, to replace good,
  he had made this beautiful evil
thing, he led her out
  where the rest of the gods and mortals
were, in the pride and glory
  that the grey-eyed daughter of a great
father had given; wonder
  seized both immortals and mortals
as they gazed on this sheer deception,
  more than mortals can deal with.
For from her originates the breed
  of female women,
and they live with mortal men,
  and are a great sorrow to them,
and hateful poverty they will not share,
  but only luxury.
As when, inside the overarching hives,
  the honeybees
feed their drones (and these are accomplished
  in doing no good,
while the bees, all day long
  until the sun goes down
do their daily hard work
  and set the white combs in order,

and the drones, spending their time
    inside the hollow skeps,
garner the hard work of others
    into their own bellies),
so Zeus of the high thunder established women,
    for mortal
men an evil thing,
    and they are accomplished in bringing
hard labours.

RICHMOND LATTIMORE (1959)

THE DESTRUCTION OF THE TITANS BY ZEUS

    ... Out of the sky
    and off Olympos
he moved flashing his fires incessantly,
    and the thunderbolts,
the crashing of them and the blaze
    together came flying, one after
another, from his ponderous hand,
    and spinning whirls of inhuman
flame, and with it the earth,
    the giver of life, cried out
aloud as she burned, and the vast forests
    in the fire screamed.
All earth was boiling with it,
    and the courses of the Ocean
and the barren sea, and the steam
    and the heat of it was engulfing
the Titans of the earth, while the flames
    went up to the bright sky
unquenchably, and the blaze
    and the glare of thunder and lightning
blinded the eyes of the Titan gods,
    for all they were mighty.
The wonderful conflagration crushed Chaos,

and to the eyes' seeing
and ears' hearing the clamour of it,
    it absolutely
would have seemed as if Earth
    and the wide Heaven above her
had collided, for such would have been
    the crash arising
as Earth wrecked and the sky came piling down
    on top of her,
so vast was the crash heard
    as the gods collided in battle.
The winds brought on with their roaring
    a quake of the earth and dust storm,
with thunder and with lightning,
    and the blazing thunderbolt,
the weapons thrown by great Zeus,
    and they carried the clamour
and outcry between the hosts opposed,
    and a horrible tumult
of grisly battle uprose,
    and both sides showed power in the fighting.
Then the battle turned; before that,
    both sides attacking
in the fury of their rage fought on
    through the strong encounters.
        But now the Three, Kottos and Briareos
        and Gyes,[1]
insatiate of battle, stirred
    the grim fighting in the foremost,
for from their powerful hands they volleyed
    three hundred boulders
one after another, and their missile flights
    overwhelmed the Titans
in darkness, and these they drove
    underneath the wide-wayed
earth, and fastened them there

1. Giant sons of Earth and Heaven, unleashed by Zeus.

in painful bondage, for now they
had beaten the Titan gods with their hands,
for all their high hearts.
They drove them as far underground
as earth is distant from heaven.
Such is the distance from earth's surface
to gloomy Tartaros.[1]
For a brazen anvil dropping out of the sky
would take nine
nights, and nine days, and land on earth
on the tenth day,
and a brazen anvil dropping off the earth
would take nine
nights, and nine days, and land in Tartaros
on the tenth day.

RICHMOND LATTIMORE (1959)

1. Hades.

THE HOMERIC HYMNS

THE thirty-three hymns with this title are addressed to various gods and goddesses but are literary rather than devotional in character. Their ancient ascription to Homer is no longer accepted; they were written at many different epochs from the eighth century B.C. onwards.

*

HYMN TO DIONYSUS

Of Bacchus[1] let me tell a sparkling story –
'Twas by the sea-side, on a promontory,
As like a blooming youth he sat one day,
His dark locks ripening in the sunny ray,
And wrapt in a loose cloak of crimson bright,
Which half gave out his shoulders, broad and white,
That making up, a ship appeared at sea,
Brushing the wine-black billows merrily, –
A Tuscan trim,[2] and pirates were the crew;
A fatal impulse drove them as they flew;
For looking hard, and nodding to each other,
Concluding him, at least, some prince's brother,
They issued forth along the breezy bay,
Seized him with jovial hearts, and bore away.

No sooner were they off, than gathering round him
They marked his lovely strength, and would have bound him;
When lo, instead of this, the ponderous bands
Snapped of themselves from off his legs and hands,
He, all the while, discovering no surprise,
But keeping, as before, his calm black eyes.

At this, the Master, struck beyond the rest,
Drew them aside, and earnestly addressed; –

1. Dionysus.   2. 'Tyrsenian' – perhaps Etruscan.

63

'O wretched as ye are, have ye your brains,
And see this being ye would hold with chains?
Trust me, the ship will not sustain him long;
For either Jove he is, terribly strong,
Or Neptune, or the silver-shafted King,[1]
But nothing, sure, resembling mortal thing.
Land then and set him free, lest by and by
He call the winds about him, and we die.'

He said; and thus, in bitterness of heart
The Captain answered, – 'Wretched that *thou* art!
Truly we've much to fear, – a favouring gale,
And all things firm behind the running sail!
Stick to thy post, and leave these things to men.
I trust, my friends, before we sail again,
To touch at Egypt, Cyprus, or the north,
And having learnt meantime our prisoner's worth,
What friends he has, and wealth to what amount,
To turn this god-send to a right account.'

He said; and hauling up the sail and mast,
Drew the tight vessel stiff before the blast;
The sailors, under arms, observe their prize,
When lo, strange doings interrupt their eyes;
For first, a fountain of sweet-smelling wine
Came gushing o'er the deck with sprightly shine;
And odours, not of earth, their senses took;
The pallid wonder spread from look to look;
And then a vine-tree over-ran the sail,
Its green arms tossing to the pranksome gale;
And then an ivy, with a flowering shoot,
Ran up the mast in rings, and kissed the fruit,
Which here and there the dipping vine let down;
On every oar there was a garland crown. –
But now the crew called out 'To shore! To shore!'
When, leaping backward with an angry roar,

1. Zeus, Poseidon and Apollo.

64

The dreadful stranger to a lion turned;
His glaring eyes beneath the hatches burned:
Then rushing forward, he became a bear,
With fearful change bewildering their despair;
And then again a lion, ramping high
From seat to seat, and looking horribly.
Heaped at the stern, and scrambling all along,
The trembling wretches round the Master throng,
Who calmly stood, for he had done no wrong.
Oh, at that minute, to be safe on land!
But now, in his own shape, the God's at hand,
And spurning first the Captain from the side,
The rest leaped after in the plunging tide;
For one and all, as they had done the same,
The same deserved; and dolphins they became.

The God then turning to the Master, broke
In happy-making smiles, and stoutly spoke:—
'Be of good courage, blest companion mine;
Bacchus am I, the roaring God of Wine;
And well shall this day be, for thee and thine.'

And so, all reverence and all joy to thee,
Son of the sparkle-smiling Semele!
Must never bard forget thee in his song,
Who makest it flow so sweetly and so strong.

LEIGH HUNT (1814)

THE HYMN TO EARTH, MOTHER OF ALL

O universal mother, who dost keep
From everlasting thy foundations deep,
Eldest of things, Great Earth, I sing of thee!
All shapes that have their dwelling in the sea,
All things that fly, or on the ground divine
Live, move, and there are nourished – these are thine;

These from thy wealth thou dost sustain; from thee
Fair babes are born, and fruits on every tree
Hang ripe and large – revered divinity!

PERCY BYSSHE SHELLEY (1818, first published 1839)

FROM THE HYMN TO APOLLO

For many thy sacred groves, many thy temples be,
And all high hills and headlands were ever dear to thee,
All peaks amid the mountains, all seaward swirling streams;
Yet Delos, O Apollo, to thy heart the dearest seems.
There gather to thy glory the long-robed Ionians,
They and their honoured wives,their daughters and their sons:
There, when the lists stand ready, faithfully they throng
To gladden thee with boxing, and with dancing, and with song.
A man might dream them ageless and deathless evermore,
Who sees the Ionians gather upon the Delian shore,
And marks with what grace they bear them, and rejoices there
In the glory of their manhood and their women girdled fair,
Their swift ships, and the riches of the proud Ionian race.
And there, too, is a wonder that the years shall not efface –
The mustered maids of Delos, who serve the Archer-king.
For first the praise of Apollo their lips in chorus sing.
The praise of Leto his mother, and his sister's deadly bow;
Then, of men and women that lived long years ago
They chant, till all who listen their life's own cares forget;
And last their quick tongues mimic the dancer's castanet,
Or the speech of many a country, till each man seems to hear
His own tongue calling to him – so subtle-sweet their ear.

Now the grace of Apollo upon us, and the grace of Artemis;
And so farewell to you, maidens; and in days after this
Remember, whenever a stranger and wanderer over earth
Hither shall come and ask you – 'What minstrel is most of worth,
Of all that sail to Delos? Whose songs have sweetest fall?'
Then shall ye make this answer to his question, one and all –

'A blind man,[1] craggy Chios is his homeland – and 'tis he
Whose songs of all are noblest, for all the years to be.'

F. L. Lucas (1951)

HYMN TO PAN

Muse, speak in me verses about the dear son of Hermes
with two goat feet and two horns who loves rattle-noise. Up through
    the valleys
of trees he goes wandering wild with nymphs whose whole life is
    dancing,
nymphs who walk light over heads of sheer rock that even the goats
    fear,
calling aloud for Pan the pasture god, hairy and bright,
dry and dusty. He is natural master of hills under snowfall,
possesses peaks of mountains and paths that wind among rocks.
This way and that way he passes among the thick tangles of bushes,
sometimes drawn in delight along the softness of rivers,
sometimes pushing his way up tall cliffs haunted in sunlight,
climbing high to the uttermost crest where shepherds keep lookout.
Often he runs leaping through long mountains like silver,
often he drives wild animals over the slopes and kills them,
his eyes like arrows. Then in the evening he cries out lonely,
moving away from the hunt, and plays low music on reed tubes,
deep and sweet. Not even the bird could surpass him in melody
who, mourning among the petals of flowered springtime,
pours out her song in a voice of mingled honey and tears.
At that hour the clear-toned nymphs of the mountains are with him:
through dense patterns of feet beside a black fountain of water
they sway to their own song; echo moans circles around the hill top.
Now on the choir's flanks, now sinuously in its centre,
the god busies staccato hooves. On his back a blood-red
lynx skin hangs, and his heart leaps to the cool sharp dance notes

1. This suggested the idea that Homer was a blind poet from Chios. This
hymn was also ascribed to Cynaethus of Chios (late sixth century B.C.), but
is older.

there in the soft pasture where countless crocus and hyacinth
swell in scent and push to make careless love in the grasses.
   Now they make hymns for towering Olympos and happy gods
like Hermes, whom they put into verse as a creature lucky
beyond any other, the quick messenger of all divinity:
how he came to rich watered Arkadia mother of sheep flocks
where his sacred place lies open on Mount Kyllene.
There, though divine, he guarded the dust-fleeced sheep in their
       pasture,
serving a mortal, for flowing desire attacked him and burst to
flower, to penetrate Dryops' lovely-haired daughter in love play.[1]
That fertile union he formed perfectly, for in the palace
the nymph bore Hermes a son – divinely peculiar to look at,
with two goat feet and two horns, loving rattle-noise, wonderfully
       laughing.
Even his nurse jumped up and ran headlong, left the dear infant
because she was frightened to look at his bony face and fine beard.
Lucky Hermes at once took the baby into his own hands
nestling him as vast pleasure stirred in his godlike thoughts.
Lightly he rushed to the thrones of the gods, having wrapped the boy
       well up
tight in the folded skins of rabbits that play in the mountains.
Taking his place by the side of Zeus and the other immortals
he showed off his young hero, and all grew gay in their deathless
moods; Dionysos lord of the Bacchai[2] was happiest of all.
Pan was the name they called him because he gave pleasure to *all*.[3]
   Greetings, lord, and find pleasure here; I entreat you with singing.
I shall remember to hymn you again and others also.

EMILY VERMEULE (1964)

1. Dryope.
2. Bacchants or Maenads.
3. '*Pan*' is the Greek for 'all'.

HYMN TO PAN[1]

Tell me, Muse, of the good son of Hermes,
the goat-footed two-horned obstreperous
loafer in wooded meadows with folkdancing
nymphs, who cavort on the sheer cliff's edge
calling on Pan, the bedraggled & longhaired
god of shepherds, who owns every snow-tipped ridge,
mountain-top & rocky peak.
      Here & there
he tramps through the thickets of brushwood, drawn
sometimes by gentle streams,
othertimes on the move among boulders & crags
climbing up to the top overlooking the herds.
Often he runs through the dazzling mountains
or sharpeyed on mountain-shoulders rampages
killing game.
      Only when he comes back
at evening from his hunt will he play his pipe
singing exquisitely – song
unexcelled even in blossoming spring by the bird
who unfolds her lament honeysoft from the leaves.
With him the mountain-nymphs move in quick time
by a spring of dark water, singing
with clear voices. And Echo grumbles around the mountains.
(The god threads either side of the group &
sidles into the middle, feet flickering.)
A sanguine lynx-pelt over his back, he loves
singing con brio in a soft meadow
where saffron & larkspur blossom together &
litter the grass in sweet-scented confusion.
They sing of the blest gods & great Olympus'
stories, especially like that of Hermes,
the gods' express messenger, how he came
to Arcadia of the Fountains, Mother of Flocks
where his precinct as god of Cyllene stands.

    1. Same as the last.

There, though a god, he used to tend sheep
as a mortal's farmhand; luxuriating desire
had grown into him to have Dryops' daughter, & he
contrived this happy marriage. In their home
she bore him a lovely son, a miraculous sight –
goat-footed two-horned obstreperous & sweetly
laughing. On seeing his bearded face
the nurse fled startled, abandoning him; but
Hermes was overjoyed & at once accepted
him in his heart, in his arms, & wrapped him
warmly in thick wild-hare-skins & took him
hurrying to the immortals' palace,
and there set him down near Zeus, displaying
him to the company.
                                They were all delighted,
Dionysus most of all, & they called him
Pan, because he amused them *all*.
And so, Greetings, master. I look for your favour
& will remember you with another song.

PETER JAY (1969)

HYMN TO DIONYSUS[1]

Dionysus, famous Semele's child, is my subject:
how he appeared by the shore of the unharvested sea
on a jutting promontory, like a young man
in the prime of youth; his beautiful dark hair
streamed about him, a purple robe
clasping his strong shoulders.

                                Then came in sight
voyaging over the wine-dark sea in a sturdy ship
pirates, Tyrsenians –

                        an ill fate led them: they saw him,
nodded among themselves, alighted, snatched him

1. cf. above, p. 63.

hastily and shoved him aboard.
                                                    And they boasted
They thought him the son of kings descended from Zeus,
and tried to bind him with uncomfortable fetters . . .
but the bonds could not hold him,
                                        the soft straps
fell from his hands and feet,
                                        and he sat smiling
flashing those dark eyes.
                                        The helmsman saw this
and shouted to his companions:
                                        ' – You fools.
'This is no ordinary mortal you've taken in,
'but a god, an Olympian – Zeus, or Apollo, Poseidon –
'he is so strong, our sleek ship cannot hold him . . .
'Come on – let's set him free on the mainland
'at once; don't anyone touch him,
                                        or in anger
'he'll rouse terrible winds and storm.'
Those were his words. But the captain spat out in spite –
'Fool, watch your weather,
                                        hoist up the mainsail,
'mind the gear, all of it
                                        – this one is for men to deal with.
'He can come with us . . . to Egypt, say, or Cyprus –
'the Hyperboreans . . . or further. Sooner or later
'he'll tell us who his friends are
                                        and his family
'*and* how much he's got. Yes sir,
                                        a god has delivered him to us.'
Those were his words, and he had the mast and sail raised.
Wind filled out the canvas,
                                        they tightened the ropes round it,
then the miracle started:
                                        a fragrant, rich-bodied wine
flowed everywhere on the ship's deck
                                        and an ambrosial

scent arose . . .
                                   at once fear froze all the sailors.
Then all along the top of the sail, a vine
stretched, and its many clusters
hung downwards; black ivy clung to the mast
which sprouted with blossom.
                         Ripe fruit sprang from it; garlands
grew round the oarlocks.
                         When the men saw it, they
begged the helmsman to make for shore.
                              At the ship's bow
the god had turned into a lion – in midship,
Proteus-like, a shaggy bear – snorting, the lion
held the deck, glaring terribly.
                         In terror they fled to the stern,
cowering there round the wise
and steadfast helmsman.
                         – Then the lion leapt out,
gripped the captain, and they all at once
jumped overboard, when they saw this, into the god-given sea,
avoiding this ghastly fate,
                         and were turned into dolphins.
But he took pity on the helmsman and spared him,
speaking these gracious words:
                         '– Be bold, my friend;
'you are dear to my heart, and I am the loud-
'roarer Dionysus whom my mother, Cadmeian
'Semele bore to Zeus when she made love with him:'
                         My greetings, child of beautiful
                         Semele.
None who forgets you can fashion
                         the unforgettable poem.

                                   PETER JAY (1968)

72

PART II

PERSONAL AND LYRIC POETRY

ARCHILOCHUS

An iambic and elegiac poet, son of a citizen and a slave-woman of the island of Paros in the Aegean. Perhaps of the early and mid seventh century B.C.

*

SHIPWRECK[1]

slammed by the surf on the beach
naked at Salmydessos, where the screw-haired men
of Thrace, taking him in
will entertain him (he will have much to undergo,
chewing on slavery's bread)
stiffened with cold, and loops of seaweed from the slime
tangling his body about,
teeth chattering as he lies in abject helplessness
flat on his face like a dog
beside the beach-break where the waves come shattering in.
And let me be there to watch;
for he did me wrong and set his heel on our good faith,
he who had once been my friend.

RICHMOND LATTIMORE (1955)

LOSS OF SHIELD

Some barbarian is waving my shield, since I was obliged to
     leave that perfectly good piece of equipment behind
under a bush. But I got away, so what does it matter?
     Let the shield go; I can buy another one equally good.

RICHMOND LATTIMORE (1955)

1. The authorship of this poem is regarded as doubtful.

DRUNK ON DUTY

Kindly pass the cup down the deck
And keep it coming from the barrel,
Good red wine, and don't stir up the dregs,
And don't think why we shouldn't be,
More than any other, drunk on guard duty.

GUY DAVENPORT (1964)

STAND FAST

Soul, soul,
Torn by perplexity
On your feet now.
Throw forward your chest
To the enemy;
Keep close in the attack;
Move back not an inch.
But never crow in victory,
Nor mope hang-dog in loss.
Overdo neither sorrow nor joy:
A measured motion governs man.

GUY DAVENPORT (1964)

BOREDOM

What breaks me,
Young friend,
Is tasteless desire,
Dead iambics,[1]
Boring dinners.

GUY DAVENPORT (1964)

1. Archilochus himself wrote both iambics and elegiacs, the former metre being specially used for personal invective.

ALCMAN

Lyric poet, who lived at Sparta in the second half of the seventh century B.C. He may have come from Sardis (Sart) in Lydia (Asia Minor).

*

NIGHT

The hills have fallen asleep.
    O'er cleft and crag
      One quiet spreads,
O'er rocks that face the deep
      And stony torrent beds.

A. E. ZIMMERN (1911)

OLD AGE

O girls of honey-sweet voices, my limbs are weak.
They will not bear me. I wish, ah, I wish I were
a carefree kingfisher flying over flowering foam
with the halcyons – sea-blue holy birds of spring.

WILLIS BARNSTONE (1962)

YOU MADE MILK AND CHEESE

Often at night along the mountain tops,
when gods are revelling by torch light,
you came carrying a great jar
(like one shepherds use) but of heavy gold.
You filled the jar with milk
drawn from a lioness, and made a great cheese
unbroken and gleaming white.

WILLIS BARNSTONE (1962)

ALCMAN'S SUPPER

Get him that enormous cauldron on the tripod
so he can bloat his stomach with every food.
It is cool but soon will boil with good soup
which gobbler Alkman likes sparkling hot,
especially in the cold season of the solstice.
The glutton Alkman abstains from fancy dishes
but like the demos eats a plain massive meal.

WILLIS BARNSTONE (1962)

ANACREON

Lyric poet, *c.* 570 – after 500 B.C. Left his home Teos, in Ionia, when it was threatened by the Persians (545), and lived in Samos, Athens and Thessaly.

*

OLD AGE

Sweet Youth no more will tarry,
    My friend a while ago;
Now white's the head I carry,
    And grey my temples grow,
    My teeth – a ragged row.

To taste the joy of living
    But little space have I,
And torn with sick misgiving
    I can but sob and sigh,
    So deep the dead men lie.

So deep their place and dismal,
    All means, be sure, they lack
Down in the murk abysmal
    To scale the upward track
    And win their journey back.

T. F. Higham (1938)

ON THE FORTUNES OF ARTEMON

Once he went about in filthy clothes and waspy hair,
with wooden rings on his ears, and wore around his ribs
an unwashed hairy oxhide from an old miserable shield.

79

Our con-man pimped a living from bakery girls and whores,
and got his neck bound to a whipping block where the leather
made raw meat of his back – and best, he rode the wheel
so that hairs could be torn from his beard and scalp.

But now the good Artemon rides like a generous lord
in an excellent coach or litter; he wears gold ear-rings
and carries a special ivory parasol like a grand lady.

WILLIS BARNSTONE (1962)

ALCAEUS

Lyric poet, of Mytilene on the island of Lesbos. Born *c.* 620 B.C.

*

WINTER[1]

Zeus rains upon us, and from the sky comes down
enormous winter. Rivers have turned to ice . . .

Dash down the winter! Throw a log on the fire
and mix the flattering wine (do not water it
    too much) and bind on round our foreheads
      soft ceremonial wreaths of spun fleece.

We must not let our spirits give way to grief.
By being sorry we get no further on,
    my Bukchis. Best of all defences
      is to mix plenty of wine, and drink it.

RICHMOND LATTIMORE (1955)

SUMMER

Wash your gullet with wine for the Dog-Star returns
with the heat of summer searing a thirsting earth.
Cicadas cry softly under high leaves, and pour down
shrill song incessantly from under their wings.
The artichoke blooms, and women are warm and wanton –
but men turn lean and limp for the burning Dog-
    Star parches their brains and knees.

WILLIS BARNSTONE (1962)

1. Best known as the partial model of a poem of Horace, *Odes,* 1, 9.

THE SHIP OF STATE IN ROUGH WATERS[1]

I can't tell you which way the gale has turned
for waves crash in from west and east, and we
are tossed and driven between, our black ship
      labouring under the giant storm.

The sea washes across the decks and maststep
and dark daylight already shows through long rents
in the sails. Even the halyards slacken as
      windward waves coil above the hull.

What sore labour to bale the water we've shipped!
Let us raise bulwarks and ride out the storm,
heeding my words: 'Let each man now be famous.'
      Yet base cowards betray the state.

WILLIS BARNSTONE (1962)

HELEN OF TROY[2]

... and Helen
      heart
crumbling
      mind blurred
took ship
      left
house & daughter
husband
      bed
for him
whose dead
      brothers

1. Echoed by Horace, *Odes*, I, 14.
2. This is a reconstruction of fragments that may not have formed a continuous run of text.

ALCAEUS

now lie caught
       deep
in Troy's
black earth
       the chariots
shivered in dust
bodies torn
       blood
death . . .
       Achilles . . .

ANDREW MILLER (1970)

EPITAPH

You also, Cleanor's son, are one who gave
Life for your country's love. This was the reason
You challenged tempests of the lawless season
And left youth's flower in the disfiguring wave.

WILLIAM J. PHILBIN (1972)

SAPPHO

POETESS, of Eresus and Mytilene on Lesbos. Born *c.* 612 B.C.

★

FORGOTTEN

Dead shalt thou lie; and nought
    Be told of thee or thought,
For thou hast plucked not of the Muses' tree:
    And even in Hades' halls
    Amidst thy fellow-thralls
No friendly shade thy shade shall company!

THOMAS HARDY (1901)

AN ABSENT FRIEND

A glorious goddess in her eyes
Were you, her comrade, and your songs
Above all other songs she'd prize.

With Lydian women now she dwells
Surpassing them, as when day dies
The rosy-fingered moon excels

The host of stars, and light illumes
The salt sea and the cornland glows
With light upon its thousand blooms.

In loveliness the dew spills over
And with new strength revives the rose,
Slim grasses and the flowering clover.

SAPPHO

But sadly up and down she goes,
Remembering Atthis, once her lover,
And in her heart sick longing grows.

C. M. BOWRA (1957)

LOVE

To me he seems like a god
as he sits facing you and
hears you near as you speak
softly and laugh

in a sweet echo that jolts
the heart in my ribs. For now
as I look at you my voice
is empty and

can say nothing as my tongue
cracks and slender fire is quick
under my skin. My eyes are dead
to light, my ears

pound, and sweat pours over me.
I convulse, paler than grass,
and feel my mind slip as I
go close to death.

WILLIS BARNSTONE (1962)

DESIRE

Desire shakes me once again,
here is that melting of my limbs.
It is a creeping thing, and bittersweet.
I can do nothing to resist.

SUZY Q. GRODEN (1964)

THE ORCHARD

Cold water falls between the apple-trees
And climbing roses over-arch their shade,
And rustling in the leafy boughs the breeze
      Lulls every sense.

A. R. BURN (1965)

SIMONIDES

LYRIC and elegiac poet, of Iulis on the Aegean island of Ceos. Lived
c. 556–468 B.C.

*

THE PRECARIOUSNESS OF PROSPERITY

Being no more than a man, you cannot tell what will happen tomorrow,
Nor, when you see one walk in prosperity, know for how much
   time it will be.
For overturn on the light-lifting wings of a dragonfly
Is not more swift.

RICHMOND LATTIMORE (1955)

THE TRAGEDY OF WAR

We were slaughtered in a Dirphian gully, and our graves,
   near Euripos, were paid for by our nation.
Justice. For in confronting the cruel clouds of war,
   we gave away our years of lovely youth.[1]

WILLIS BARNSTONE (1962)

THE WAR-GOD[2]

With mindless bravura Ares washed his long sleek
   arrowheads.

1. Mount Dirphys is on the island of Euboea, and the Euripus is the channel
that separates it from the mainland. The passage may refer to operations
against Chalcis (*c.* 506).
2. Ascription uncertain. This epitaph was attributed to the Greek victory
over the Persians at the mouth of the river Eurymedon (Köprüçayi) in Asia
Minor in *c.* 467 B.C., but it is doubtful if Simonides was still alive at the time
of the battle.

in the crimson waters within their chests,
and dust now lies not on the living flesh
   of javelineers,
but on the vivid remnants of lifeless bodies.

WILLIS BARNSTONE (1962)

THEY FOUGHT FOR THEIR COUNTRY[1]

Through valour of these men, no smoke on high
from burning Tegea rose to foul the sky.
Death in the line, to leave her free for those
who should come after them, was what they chose.

A. R. BURN (1965)

THE WAR-GOD[2]

The God of War once washed his long-barbed arrows
In rain that was red on the breasts of these.
The standing ranks now lie beneath the barrows,
The living men are lifeless memories.

ANDREW SINCLAIR (1967)

1. Tegea is in Arcadia, but the epitaph was perhaps engraved on a tomb at the battlefield of Plataea (479 B.C.), or was proposed for it.
2. The same as the last but one.

IBYCUS

LYRIC poet from Rhegium (Reggio in Calabria). Mid sixth century B.C.

*

LOVE KNOWS NO WINTER SLEEP

In spring the quince trees
ripen in the girls' holy orchard
with river waters;
and grapes turn violet
under the shade of luxuriant leafage
and newborn shoots.

But for me, Eros
knows no winter sleep, and as north winds
burn down from Thrace
with searing lightning,
Kypris[1] mutilates my heart with black
and baleful love.

WILLIS BARNSTONE (1962)

---

1. Aphrodite.

XENOPHANES

Philosopher-poet, *c.* 570–*c.* 503 (?) B.C. Left his home Colophon in Ionia when it was annexed by the Persians (545), and settled in Sicily.

*

KNOWLEDGE

The gods did not enrich man
with a knowledge of all things
from the beginning of life . . .
Yet man seeks, and in time
invents what may be better . . .

The truth is that no man ever was or will be
who understands the gods and all I speak of.
If you stumble on some rocks of the whole truth
you never know it. There is always speculation.

WILLIS BARNSTONE (1962)

THE NATURE OF THE GODS

Man made his gods, and furnished them
with his own body, voice and garments . . .
If a horse or lion or a slow ox
had agile hands for paint and sculpture,
the horse would make his god a horse,
the ox would sculpt an ox . . .
Our gods have flat noses and black skins
say the Ethiopians. The Thracians say
our gods have red hair and hazel eyes.

WILLIS BARNSTONE (1962)

SOLON[1]

ATHENIAN statesman, legislator and poet. Held office in 594/3 B.C.

★

THE MIDDLE COURSE

I gave the people as much privilege as they have a right to:
   I neither degraded them from rank nor gave them free hand;
and for those who already held the power and were envied for money,
   I worked it out that they also should have no cause for complaint.
I stood there holding my sturdy shield over both the parties;
   I would not let either side win a victory that was wrong.

RICHMOND LATTIMORE (1955)

---

1. See also p. 401.

THEOGNIS

Elegiac poet, of Megara. Mid sixth century B.C.

*

DANGERS OF A YOUNG WIFE

Shun when you be grey and old
    A wife whose locks are raven:
Like boat whose anchors never hold
That ne'er obeys the helm aright,
She'll slip her moorings any night
    And make another haven.

J. M. EDMONDS (1937)

POVERTY

Nothing destroys a good man quicker than
    poverty:
not malarial fever, Kyrnos, nor old age.
Better to hurl oneself into the abysmal sea
    or over a blunt cliff – than be a victim
of poverty. The poor man can do or say nothing
    worthwhile. Even his mouth is gagged.

WILLIS BARNSTONE (1962)

GLOOM

Best of all things – is never to be born,
never to know the light of sharp sun.
But being born, then best

to pass quickly as one can through the gates of
    Hell,
and there lie under the massive shield of earth.

WILLIS BARNSTONE (1962)

HAPPINESS

Blessed is the man who knows how to make love
   as one wrestles in a gym,
and then goes home happy to sleep the day
   with a delicious young boy.

WILLIS BARNSTONE (1962)

THE REWARD

I gave you wings
    to soar on,
deft grace over earth & sea,
   a name
through feast-nights
    to ring from all lips,
the grave
    & smiling,
that nimble
    pipes & the melody
of young throats
   will celebrate.
Die you may
   and go
through dusk into lamentation,
    but O Kyrnos
sprung
    warm
of glad mouths,

wheeling over
the Greek earth
    & blue shifting sea
faster than horse
    or north-wind,
your name
    will live by song's grace
& you in song's
    body
till earth burn
    under sun.

You give me
    insolence, nothing more.
You fob me off like a child
    with thin lies.

ANDREW MILLER (1970)

EXILE

Yes
I have been there
        Sicily
Eretrian winelands rust-red

and Sparta
        tall torch
kindled in river reeds.

I went there
I found men with frank hearts
        who took me in
I found kind hands

94

but no joy
and no rest.

Home hugs close.

ANDREW MILLER (1970)

BACCHYLIDES

LYRIC poet, of Iulis on Ceos; nephew of Simonides. Early fifth century
B.C.

*

THE TROJAN WAR

But I'll sing their sons
Who spring war,
Fleet Achilles
And fair Eriboea's Ajax,[1]
Daring comrade-at-arms
Who braced a shield
And stood his stern
As Hector, hurtling on
In his kilt of bronze,
Went for the hulls
With hideous fire;
Achilles' bullneck wrath
Attacked the Greeks,
And slacked the fall of Troy:

Till then her troops
Had kept to Ilium,
Town towered to wonders;
Stunned, they'd flinched
From the slash of fight
When Achilles ramped
On the raging plains,
    Flailing a spear
He launched to kill.
But when the rocksure son

1. Eriboea was the wife of Telamon of Salamis and mother of Ajax.

Of the Nereid crowned in violets
Quit that war –

As Boreas whips the Sea of Thrace
Through a spindrift night, pelting
A crew with craggy swells,
But dies down
When the dawn climbs up to light,
A sweet breeze skims the combers smooth,
The sheets puff out on a breath from south,
And seamen break to take the dear land in –

So when they heard
That spearing Achilles
Held to his tents
For blonde Briseis[1]
And lovely limbs,
The Trojans flung
Their hands to the gods –
Lured by a light
That dazzled them
Blind in cloudburst –
They streamed
From Laomedon's walls
To the plains,
Mounting assault
To smash the Greeks
And churn their fear;
Ares the Lancer,
And Lord of the Lycians
Apollo impelled them
To storm the beaches
And sturdy ships;
Black earth ran red
With the blood of Achaeans

1. Briseis was the slave-concubine of Achilles, taken from him by Agamemnon and afterwards restored.

Brought under by Hector,
Heroes mauled on the brunt
Of men turned gods.

Those poor fools!
Big hopes swelled
The Trojan horsemen's pride,
Sure of gutting
The dark-eyed prows,
And putting their city,
Built by the gods,
Under sway of the dancers
Days and nights.
But first Scamander
Would swirl their blood,
Shed by Aeacus' sons[1]
Who raze walls.

And if the Aeacids' bodies
Are gone in the woody pyres,
Or lost down mounding tombs,
Theirs perpetual glory,
Thanks to the eloquent Muses,
Thanks to deathless song.
Excellence flaming to all
Does not black out,
Not even dim
Under night's folding drifts,
But alive with esteem
Irrepressibly wings the earth
And trackless sea.

ROBERT FAGLES (1961)

1. Achilles, Ajax, Peleus and Telamon are described as the sons or descendants of Aeacus.

EMPEDOCLES

LEGENDARY philosopher-poet of Acragas (Agrigento) in Sicily; *c.* 493–*c.* 433 B.C.

*

BLOOD-GUILT

There is a law of stern Necessity,
The immemorial ordinance of the gods
Made fast for ever, bravely sworn and sealed: –
Should any Spirit, born to enduring life,
Be fouled with sin of slaughter, or transgress
By disputation, perjured and forsworn,
Three times ten thousand years that soul shall wander
An outcast from Felicity, condemned
To mortal being, and in diverse shapes
With interchange of hardship go his ways.
The Heavens force him headlong to the Sea;
And vomited from the Sea, dry land receives him,
But flings unwanted to the burning Sun;
From there, to the heavenly vortex backward thrown,
He makes from host to host, by all abhorred.

T. F. HIGHAM (1938)

PINDAR

Lyric poet, of Cynoscephalae in Boeotia, 518–438 B.C. Writer of
Pythian, Isthmian, Olympian and Nemean Odes, and many other
sorts of poem.

*

FOR ARISTOMENES OF AEGINA, CHAMPION BOY WRESTLER IN THE PYTHIAN GAMES[1]

And now four times you came down with bodies
    beneath you,
(You meant them harm),
To whom the Pythian feast has given
No glad home-coming like yours.
They, when they meet their mothers,
Have no sweet laughter around them moving delight.
In back streets out of their enemies' way,
They cower; disaster has bitten them.

But who, in his tenderest years,
Finds some new lovely thing,
His hope is high, and he flies
On the wings of his manhood:

Better than riches are his thoughts.
– But man's pleasure is a short time growing
And it falls to the ground
As quickly, when an unlucky twist of thought
Loosens its roots.

Man's life is a day. What is he?
What is he not? A shadow in a dream

1. The Pythian Festival was held every four years at Delphi.

100

Is man: but when God sheds a brightness,
Shining life is on earth
And life is sweet as honey.

C. M. BOWRA (1928)

FOR KING HIERO OF SYRACUSE, WINNER OF THE HORSE RACE AT OLYMPIA

Water is the best thing of all, and gold
Shines like flaming fire at night,
More than all a great man's wealth.
But if, my heart, you would speak
Of prizes won in the Games,[1]
Look no more for another bright star
By day in the empty sky
More warming than the sun,
Nor shall we name any gathering
Greater than the Olympian.
The glorious song of it is clothed by the wits of the
        wise:
They sing aloud of Kronos' son,[2]
When they come to the rich and happy hearth of
        Hieron,[3]

Who sways the sceptre of law
In Sicily's rich sheep-pasture.
He gathers the buds of all perfections,
And his splendour shines in the festal music,
Like our own merry songs
When we gather often around that table of friends.

C. M. BOWRA (1928-69)

1. The Olympic Games, the oldest of the major festivals, were believed to have been founded in 776 B.C.
2. Zeus.
3. Tyrant of Syracuse from 478 to 467 B.C.

THE OLYMPIC GAMES

The strong son of Zeus[1] drove the whole of his host
And all his booty to Pisa,[2]
And measured a holy place
For his mighty Father.
He fenced the Altis[3] and marked it off
In a clean space, and the ground encircling it
He set for rest at supper,
In honour of the ford of Alpheos

And the twelve Kings of the Gods.
To Kronos' Hill[4] he gave a name; for before
It was nameless when Oinomaos ruled,
And drenched with many a snowstorm.
In this first birthday-rite
The Fates stood near at hand,
And he who alone proves the very truth,

Time. In his forward march
He has revealed all clearly:
How Herakles portioned the booty, war's gift,
Made sacrifice and founded
The fourth year's feast
With the first Olympiad
And the winning of victories.

C. M. BOWRA (1928–69)

1. Heracles.
2. The region of Elis round Olympia. It is doubtful if there was a town of that name.
3. The precinct of Olympian Zeus, between the rivers Alpheus and Cladeus.
4. The father of Zeus.

FREED FROM THE PERILS OF THE PERSIAN WAR[1]

Wherefore I also, though with anguish at heart,
Am called to summon the golden Muse.
We have been freed from vast griefs;
So let us not give in and go without garlands;
Nor should you nurse sorrows. We have ended
Evils beyond contrivance
And shall give the people a sweet song
Even after our suffering;
For the stone of Tantalos[2]
That hung over our head
Has been turned aside from us by some God,

An unendurable torment for Hellas. Yet
The passing of fear has delivered men
From overmastering cares. It is always best
To look at whatever lies before our feet;
For treacherous Time hangs over men
And twists awry the path of life. But even those things
Can be healed by men if freedom is with them;
And a man should give care to noble hope.

C. M. BOWRA (1928–69)

THE POET GIVES IMMORTALITY[3]

If any man's actions prosper, he strikes
A honey-hearted well of the Muses' streams.
Even high deeds of bravery

1. For Cleandrus of Aegina, winner in boys' trial of strength at the Isthmian Games, held at Corinth. The Ode was probably written in 478 B.C., soon after the withdrawal of the Persian army from Greece. Pindar's own city, Thebes, had collaborated with the Persians, but Aegina actively resisted them.

2. Punished by the gods for a crime. Pindar's version of his punishment differs from that of Homer, who makes him 'tantalized' by hunger and thirst.

3. The Ode is written for Sogenes, winner in the boys' five events in the Nemean Games (north-east Peloponnese).

Have a great darkness if they lack song;
We can hold a mirror to fine doings
In one way only,
If with the help of Memory in her glittering crown
Recompense is found for labour
In echoing words of song.
Wise sailors have learned
Of the wind that comes on the third day,
And lust for profit brings them to no harm.
The rich man and poor man together
Come to death's boundary.
But I hold that the name of Odysseus
Is more than his sufferings
Because of Homer's sweet singing;

For on his untruths and winged cunning
A majesty lies.

C. M. BOWRA (1928–69)

MEN AND GODS[1]

Single is the race, single
Of men and of gods;
From a single mother we both draw breath.
But a difference of power in everything
Keeps us apart;
For the one is as Nothing, but the brazen sky
Stays a fixed habitation for ever.
Yet we can in greatness of mind
Or of body be like the Immortals,
Tho' we know not to what goal
By day or in the nights
Fate has written that we shall run.

C. M. BOWRA (1928–69)

1. Alkimidas of Aigina, winner in the boys' wrestling at the Nemean Games.

THE ELYSIAN FIELDS

For them the sun shines at full strength – while we here walk in
    night.
The plains around their city are red with roses
and shaded by incense trees heavy with golden fruit.
And some enjoy horses and wrestling, or table games and the lyre,
and near them blossoms a flower of perfect joy.
Perfumes always hover above the land
from the frankincense strewn in deep-shining fire of the gods'
    altars.

And across from them the sluggish rivers of black night
vomit forth a boundless gloom.

WILLIS BARNSTONE (1962)

PRAXILLA

Poetess of Sicyon in the mid fifth century B.C.

*

PLEASURES

Loveliest of what I leave behind is the sunlight,
And loveliest after that the shining stars, and
    the moon's face,
But also cucumbers that are ripe, and pears, and
    apples.

RICHMOND LATTIMORE (1955)

TIMOTHEUS

Poet from Miletus in Ionia; worked in Athens. Lived *c.* 450–*c.* 360 B.C.

*

A NEW PROGRAMME

Old songs I will not sing.
Now better songs are sung.
Zeus reigns now, and is young,
Where Kronos once was king.[1]
Old Muse, your knell is rung.

GILBERT HIGHET (1938)

[1]. He was overthrown by his son Zeus.

ARIPHRON

THE 'Hymn to Health' of this poet of Sicyon (*c*. 400 B.C.) is preserved on an inscription.

*

IN PRAISE OF HEALTH

Health, best of the Blessed Ones to men,
May I dwell with you for the rest of my days,
And may you be kind and stay with me.
For if there is any joy in wealth or in children,
Or in royal rule which makes men like the gods,
Or in the desires which we hunt
With Aphrodite's secret snares,
Or if men have any other delight
From the gods or respite from their labours,
With you, blessed Health,
All things are strong and shine with the converse of the Graces,
And without you no man is happy.

C. M. BOWRA (1957)

ANONYMOUS

LONELINESS

The moon has set,
And the Pleiades as well.
In the deep middle of the night
The time is passing,
And I lie alone.

SUZY Q. GRODEN (1964)

DO GET UP QUICKLY

Oh. What is the matter?
Please be quiet. Get up
And go before he comes
Or he will do something
Terrible to you and
Worse to me. It is dawn
Already. Can't you see
The light through the window?

KENNETH REXROTH (1962)

PART III

FIFTH-CENTURY ATHENIAN DRAMA

AESCHYLUS

THE first great Athenian tragic poet; from Eleusis in Attica. Born 525/4 B.C.; his last prize-winning was in 458. Seven of his ninety plays have survived.

*

THE CHORUS, MOURNING FOR PROMETHEUS, TELLS OF ANOTHER VICTIM OF A DIVINE CURSE

But one other before have I seen to remain
          By invincible pain
Bound and vanquished – one Titan![1] 'twas Atlas, who
     bears
In a curse from the gods, by that strength of his own
          Which he evermore wears,
The weight of the heaven on his shoulder alone,
          While he sighs up the stars;
And the tides of the ocean wail bursting their bars –
          Murmurs still the profound,
And black Hades roars up through the chasm of the ground.
And the fountains of pure-running rivers moan low
          In a pathos of woe.

ELIZABETH BARRETT BROWNING (1833)

THE SONS OF OEDIPUS, ETEOCLES AND POLYNEICES, HAVE SLAIN EACH OTHER IN A DUEL OUTSIDE THEBES

Now do our eyes behold
The tidings which were told:

1. The Titans, among whom Atlas is sometimes included, were older gods before the Olympians (p. 60).

Twin fallen kings, twin perished hopes to mourn,
 The slayer, the slain,
The entangled doom forlorn
 And ruinous end of twain.
Say, is not sorrow, is not sorrow's sum
On home and hearthstone come?
 O waft with sighs the sail from shore,
 O smite the bosom, cadencing the oar
That rows beyond the rueful stream for aye
  To the far strand,
 The ship of souls, the dark,
 The unreturning bark
Whereon light never falls nor foot of Day,
Ev'n to the bourne of all, to the unbeholden land.

A. E. HOUSMAN (1928)

BEWARE OF SUCCESS AND GOOD NEWS

A people's wrath voiced abroad bringeth grave
Danger, no less than public curse pronounced.
It still abideth for me, a hidden fear wrapped in night.
Watchful are the Gods of all
Hands with slaughter stained. The black
Furies wait, and when a man
Has grown by luck, not justice, great,
With sudden overturn of chance
They wear him to a shade, and, cast
Down to perdition, who shall save him?
In excess of fame is danger.
With a jealous eye the Lord Zeus in a flash shall smite him.
 Mine be the life unenvied,
 Neither to plunder cities
 Nor myself a prisoner bow
 Down to the will of others.

– The tale of glad news afire
Throughout the town spreads its fleet

Rumour; yet if this be true,
Who knows? It is perhaps a trick played by God.
– Who is so childish or so maimed of wit
To let a mere fiery word
Inflame the heart, then with swiftly-changed import
Flicker out and fade to nought?
– A woman's heart ever thus
Accepteth joy ere the joy is brought to light.
– Too credulous a woman's longing flies
And spreading swiftly, swiftly dies,
An idle word noised abroad on woman's lips.

GEORGE THOMSON (1938)

THE RELIGIOUS ORGIES OF THE THRACIANS

Kotytto's ritual feast they keep.[1]
One handles the chiselled wood that hums
Its droning music full and deep
To work on the soul till frenzy comes;
The brasses clash as a second sings;
Another howls to the twang of strings;
And the roar of a terrible bull-like note
Keeps time, from some invisible throat,
While tom-tom beats with a fearful sound
Like the voice of a thunderclap underground.

ANONYMOUS (1938)

PROMETHEUS DEFIES ZEUS

PROMETHEUS: I swear to you that Zeus, for all his stubborn mind,
Will yet be lowly; such a marriage is that he plans
To make, one that will hurl him from his dictatorship,
A thing of nothing from his throne. The curse of Kronos
His father then indeed will come true utterly,

1. Cotys, or Cotytto, was a Thracian goddess worshipped with orgiastic rites.

That curse he made when hurled from his established throne.
And from these troubles none of the gods but I
Can clearly show him how he can escape. I know
The means and how to accomplish it. And therefore now
Let him sit confident, and in his airy noise
Put faith, and brandish in his hands the fire-breathed bolt.
In no way will all this avail him to escape
Falling into shame an intolerable fall.
So mighty is the wrestler that now he seeks
To equip against himself, an invincible wonder,
One that will find a mightier flame than the lightning,
And heavy crashes that go beyond the thunder.
And as for that plague of the sea that shakes the earth,
Poseidon's spear, the trident, he will brush it aside.
Zeus, stumbling on this misadventure, will find out
How far apart are supreme power and slavery.

CHORUS: What you would have yourself you mouth out
    against Zeus.

PROMETHEUS: I say what will come true and also what I wish.

REX WARNER (1947)

A MESSENGER TELLS THE PERSIAN QUEEN MOTHER
ATOSSA OF THE BATTLE OF SALAMIS (480 B.C.)

    O Queen, the whole disaster first began
    surely with coming of some fiend or devil!

    There came a Greek from the Athenian camp,
    and said to your son Xerxes: come the night,
    the Greeks would wait no longer, but embark
    and sail in secret, scattering for their lives.
    He, not suspecting the deceitfulness
    of that Greek, nor the envy of high heaven,

forthwith gave order to his admirals
at sunset to embark, in three divisions,
and guard the outlets well, while other ships
encircled all the island round about.
And should the Greeks escape, their heads should fall;
– so said he, confident and glad at heart.
Little he knew what the gods had in store!

   Then they in order took their evening meal,
and sailors set in rowlocks each his oar,
and when night fell, each master of the oar
embarked, and every skilful man-at-arms,
and rank hailed rank as the long ships went forth.

   Then all night long the captains kept their crews
patrolling in the fairway. Night wore on,
and still no Greeks came out in secret flight;
but when at last the sun's bright chariot rose,
then we could hear them – singing; loud and strong
rang back the echo from the island rocks,
and with the sound came the first chill of fear.
Something was wrong. This was not flight; they sang
the deep-toned hymn, *Apollo, Saving Lord,*
that cheers the Hellene armies into battle.

   Then trumpets over there set all on fire;
then the sea foamed as oars struck all together,
and swiftly, there they were! The right wing first
led on the ordered line, then all the rest
came on, came out, and now was to be heard
a mighty shouting: 'On, sons of the Greeks!
Set free your country, set your children free,
your wives, the temples of your country's gods,
your fathers' tombs; now they are all at stake.'
And from our side the Persian battle-cry
roared back the answer; and the time was come.

   Then ship on ship rammed with her beak of bronze;
but first a Greek struck home; full on the quarter
she struck and shattered a Phoenician's planks;
then all along the line the fight was joined.

117

At first, the torrent of the Persian fleet
bore up; but when the press of shipping jammed
there in the narrows, none could help another,
but our ships rammed each other, fouled each other
and broke each other's oars. But those Greek ships,
skilfully handled, kept the outer station
ringing us round and striking in, till ships
turned turtle, and you could not see the water
for blood and wreckage; and the dead were strewn
thickly on all the beaches, all the reefs;
and every ship in all the fleet of Asia
in grim confusion fought to get away.

Meanwhile the enemy, as men gaff tunnies
or some great shoal of fish, with broken oars
and bits of wreckage hacked and killed; and shrieks
and cries filled the whole sea, till night came down.

A. R. BURN (1965)

SOPHOCLES

ATHENIAN tragic poet; from Colonus in Attica. Lived *c.* 496–406
B.C. Seven of his 120 plays have survived.

*

THE PUNISHMENT OF SIN

O may it ever be my Fate
Justly those sacred Truths to rate;
And those blest Laws that have their Rise
From Wisdom lodged above the Skies,
Those which the Olympian King alone
Dictates from his eternal Throne,
(Unlike to those weak mortals frame),
Live unabolished, still the same!
Sprung from the God, replete with heavenly Fire,
They baffle Time, and keep their Strength entire.

The Tyrant and illegal Man
From Pride and rash Contempt began;
Pride and Contempt that left him high
O'er Mountains of Impiety;
Till placed aloft he dazzled grows,
And in his Fear his Hold foregoes.
O! may the City's Cares succeed,
Nor envying Fates their search mislead.
With ardent humble Prayers the Gods I'll move;
The Gods shall still my kind Protectors prove!

But whoe'er in Word or Deed
Does from the sacred Laws recede,
No divine Resentments fearing,
Nor the hallowed Shrines revering,
If licentious Ease beguile him,

If dishonest Gains defile him,
If he pursue corrupting Pleasure,
Or grasps at unpermitted Treasure,
    Some rigid Doom his Guilt o'ertake!
    Else who hereafter will control
    The Sallies of his impious Soul?
    If no avenging Judgements shake
    The triumphs of the dissolute,
    'Tis time the instructive Choirs be mute.

LEWIS THEOBALD (1715)

PRAYER FOR THE SAFE RETURN OF HERACLES

On thee we call, great god of day
To whom the night, with all her starry train,
    Yields her solitary reign,
To send us some propitious ray:
Say thou, whose all-beholding eye
    Doth nature's every part descry,
What dangerous ocean, or what land unknown
From Deianira keeps Alcmena's valiant son.[1]

For she nor joy nor comfort knows,
But weeps her absent lord, and vainly tries
To close her ever-streaming eyes,
    Or sooth her sorrows to repose:
Like the sad bird of night, alone
She makes her solitary moan;
And still, as on her widowed bed reclined
She lies, unnumbered fears perplex her anxious mind.

Even as the troubled billows roar,
When angry Boreas rules the inclement skies
And waves on waves tumultuous rise
    To lash the Cretan shore:
Thus sorrows still on sorrows prest,

1. Deianira was the wife and Alcmena the mother of Heracles.

Fill the great Alcides' breast;[1]
Unfading yet shall his fair virtues bloom,
And some protecting god preserve him from the tomb.

THOMAS FRANCKLIN (1758)

AJAX OF SALAMIS, RECOVERED FROM HIS MADNESS, BIDS FAREWELL FOR EVER

All strangest things the multitudinous years
Bring forth, and shadow from us all we know.
Falter alike great oath and steeled resolve;
And none shall say of aught, 'This may not be.'
Lo! I myself, but yesterday so strong,
As new-dipt steel am weak and all unsexed
By yonder woman: yea I mourn for them,
Widow and orphan, left amid their foes.
But I will journey seaward – where the shore
Lies meadow-fringed – so haply wash away
My sin, and flee that wrath that weighs me down.
And, lighting somewhere on an untrodden way,
I will bury this my lance, this hateful thing,
Deep in some earth-hole where no eye shall see –
Night and Hell keep it in the underworld!
For never to this day, since first I grasped
The gift that Hector gave, my bitterest foe,
Have I reaped aught of honour from the Greeks.
So true that byword in the mouths of men,
'A foeman's gifts are no gifts, but a curse.'
  Wherefore henceforward shall I know that God
Is great; and strive to honour Atreus' sons.[2]
Princes they are, and should be obeyed. How else?
Do not all terrible and most puissant things
Yet bow to loftier majesties? The Winter,

1. Heracles was known as 'the son [descendant] of Alcaeus', who was the father of his earthly father Amphitryon.
2. Agamemnon and Menelaus.

Who walks forth scattering snows, gives place anon
To fruitage-laden Summer; and the orb
Of weary Night doth in her turn stand by,
And let shine out, with his white steeds, the Day.
Stern tempest-blasts at last sing lullaby
To groaning seas: even the archtyrant, Sleep,
Doth loose his slaves, not hold them chained for ever.
And shall not mankind too learn discipline?
I know, of late experience taught, that him
Who is my foe I must but hate as one
Whom I may yet call Friend: and him who loves me
Will I but serve and cherish as a man
Whose love is not abiding. Few be they
Who, reaching Friendship's port, have there found rest.
  But, for these things, they shall be well. Go thou,
Lady, within, and there pray that the Gods
May fill unto the full my heart's desire.
And ye, my mates, do unto me with her
Like honour: bid young Teucer,[1] if he come,
To care for me, but to be *your* friend still.
For where my way leads, thither I shall go:
Do ye my bidding; haply ye may hear,
Though now is my dark hour, that I have peace.

                                    C. S. CALVERLEY (1866)

QUEEN JOCASTA GUESSES THAT HER HUSBAND OEDIPUS IS HER SON

MESSENGER FROM CORINTH:
          Can you direct me, strangers, to the house
          Of Oedipus, your Master – Better still,
          Perchance you know where I may find the King?
CHORUS: This is the house, and he within. The Queen,
          His wife and mother of his home, is here.
MESSENGER: His wife, and blest with offspring! Happiness
          1. The half-brother of Ajax.

122

Wait on her always, and on all her home!

JOCASTA: I wish you happy too. Your gracious speech
Deserves no less. Tell me, with what request
You are come hither, or what news you bring.

MESSENGER: Lady, good news for him and all his house.

JOCASTA: Why, what good news is this? Who sent you here?

MESSENGER: I come from Corinth, and have that to tell
I think will please, though it be partly sad.

JOCASTA: What? Can a sad tale please? How? Tell it me!

MESSENGER: The people of that country, so men said,
Will choose him monarch of Corinthia.

JOCASTA: What? Is old Polybus no longer King?

MESSENGER: No longer King. Death has him in the grave.

JOCASTA: Death! Say you so? Oedipus' father dead?

MESSENGER: If he be not so, may I die myself!

JOCASTA: Quick! To your master, girl; tell him this news!
O oracles of the gods, where are you now!
This was the man that Oedipus so feared
To slay, he needs must leave his country. Dead!
And 'tis not Oedipus, but Fortune slew him!

OEDIPUS: Tell me, Jocasta, wife of my dear love,
Why you have called me hither, out of doors.

JOCASTA: Let this man speak; and as you listen, judge
The issue of the god's grand oracles!

OEDIPUS: This man, who is he? What has he to tell?

JOCASTA: He comes from Corinth, and will tell you this: –
Polybus is no more. Your father's dead.

OEDIPUS: What! Is this true, sir? Answer for yourself!

MESSENGER: If this must needs come first in my report,
'Tis true enough. King Polybus is dead.

OEDIPUS: By treachery? Or did sickness visit him?

MESSENGER: A little shift of the scale, and old men sleep.

OEDIPUS: Ah! My poor father died, you say, by sickness?

MESSENGER: Yes, and by reason of his length of days.

OEDIPUS: Ah me! Wife, why should any man regard
The Delphic Hearth oracular, and the birds
That scream above us – guides, whose evidence

Doomed me to kill my father, who is dead,
Yes, buried under ground, and I stand here,
And have not touched my weapon. – Stay! Perchance
'Twas grief for me. I may have slain him so.
Anyhow, he is dead, and to his grave
Has carried all these oracles – worth nought!

JOCASTA: Worth nought. Did I not tell you so long since?

OEDIPUS: You told me, but my fears misguided me.

JOCASTA: Banish these thoughts for ever from your soul.

OEDIPUS: No, no! Shall I not fear my mother's bed?

JOCASTA: Why, what should a man fear? Luck governs all!
There's no foreknowledge, and no providence!
Take life at random. Live as you best can.
That's the best way. What! Fear that you may wed
Your mother? Many a man has dreamt as much,
And so may you! The man who values least
Such scruples, lives his life most easily.

OEDIPUS: All this were well enough, that you have said,
Were not my mother living. Though your words
Be true, my mother lives, and I must fear.

JOCASTA: At least your father's death is a great hope.

OEDIPUS: I know. Yet she that lives makes me afraid.

MESSENGER: What woman is the cause of all these fears?

OEDIPUS: Merope, sir, that dwelt with Polybus.

MESSENGER: What find you both to fear in Merope?

OEDIPUS: An oracle from the gods, most terrible.

MESSENGER: May it be told, or did the gods forbid?

OEDIPUS: No, you may hear. Phoebus[1] hath said that I
Must come to know my mother's body, come
To shed with my own hand my father's blood.
Therefore have I put Corinth this long time
Far from me. Fortune has been kind, and yet
To see a parent's face is best of all.

MESSENGER: Was this the fear that drove you from your home?

OEDIPUS: This, and my will never to slay my father.

MESSENGER: Then since I came only to serve you well,

1. Apollo.

Why should I hesitate to end that fear?

OEDIPUS: Ah! If you could, you should not miss your thanks!

MESSENGER: Ah! That was my chief thought in coming here,
To do myself some good on your return.

OEDIPUS: No, where my parents are, I'll not return!

MESSENGER: Son, I can see, you know not what you do.

OEDIPUS: 'Fore God, what mean you, sir? Say what you know.

MESSENGER: If this be all that frightens you from home! –

OEDIPUS: All? 'Tis the fear Apollo may prove true –

MESSENGER: And you polluted, and your parents wronged?

OEDIPUS: Aye, it is that, good man! Always that fear!

MESSENGER: Can you not see the folly of such thoughts?

OEDIPUS: Folly? Why folly, since I am their son?

MESSENGER: Because King Polybus was nought to you!

OEDIPUS: How now? The father that begot me, nought?

MESSENGER: No more, no less, than I who speak to you!

OEDIPUS: How should my father rank with nought – with you?

MESSENGER: He never was your father, nor am I.

OEDIPUS: His reason, then, for calling me his son?

MESSENGER: You were a gift. He had you from these arms.

OEDIPUS: He gave that great love to a stranger's child?

MESSENGER: Because he had none of his own to love.

OEDIPUS: So. Did you buy this child, – or was it yours?

MESSENGER: I found you where Cithaeron's valleys wind.

OEDIPUS: Our Theban hills! What made you travel here?

MESSENGER: Once on these very hills I kept my flocks.

OEDIPUS: A shepherd? Travelling to earn your wages?

MESSENGER: Yes, but your saviour too, my son, that day!

OEDIPUS: What ailed me, that you found me in distress?

MESSENGER: Ask your own feet. They best can answer that.

OEDIPUS: No, no! Why name that old familiar hurt?

MESSENGER: I set you free. Your feet were pinned together!

OEDIPUS: A brand of shame, alas! from infancy!

MESSENGER: And from that fortune comes the name you bear.

OEDIPUS: Who named me? Who? Father or mother? Speak!

MESSENGER: I know not. He that gave you to me – may!

OEDIPUS: You found me not? You had me from another?

MESSENGER: Another shepherd bade me take you. True.

OEDIPUS: What shepherd? Can you tell me? Do you know?

MESSENGER: I think they called him one of Laïus' people.

OEDIPUS: Laïus? The same that once was King in Thebes?

MESSENGER: Aye. 'Twas the same. For him he shepherded.

OEDIPUS: Ah! Could I find him? Is he still alive?

MESSENGER: You best can tell, you, natives of the place!

OEDIPUS: Has any man here present knowledge of
The shepherd he describes? Has any seen,
Or here or in the pastures, such an one?
Speak! 'Tis the time for full discovery!

CHORUS: I think, my lord, he means that countryman
Whose presence you desired. But there is none,
Perchance, can tell you better than the Queen.

OEDIPUS: You heard him, wife. Think you he means the man
Whom we await already? Was it he?

JOCASTA: What matter what he means? Oh, take no heed,
And waste no thoughts, I beg you, on such tales.

OEDIPUS: For me it is not possible – to hold
Such clues as these, and leave my secret so.

JOCASTA: No! By the gods, no; leave it, if you care
For your own life. I suffer. 'Tis enough.

OEDIPUS: Take heart. *Your* noble blood is safe, although
I prove thrice bastard, and three times a slave!

JOCASTA: Yet, I beseech you, yield, and ask no more.

OEDIPUS: I cannot yield my right to know the truth.

JOCASTA: And yet I speak – I think – but for your good.

OEDIPUS: And this same good, I find, grows tedious.

JOCASTA: Alas! I pray you may not know yourself.

OEDIPUS: Go, someone, fetch the herdsman! Let the Queen
Enjoy her pride in her fine family!

JOCASTA: O Wretched, Wretched utterly! That name
I give you, and henceforth no other name!

CHORUS: Why went the Queen so swiftly, Oedipus,
As by some anguish moved? Alas! I fear
Lest from that silence something ill break forth.

J. T. SHEPPARD (1920)

DEATH IS WELCOME

What man is he that yearneth
For length unmeasured of days?
Folly mine eye discerneth
   Encompassing all his ways,
For years over-running the measure
   Shall change thee in evil wise:
Grief draweth nigh thee; and pleasure,
   Behold, it is hid from thine eyes.
   This is their wage have they
   Which overlive their day.
And He that looseth from labour
   Doth one with other befriend,
   Whom bride nor bridesmen attend,
Song, nor sound of the tabor,
   Death, that maketh an end.

Thy portion esteem I highest,
   Who wast not ever begot;
Thine next, being born who diest
   And straightway again art not.
With follies light as the feather
   Doth Youth to man befall;
Then evils gather together,
   There wants not one of them all –
   Wrath, envy, discord, strife,
   The sword that seeketh life.
And sealing the sum of trouble
   Doth tottering Age draw nigh,
   Whom friends and kinsfolk fly,
Age, upon whom redouble
   All sorrows under the sky.
This man, as me, even so,
Have the evil days overtaken;
And like as a cape sea-shaken

With tempest at earth's last verges
And shock of all winds that blow,
His head the seas of woe,
The thunders of awful surges
Ruining overflow;
Blown from the fall of even,
 Blown from the dayspring forth,
Blown from the noon in heaven,
 Blown from night and the North.

A. E. HOUSMAN (1928)

DEATH IS WELCOME[1]

Endure what life God gives and ask no longer span;
Cease to remember the delights of youth, travel-wearied aged man;
Delight becomes death-longing if all longing else be vain.

Even from that delight memory treasures so,
Death, despair, division of families, all entanglements of mankind
 grow,
As that old wandering beggar and these God-hated children know.

In the long echoing street the laughing dancers throng,
The bride is carried to the bridegroom's chamber
 through torchlight and tumultuous song;
I celebrate the silent kiss that ends short life or long.

Never to have lived is best, ancient writers say;
Never to have drawn the breath of life, never to have looked into
 the eye of day;
The second best's a gay goodnight and quickly turn away.

W. B. YEATS (1928)

1. A looser adaptation of the first part of the same passage. cf. p. 92.

PHILOCTETES DESERTED ON LEMNOS

Gladly they saw me sleeping on the shore,
Worn with long hours at sea; in a deep cave
They left me and went off, by my side
Set some few rags fit for a luckless man
And scanty food-scraps. May they have the like!
Think of the manner of my waking then
When I woke up from sleep and found them gone,
What tears were mine, what injuries to weep.
I saw the ships which had been mine at sea
All gone, no living being in the place,
None to give help, none to relieve my pains
In sickness. Though I looked on every side
I could find nothing but calamity,
But that in great abundance, O my son.

    Time followed in the footsteps of time past,
And in this narrow dwelling I must sate
My wants. My belly's need this bow would find,
Shooting the doves that darted on the wing,
And everything my bow-sped arrow shot
Myself would in great anguish creep to it,
Dragging my miserable foot to it.
At times there would be need of drink, at times
In winter when the frost was spread abroad
Wood must be broken. I would creep in pain
And manage it. Then there would be no fire,
But rubbing with great labour stone on stone
I struck a phantom flame. This saves my life.
This roof which gives me shelter and my fire
Give all I need, save freedom from disease.

C. M. BOWRA (1938)

THE FATE OF WOMEN

Away from home I am nothing. Oftentimes
Have I considered what is womankind
And seen that we are nothing. In girlhood's days
Ours is the sweetest of all lives at home, –
For thoughtlessness is a kind nurse to children.
But when we reach maturity and wisdom,
We are driven abroad and made a traffic of,
Far from our parents and our country's gods,
Some to strange men and some to foreigners,
Some to true homes and some to contumely,
And just because a single night has joined us,
We must give praise and think that all is well.

C. M. BOWRA (1938)

THE GLORY OF ATHENS

And our land has a thing unknown
On Asia's sounding coast
Or in the sea-surrounded west
Where Agamemnon's race has sway:[1]
The olive, fertile and self-sown,
The terror of our enemies
That no hand tames nor tears away –
The blessed tree that never dies! –
But it will mock the swordsman in his rage.

Ah, how it flourishes in every field,
Most beautifully here!
The grey-leafed tree, the children's nourisher!
No young man nor one partnered by his age

1. The original speaks of 'the Dorian isle of Pelops', the grandfather of
Agamemnon, i.e. the Peloponnese.

Knows how to root it out nor make
Barren its yield;
For Zeus the Father smiles on it with sage
Eyes that forever are awake,
And Pallas[1] watches with her sea-pale eyes.

Last and grandest praise I sing
To Athens, nurse of men,
For her great pride and for the splendour
Destiny has conferred on her.
Land from which fine horses spring!
Land where foals are beautiful!
Land of the sea and the sea-farer!
Upon whose lovely littoral
The god of the sea moves, the son of Time.

That lover of our land I praise again,
Who found our horsemen fit
For first bestowal of the curb and bit,
To discipline the stallion in his prime;
And strokes to which our oarsmen sing,
Well-fitted, oak and men,
Whose long sea-oars in wondrous rhyme
Flash from the salt foam, following
The hundred-footed sea-wind and the gull.

ROBERT FITZGERALD (1941)

THE ACHIEVEMENTS OF MAN

Wonders are many, but none there be
    So strange, so fell, as the Child of Man.
He rangeth over the whitening sea,
    Of the winds of winter he makes his plan;
About his going the deeps unfold,
    The crests o'erhang, but he passeth clear.
Oh, Earth is patient, and Earth is old,

1. Pallas Athene.

And a mother of Gods, but he breaketh her,
To-ing, fro-ing, with the plough-teams going,
   Tearing the soil of her, year by year.

Light are the birds and swift with wings,
   But his hand is round them and drags them low;
He prisons the tribes of the wild-wood things,
   And the salt sea-swimmers that dart and glow.
The nets of his weaving are cast afar,
   And his Thought in the midst of them circleth full,
Till his engines master all beasts that are.
   Where drink the horses at the desert pool,
That mane that shaketh for his slave he taketh,
   And the tireless shoulder of the mountain Bull.

Speech he hath taught him and wind-swift thought
   And the temper that buildeth a City's Wall,
Till the arrows of winter he sets at naught,
   The sleepless cold and the long rainfall.
All-armed he: unarmed never
   To meet new peril he journeyeth;
Yea, his craft assuageth each pest that rageth,
   And help he hath gotten against all save Death.

The craft of his engines hath passed his dream,
   In haste to the good or the evil goal.
One holdeth his City's Law supreme
   And the Oath of God in his inmost soul;
High-citied he: citiless that other
   Who striveth, grasping at things of naught,
On the road forbidden. From him be hidden
   The fire that comforts and the light of thought!

GILBERT MURRAY (1952)

OEDIPUS HAS KILLED HIS FATHER LAIUS (cf. p. 122)

My father was Corinthian, Polybus.
My mother Dorian, called Merope.
I was the city's foremost man until
    a certain incident befell – a curious
    incident, though hardly worth the ferment
    that it put me in.
                At dinner once
    a drunkard in his cups bawled out,
    'Aha! Sham father's son!' And all that day
I fretted, hardly able to contain my hurt.
But on the next I went straightway to ask
    my mother and my father; who were shocked
    to hear that anyone should say such things.

I was relieved by their response; and yet,
    the thing had hatched a scruple in my mind –
    so deep it made me steal away from home
    to Delphi, to the oracle, and there
    Apollo – never hinting what I came to hear –
    packs me home again with ears ringing
    with some other things he blurted out;
    horrible disgusting things:
How mating with my mother I must spawn
    a progeny to make men shudder; then,
    be my very father's murderer.

O I fled from there. I measured out
    the stars to put all heaven in between
    the land of Corinth and such a damnéd destiny.
And as I went, I stumbled on the very spot
    where this king you say had met his end.

I'll . . . I'll tell the truth to you my wife.
As I reached this triple parting of the ways,

a herald and a man like you described
in a colt-drawn chariot came.
The leading groom – the old man urging him –
tried to force me off the road. The groom
jostled me and I, infuriated,
landed him a blow. Which when the old man sees,
he waits till I'm abreast,
then from his chariot cracks a double-pointed
goad full down upon my head.
He more than paid for it. For in a trice
this hand of mine had felled him with a stick
and rolled him from the chariot stunned.
I killed them all.

Ah! If Laius is this unknown man,
there's no one in the world so doomed as I.
There's no one born so ever cursed of God:
a man, yes, whom no citizen nor even alien
can let into his house; and no one greet;
a man to force from homes.

PAUL ROCHE (1958)

THE ACHIEVEMENTS OF MAN[1]

Many marvels walk through the world,
terrible, wonderful,
but none more than Humanity,
which makes a way under winter rain,
over the grey deep of the sea,
proceeds where it swells and swallows;
that grinds at the Earth –
undwindling, unwearied, first of the Gods –
to its own purpose,
as the plough is driven, turning year into year,
through generations as colt follows mare.

1. cf. above, p. 131 – an enlightening contrast between two translations of
different generations.

Weaves and braids the meshes to hurl –
circumspect Man –
and to drive lightheaded tribes of birds his prisoners,
and the animals,
nations in fields, race of the salty ocean;
and fools and conquers the monsters
whose roads and houses are hills,
the shaggy-necked horse that he holds subject,
and the mountain-oxen that he yokes under beams,
bowing their heads,
his unwearying team.

The breath of his life
he has taught to be language,
the spirit of thought;
griefs, to give laws to nations;
fears, to dodge the weapons
of rains and winds and the homeless cold –
always clever.
He never fails to find ways
for whatever future;
manages cures for the hardest maladies;
from death alone he has secured no refuge.

With learning and with ingenuity
over his horizon of faith
Mankind crawls,
now to failure, now to worth.
And when he has bound the laws of this earth
beside Justice pledged to the Gods,
he rules his homeland;
but he has no home
whenever his recklessness weds injustice to him.
Fend this stranger from my mind's and home's hearth.

R. E. BRAUN (1962)

ANTIGONE HAS PERFORMED THE RITES OVER HER
DEAD BROTHER POLYNEICES THAT KING CREON
HAD FORBIDDEN

GUARD: My Lord, I cannot say that I have hurried,
Or that my running has made me lose my breath.
I often stopped to think, and turned to go back.
I stood there talking to myself: 'You fool,'
I said, 'Why do you go to certain death?'
And then: 'You idiot, are you still delaying?
If someone else tells Creon, you will suffer.'
I changed my mind this way, getting here slowly,
Making a short road long. But still, at last,
I did decide to come. And though my story
Is nothing much to tell, yet I will tell it.
One thing I know. I must endure my fate,
But nothing more than that can happen to me.

CREON: What is the matter? What is troubling you?

GUARD: Please let me tell you first about myself.
I did not do it. I did not see who did.
It is not right for me to be punished for it.

CREON: You take good care not to expose yourself.
Your news must certainly be something strange.

GUARD: Yes, it is strange – dreadful. I cannot speak.

CREON: Oh, tell it, will you? Tell it and go away!

GUARD: Well, it is this. Someone has buried the body,
Just now, and gone – has sprinkled it with dust
And given it other honours it should have.

CREON: What are you saying? Who has dared to do it?

GUARD: I cannot tell. Nothing was to be seen:
No mark of pickaxe, no spot where a spade
Had turned the earth. The ground was hard and dry,
Unbroken – not a trace of any wheels –
No sign to show who did it. When the sentry
On the first watch discovered it and told us,
We were struck dumb with fright. For he was hidden

Not by a tomb but a light coat of dust,
As if a pious hand had scattered it.
There were no tracks of any animal,
A dog or wild beast that had come to tear him.
We all began to quarrel, and since no one
Was there to stop us, nearly came to blows.
Everyone was accused, and everyone
Denied his guilt. We could discover nothing.
We were quite willing to handle red-hot iron,
To walk through fire, to swear by all the gods
That we were innocent of the deed itself,
And innocent of taking any part
In planning it or doing it. At last
One of us spoke. We trembled and hung our heads,
For he was right; we could not argue with him,
Yet his advice was bound to cause us trouble.
He told us all this had to be reported,
Not kept a secret. We all agreed to that.
We drew lots for it, and I had no luck.
So here I stand, unwilling, because I know
The bringer of bad news is never welcome.

CHORUS: Sir, as he spoke, I have been wondering.
Can this be, possibly, the work of gods?

CREON: Be silent! Before you madden me! You are old.
Would you be senseless also? What you say
Is unendurable. You say the gods
Cared for this corpse. Then was it for reward,
Mighty to match his mighty services,
That the gods covered him? He who came to burn
Their pillared temples and their votive offerings,
Ravage their land, and trample down the state.
Or is it your opinion that the gods
Honour the wicked? Inconceivable!
However, from the first, some citizens
Who found it difficult to endure this edict,
Muttered against me, shaking their heads in secret,
Instead of bowing down beneath the yoke,

Obedient and contented with my rule.
These are the men who are responsible,
For I am certain they have bribed the guards
To bury him. Nothing is worse than money.
Money lays waste to cities, banishes
Men from their homes, indoctrinates the heart,
Perverting honesty to works of shame,
Showing men how to practise villainy,
Subduing them to every godless deed.
But all those men who got their pay for this
Need have no doubt their turn to pay will come.
[*To the* GUARD] Now, you. As I still honour Zeus the King,
I tell you, and I swear it solemnly,
Either you find the man who did this thing,
The very man, and bring him here to me,
Or you will not just die – before you die,
You will be tortured until you have explained
This outrage; so that later when you steal
You will know better where to look for money
And not expect to find it everywhere.
Ill-gotten wealth brings ruin and not safety.

THEODORE H. BANKS (1966)

EURIPIDES

ATHENIAN tragic poet; from Phlya in Attica. Lived *c.* 485–406 B.C.
Eighteen of his eighty or ninety plays have survived.

*

THE CYCLOPS POLYPHEMUS

For your gaping gulph, and your gullet wide
The ravin is ready on every side,
The limbs of the strangers are cooked and done,
   There is boiled meat, and roast meat,
     and meat from the coal,
You may chop it, and tear it, and gnash it for fun,
   An hairy goat's-skin contains the whole.
Let me but escape, and ferry me o'er
The stream of your wrath to a safer shore.
The Cyclops Aetnean[1] is cruel and bold,
      He murders the strangers
        That sit on his hearth,
      And dreads no avengers
        To rise from the earth.
He roasts the men before they are cold,
He snatches them broiling from the coal,
And from the cauldron pulls them whole,
And minces their flesh and gnaws their bone
With his cursèd teeth, till all be gone.

PERCY BYSSHE SHELLEY (1819)

1. The island on which the savage race of Cyclopes lived was identified with Sicily.

THERE ARE NO GODS

Doth some one say that there be gods above?
There are not; no, there are not. Let no fool,
Led by the old false fable, thus deceive you.
Look at the facts themselves, yielding my words
No undue credence: for I say that kings
Kill, rob, break oaths, lay cities waste by fraud,
And doing thus are happier than those
Who live calm pious lives day after day.
How many little States that serve the gods
Are subject to the godless but more strong,
Made slaves by might of a superior army!

J. A. SYMONDS (1873–6)

THE LABOURS OF HERACLES[1]

First, then, he made the wood
Of Zeus a solitude,
Slaying its lion-tenant; and he spread
The tawniness behind – his yellow head
Enmuffled by the brute's, backed by that grin of dread.

The mountain-roving savage Kentaur-race
He strewed with deadly bow about their place,
Slaying with winged shafts: Peneios knew,
Beauteously-eddying, and the long tracts too
Of pasture trampled fruitless, and as well
Those desolated haunts Mount Pelion under,
And, grassy up to Homole,[2] each dell

1. The labours are listed as follows: (1) the Nemean lion, (2) the fight with the Centaurs, (3) the golden-horned hind, (4) the horses of Diomede, (5) Cycnus the robber, (6) the golden apples of the Hesperides, (7) the extirpation of pirates, (8) the holding up of the pillars of heaven in place of Atlas, (9) the Amazon's girdle, (10) the Hydra of Lerna, (11) the three-bodied giant Geryon, and (12) Cerberus. For (2), (5), (7) and (8) later writers substitute the Erymanthian boar, the Augean stables, the birds of Stymphalus and the Cretan bull.

2. A mountain near the river Peneus in Thessaly.

Whence, having filled their hands with pine tree plunder,
Horse-like was wont to prance from, and subdue
The land of Thessaly, that bestial crew.

The golden-headed spot-backed stag he slew,
That robber of the rustics: glorified
Therewith the goddess who in hunter's pride
Slaughters the game along Oino's side.[1]

And, yoked abreast, he brought the chariot-bred
To pace submissive to the bit, each steed
That in the bloody cribs of Diomede
Champed and, unbridled, hurried down that gore
For grain, exultant the dread feast before –
Of man's flesh: hideous feeders they of yore!

All as he crossed the Hebros' silver-flow
Accomplished he such labour, toiling so
For Mukenaian tyrant; ay, and more –
He crossed the Melian shore
And, by the sources of Amauros,[2] shot
To death that strangers' pest
Kuknos, who dwelt in Amphanaia: not
Of fame for good to guest!

And next, to the melodious maids he came,
Inside the Hesperian court-yard: hand must aim
At plucking gold fruit from the appled leaves,
Now he had killed the dragon, backed like flame,
Who guards the unapproachable he weaves
Himself all round, one spire[3] about the same.

---

1. Artemis had a shrine at Oenoe in Argolid (north-east Peloponnese).
2. This stream flows into the Pagassean gulf, near Mount Pelion (which, according to one reading, is referred to instead of Melis or Malis in the preceding line). Amphanaea is the region of Amphanae, a town near Pagasae.
3. Coil.

And into those sea-troughs of ocean dived
The hero, and for mortals calm contrived,
Whatever oars should follow in his wake.

And under heaven's mid-seat his hands thrust he,
At home with Atlas: and, for valour's sake,
Held the gods up their star-faced mansionry.

Also, the rider-host of Amazons
About Maiotis[1] many-streamed, he went
To conquer through the billowy Euxin[2] once,
Having collected what an armament
Of friends from Hellas, all on conquest bent
Of that gold-garnished cloak, dread girdle-chase!
So Hellas gained the girl's barbarian grace
And at Mukenai saves the trophy still –
Go wonder there – who will.

And the ten thousand-headed hound
Of many a murder, the Lernaian snake
He burned out, head by head, and cast around
His darts a poison thence, – darts soon to slake
Their rage in that three-bodied herdsman's gore
Of Erutheia.[3] Many a running more
He made for triumph and felicity,

And, last of toils, to Haides,[4] never dry
Of tears, he sailed: and there he, luckless, ends
His life completely, nor returns again.
The house and home are desolate of friends,
And where the children's life-path leads them, plain
I see, – no step retraceable, no god

1. The Sea of Azov.
2. The Black Sea.
3. The herdsman is Geryon, and his isle 'sunset red' was identified with the island on which Gades (Cadiz) was built.
4. Hades, the underworld.

Availing, and no law to help the lost!
The oar of Charon[1] marks their period,
Waits to end all. Thy hands, these roofs accost –
To thee, though absent, look their uttermost!

ROBERT BROWNING (1875)

PHAEDRA TELLS OF TEMPTATIONS

How oft, in other days than these, have I
Through night's long hours, thought of man's misery,
And how this life is wrecked. And, to mine eyes,
Not in man's knowledge, not in wisdom, lies
The lack that makes for sorrow. Nay, we scan
And know the right – for wit hath many a man –
But will not to the last end strive and serve.
For some grow too soon weary, and some swerve
To other paths, setting before the Right
The diverse far-off image of Delight;
And many are delights beneath the sun.
Long hours of converse; and to sit alone
Musing – a deadly happiness, and Shame:
Though two things there be hidden in one name,
And Shame can be slow poison if it will.
      This is the truth I saw then, and see still;
Nor is there any magic that can stain
That white truth for me, or make me blind again.

GILBERT MURRAY (1900–2)

THE ISLAND OF SALAMIS

In Salamis, filled with the foaming
    Of billows and murmur of bees,
Old Telamon stayed from his roaming,
      1. The aged ferryman of Hades.

143

Long ago, on a throne of the seas;
Looking out on the hills olive-laden,
        Enchanted, where first from the earth
        The grey-gleaming fruit of the Maiden
                        Athena had birth.[1]

GILBERT MURRAY (1900–2)

LIFE AND DEATH

Who knoweth if the thing that we call death
Be Life, and our Life dying – who knoweth?
Save only that all we beneath the sun
Are sick and suffering, and those foregone
Not sick, nor touched with evil any more.

GILBERT MURRAY (1913)

CREUSA LAMENTS HER RAPE BY APOLLO[2]

Soul,
soul,
speak;
nay, soul, O, my soul,
be silent;
how can you name an act
of shame,
an illicit act?
soul,
soul,
be silent;
nay, nay, O, my soul,
speak;

1. Banished from the island of Aegina, Telamon settled on Salamis, which
looks out over Attica.
2. This is an imitation rather than a translation.

what can stop you,
what can prevent?
is not your husband traitorous?
he has stolen your hope
and your house;
all hope of a child is lost;

great Zeus,
O, great Zeus,
be my witness;
O, goddess
who haunts my rocks,
by Tritonis
your holy lake[1]
be witness;
O, witness and help,
O, stars,
O, star–throne of Zeus;

I have hidden too long
this truth,
I must lighten my heart
of this secret;
I must be rid of it.

O, eyes,
eyes weep,
O, heart,
heart break,
you fell in a trap of men,
you were snared in a god's net;
(are gods or are men more base?)

O, eyes,
eyes weep,
O, heart,

1. A lake in Libya sacred to Pallas Athene.

O, my heart
cry out
against him of the seven-strung lyre,
against him of the singing voice;

yes,
to you, you, you
I shout,
harmony, rhythm, delight
of the Muses,
you I accuse;
you, born of Leto,[1]
you bright
traitor within the light;

why did you seek me out,
brilliant, with gold hair?
vibrant,
you seized my wrists,
while the flowers fell from my lap,
the gold and the pale-gold crocus,
while you fulfilled your wish;
what did it help, my shout
of mother,
mother?
no help
came to me
in the rocks;
O, mother,
O, white hands caught;
O, mother,
O, gold flowers lost;

O, terror,
O, hopeless loss,
O, evil union,

1. A Titaness, mother of Apollo.

O, fate;
where is he whom you begot?
(for fear of my mother,
I left
that child
on those bride-rocks;)

O, eyes,
eyes weep,
but that god will not relent,
who thought of the harp-note
while his child was done to death
by hovering eagles or hawks;
O, heart,
heart break,
but your heart will never break,
who sit apart
and speak
prophecies;
I will speak
to you on your golden throne,
you devil
at earth-heart,
your golden tripod
is cursed;

O, evil lover,
you grant
my husband who owes you naught,
his child to inherit my house,
while my child
and your child
is lost;
our son was torn by beaks
of ravaging birds,
he was caught
out of the little robes

I wrapped him in,
and lost;

O, terror,
O, hopelessness,
O, evil union,
O, fate,
I left him there on the rocks,
alone
in a lonely place,
be witness,
O, Delos,[1]
and hate,
hate him, O, you laurel-branch,
hate,
hate him
you palm-branch,
caught
with the leaves of the laurel to bless
that other so-holy birth,
yours,
Leto's child
with Zeus.

HILDA DOOLITTLE (1937)

ION DEDICATES HIMSELF TO APOLLO

See, already over the earth
The Sun lights up his four-horsed team;
His flames put the stars to flight from the sky
Into holy night.
Parnassus' untrodden mountain-peaks
Are lit with his fires,[2] and welcome for men

1. The Aegean island sacred to Apollo.
2. Delphi lies on the lower southern slopes of this sacred mountain.

The chariot-wheels of day.
Smoke of rainless frankincense
Spreads over Apollo's roof;
The Delphian woman is taking her seat
On the holy tripod and sings to the Greeks
The dooms that ring from Apollo.
      Come, Apollo's Delphian servants.
Come to Castalia's whirling waters
Silver-shining.[1] Wash yourselves
In the pure spring and come to the shrine.
Seal your lips in reverent silence;
To all who would question the oracle
Nothing unseal
But holy words from your lips.
      And I, who from my childhood's days
Have done this task, will sanctify
With laurel branches and holy crowns
Apollo's doorway and cleanse the floor
With splash of water. Flocks of birds,
Who spoil the sacred offerings,
My bow and arrow shall put to flight.
For, since I have neither mother nor father,
I give my service
To Apollo's house which has nursed me.

C. M. BOWRA (1938)

THE STUDY OF NATURE

Happy is he who has knowledge
That comes from inquiry. No evil he stirs
For his townsmen, nor gives himself
To unjust doings,
But surveys the unageing order
Of deathless nature, of what it is made,
And whence, and how.

1. A spring beside Delphi, sacred to Apollo and the Muses.

In men of this kind the study
Of base acts never finds a home.

C. M. BOWRA (1957)

ATHENS

From old the sons of Erechtheus[1] know felicity;
The children of blessed gods,
Born from a land holy and undespoiled,
They pasture on glorious Wisdom,
Ever walking gracefully through the brightest of skies,
Where once, men tell, the Holy Nine,
The Pierian Muses,[2]
Created golden-haired Harmony.

On the fair-flowing waters of Cephisus[3]
They say that Aphrodite fills her pitcher
And breathes over the land
The sweet gentle air of winds,
And ever she crowns her hair
With a fragrant wreath of roses;
She sends her Loves[4] to be throned at Wisdom's side,
And with her to work all manner of excellence.

C. M. BOWRA (1957)

MEDEA SPEAKS OF HER DESERTION BY JASON

... And those who live
Quietly, as I do, get a bad reputation.
For a just judgement is not evident in the eyes

1. Erechtheus, a mythical king of Athens, the son of Earth, brought up by Pallas Athene.
2. Pieria was a spring on the slopes of Mount Olympus, near which the Muses and Orpheus were born.
3. The river of Athens.
4. The Erotes, multiplications or companions of Eros (Cupid), the son of Aphrodite.

When a man at first sight hates another, before
Learning his character, being in no way injured;
And a foreigner especially must adapt himself.
I'd not approve of even a fellow-countryman
Who by pride and want of manners offends his neighbours.
But on me this thing has fallen so unexpectedly,
It has broken my heart. I am finished. I let go
All my life's joy. My friends, I only want to die.
It was everything to me to think well of one man,
And he, my own husband, has turned out wholly vile.
Of all things which are living and can form a judgement
We women are the most unfortunate creatures.
Firstly, with an excess of wealth it is required
For us to buy a husband and take for our bodies
A master; for not to take one is even worse.
And now the question is serious whether we take
A good or bad one; for there is no easy escape
For a woman, nor can she say no to her marriage.
She arrives among new modes of behaviour and manners,
And needs prophetic power, unless she has learnt at home,
How best to manage him who shares the bed with her.
And if we work out all this well and carefully,
And the husband lives with us and lightly bears his yoke,
Then life is enviable. If not, I'd rather die.
A man, when he's tired of the company in his home,
Goes out of the house and puts an end to his boredom
And turns to a friend or companion of his own age.
But we are forced to keep our eyes on one alone.
What they say of us is that we have a peaceful time
Living at home, while they do the fighting in war.
How wrong they are! I would very much rather stand
Three times in the front of battle than bear one child.

REX WARNER (1944)

THE TWO FACES OF WAR

MENELAUS: It was, I think, the greatest force on earth I led
(and here I do not boast) across the sea to Troy;
nor was it by compulsion that I ruled my troops;
no, it was freely that the youth of Greece obeyed ...
Troy's burning is a human's act: I, Menelaus,
who lit the fire am not unknown throughout the
earth ...

HELEN: O unhappy Troy, destroyed
by deeds that should not have been done!
How have you suffered? The gifts
of Cypris[1] to me have brought forth blood,
have brought forth tears, sorrow on sorrow,
weeping on weeping and pain upon pain.
Mothers have lost their children,
maidens have cut from their heads
their tresses in mourning for brothers,
dead men in the Phrygian stream
of Scamander.[2] And Greece has let loose
a cry and a wailing for death.
Hands are laid to the head;
finger nails tear the delicate skin of the cheek
which is wet from the flowing of blood.

REX WARNER (1951)

THE GREEK CAPTIVE WOMEN IN TAURIS SING OF THEIR EXILE AND IPHIGENIA'S RESCUE

Bird of the rocky reefs, desolate halcyon,
Sweet dirge that hovers
Above the ocean wave,
A song that speaks to the ear well tuned to sorrow,
Crying for your mate who is lost forever,

1. Aphrodite.   2. The river of Troy.

Bird of repining, listen while I sing
A wingless mourner
Who yearns for the friendly throng
Of a market-place in Hellas,
For Artemis, our help in childbirth
Whose shrine is the island hill of Delos
Shelter of Leto's travail[1] —
The cool grove of soft-tressed palms
Sweet-scented laurel and the silver veil of the olive
That shades the curving waters of the lake
Where drifts the coiléd swan
Prophetic singer of the Muses
At rest on the windless flood.

I remember the hot tears upon my cheek
The fractured towers, the walls thrown down
Oars and spears of our enemies
And ships that bore us to exile far away
Marketed for gold.
They led me to this savage coast
Servant to Artemis of the dark forest
And her virgin priestess Agamemnon's daughter[2]
Tending the altars of this temple of death
Where no beast-offering thicks the stones
But the blood of men.
Now I have come to envy
Those who have never known happiness:
A cruel fate may relent
But to fall from joy to misery
This is the hardest lot for mortal man.

But you, daughter of Agamemnon, shall come again to Argos
A fifty-oared ship to speed you home.
For you the wax-stopped pipes

1. Mother of Apollo and Artemis.
2. Iphigenia.

Of Pan-of-the-mountain-side
Shall pierce the ocean breeze
Calling the time to your rowers
And Phoebus the prophet-god[1]
Shall bless your voyage with music
Striking the deep chords of his seven-toned lyre
And guide you to the shining rock of Athens
While I shall gaze
On the fading foam of your oar-blades
The white curve of your sails
And the wake of a fleeing keel.

O to tread that fiery chariot-course
Of the burning horses of the sun, westward and home
And come to rest, folding impetuous wings
Above my beloved roof.
O to call back
Bright years behind me
Days of great weddings and the marriage music
When I would steal from my mother's side
Into the winding circle of the dancers
The gay challenge of my dear companions
Sweet strife of smooth tresses, whispered words
And the flushed cheek of happiness half-hidden
In the bright fall of my scarf
Or by my tumbling hair.

IAN SCOTT-KILVERT (1955)

THE MADNESS OF HERACLES

Ah, all this has no bearing on my grief;
But I do not believe the gods commit
Adultery, or bind each other in chains.
I never did believe it; I never shall;
Nor that one god is tyrant of the rest.

1. Apollo.

154

If god is truly god, he is perfect,
Lacking nothing. These are poets' wretched lines.

WILLIAM ARROWSMITH (1959)

A MESSENGER TELLS KING PENTHEUS OF THEBES OF THE BACCHIC FRENZY

About that hour
when the sun lets loose its light to warm the earth,
our grazing herds of cows had just begun to climb
the path along the mountain ridge. Suddenly
I saw three companies of dancing women,
one led by Autonoë, the second captained
by your mother Agave, while Ino led the third.[1]
There they lay in the deep sleep of exhaustion,
some resting on boughs of fir, others sleeping
where they fell, here and there among the oak leaves –
but all modestly and soberly, not, as you think,
drunk with wine, nor wandering, led astray
by the music of the flute, to hunt their Aphrodite
through the woods.

But your mother heard the lowing
of our hornéd herds, and springing to her feet,
gave a great cry to waken them from sleep.
And they too, rubbing the bloom of soft sleep
from their eyes, rose up lightly and straight –
a lovely sight to see: all as one,
the old women and the young and the unmarried girls.
First they let their hair fall loose, down
over their shoulders, and those whose straps had slipped
fastened their skins of fawn with writhing snakes
that licked their cheeks. Breasts swollen with milk,
new mothers who had left their babies behind at home
nestled gazelles and young wolves in their arms,
suckling them. Then they crowned their hair with leaves,

1. The three were sisters.

ivy and oak and flowering bryony. One woman
struck her thyrsus[1] against a rock and a fountain
of cool water came bubbling up. Another drove
her fennel in the ground, and where it struck the earth,
at the touch of god, a spring of wine poured out.
Those who wanted milk scratched at the soil
with bare fingers and the white milk came welling up.
Pure honey spurted, streaming, from their wands.
If you had been there and seen these wonders for yourself,
you would have gone down on your knees and prayed
to the god you now deny.

      We cowherds and shepherds
gathered in small groups, wondering and arguing
among ourselves at these fantastic things,
the awful miracles those women did.
But then a city fellow with the knack of words
rose to his feet and said, 'All you who live
upon the pastures of the mountain, what do you say?
Shall we earn a little favour with King Pentheus
by hunting his mother Agave out of the revels?'
Falling in with his suggestion, we withdrew
and set ourselves in ambush, hidden by the leaves
among the undergrowth. Then at a signal
all the Bacchae whirled their wands for the revels
to begin. With one voice they cried aloud:
'O Iacchus! Son of Zeus!' 'O Bromius!'[2] they cried
until the beasts and all the mountain seemed
wild with divinity. And when they ran,
everything ran with them.

      It happened, however,
that Agave ran near the ambush where I lay
concealed. Leaping up, I tried to seize her,
but she gave a cry: 'Hounds who run with me,
men are hunting us down! Follow, follow me!

---

1. The staff of Dionysus, wreathed with ivy and vine leaves.
2. Names of Dionysus (Bacchus).

Use your wands for weapons.'

At this we fled
and barely missed being torn to pieces by the women.
Unarmed, they swooped down upon the herds of cattle
grazing there on the green of the meadow. And then
you could have seen a single woman with bare hands
tear a fat calf, still bellowing with fright,
in two, while others clawed the heifers to pieces.
There were ribs and cloven hooves scattered everywhere,
and scraps smeared with blood hung from the fir trees.
And bulls, their raging fury gathered in their horns,
lowered their heads to charge, then fell, stumbling
to the earth, pulled down by hordes of women
and stripped of flesh and skin more quickly, sire,
than you could blink your royal eyes.

WILLIAM ARROWSMITH (1959)

ARISTOPHANES

The outstanding poet of the Athenian Old Comedy. Born between 457 and 445 B.C., and died in, or shortly before, 385. His plays perhaps numbered more than forty; eleven have survived.

*

THE HYMN OF THE CLOUDS

Cloud-maidens that float on for ever,
 Dew-sprinkled, fleet bodies, and fair,
Let us rise from our Sire's loud river,
 Great Ocean, and soar through the air
To the peaks of the pine-covered mountains where the
  pines hang as tresses of hair.
Let us seek the watchtowers undaunted,
 Where the well-watered cornfields abound,
And through murmurs of rivers nymph-haunted
 The songs of the sea-waves resound;
And the sun in the sky never wearies of spreading his
  radiance around.
   Let us cast off the haze
    Of the mists from our band,
   Till with far-seeing gaze
    We may look on the land . . .

Cloud-maidens that bring the rain-shower,
 To the Pallas-loved land let us wing,
To the land of stout heroes and Power,
 Where Kekrops was hero and king,[1]
Where honour and silence is given
 To the mysteries that none may declare,
Where are gifts to the high gods in heaven

1. The mythical first king of Athens.

158

When the house of the gods is laid bare,
Where are lofty roofed temples, and statues well
    carven and fair;
    Where are feasts to the happy immortals
When the sacred procession draws near,
    Where garlands make bright the bright portals
At all seasons and months in the year;
           And when spring days are here,
           Then we tread to the wine-god a measure,
           In Bacchanal dance and in pleasure,
           'Mid the contests of sweet singing choirs,
           And the crash of loud lyres.

OSCAR WILDE (1874)

THE HYMN OF THE BIRDS

Come on then, ye dwellers by nature in darkness,
    and like to the leaves' generations,
That are little of might, that are moulded of mire,
    unenduring and shadow-like nations,
Poor plumeless ephemerals, comfortless mortals,
    as visions of shadows fast fleeing,
Lift up your mind unto us that are deathless,
    and dateless the date of our being:
Us, children of heaven, us, ageless for aye,
    us, all of whose thoughts are eternal;
That ye may from henceforth, having heard of us
    all things aright as to matters supernal,
Of the being of birds, and beginning of gods,
    and of streams, and the dark beyond reaching,
Truthfully knowing aright, in my name
    bid Prodicus pack with his preaching . . .[1]
  It was Chaos and Night at the first, and the blackness
    of darkness, and Hell's broad border,
Earth was not, nor air, neither heaven; when in depths

1. Prodicus of Ceos, a sophist and a friend of Socrates.

of the womb of the dark without order
First thing first-born of the black-plumed Night
    was a wind-egg hatched in her bosom,
Whence timely with seasons revolving again
    sweet Love burst out as a blossom,
Gold wings gleaming forth of his back,
    like whirlwinds gustily turning.
He, after his wedlock with Chaos, whose wings
    are of darkness, in Hell broad-burning,
For his nestling begat him the race of us first,
    and upraised us to light new-lighted,
And before this was not the race of the gods,
    until all things by Love were united:
And of kind united with kind in communion
    of nature the sky and the sea are
Brought forth, and the earth, and the race of the gods
    everlasting and blest. So that we are
Far away the most ancient of all things blest.
    And that we are of Love's generation
There are manifest manifold signs. We have wings,
    and with us have the Loves habitation . . .
    All best good things that befall men come
    from us birds, as is plain to all reason;
For first we proclaim and make known to them spring,
    and the winter and autumn in season:
Bid sow, when the crane starts clanging for Afric,
    in shrill-voiced emigrant number,
And calls to the pilot to hang up his rudder
    again for the season, and slumber;
And then weave cloak for Orestes the thief,[1]
    lest he strip men of theirs if it freezes.
And again thereafter the kite reappearing
    announces a change in the breezes,
And that here is the season for shearing your sheep
    of their spring wool. Then does the swallow
Give you notice to sell your greatcoat, and provide

    1. Nickname of a well-known robber of travellers.

something light for the heat that's to follow.
Thus are we as Ammon or Delphi unto you,
  Dodona, nay, Phoebus Apollo.[1]
For, as first ye come all to get auguries of birds,
  even such is in all things your carriage,
Be the matter a matter of trade or of earning
  your bread, or of any one's marriage.
And all things ye lay to the charge of a bird
  that belong to discerning prediction:
Winged fame is a bird, as you reckon: you sneeze,
  and the sign's as a bird for conviction:
All tokens are 'birds' with you – sounds too, and lackeys,
  and donkeys. Then must it not follow
That we ARE to you all as the manifest godhead
  that speaks in prophetic Apollo?

A. C. SWINBURNE (1880)

THE POET'S SELF-DEFENCE

From the time Aristophanes first began to write,
He's never come into the open as frankly as this.
And you Athenians, renowned for your quicksilver wit,
– You've seen him attacked by unprincipled enemies
Who say he slanders the State (and so, you) in his plays.
He's ready to answer; he knows you, quicksilver, too,
For the truth if it's offered you. Hear what he says. He says
He deserves your approval: hasn't he held before you
The mirror in which you see yourselves flattered and tricked
By any slick foreign envoy? – right from the time
Some smarmy called Athens 'violet crowned' and you stuck
Yourselves up, and sat on your bottoms and beamed?
And if anyone sucked up and simpered 'Athens so glistening'
You'd do *anything* for them (though the epithet better applies

1. Ammon (in the Siwa oasis) and Dodona (north-west Greece) were oracles
of Zeus, Delphi the oracle of Apollo. 'Nay, Phoebus Apollo' means 'We
are your Phoebus Apollo himself'.

To a sardine).[1] But now, as you listen
To the Truth from your poet, won't you reward him for this?
– And for showing the world how a *real* democracy works? If
I told you they'll come simply *pressing* tribute upon you
– Just for a glimpse of the poet who risked his life
To tell the Athenians the truth – it'd *be* the truth.
Why, the report of his courage has spread so widely already:
The King of Persia asked the envoys from Sparta,
First, what nation was the greatest power at sea?
And then, *whose* poet was the hardest hitter,
The most fearless satirist. Then the King added this:
'The people that have *his* advice will fight better, they'll win
'The war for a cert!' – Aren't the Spartans sueing for peace,
At the moment, because of this?[2] Demanding the cession of
    Aegina,[3]
Yes (though they don't give a damn for the place)
But hoping to whittle the poet away with it. Y O U
Must never allow that! For he tells the truth in his plays
And he's still got a packet to say, and *all for your good.*
And you know him: he doesn't toady, suck up, blather, or lie;
He has only the best to offer you. He offers it fearlessly!

> Let Kleon[4] direct against me
> As much smear and smut as he likes –
> I've got Right on my side, I don't mind!
> My conscience is clean, as regards the State.
> *Him!* Well, you know what a coward *he* is,
> And what sort of jobs for the boys *he* finds . . .
> You know I am not like that!

PATRIC DICKINSON (1957)

1. 'Violet crowned' and 'Athens so glistening', are the traditional complimentary epithets of the city.

2. *The Acharnians*, from which this passage comes, was written in 425 B.C., during the first phase of the Peloponnesian War. Acharnae was a small town in Attica.

3. The conquest of the island of Aegina by Athens in 457 B.C. was regarded as one of the causes of the Peloponnesian War.

4. The Athenian political leader and demagogue.

THE UNNECESSARY WAR

DIKAIOPOLIS: I trust that none of you here will think ill of me
    If, dressed as a beggar, I'm bold enough to speak
    To the Athenian people about the State
    – And in a comedy. Even a comedy
    Can tell the truth. Nor can Kleon accuse me –
    Of inveighing against the State with strangers present.
    There are no strangers present. We are alone here.
    There are no emissaries from the allies. No one.
    We are here; the people, the winnowed grain of us.
    Our resident aliens are not in this. We are alone.

    So – just let me tell you that I loathe the Spartans,
    And if Poseidon wrecked, in a bumper earthquake,
    Every single one of their homes – I shouldn't worry.
    But are we, I say, – and we're all friends here, –
    (I, like you, have had my vines cut down)
    Are *we* to blame the Spartans for everything?
    There are those among us – I do not say the State,
    Remember that, please, – I do not say the State,
    There are those among us, men of a sort I suppose,
    Crooked, dishonest, degenerate, doubledealers,
    And what have they done?
    – They kept on objecting and informing against
    The Megarian trade in tunics[1] – their staple trade –
    And if they saw a cucumber, or a hare,
    Or a sucking pig, a garlic-corm, a block of salt,
    And they came from Megara – what did they do?
    Had them confiscated! and then knocked down for a song ...
    I suppose these were mere nothings – just our
    Athenian way – the Megarians shouldn't have
        minded?

PATRIC DICKINSON (1957)

1. Shortly before the Peloponnesian War the Athenians passed a decree excluding the Megarians from every port and market in Athenian jurisdiction.

AN UNFORTUNATE MATCH

Oh curse the confounded matchmaker
Who jockeyed me into marrying
Your mother! There was I, leading
A blissful country-life, shabby
And dirty and happy-go-lucky with piles
Of olives, flocks in my folds,
Bees in my hives – and then I had
To marry this blue-blooded bit.
Me a farmer, she the niece
Of nobility, a town-bred,
Stuck-up, finicky, classy lady
and *I* married her! Me, stinking of wine
And fig-boards and oily with raw wool,
And she all cloyed with expensive
Scents and saffrons, and tricksy kisses,
And parties, and stuffing herself, and sex.
I don't say she did nothing, no!
She went the pace and I told her so,
Showing her my more-than-worn-out cloak:
'You're burning it up too fast,' I said.

PATRIC DICKINSON (1970)

SEARCH FOR UTOPIA

EUELPIDES: Yes, dear people, we confess we're completely mad.
But it's not like Sakas'[1] madness. Not a bit.
For he, poor dumb foreigner, wants in, while we,
born and bred Athenians both, true blue,
true citizens, not afraid of any man,
want out.

1. The Scythians (from South Russia) were called 'Sakai', i.e. a nickname for foreigners who managed to get Athenian citizenship. Here the term is said to refer to a tragic poet called Acestor.

Yes, we've spread our little feet
and taken off. Not that we hate Athens –
heavens, no. And not that dear old Athens
isn't grand, that blessed land where men are free –
to pay their taxes.

No, look to the locust
who, one month or two, drones and shrills
among the little thickets, while the men of Athens,
perched upon the thorny thickets of the law, sit
shrilling out their three score years and ten.
Because of legal locusts, gentlemen, we have left,
lugging these baskets and pots and boughs of myrtle,
looking for some land of soft and lovely leisure
where a man may loaf and play and settle down
for good. Tereus the Hoopoe is our journey's end.
From him we hope to learn if he has seen
in all his many travels such a place
on earth.

WILLIAM ARROWSMITH (1961)

THE BIRDS HAVE LOST THEIR ANCIENT GREATNESS

Such were the honours you held in the days of your soaring
    greatness.

But now you've been downgraded.
You're the slaves, not lords, of men.
They call you brainless or crazy.
They kill you whenever they can.

The temples are no protection:
The hunters are lying in wait
with traps and nooses and nets
and little limed twigs and bait.

And when you're taken, they sell you
as tiny *hors d'oeuvres* for a lunch.
And you're not even sold alone
but lumped and bought by the bunch.

And buyers come crowding around
and pinch your breast and your rump,
to see if your fleshes are firm
and your little bodies are plump.

And as if that wasn't enough,
they refuse to roast you whole,
but dump you down in a dish
and call you a *casseróle*.

They grind up cheese and spices
with some oil and other goo,
and they take this slimy gravy
and they pour it over you! . . .

It's like a disinfectant,
and they pour it piping hot
as though your meat were putrid,
to sterilize the rot!

WILLIAM ARROWSMITH (1961)

THE GRIEVANCE OF THE WOMEN

COMMISSIONER:
    Now, Lysistrata: tell me what you're thinking.
LYSISTRATA:
    Glad to.
                Ever since this war began[1]
    We women have been watching you men, agreeing with you,

1. The *Lysistrata* was written in 411 B.C., in the later stages of the Peloponnesian War.

keeping our thoughts to ourselves. That doesn't mean
we were happy: we weren't, for we saw how things were
    going;
but we'd listen to you at dinner
arguing this way and that.
                   – Oh you, and your big
Top Secrets! –
             And then we'd grin like little patriots
(though goodness knows we didn't feel like grinning) and
    ask you:
'Dear, did the Armistice come up in Assembly today?'
And you'd say, 'None of your business! Pipe down!',
    you'd say.
And so we would.

                          DUDLEY FITTS (1962)

ATTACK ON EURIPIDES

A WOMAN: . . . No; I have long
  viewed with alarm the reprehensible conduct
  of the vegetable dealer's son Euripides.
  The vicious
  contumely he has indulged in, dragging us
  through the cloacine seepage of his mind!
  Evil? Can you think of any evil
  that he has left unsaid? Give him some actors,
  a Chorus, an audience, and there he goes
  proving that women are good-for-nothing, incarnate
  wine-jugs, walking sinks of lust, deceivers,
  babblers, fly-by-nights, knives in the flesh
  of honest men. And what is the result?
  You know perfectly well. When those husbands of ours
  come home from one of his plays,
  first they look at us queerly, and then,
  why, they simply tear the house apart
  hunting for lovers hidden in some closet.

It's no use,
we can't do things we've been doing all our lives
but they get suspicious, thanks to Euripides
and his Advice to Husbands.
                          Suppose a woman
buys a flower for her hair: that means she's in love.
Or she drops a pot or two on the way to the kitchen:
immediately her husband finds significance
in the broken crockery, and he quotes Euripides:
The trembling hand betrays th' adult'rous guest.
Or say a girl gets sick,
here comes big brother with his Euripides:
This morning greenness augureth no maid.

DUDLEY FITTS (1962)

THE EFFEMINATE POET AGATHON[1]

MNESILOCHUS:

I wouldn't have believed it, you move me to poetry, you do,
Speaking as spicily as though you'd just grazed on orchids.
As I listened I felt such a melodious itch of the bum.
And now, dear boy, let me ask you in the words of Aeschylus
Who the Devil are you? Where the Devil do you come from
And what the Devil are you doing crusted up like a
      cloud-cuckoo?
Is your sex prismatic? One little rosy nail
Prattles over the lyre, one little tepid hand
Coyly arched with silks and your hair not rank merely but
      netted.
A woman's girdle, a skin smarmed up with oil like a wrestler,
Dangling a sword in one hand, a looking glass in the other.
Are you horned or slatted, you twilight of the genders?
Because if you're a man your hinge doesn't give you away
And if you're a woman what have you done with those titties?

1. After the three great masters – Aeschylus, Sophocles, Euripides – Agathon
was the most distinguished Athenian tragic poet.

Well, say something can't you. Mum? If you don't speak to me
I shall have to track your gender down from your poem.

AGATHON:

You're
Just madly jealous, dearie. Don't talk to me about empathy,
So *triste*-making. Whatever a poet writes about, he becomes.
We're as volatile as acids, a mere wardrobe of identities.
I'm writing a Kassandra now, that's a play about women
With a chorus of women: so of course I *become* a woman.

MNESILOCHUS:

When you're trying a Phaedra who wanted a boy mad
On horses you make love, I suppose, in the horse position.

AGATHON:

But of course if one's writing about men one becomes
Profoundly male and all that. *Le style c'est l'homme.*

MNESILOCHUS:

I'd like to have seen you, Euripides, when writing the Satyrs,
Did you spend several weeks buttoned up in a foreskin?
[*To* AGATHON] If you should think of turning to Satyric drama
Just tell me and I'll help you from behind.

AGATHON:

He should be dandified in clothes as well as in metres.
Take Ibycus or Anacreon, all those delicious Ionians,
Alcaeus too, who sophisticated poetry.[1]
Well! all of them wore headscarves and must have looked
    rather like me;
And there's Phrynichus, well, you've heard of him surely,[2]
Such an elegant dear and just as elegantly dressed.
That's why his plays are so elegant, because naturally
One writes as one is. The play is more or less the man.

MNESILOCHUS:

I get it. That's why Philocles who looks like an ape
Writes like an ape – or would if an ape could write. Xenocles,

1. Specimens of the lyric poetry of Ibycus, Anacreon and Alcaeus appear elsewhere in this book.
2. Phrynichus was one of the originators of Athenian tragedy.

Rather an outsider, scribbles like a cad and
Theognis' veins run ice-water so his plays are all pompous.

AGATHON:

What a critic! Well, wishing to follow a feminine idiom
I dress myself up like a woman.

MNESILOCHUS:

Do you, you bitch.

EURIPIDES:

O stop yapping. When I was a promising younger poet
I was full of these florid gestures too.

MNESILOCHUS:

I won't say I envy
Your literary milyew – if that's the O.K. phrase.

IAN FLETCHER (1963)

HOW WE TREAT OUR GOOD MEN

I'll tell you what I think about the way
This city treats her soundest men today:
By a coincidence more sad than funny,
It's very like the way we treat our money.
The noble silver drachma, that of old
We were so proud of, and the recent gold,
Coins that rang true, clean-stamped and worth their weight
Throughout the world, have ceased to circulate.
Instead, the purses of Athenian shoppers
Are full of shoddy silver-plated coppers.
Just so, when men are needed by the nation,
The best have been withdrawn from circulation.
Men of good birth and breeding, men of parts,
Well schooled in wrestling and in gentler arts,
These we abuse, and trust instead to knaves,
Newcomers, alien, copper-pated slaves,
All rascals – honestly, what men to choose!
There was a time when you'd have scorned to use
Men so debased, so far beyond the pale,
Even as scapegoats to be dragged from jail

And flogged to death outside the city gate.
My foolish friends, change now, it's not too late!
Try the good ones again: if they succeed,
You will have proved that you have sense indeed;
And if things don't go well, if these good men
All fail, and Athens comes to grief, why then
Discerning folk will murmur (let us hope):
'She's hanged herself – but what a splendid rope!'

DAVID BARRETT (1964)

WE ARE JUST LIKE WASPS

Now anyone who studies us from various points of view
Will find that we resemble wasps in everything we do.
No creature, to begin with, is more savage and irate,
When once provoked, than we are, or less easy to placate.
Observe our social structure and you'll see that it conforms
To that of wasps exactly – we are organized in swarms;
And according to the jury that we're privileged to be on
We buzz about the Archon's Court, or nest in the Odeon.
And some, like grublets in their cells, are packed around the wall:
They nod their heads, but otherwise they scarcely move at all.
Our economic system, too, is practical and neat:
By stinging all and sundry we contrive to make ends meet.
Of course we have our drones as well, dull stingless brutes who shirk
Their military duties, letting others do the work –
And sure enough they gobble up as much as they can get
Of the income *we* have earned them with no end of toil and sweat.
It makes us wild to think that those who've never raised a hand
Or risked a single blister to defend their native land
Can draw their pay with all the rest: I think the rule should be
That if you haven't got a sting you get no jury fee.

DAVID BARRETT (1964)

PART IV

_____

THE HISTORIANS

HERODOTUS

THE first great historian, from Halicarnassus (Bodrum) in Caria (western Asia Minor); settled at the pan-Hellenic colony in Thurii (southern Italy). Born *c.* 484 B.C. (?), died between 430 and 420. His history is a wide-ranging account of the wars between the Greeks and Persians.

*

THE BUILDING OF THE PYRAMIDS

When Cheops succeeded to the throne, the priests said, he plunged into all manner of wickedness.[1] He closed the temples, and forbade the Egyptians to offer sacrifice, compelling them instead to labour, one and all, in his service. Some were required to drag blocks of stone down to the Nile from the quarries in the Arabian range of hills;[2] others received the blocks after they had been conveyed in boats across the river, and drew them to the range of hills called the Libyan. A hundred thousand men laboured constantly, and were relieved every three months by a fresh lot. It took ten years' oppression of the people to make the causeway for the conveyance of the stones, a work not much inferior, in my judgement, to the pyramid itself. This causeway is five furlongs in length, ten fathoms wide, and in height, at the highest part, eight fathoms. It is built of polished stone, and is covered with carvings of animals. To make it took ten years, as I said – or rather to make the causeway, the works on the mound where the pyramids stand, and the underground chambers, which Cheops intended as vaults for his own sepulchre: these last were built on a sort of island, surrounded by water introduced from the Nile by a canal. The pyramid itself was twenty years in building. It is a square, eight hundred feet each way, and the height the same, built entirely of polished stones, perfectly joined; no stone is less than thirty feet in length.

1. King Khufu of Egypt (twenty-sixth century B.C.).
2. i.e. on the east bank of the Nile.

The pyramid was built in steps, battlement-wise, as it is called, or, according to others, altar-wise. After laying the stones for the base they raised the remaining stones to their places by means of machines formed of short wooden planks. The first machine raised them from the ground to the top of the first step. On this there was another machine, which received the stone upon its arrival, and conveyed it to the second step, whence a third machine advanced it still higher. Either they had as many machines as there were steps in the pyramid, or possibly they had but a single machine, which, being easily moved, was transferred from tier to tier as the stone rose – both accounts are given, and therefore I mention both. The upper portion of the pyramid was finished first, then the middle, and finally the part which was lowest and nearest the ground. There is an inscription in Egyptian characters on the pyramid which records the quantity of radishes, onions, and garlic consumed by the labourers who constructed it; and I perfectly well remember that the interpreter who read the writing to me said that the money expended in this way was sixteen hundred talents of silver. If this then is a true record, what a vast sum must have been spent on the iron tools used in the work, and on the feeding and clothing of the labourers, considering the length of time the work lasted, which has already been stated, and the additional time – no small space, I imagine – which must have been occupied by the quarrying of the stones, their conveyance, and the cutting of the underground canal.

The wickedness of Cheops reached to such a pitch that, lacking funds, he placed his own daughter in a brothel, with orders to procure him a certain sum – how much I cannot say, for I was not told; she procured it, however, and at the same time, bent on leaving a monument which should perpetuate her own memory, she required each man to make her a present of a stone. With these stones she built the pyramid which stands midmost of the three that are in front of the great pyramid, measuring along each side a hundred and fifty feet.

GEORGE RAWLINSON (1858–60)

THE SPARTANS AT THERMOPYLAE[1]

The Greek forces at Thermopylae, when the Persian army drew near to the entrance of the pass, were seized with fear; and a council was held to consider about a retreat. It was the wish of the Peloponnesians generally that the army should fall back upon the Peloponnesus, and there guard the Isthmus. But Leonidas, who saw with what indignation the Phocians and Locrians heard of this plan, gave his voice for remaining where they were, while they sent envoys to the several cities to ask for help, since they were too few to make a stand against an army like that of the Medes.[2]

While this debate was going on, Xerxes[3] sent a mounted spy to observe the Greeks, and note how many they were, and see what they were doing. He had heard, before he came out of Thessaly, that a few men were assembled at this place, and that at their head were certain Lacedaemonians,[4] under Leonidas, a descendant of Hercules. The horseman rode up to the camp, and looked about him, but did not see the whole army, for such as were on the farther side of the wall (which had been rebuilt and was now carefully guarded) it was not possible for him to behold; but he observed those on the outside, who were encamped in front of the rampart. It chanced that at this time the Lacedaemonians held the outer guard, and were seen by the spy, some of them engaged in gymnastic exercises, others combing their long hair. At this the spy greatly marvelled, but he counted their number, and when he had taken accurate note of everything he rode back quietly; for no one pursued after him, nor paid any heed to his visit. So he returned, and told Xerxes all that he had seen.

Upon this Xerxes, who had no means of surmising the truth – namely, that the Spartans were preparing to die manfully – but thought it laughable that they should be engaged in such employments, sent and called to his presence Demaratus the son of Ariston, who still remained with the army. When he appeared, Xerxes told him all that he had heard, and questioned him concerning the news,

1. 480 B.C.   2. i.e. the Persians.
3. King of Persia, 486–465 B.C.
4. i.e. Spartans.

since he was anxious to understand the meaning of such behaviour on the part of the Spartans. Then Demaratus said:

'I spoke to you concerning these men long since, when we had just begun our march upon Greece; you, however, only laughed at my words, when I told you of all this, which I saw would come to pass. Earnestly do I struggle at all times to speak truth to you, O King, and now listen to it once more. These men have come to dispute the pass with us; and it is for this that they are now making ready. It is their custom, when they are about to hazard their lives, to adorn their heads with care. Be assured, however, that if you can subdue the men who are here and the Lacedaemonians who remain in Sparta, there is no other nation in all the world which will venture to lift a hand against you. You have now to deal with the first kingdom in Greece, and with the bravest men.'

Then Xerxes, to whom what Demaratus said seemed altogether to surpass belief, asked further how it was possible for so small an army to contend with his.

'O King,' Demaratus answered, 'let me be treated as a liar if matters fall not out as I say.'

GEORGE RAWLINSON (1858–60)

THE LYDIANS[1]

Apart from the fact that they prostitute their daughters, the Lydian way of life is not unlike our own. The Lydians were the first people we know of to use a gold and silver coinage and to introduce retail trade, and they also claim to have invented the games which are now commonly played both by themselves and by the Greeks. These games are supposed to have been invented at the time when they sent a colony to settle in Tyrrhenia,[2] and the story is that in the reign of Atys, the son of Manes, the whole of Lydia suffered from a severe famine. For a time the people lingered on as patiently as they

1. A powerful country in western Asia Minor; flourished c. 700–550 B.C.
2. i.e. Etruria. Herodotus thus sponsors the greatly disputed theory that the Etruscans came from Asia Minor.

could, but later, when there was no improvement, they began to look for something to alleviate their misery. Various expedients were devised: for instance, the invention of dice, knucklebones, and ball-games. In fact they claim to have invented all games of this sort except draughts. The way they used these inventions to help them endure their hunger was to eat and play on alternate days – one day playing so continuously that they had no time to think of food, and eating on the next without playing at all. They managed to live like this for eighteen years. There was still no remission of their suffering – indeed it grew worse; so the King divided the population into two groups and determined by drawing lots which should emigrate and which should remain at home. He appointed himself to rule the section whose lot determined that they should remain, and his son Tyrrhenus to command the emigrants. The lots were drawn, and one section went down to the coast at Smyrna, where they built vessels, put aboard all their household effects and sailed in search of a livelihood elsewhere. They passed many countries and finally reached Umbria in the north of Italy, where they settled and still live to this day. Here they changed their name from Lydians to Tyrrhenians, after the king's son Tyrrhenus, who was their leader.

AUBREY DE SELINCOURT (1954)

HOW GYGES SUCCEEDED CANDAULES AS KING OF LYDIA (c. 685 B.C.)

Now Candaules conceived a passion for his own wife, and thought she was the most beautiful woman on earth. To this fancy of his there was an unexpected sequel.

In the king's bodyguard was a fellow he particularly liked whose name was Gyges, son of Dascylus. With him Candaules not only discussed his most important business, but even used to make him listen to eulogies of his wife's beauty.

One day the king (who was doomed to a bad end) said to Gyges: 'It appears you don't believe me when I tell you how lovely my wife is. Well, a man always believes his eyes better than his ears; so do as I tell you – contrive to see her naked.'

Gyges gave a cry of horror. 'Master,' he said, 'what an improper suggestion! Do you tell me to look at the queen when she has no clothes on? No, no: "off with her skirt, off with her shame" – you know what they say of women. Let us learn from experience. Right and wrong were distinguished long ago – and I'll tell you one thing that is right: a man should mind his own business. I do not doubt that your wife is the most beautiful of women; so for goodness' sake do not ask me to behave like a criminal.'

Thus he did his utmost to decline the king's invitation, because he was afraid of what might happen if he accepted it.

The king, however, told him not to distress himself. 'There is nothing to be afraid of,' he said, 'either from me or my wife. I am not laying a trap for you; and as for her, I promise she will do you no harm. I'll manage so that she doesn't even know that you have seen her. Look: I will hide you behind the open door of our bedroom. My wife will follow me in to bed. Near the door there's a chair – she will put her clothes on it as she takes them off, one by one. You will be able to watch her with perfect ease. Then, while she's walking away from the chair towards the bed with her back to you, slip away through the door – and mind she doesn't catch you.'

Gyges, since he was unable to avoid it, consented, and when bed-time came Candaules brought him to the room. Presently the queen arrived, and Gyges watched her walk in and put her clothes on the chair. Then, just as she had turned her back and was going to bed, he slipped softly out of the room. Unluckily, the queen saw him.

At once she realized what her husband had done. But she did not betray the shame she felt by screaming, or even let it appear that she had noticed anything. Instead she silently resolved to have her revenge. For with the Lydians, as with most barbarian races, it is thought highly indecent even for a man to be seen naked.

For the moment she kept her mouth shut and did nothing; but at dawn the next morning she sent for Gyges after preparing the most trustworthy of her servants for what was to come. There was nothing unusual in his being asked to attend upon the queen; so Gyges answered the summons without any suspicion that she knew what had occurred on the previous night.

'Gyges,' she said, as soon as he presented himself, 'there are two courses open to you, and you may take your choice between them. Kill Candaules and seize the throne, with me as your wife; or die yourself on the spot, so that never again may your blind obedience to the king tempt you to see what you have no right to see. One of you must die; either my husband, the author of this wicked plot; or you, who have outraged propriety by seeing me naked.'

For a time Gyges was too much astonished to speak. At last he found words and begged the queen not to force him to make so difficult a choice. But it was no good; he soon saw that he really was faced with the alternatives, either of murdering his master, or of being murdered himself. He made his choice – to live.

'Tell me,' he said, 'since you drive me against my will to kill the king, how shall we set on him?'

'We will attack him when he is asleep,' was the answer; 'and on the very spot where he showed me to you naked.'

All was made ready for the attempt. The queen would not let Gyges go or give him any chance of escaping the dilemma: either Candaules or he must die. Night came, and he followed her into the bedroom. She put a knife into his hand, and hid him behind the same door as before. Then, when Candaules was asleep, he crept from behind the door and struck.

Thus Gyges usurped the throne and married the queen.

AUBREY DE SELINCOURT (1954)

THE ARGIPPAEI OF SOUTH RUSSIA

Further to the north and east lives another Scythian tribe, which moved into these parts after some trouble with the Royal Scythians[1] to which it originally belonged. As far as this, the country I have been describing is a level plain with good deep soil, but further on it becomes rugged and stony; beyond this region, which is of great extent, one comes to the foothills of a lofty mountain chain, and a nation of bald men. They are said to be bald from birth, women and men alike, and to have snub noses and long chins; they speak a peculiar language, dress in the Scythian fashion, and live on the fruit of a

1. These were based on the lower reaches of the River Borysthenes (Dnieper).

tree called ponticum – a kind of cherry – which is about the size of a fig-tree and produces a stoned fruit as large as a bean. They strain the ripe fruit through cloths and get from it a thick dark-coloured juice which they call *aschy*. They lap the juice up with their tongues, or mix it with milk for a drink, and make cakes out of the thick sediment which it leaves. They have but few sheep, as the grazing is poor. Every man lives under his ponticum-tree, which he protects in winter with bands of thick white felt, taking them off in the summer. These people are supposed to be protected by a mysterious sort of sanctity; they carry no arms and nobody offers them violence; they settle disputes amongst their neighbours, and anybody who seeks asylum amongst them is left in peace. They are called Argippaei.

As far as the bald men, a great deal is known of the country and of the people to the south and west from the reports, which are easy enough to come by, of Scythians who visit them, and of Greeks who frequent the port on the Dnieper and other ports along the Black Sea coast. The Scythians who penetrate as far as this do their business through interpreters in seven languages.

AUBREY DE SELINCOURT (1954)

THE BURIAL CUSTOMS OF THE SCYTHIAN KINGS

The burial-place of the Scythian kings is in the country of the Gerrhi, near the spot where the Borysthenes first becomes navigable. When a king dies, they dig a great square pit, and, when it is ready, they take up the corpse, which has been previously prepared in the following way: the belly is slit open, cleaned out, and filled with various aromatic substances, crushed galingale, parsley-seed, and anise; it is then sewn up again and the whole body coated over with wax. In this condition it is carried in a waggon to a neighbouring tribe within the Scythian dominions, and then on to another, taking the various tribes in turn; and in the course of its progress, the people who successively receive it follow the custom of the Royal Scythians and cut a piece from their ears, shave their hair, make circular incisions on their arms, gash their foreheads and noses, and thrust arrows through their left hands. On each stage of the journey those who have already been visited join the procession, until at last the funeral cortège, after passing through every part of the Scythian dominions, finds itself at the place of burial amongst the Gerrhi, the most northerly and remote of Scythian tribes. Here the corpse is laid in the tomb on a mattress, with spears fixed in the ground on either side to support a roof of withies laid on wooden poles, while in other parts of the great square pit various members of the king's household are buried beside him: one of his concubines, his butler, his cook, his groom, his steward, and his chamberlain – all of them strangled. Horses are buried too, and gold cups (the Scythians do not use silver or bronze), and a selection of his other treasures. This ceremony over, everybody with great enthusiasm sets about raising a mound of earth, each competing with his neighbour to make it as big as possible. At the end of a year another ceremony takes place: they take fifty of the best of the king's remaining servants, strangle and gut them, stuff the bodies with chaff, and sew them up again – these servants are native Scythians, for the king has no bought slaves, but chooses people to serve him from amongst his subjects. Fifty of the finest horses are then subjected to the same treatment.

AUBREY DE SELINCOURT (1954)

WESTERN AND NORTHERN EUROPE

About the far west of Europe I have no definite information, for I cannot accept the story of a river called by non-Greek peoples the Eridanus,[1] which flows into the northern sea, where amber is supposed to come from; nor do I know anything of the existence of islands called the Tin Islands,[2] whence we get our tin. In the first place, the name Eridanus is obviously not foreign but Greek, and was invented by some poet or other; and, secondly, in spite of my efforts to do so, I have never found anyone who could give me first-hand information of the existence of a sea beyond Europe to the north and west. Yet it cannot be disputed that tin and amber do come to us

1. A mythical river, identified with the Po.
2. The Cassiterides, a name applied generically to all the north Atlantic tin lands, but especially to Cornwall and the Scilly Isles.

from what one might call the ends of the earth. It is clear that it is the northern parts of Europe which are richest in gold, but how it is procured is another mystery. The story goes that the one-eyed Arimaspians[1] steal it from the griffins who guard it; personally however, I hesitate to believe in one-eyed men who in other respects are like the rest of us. In any case it does seem to be true that the countries which lie on the circumference of the inhabited world produce the things which we believe to be most rare and beautiful.

AUBREY DE SELINCOURT (1954)

KING CLEISTHENES OF SICYON (c. 600–570 B.C.) REJECTS HIPPOCLEIDES AS A SUITOR FOR HIS DAUGHTER

At last the day came which had been fixed for the betrothal, and Cleisthenes had to declare his choice. He marked the day by the sacrifice of a hundred oxen, and then gave a great banquet, to which not only the suitors but everyone of note in Sicyon was invited. When dinner was over, the suitors began to compete with each other in music and in talking on a set theme to the assembled company. In both these accomplishments it was Hippocleides who proved by far the doughtiest champion, until at last, as more and more wine was drunk, he asked the flute-player to play him a tune and began to dance to it. Now it may well be that he danced to his own satisfaction; Cleisthenes, however, who was watching the performance, began to have serious doubts about the whole business. Presently, after a brief pause, Hippocleides sent for a table; the table was brought, and Hippocleides, climbing on to it, danced first some Laconian dances, next some Attic ones, and ended by standing on his head and beating time with his legs in the air. The Laconian and Attic dances were bad enough; but Cleisthenes, though he already loathed the thought of having a son-in-law who could behave so disgracefully in public, nevertheless restrained himself and managed to avoid an outburst; but when he saw Hippocleides beating time with his legs, he could

1. A mythical people about whom the legendary Aristeas was said to have written an epic.

bear it no longer. 'Son of Tisander,' he cried, 'you have danced away your wife.' 'I could hardly care less,' was the cheerful reply.[1]

AUBREY DE SELINCOURT (1954)

KING XERXES OF PERSIA BUILDS BRIDGES ACROSS THE HELLESPONT (DARDANELLES) IN 480 B.C.

This headland was the point to which Xerxes' engineers carried their bridges from Abydos – a distance of seven furlongs. One was constructed by the Phoenicians using flax cables, the other by the Egyptians with papyrus cables. The work was successfully completed, but a subsequent storm of great violence smashed it up and carried everything away. Xerxes was very angry when he learned of the disaster, and gave orders that the Hellespont should receive three hundred lashes and have a pair of fetters thrown into it. And I have heard before now that he also sent people to brand it with hot irons. He certainly instructed the men with the whips to utter, as they wielded them, the following words: 'You salt and bitter stream, your master lays this punishment upon you for injuring him, who never injured you. But Xerxes the King will cross you, with or without your permission. No man sacrifices to you, and you deserve the neglect by your acrid and muddy waters' – a highly presumptuous way of addressing the Hellespont, and typical of a barbarous nation. In addition to punishing the Hellespont Xerxes gave orders that the men responsible for building the bridges should have their heads cut off. This unseemly order was duly carried out.

AUBREY DE SELINCOURT (1954)

KING XERXES REVIEWS HIS ARMY

It now occurred to Xerxes that he would like to hold a review of his army. On a rise of ground near by, a throne of white marble had

1. Hence the common saying, 'It's all one to Hippocleides'.

already been prepared for his use, and at his orders, by the people of Abydos; so the king took his seat upon it and, looking down over the shore, was able to see the whole of his army and navy at a single view. Suddenly as he watched them he was seized with the whim to witness a rowing-match. The match took place and was won by the Phoenicians of Sidon,[1] to the great delight of Xerxes who was as pleased with the race as with his army. Still the king watched the spectacle below, and when he saw the whole Hellespont hidden by ships, and all the beaches of Abydos and all the open ground filled with men, he congratulated himself – and the moment after burst into tears. Artabanus his uncle, the man who in the first instance had spoken his mind so freely in trying to dissuade Xerxes from undertaking the campaign, was by his side; and when he saw how Xerxes wept, he said to him: 'My lord, surely there is a strange contradiction in what you do now and what you did a moment ago. Then you called yourself a lucky man – and now you weep.'

'I was thinking,' Xerxes replied; 'and it came into my mind how pitifully short human life is – for of all these thousands of men not one will be alive in a hundred years' time.'

'Yet,' said Artabanus, 'there are sadder things in life even than that. Short as it is, there is not a man in the world, either here or elsewhere, who is happy enough not to wish – not once only but again and again – to be dead rather than alive. Troubles come, diseases afflict us; and this makes life, despite its brevity, seem all too long. So heavy is the burden of it that death is a refuge which we all desire, and it is common proof amongst us that God who gave us a taste of this world's sweetness has been a niggard in his giving.'

AUBREY DE SELINCOURT (1954)

1. Now Saida in Lebanon. Sidon and Tyre were formerly great maritime and colonizing powers.

THUCYDIDES

The second great historian; an Athenian, perhaps part-Thracian, born between 460 and 455 B.C., died in *c.* 400, wrote an incomplete history of the Peloponnesian War between Athens and Sparta (431–404 B.C.).

*

THE SPEECH OF PHORMIO TO HIS SOLDIERS AND THE BATTLE OF NAUPACTUS (429 B.C.)

'Soldiers, having observed your fear of the enemies' number, I have called you together, not enduring to see you terrified with things that are not terrible. For first they have prepared this great number and odds of galleys, for that they were overcome before, and because they are even in their own opinions too weak for us. And next, their present boldness proceeds only from their knowledge in land service, in confidence whereof (as if to be valiant were peculiar unto them) they are now come up; wherein having the most part prospered, they think to do the same in service by sea. But in reason the odds must be ours in this, as well as it is theirs in the other kind. For in courage they exceed us not, and as touching the advantage of either side, we may better be bold now than they. And the Lacedaemonians,[1] who are the leaders of the confederates, bring them to fight, for the greatest part (in respect of the opinion they have of us) against their wills; for else they would never have undertaken a new battle after they were once so clearly overthrown. Fear not therefore any great boldness on their part. But the fear which they have of you is far both greater and more certain, not only for that you have overcome them before, but also for this, that they would never believe you would go about to resist, unless you had some notable thing to put in practice upon them. For when the enemy is the greater number, as these are now, they invade chiefly upon confidence on their strength. But they that are much the fewer must have some great and sure

1. The Spartans.

187

design when they dare fight unconstrained. Wherewith these men now amazed, fear us more for our unlikely preparation, than they would if it were more proportionable. Besides, many great armies have been both overcome by the lesser through unskilfulness, and some also by timorousness, both which we ourselves are free from. As for the battle, I will not willingly fight in the gulf; nor go in thither; seeing that to a few galleys with nimbleness and art, against many without art, straitness of room is disadvantage. For neither can one charge with the beak of the galley as is fit, unless he have sight of the enemy afar off, or if he be himself over-pressed, again get clear. Nor is there any getting through them, or turning to and fro at one's pleasure, which are all the works of such galleys as have their advantage in agility; but the sea fight would of necessity be the same with a battle by land, wherein the greater number must have the better. But of this, I shall myself take the best care I am able. In the mean time keep you your order well in the galleys, and every man receive his charge readily, and the rather because the enemy is at anchor so near us. In the fight, have in great estimation, order and silence, as things of great force in most military actions, especially in a fight by sea, and charge these your enemies according to the worth of your former acts. You are to fight for a great wager, either to destroy the hope of the Peloponnesian navies, or to bring the fear of the sea nearer home to the Athenians. Again, let me tell you, you have beaten them once already; and men once overcome, will not come again to the danger so well resolved as before.'

Thus did Phormio also encourage his soldiers.

The Peloponnesians, when they saw the Athenians would enter the gulf and strait, desiring to draw them in against their wills, weighed anchor, and betime in the morning having arranged their galleys by four and four in a rank, sailed along their own coast, within the gulf, leading the way, in the same order as they had lain at anchor with their right-wing. In this wing they had placed twenty of their swiftest galleys, to the end that if Phormio, thinking them going to Naupactus,[1] should for safeguard of the town sail along his own

1. A harbour town commanding the narrowest part of the entrance to the Gulf of Corinth.

coast likewise, within the strait, the Athenians might not be able to get beyond that wing of theirs and avoid the impression, but be enclosed by their galleys on both sides. Phormio fearing (as they expected) what might become of the town now without guard, as soon as he saw them from anchor, against his will and in extreme haste went aboard, and sailed along the shore with the land forces of the Messenians marching by to aid him.[1] The Peloponnesians when they saw them sail in one long file, galley after galley, and that they were now in the gulf, and by the shore (which they most desired), upon one sign given turned suddenly, every one as fast as he could upon the Athenians, hoping to have intercepted them every galley. But of those, the eleven foremost, avoiding that wing and the turn made by the Peloponnesians, got out into the open sea. The rest they intercepted, and driving them to the shore, sunk them.

The men, as many as swam not out, they slew, and the galleys some they tied to their own, and towed them away empty, and one with the men and all in her they had already taken. But the Messenian succours on land, entering the sea with their arms, got aboard of some of them, and fighting from the decks, recovered them again, after they were already towing away. And in this part the Peloponnesians had the victory, and overcame the galleys of the Athenians. Now the twenty galleys that were their right wing, gave chase to those eleven Athenian galleys, which had avoided them when they turned, and were gotten into the open sea. These flying toward Naupactus, arrived there before the enemies all save one, and when they came under the temple of Apollo, turned their beak-heads, and put themselves into readiness for defence, in case the enemy should follow them to the land. But the Peloponnesians as they came after, were paeanizing, as if they had already the victory; and one galley, which was of Leucas,[2] being far before the rest, gave chase to one Athenian galley that was behind the rest of the Athenians. Now it chanced that there lay out into the sea a certain ship at anchor, to which the Athenian galley first coming, fetched a compass about her,

1. Refugees from Spartan rule settled by the Athenians at Naupactus. Messenia is the south-western part of the Peloponnese.
2. A large island off north-western Greece.

and came back full butt against the Leucadian galley that gave her chase, and sunk her. Upon this unexpected and unlikely accident they began to fear, and having also followed the chase, as being victors, disorderly, some of them let down their oars into the water and hindered the way of their galleys (a matter of very ill consequence, seeing the enemy was so near) and stayed for more company. And some of them, through ignorance of the coast, ran upon the shelves. The Athenians seeing this, took heart again, and together with one clamour set upon them; who resisted not long, because of their present errors committed, and their disarray; but turned and fled to Panormus, from whence at first they set forth. The Athenians followed, and took from them six galleys, that were hindmost, and recovered their own which the Peloponnesians had sunk by the shore, and tied astern of theirs. Of the men, some they slew, and some also they took alive. In the Leucadian galley that was sunk near the ship, was Timocrates a Lacedaemonian, who when the galley was lost, run himself through with his sword, and his body drove into the haven of Naupactus. The Athenians falling off, erected a trophy in the place from whence they set forth to this victory, and took up their dead, and the wreck, as much as was on their own shore, and gave truce to the enemy to do the like. The Peloponnesians also set up a trophy, as if they also had had the victory, in respect of the flight of those galleys which they sunk by the shore; and the galley which they had taken they consecrated to Neptune[1] in Rhium of Achaia, hard by their trophy.

THOMAS HOBBES (1629)

CIVIL WAR AT CORCYRA (CORFU) (427 B.C.)

So bloody was the march of the revolution, and the impression which it made was the greater as it was the first to occur. Later on, one may say, the whole Hellenic world was convulsed, struggles being everywhere made by the popular chiefs to bring in the Athenians, and by the oligarchs to introduce the Lacedaemonians. In peace there would have been neither the pretext nor the wish to make such an invitation; but in war, with an alliance always at the command of either faction

1. Poseidon.

for the hurt of their adversaries and their own corresponding advantage, opportunities for bringing in the foreigner were never wanting to the revolutionary parties. The sufferings which revolution entailed upon the cities were many and terrible, such as have occurred and always occur, as long as the nature of mankind remains the same; though in a severer or milder form, and varying in their symptoms, according to the variety of the particular cases. In peace and prosperity states and individuals have better sentiments, because they do not find themselves suddenly confronted with imperious necessities; but war takes away the easy supply of daily wants, and so proves a rough master, that brings most men's characters to a level with their fortunes.

Revolution thus ran its course from city to city, and the places at which it arrived at last, from having heard what had been done before, carried to a still greater excess the refinement of their inventions, as manifested in the cunning of their enterprises and the atrocity of their reprisals. Words had to change their ordinary meaning and to take that which was now given them. Reckless audacity came to be considered the courage of a loyal ally; prudent hesitation, specious cowardice; moderation was held to be a cloak for unmanliness; ability to see all sides of a question inaptness to act on any. Frantic violence became the attribute of manliness, cautious plotting a justifiable means of self-defence. The advocate of extreme measures was always trustworthy, his opponent a man to be suspected. To succeed in a plot was to have a shrewd head, to divine a plot a still shrewder; but to try to provide against having to do either was to break up your party and to be afraid of your adversaries. In fine, to forestall an intending criminal, or to suggest the idea of a crime where it was wanting, was equally commended, until even blood became a weaker tie than party, from the superior readiness of those united by the latter to dare everything without reserve; for such associations had not in view the blessings derivable from established institutions but were formed by ambition for their overthrow; and the confidence of their members in each other rested less on any religious sanction than upon complicity in crime. The fair proposals of an adversary were met with jealous precautions by the stronger of the two, and not with a generous confidence. Revenge also was held of more account than self-preservation. Oaths of reconciliation, being proffered on either side only to meet an immediate difficulty, held good only so long as no other weapon was at hand; but when opportunity offered, he who first ventured to seize it and to take his enemy off his guard, thought this perfidious vengeance sweeter than an open one, since, considerations of safety apart, success by treachery won him the palm of superior intelligence. Indeed it is generally the case that men are readier to call rogues clever than simpletons honest, and are as ashamed of being the second as they are proud of being the first.

The cause of all these evils was the lust for power arising from greed and ambition; and from these passions proceeded the violence of parties once engaged in contention. The leaders in the cities, each provided with the fairest professions, on the one side with the cry of political equality of the people, on the other of a moderate aristocracy, sought prizes for themselves in those public interests which they pretended to cherish, and, recoiling from no means in their struggles for ascendancy, engaged in the direst excesses; in their acts of vengeance they went to even greater lengths, not stopping at what justice or the good of the state demanded, but making the party caprice of the moment their only standard, and invoking with equal readiness the condemnation of an unjust verdict or the authority of the strong arm to glut the animosities of the hour. Thus morality was in honour with neither party; but the use of fair phrases to arrive at guilty ends was in high reputation. Meanwhile the moderate part of the citizens perished between the two, either for not joining in the quarrel or because envy would not suffer them to escape.

RICHARD CRAWLEY (1874)

THE DEFEAT OF THE ATHENIANS OFF SYRACUSE (413 B.C.)

The huge din caused by the number of ships crashing together not only spread terror, but made the orders of the boatswains inaudible. The boatswains on either side in the discharge of their duty and in the heat of the conflict shouted incessantly orders and appeals to their men; the Athenians they urged to force the passage out, and now if ever to show their mettle and lay hold of a safe return to their country; to the Syracusans and their allies they cried that it would be glorious to prevent the escape of the enemy, and, conquering, to exalt the countries that were theirs. The generals, moreover, on either side, if they saw any in any part of the battle backing ashore without being forced to do so, called out to the trierach[1] by name and asked him – the Athenians, whether they were retreating because they thought the thrice hostile shore more their own than that sea which had cost them so much labour to win; the Syracusans, whether they were flying from the flying Athenians, whom they well knew to be eager to escape in whatever way they could.

Meanwhile the two armies on shore, while victory hung in the balance, were a prey to the most agonizing and conflicting emotions, the natives thirsting for more glory than they had already won, while the invaders feared to find themselves in even worse plight than before. Since all the Athenians were set upon their fleet, their fear for the event was like nothing they had ever felt; while their view of the struggle was necessarily as checkered as the battle itself. Close to the scene of action and not all looking at the same point at once, some saw their friends victorious and took courage, and fell to calling upon heaven not to deprive them of salvation, while others who had their eyes turned upon the losers wailed and cried aloud, and, although spectators, were more overcome than the actual combatants. Others, again, were gazing at some spot where the battle was evenly disputed; as the strife was protracted without decision, their swaying bodies reflected the agitation of their minds, and they suffered the worst agony of all, ever just within reach of safety or just on the point of destruction. In short, in that one Athenian army as long as the sea fight remained doubtful there was every sound to be heard at once, shrieks, cheers, 'We win,' 'We lose,' and all the other manifold exclamations that a great host would necessarily utter in great peril.

And with the men in the fleet it was nearly the same, until at last the Syracusans and their allies, after the battle had lasted a long while,

1. Commander of a trireme.

put the Athenians to flight, and with much shouting and cheering chased them in open rout to the shore. The naval force, one one way, one another, as many as were not taken afloat, now ran ashore and rushed from on board their ships to their camp; while the army, no more divided, but carried away by one impulse, all with shrieks and groans deplored the event, and ran down, some to help the ships, others to guard what was left of their wall, while the remaining and most numerous part already began to consider how they should save themselves. Indeed, the panic of the present moment had never been surpassed.

RICHARD CRAWLEY (1874)

THEMISTOCLES, VICTOR OF SALAMIS (c. 528–462 B.C.)

Indeed, Themistocles was a man who showed an unmistakable natural genius; in this respect he was quite exceptional, and beyond all others deserves our admiration. Without studying a subject in advance or deliberating over it later, but using simply the intelligence that was his by nature, he had the power to reach the right conclusion in matters that have to be settled on the spur of the moment and do not admit of long discussions, and in estimating what was likely to happen, his forecasts of the future were always more reliable than those of others. He could perfectly well explain any subject with which he was familiar, and even outside his own department he was still capable of giving an excellent opinion. He was particularly remarkable at looking into the future and seeing there the hidden possibilities for good or evil. To sum him up in a few words, it may be said that through force of genius and by rapidity of action this man was supreme at doing precisely the right thing at precisely the right moment.

REX WARNER (1954)

THE UNIQUE IMPORTANCE OF THE PELOPONNESIAN WAR (431–404 B.C.)

I began my history at the very outbreak of the war, in the belief that it was going to be a great war and more worth writing about than any of those which had taken place in the past. My belief was based on the fact that the two sides were at the very height of their power and preparedness, and I saw, too, that the rest of the Hellenic world was committed to one side or the other; even those who were not immediately engaged were deliberating on the courses which they were to take later. This was the greatest disturbance in the history of the Hellenes, affecting also a large part of the non-Hellenic world, and indeed, I might almost say, the whole of mankind. For though I have found it impossible, because of its remoteness in time, to acquire a really precise knowledge of the distant past or even of the history preceding our own period, yet, after looking back into it as far as I can, all the evidence leads me to conclude that these periods were not great periods either in warfare or in anything else.

It appears, for example, that the country now called Hellas had no settled population in ancient times; instead there was a series of migrations, as the various tribes, being under the constant pressure of invaders who were stronger than they were, were always prepared to abandon their own territory. There was no commerce, and no safe communication either by land or sea; the use they made of their land was limited to the production of necessities; they had no surplus left over for capital, and no regular system of agriculture, since they lacked the protection of fortifications and at any moment an invader might appear and take their land away from them. Thus, in the belief that the day-to-day necessities of life could be secured just as well in one place as in another, they showed no reluctance in moving from their homes, and therefore built no cities of any size or strength, nor acquired any important resources.

REX WARNER (1954)

THE CORINTHIANS WARN THE SPARTANS ABOUT THE ATHENIANS (431 B.C.)

'We think we have as much right as anyone else to point out faults in our neighbours, especially when we consider the enormous difference between you and the Athenians. To our minds, you are quite unaware of this difference; you have never yet tried to imagine what sort of people these Athenians are against whom you will have to fight – how much, indeed how completely, different from you. An Athenian is always an innovator, quick to form a resolution and quick at carrying it out. You, on the other hand, are good at keeping things as they are; you never originate an idea, and your action tends to stop short of its aim. Then again, Athenian daring will outrun its own resources; they will take risks against their better judgement, and still, in the midst of danger, remain confident. But your nature is always to do less than you could have done, to mistrust your own judgement, however sound it may be, and to assume that dangers will last for ever. Think of this, too: while you are hanging back, they never hesitate; while you stay at home, they are always abroad; for they think that the farther they go the more they will get, while you think that any movement may endanger what you have already. If they win a victory, they follow it up at once, and if they suffer a defeat, they scarcely fall back at all. As for their bodies, they regard them as expendable for their city's sake, as though they were not their own; but each man cultivates his own intelligence, again with a view to doing something notable for his city. If they aim at something and do not get it, they think that they have been deprived of what belonged to them already; whereas, if their enterprise is successful, they regard that success as nothing compared to what they will do next. Suppose they fail in some undertaking; they make good the loss immediately by setting their hopes in some other direction. Of them alone it may be said that they possess a thing almost as soon as they have begun to desire it, so quickly with them does action follow upon decision. And so they go on working away in hardship and danger all the days of their lives, seldom enjoying their possessions because they are always adding to them. Their view of a holiday is to do what needs doing;

they prefer hardship and activity to peace and quiet. In a word, they are by nature incapable of either living a quiet life themselves or of allowing anyone else to do so.

'That is the character of the city which is opposed to you.'

REX WARNER (1954)

PERICLES ON THE ATHENIAN WAY OF LIFE

'Our love of what is beautiful does not lead to extravagance; our love of the things of the mind does not make us soft. We regard wealth as something to be properly used, rather than as something to boast about. As for poverty, no one need be ashamed to admit it: the real shame is in not taking practical measures to escape from it. Here each individual is interested not only in his own affairs but in the affairs of the state as well: even those who are mostly occupied with their own business are extremely well-informed on general politics – this is a peculiarity of ours: we do not say that a man who takes no interest in politics is a man who minds his own business; we say that he has no business here at all. We Athenians, in our own persons, take our decisions on policy or submit them to proper discussions: for we do not think that there is an incompatibility between words and deeds; the worst thing is to rush into action before the consequences have been properly debated. And this is another point where we differ from other people. We are capable at the same time of taking risks and of estimating them beforehand. Others are brave out of ignorance; and, when they stop to think, they begin to fear. But the man who can most truly be accounted brave is he who best knows the meaning of what is sweet in life and of what is terrible, and then goes out undeterred to meet what is to come.

'Again, in questions of general good feeling there is a great contrast between us and most other people. We make friends by doing good to others, not by receiving good from them. This makes our friendship all the more reliable, since we want to keep alive the gratitude of those who are in our debt by showing continued goodwill to them: whereas the feelings of one who owes us something lack the same enthusiasm, since he knows that, when he repays our kindness, it will be more like paying back a debt than giving something spontaneously. We are unique in this. When we do kindnesses to others, we do not do them out of any calculations of profit or loss: we do them without afterthought, relying on our free liberality. Taking everything together then, I declare that our city is an education to Greece, and I declare that in my opinion each single one of our citizens, in all the manifold aspects of life, is able to show himself the rightful lord and owner of his own person, and do this, moreover, with exceptional grace and exceptional versatility.'

REX WARNER (1954)

CLEON ADVISES THE ATHENIANS TO BE HARSH TO THE MYTILENIAN REBELS (427 B.C.)

Cleon, the son of Cleaenetus, spoke again. It was he who had been responsible for passing the original motion for putting the Mytilenians to death. He was remarkable among the Athenians for the violence of his character, and at this time he exercised far the greatest influence over the people. He spoke as follows:

'Personally I have had occasion often enough already to observe that a democracy is incapable of governing others, and I am all the more convinced of this when I see how you are now changing your minds about the Mytilenians. Because fear and conspiracy play no part in your daily relations with each other, you imagine that the same thing is true of your allies, and you fail to see that when you allow them to persuade you to make a mistaken decision and when you give way to your own feelings of compassion you are being guilty of a kind of weakness which is dangerous to you and which will not make them love you any more. What you do not realize is that your empire is a dictatorship exercised over subjects who do not like it and who are always plotting against you; you will not make them obey you by injuring your own interests in order to do them a favour; your leadership depends on superior strength and not on any goodwill of theirs. And this is the very worst thing – to pass measures and then not to abide by them. We should realize that a city is better off with bad laws, so long as they remain fixed, than with good laws that are constantly being altered, that lack of learning combined with sound common sense is more helpful than the kind of cleverness that gets out of hand, and that as a general rule states are better governed by the man in the street than by intellectuals.'

REX WARNER (1954)

THE FINAL DEFEAT OF THE ATHENIAN EXPEDITIONARY FORCE TO SICILY (413 B.C.)

When day came Nicias[1] led his army on, and the Syracusans and their allies pressed them hard in the same way as before, showering missiles and hurling javelins in upon them from every side. The Athenians hurried on towards the river Assinarus,[2] partly because they were under pressure from the attacks made upon them from every side by the numbers of cavalry and the masses of other troops, and thought that things would not be so bad if they got to the river, partly because they were exhausted and were longing for water to drink. Once they reached the river, they rushed down into it, and now all discipline was at an end. Every man wanted to be the first to get across, and, as the enemy persisted in his attacks, the crossing now became a difficult matter. Forced to crowd in close together, they fell upon each other and trampled each other underfoot; some were killed immediately by their own spears, others got entangled among themselves and among the baggage and were swept away by the river. Syracusan troops were stationed on the opposite bank, which was a steep one. They hurled down their weapons from above on the Athenians, most of whom, in a disordered mass, were greedily drinking in the deep river-bed. And the Peloponnesians came down and slaughtered them, especially those who were in the river. The water immediately became foul, but nevertheless they went on drinking it, all muddy as it was and stained with blood; indeed, most of them were fighting among themselves to have it.

1. The general and politician who was in command of the Athenian forces retreating from Syracuse. See also p. 192 above, and pp. 409ff. below (Plutarch).

2. A stream some miles south of Syracuse, perhaps the Tellaro (Atiddaru).

Finally, when the many dead were by now heaped upon each other in the bed of the stream, when part of the army had been destroyed there in the river, and the few who managed to get away had been cut down by the cavalry, Nicias surrendered himself to Gylippus,[1] whom he trusted more than he did the Syracusans, telling him and the Spartans to do what they liked with him personally, but to stop the slaughter of his soldiers.

REX WARNER (1954)

1. A Spartan general who was fighting for the Syracusans.

XENOPHON

Athenian historian, moralist, political and military theorist, and biographer. Lived c. 428/7–c. 354 B.C.

*

HUNTING IN MESOPOTAMIA

From here, with the Euphrates on the right, he moved forward through Arabia.[1] It was a five days' march of a hundred and five miles through the desert. In this part of the world the ground was all one level plain, like the sea. Wormwood was plentiful, and all the other shrubs and reeds which grew there smelt as sweetly as perfume. There were no trees, but there was a great variety of animal life. Wild asses were very common and there were many ostriches; also there were bustards and gazelles. The cavalry hunted all these animals on various occasions. In the case of the wild asses, when anyone chased them, they ran ahead and then stopped still; for they ran much faster than the horses. Then again, when the horses got near, they would do the same thing, and it was impossible to catch them except by stationing the horsemen at intervals from each other and hunting in relays. The flesh of those that were caught was very like venison, only more tender. No one succeeded in catching an ostrich. Indeed the horsemen who tried soon gave up the pursuit, as it made them go a very great distance when it ran from them. It used its feet for running and got under way with its wings, just as if it was using a sail. But one can catch bustards if one puts them up quickly, as they only fly a little way, like partridges, and soon get tired. Their flesh was delicious.

REX WARNER (1949)

1. Loosely used for Mesopotamia. Cyrus II, with his Greek mercenaries (including Xenophon, who describes the expedition in his *Anabasis*), is moving against his brother Artaxerxes II, from whom he hopes to seize the Persian throne.

PERSIAN NOBLEMEN AT WORK

Cyrus made some of these marches extremely long, when it was a case of wanting to reach water or fodder. And there was one occasion on which the road got narrow and muddy and difficult for the waggons, when Cyrus halted with the nobles and richest of his company and ordered Glous and Pigres to take a detachment of native troops and help in getting the waggons out of the mud; and when he thought that they were going slow on it, he looked angry and ordered the most important Persians in his company to give a hand with the waggons. Then certainly one saw a bit of discipline. Wherever they happened to be standing, they threw off their purple cloaks and rushed forward as though it was a race down a very steep hill, too, and wearing those expensive tunics which they have, and embroidered trousers. Some also had chains round their necks and bracelets on their wrists. But with all this on they leapt straight down into the mud and got the waggons on to dry ground quicker than anyone would have thought possible.

REX WARNER (1949)

AN ARMENIAN VILLAGE[1]

On this occasion Polycrates, an Athenian captain, asked leave to go on independently and, taking with him the men who were quickest on their feet, ran to the village which had been allotted to Xenophon and surprised all the villagers, with their head-man, inside the walls, together with seventeen colts which were kept there for tribute to the King, and the head-man's daughter, who had only been married nine days ago. Her husband had gone out to hunt hares and was not captured in the village.

The houses here were built underground; the entrances were like wells, but they broadened out lower down. There were tunnels

1. Cyrus had been defeated and killed at Cunaxa, and his Greek soldiers, the Ten Thousand, are on their long journey back to the Black Sea. They have come to a village in Armenia.

dug in the ground for the animals while the men went down by ladder. Inside the houses there were goats, sheep, cows and poultry with their young. All these animals were fed on food that was kept inside the houses. There was also wheat, barley, beans and barley-wine in great bowls. The actual grains of barley floated on top of the bowls, level with the brim, and in the bowls there were reeds of various sizes and without joints in them. When one was thirsty, one was meant to take a reed and suck the wine into one's mouth. It was a very strong wine, unless one mixed it with water, and, when one got used to it, it was a very pleasant drink.

Xenophon invited the chief of the village to have supper with him, and told him to be of good heart, as he was not going to be deprived of his children, and that, if he showed himself capable of doing the army a good turn until they reached another tribe, they would restock his house with provisions when they went away. He promised to cooperate and, to show his good intentions, told them of where some wine was buried. So for that night all the soldiers were quartered in the villages and slept there with all sorts of food around them, setting a guard over the head-man of the village and keeping a watchful eye on his children too.

On the next day Xenophon visited Chirisophus and took the head-man with him. Whenever he went past a village he turned into it to see those who were quartered there. Everywhere he found them feasting and merry-making, and they would invariably refuse to let him go before they had given him something for breakfast. In every single case they would have on the same table lamb, kid, pork, veal and chicken, and a number of loaves, both wheat and barley. When anyone wanted, as a gesture of friendship, to drink to a friend's health, he would drag him to a huge bowl, over which he would have to lean, sucking up the drink like an ox. They invited the head-man too to take what he liked, but he refused their invitations, only, if he caught sight of any of his relatives, he would take them along with him.

When they came to Chirisophus, they found his men also feasting, with wreaths of hay round their heads, and with Armenian boys in native dress waiting on them. They showed the boys what to do by signs, as though they were deaf mutes. After greeting each other,

Chirisophus and Xenophon together interrogated the head-man through the interpreter who spoke Persian, and asked him what country this was. He replied that it was Armenia. Then they asked him for whom the horses were being kept, and he said that they were a tribute paid to the King. The next country, he said, was the land of the Chalybes,[1] and he told them the way there.

Xenophon then went away and took the head-man back to his own people. He gave him back the horse (rather an old one) which he had taken, and told him to fatten it up and sacrifice it. This was because he had heard that it was sacred to the Sun and he was afraid that it might die, as the journey had done it no good. He took some of the colts himself, and gave one colt to each of the generals and captains. The horses in this part of the world were smaller than the Persian horses, but much more finely bred. The head-man told the Greeks to tie small bags round the feet of the horses and baggage animals whenever they made them go through snow, as, without these bags, they sank in up to their bellies.

REX WARNER (1949)

XENOPHON THE ATHENIAN AND CHIRISOPHUS THE SPARTAN[2]

'I gather that you Spartans, Chirisophus – I mean the real officer class – study how to steal from your earliest boyhood, and think that so far from it being a disgrace it is an actual distinction to steal anything that is not forbidden by law. And, so that you may become expert thieves and try to get away with what you steal, it is laid down by law that you get a beating if you are caught stealing. Here then is an excellent opportunity for you to give an exhibition of the way in which you were brought up, and to preserve us from blows, by seeing to it that we are not caught stealing our bit of mountain.'

'Well,' said Chirisophus, 'what I have gathered about you

1. i.e. ironworkers – famous as the alleged first workers of iron.
2. Somewhat perilous badinage only a few years after the Peloponnesian War! They are discussing how best to 'steal' an Armenian mountain, i.e. take it by subterfuge.

Athenians is that you are remarkably good at stealing public funds, even though it is a very risky business for whoever does so; and your best men are the greatest experts at it, that is if it is your best men who are considered the right people to be in the government. So here is a chance for you too to give an exhibition of the way in which you were brought up.'

REX WARNER (1949)

THE SEA! THE SEA!

They came to the mountain on the fifth day, the name of the mountain being Thekes.[1] When the men in front reached the summit and caught sight of the sea there was great shouting. Xenophon and the rearguard heard it and thought that there were some more enemies attacking in the front, since there were natives of the country they had ravaged following them up behind, and the rearguard had killed some of them and made prisoners of others in an ambush, and captured about twenty raw ox-hide shields, with the hair on. However, when the shouting got louder and drew nearer, and those who were constantly going forward started running towards the men in front who kept on shouting, and the more there were of them the more shouting there was, it looked then as though this was something of considerable importance. So Xenophon mounted his horse and, taking Lycus and the cavalry with him, rode forward to give support, and, quite soon, they heard the soldiers shouting out 'The sea! The sea!' and passing the word down the column. Then certainly they all began to run, the rearguard and all, and drove on the baggage animals and the horses at full speed; and when they had all got to the top, the soldiers, with tears in their eyes, embraced each other and their generals and captains. In a moment, at somebody or other's suggestion, they collected stones and made a great pile of them. On top they put a lot of raw ox-hides and staves and the shields which they had captured. The guide himself cut the shields into pieces and

1. Above Trapezus (Trabzon, Trebizond) on the Black Sea. The Ten Thousand were on their way back from Mesopotamia (p. 202).

urged the others to do so too. Afterwards the Greeks sent the guide back and gave him as presents from the common store a horse, and a silver cup and a Persian robe and ten darics.[1] What he particularly wanted was the rings which the soldiers had and he got a number of these from them. He pointed out to them a village where they could camp, and showed them the road by which they had to go to the country of the Macrones. It was then evening and he went away, travelling by night.

REX WARNER (1949)

HABITS IN NORTH-EASTERN ASIA MINOR

When the Greeks advanced further and reached the country of the allies of the Mossynoeci[2] they pointed out to them some boys belonging to the wealthy class of people, who had been specially fatted up by being fed on boiled chestnuts. Their flesh was soft and very pale, and they were practically as broad as they were tall. Front and back were brightly coloured all over, tattooed with designs of flowers. These people wanted to have sexual intercourse in public with the mistresses whom the Greeks brought with them, this being actually the normal thing in their country. Both men and women were pale skinned. Those who were on the expedition used to say that these people were the most barbarous and the furthest removed from Greek ways of all those with whom they came in contact. When they were in a crowd they acted as men would act when in private, and when they were by themselves, they used to behave as they might do if they were in company; they used to talk to themselves, and laugh to themselves, and stop and dance wherever they happened to be, just as if they were giving a display to others.

REX WARNER (1949)

1. A silver coin.
2. South of Cerasus (Giresun).

THE FINAL DEFEAT OF THE ATHENIANS BY THE SPARTAN LYSANDER IN THE PELOPONNESIAN WAR: AEGOSPOTAMI (405 B.C.)

The Athenian fleet set out at once for Sestus[1] where they took provisions aboard and then went straight on to Aegospotami, which is opposite Lampsacus. The Hellespont here is about two miles wide. It was here that the Athenians had their evening meal.

The night passed and at dawn Lysander[2] ordered his men to have breakfast and embark. He had the side-screens put up on the ships and made all preparations for battle, but gave orders that no one should leave his position or put out into the open sea.

As soon as the sun rose the Athenians came up with their fleet in line of battle to the mouth of the harbour. However, Lysander did not put to sea against them, so, when it was late in the day, they sailed back again to Aegospotami. Lysander then instructed some of his fastest ships to follow the Athenians and, when they had disembarked, to observe what they were doing and then to report back to him. He did not allow his own men to go ashore until these ships had returned.

Both he and the Athenians did the same thing for four days. All this time Alcibiades[3] was in his castle and he could see from there that the Athenians were moored on an open shore with no city behind them and that they were getting their supplies from Sestus, which was about two miles away from the ships, while the enemy, inside a harbour and with a city at their backs, had everything they wanted. He therefore told the Athenians that they were in a very poor position and advised them to shift their anchorage to Sestus, where they would have the advantages of a harbour and a city 'Once you are there,' he said, 'you can fight whenever you please.'

The generals, however – particularly Tydeus and Menander –

1. On the Chersonese (Gallipoli or Gelibolu) peninsula, on the European shore of the Hellespont (Dardanelles).
2. The Spartan commander and statesman (died 395 B.C.).
3. The Athenian statesman, now in exile for the second time. In the following year he was murdered. For him see also p. 241 (Plato) and p. 412 (Plutarch).

told him to go away. 'We are in command now,' they said, 'not you.' So Alcibiades went away.

On the fifth day as the Athenians sailed up, Lysander gave special instructions to the ships that were to follow them. As soon as they saw that the Athenians had disembarked and had scattered in various directions over the Chersonese – as they were now doing more freely every day, since they had to go a long way to get their food and were now actually contemptuous of Lysander for not coming out to fight – they were to sail back and to signal with a shield when they were half-way across the straits. These orders were carried out and, as soon as he got the signal, Lysander ordered the fleet to sail at full speed. Thorax and his men went with the fleet.

When Conon[1] saw that the enemy were attacking, he signalled to the Athenians to hurry back as fast as they could come to their ships. But they were scattered in all directions; some of the ships had only two banks of oars manned, some only one, and some were not manned at all. Conon himself in his own ship with seven others and also the state trireme *Paralus* did get to sea fully manned and in close order. All the rest were captured by Lysander on land. He also rounded up nearly all the crews, though a few managed to escape into various fortified places in the neighbourhood.

Conon, escaping with his nine ships, could see that for the Athenians all was over. He put in at Abarnis, the headland off Lampsacus, and there seized the cruising sails of Lysander's fleet. Then, with eight ships, he sailed away to King Evagoras in Cyprus.[2] The *Paralus* sailed to Athens to report what had happened.

It was at night that the *Paralus* arrived at Athens. As the news of the disaster was told, one man passed it on to another, and a sound of wailing arose and extended first from Piraeus, then along the Long Walls until it reached the city. That night no one slept. They mourned for the lost, but more still for their own fate. They thought that they themselves would now be dealt with as they had dealt with others.

REX WARNER (1966)

1. One of the Athenian admirals.
2. The ruler of Salamis in Cyprus (died *c.* 374–373 B.C.).

DID SOCRATES CORRUPT THE YOUNG?

It also seems extraordinary to me that any people should have been persuaded that Socrates had a bad influence upon young men. Besides what I have said already, he was in the first place the most self-controlled of men in respect of his sexual and other appetites; then he was most tolerant of cold and heat and hardships of all kinds; and finally he had so trained himself to be moderate in his requirements that he was very easily satisfied with very slight possessions. So if he himself was like this, how could he have made others irreverent or criminal or greedy or sensual or work-shy? On the contrary, he rescued many from this sort of state by inspiring them with a desire for goodness and offering them hopes that if they took themselves in hand they would become decent citizens. At the same time he never undertook to teach how this could be done; but by obviously *being* such a person he made those who spent their time with him hope that if they followed his example they would develop the same character.

He neither neglected the body himself nor commended others for doing so. He disapproved of over-eating followed by violent exercise, but he approved of taking enough exercise to work off the amount of food that the appetite accepts with pleasure; he said that this was quite a healthy practice and did not hinder the cultivation of the mind. He was certainly not foppish or ostentatious either in his clothing or in his footwear or in the rest of his daily life. Nor again did he make his associates money-lovers; he rid them of all other desires except for his company, and for that he charged no fee. In exercising this restraint he considered that he was consulting his own independence; those who accepted a fee in return for their services he nicknamed 'self-enslavers', because they were bound to converse with those who paid the fee. He expressed surprise that a man who offered to teach goodness should demand to be paid for it and, instead of anticipating the greatest possible gain through obtaining a good friend, should be afraid that the person who has become a model of virtue will feel less than the deepest gratitude to his supreme benefactor. Socrates never made any such offer to anyone, but he believed that those of his associates who accepted the principles which he himself approved would be good friends all their life long to himself and to one another. How, then, could such a person have a corrupting influence upon the young? Unless the cultivation of goodness is a form of corruption.

HUGH TREDENNICK (1970)

THE ADVANTAGES OF KNOWLEDGE

When Glaucon the son of Ariston[1] was trying to become a popular orator, because he was set on being the head of the state although he was not yet twenty years old, none of his friends and intimates could stop him; he was always getting dragged off the public platform and laughed at. The one person who prevailed upon him was Socrates, who was kindly disposed towards him for the sake of two persons, Charmides, the son of Glaucon,[2] and Plato. Socrates happened to meet him, and he first won his attention by addressing him in the following way:

'Glaucon,' he said, 'have you made up your mind to become the head of our state?'

'Yes, I have, Socrates.'

'And a fine thing too, upon my word; I don't know that there is any higher human ambition. Clearly if you succeed in it you will have the power to obtain your own desires, and be able to help your friends; you will gain distinction for your family and extend the power of your country; and you will win a name for yourself first in our city, and then in Greece, and perhaps even, like Themistocles, among foreign powers. And wherever you are, every eye will be fixed upon you.'

This description appealed to Glaucon's vanity, and he was glad to remain where he was. Socrates then went on:

'It's obvious, isn't it, Glaucon, that if you want to be held in honour you must help your country?'

'Certainly.'

1. Glaucon was Plato's elder brother.
2. Charmides was the son of another Glaucon, Plato's uncle.

XENOPHON

'Well, then,' said he, 'please don't make a secret of it, but tell us where you will start to benefit your country.'

Glaucon made no reply, as if he were considering for the first time where he should start.

'If you wanted to make the family of a friend more important, you would try to make it wealthier. On the same principle I suppose you will try to make your country wealthier.'

'Yes, of course.'

'Wouldn't it be wealthier if its revenues were increased?'

'Naturally.'

'Tell me, then: what are our country's present revenues derived from, and what do they amount to? No doubt you have looked into this, so that you may make up any of them that are inadequate and supply any that are lacking.'

'Actually,' said Glaucon, 'I haven't looked into that.'

'Well,' said Socrates, 'if you have left that aside, tell us what the country's expenditure is. You must be planning to curtail any extravagance.'

'Actually,' said Glaucon, 'I haven't had time for that yet either.'

'Then we will defer the question of making the country wealthier. You can't very well look after the expenditure and revenues if you don't know what they are.'

'But, Socrates,' said Glaucon, 'it is possible to enrich one's country from the resources of its enemies.'

'Yes, indeed, perfectly possible,' said Socrates, 'if you are stronger than they are. If you are weaker, you are likely to lose even what you have already.'

'That is true.'

'So before you start considering on whom to make war you ought to know the strength both of your own country and of her opponents, so that if your country is the stronger you may encourage her to undertake the war, and if she is weaker you may persuade her to be cautious.'

'Quite right,' said he.

'Then tell us first what our country's land and sea forces are, and then do the same for the enemy's.'

'Well, really,' he said, 'I couldn't tell you off-hand.'

'If you've got a written note, fetch it; I should very much like to hear the answer.'

'Actually,' he said, 'I haven't got a note of it yet either.'

'Very well, then,' said Socrates, 'we will put off our military discussion too, in the first instance. Probably you haven't yet had time to go carefully into the matter, because of its magnitude, besides your being so newly in office. But of course I'm sure that you have already given your attention to the defence of our territory, and know how many guard-posts are well placed and how many are not, how many of the garrisons are adequate and how many are not. And you will recommend the strengthening of those that are well placed and the abolition of those that are superfluous.'

'Actually I shall recommend abolishing the lot,' said Glaucon, 'for they are so badly manned that the produce of the land gets stolen.'

'But if the guard-posts are abolished,' said Socrates, 'don't you think that it will be open to anyone to help himself freely? By the way, have you found this out by personal inspection, or how do you know that the posts are badly manned?'

'I assume it,' he said.

'Shall we wait to discuss this subject too until we have got beyond assumptions and know the facts?'

'Perhaps that would be better,' said Glaucon.

'Then there are the silver mines,'[1] said Socrates. 'I know that you haven't visited them so as to be able to account for the decline of revenue from them.'

'No, I haven't.'

'As a matter of fact,' said Socrates, 'they say that it's an unhealthy district; so when you have to state your views about it this excuse will cover you.'

'You're making fun of me,' said Glaucon.

'But there's another problem that I'm sure you haven't neglected but investigated: how long can the country be fed on home-produced corn, and how much extra does it need per year?[2] You wouldn't like your country to incur a shortage of this kind without your realizing

1. At Laurium near Cape Sunium at the southern extremity of Attica. They furnished a great part of Athens' wealth.
2. About one third of the corn supply was imported.

it; you would wish to be able to advise from personal knowledge about essential supplies, and so to give her help and security.'

'That's an enormous task you're suggesting,' said Glaucon, 'if one is to be obliged to look after that sort of thing.'

'But surely,' said Socrates, 'a man could never manage even his own household properly unless he knows all its deficiencies and supplies them by looking after them all. As our city consists of more than ten thousand houses, and it would be difficult to look after so many households simultaneously, why don't you first try to look after one, your uncle's? It needs it. And if you can cope with that, you can try your hand on more; but if you can't do any good to one, how can you do good to many? If a man can't carry one hundredweight, surely it's obvious that he shouldn't even try to carry more than one.'

'Well,' said Glaucon, 'I would do something for my uncle's household if he would follow my advice.'

'So although you can't persuade your uncle,' said Socrates, 'you expect to be able to make the whole population of Athens, including your uncle, follow your advice? Take care, my dear Glaucon, that your craving for distinction doesn't take you in the opposite direction. Can't you see how risky it is to say or to do things that you don't know about? Consider the rest of your acquaintances, those whom you know to be the sort of people who obviously say and do things that they don't know about; do you think that they are more admired or despised for this sort of conduct? And then consider the case of those who know what they are saying and what they are doing. In my opinion you will find in every sphere of action that esteem and admiration are reserved for those who are best informed, while ignominy and contempt are the lot of the most ignorant. So if you really want to be esteemed and admired in the state, try to ensure as far as possible that you know about the things that you want to do. If you have this advantage over the rest when you try your hand at politics, I shouldn't be surprised if you realized your ambition quite easily.'

I shall next describe what his attitude was towards those who thought that they had received the best education and prided themselves on their wisdom.

He discovered that the handsome Euthydemus had collected a

great many writings of the best-known poets and sophists, and that consequently he now considered himself to be more enlightened than anyone of his age, and entertained high hopes of becoming unrivalled in eloquence and administrative ability. So first of all, realizing that because of his youth Euthydemus did not yet go into the market-place if he wanted to conduct any business but took up his position in a saddler's shop close by, Socrates went to the shop himself with some of his friends. Someone opened the conversation by inquiring whether it was through association with one of the sophists or by natural talent that Themistocles rose so far above his fellow-citizens that the state looked to him whenever it needed a man of action. Socrates wanted to stir up Euthydemus, and observed that it was silly to imagine that, although the lesser arts were not practised seriously without the help of competent teachers, the art of public administration, which was the greatest accomplishment of all, came to people of its own accord.

On another occasion when Euthydemus was present Socrates noticed that he was withdrawing from the group and taking care not to seem impressed by Socrates' wisdom. 'Gentlemen,' he said, 'it is easy to see from the way in which our friend Euthydemus spends his time that when he is old enough he won't refrain from advising the state on any political issue that comes up. And it seems to me that by carefully avoiding the appearance of learning anything from anybody he has provided himself with a splendid preface to his public speeches. Evidently when he begins to speak he will introduce what he has to say like this: "Gentlemen, I have never learned anything from anybody, nor have I sought the company of any persons whose abilities in speech and action I had heard of, nor have I troubled to acquire a teacher from among those who understand these matters. On the contrary I have consistently avoided not only learning anything from anybody but even giving the impression of doing so. However, I shall offer you whatever advice occurs to me of its own accord." Such an introduction would be appropriate for candidates applying for a public medical post. They could suitably begin their application in this way: "Gentlemen, I have never learned medicine from anyone, nor have I tried to secure any doctor as a teacher. I have consistently avoided not only learning anything from medical men, but even giving the impression of having learned this art. However, I ask you to give me this medical post. I shall try to learn by experimenting on you.""'

This introduction made everybody present laugh.

It was now obvious that Euthydemus was paying attention to what Socrates was saying, although he was still careful not to say anything himself, thinking by his silence to invest himself with an air of discretion. Socrates wanted to stop him behaving like this, and said:

'I can't understand how it is that people who want to be competent performers on a stringed or wind instrument, or on horseback, or in any other similar skill, try to practise the desired accomplishment as continuously as possible, not only by themselves but under the super-vision of acknowledged experts, going to all lengths in their anxiety to do nothing without these experts' advice, because they feel that they cannot otherwise earn recognition; whereas some of those who wish to become proficient in public speaking and administration expect to be able to do this of their own accord off-hand, without preparation or application. Yet political proficiency seems to be harder to achieve than the other kinds, inasmuch as more people pursue political ends and fewer achieve them. So obviously political ambition calls for more and closer application than other kinds.'

Socrates began by making observations of this sort in the hearing of Euthydemus. When he noticed that Euthydemus was enduring his comments more readily and listening with greater interest, he went alone to the saddler's shop, and when Euthydemus sat down near him he said, 'Tell me, Euthydemus, is it true what I hear, that you have collected a large number of books by reputed experts?'

'Indeed it is, Socrates,' replied Euthydemus, 'and I'm going on collecting them still, until I have got as many as I can.'

'Upon my word,' said Socrates, 'I do admire you for not preferring hoards of silver and gold to the possession of wisdom. Evidently you think that silver and gold make people no better, whereas the maxims of the wise enrich their possessors with moral goodness.'

Euthydemus cheered up as he heard this, thinking that Socrates approved of his method of pursuing wisdom; but when Socrates noted that he was pleased at this commendation, he said,

'What exactly is it that you want to become good at, Euthydemus, by collecting these books?'

When Euthydemus remained silent, wondering what he should reply, Socrates went on: 'Can it be medicine? There are a great many treatises written by doctors.'

'That's not my idea at all,' said Euthydemus.

'Perhaps you want to become an architect? That's another profession that calls for a skilled mind.'

'Not for my taste,' he said.

'Perhaps you are keen to become a good geometrician, like Theodorus?'

'Not that either,' he said.

'Perhaps you want to be an astronomer?'

When he denied this too, 'Perhaps a reciter? They say that you have got all the poems of Homer.'

'Certainly not,' he said. 'I know that professional reciters are word-perfect, but they have very little intelligence themselves.'

At this Socrates said, 'You don't mean to tell me, Euthydemus, that you are aiming at that kind of proficiency that makes people politicians and administrators and capable of governing, and helpful both to others and to themselves?'

'I am very anxious to acquire this kind of proficiency,' replied Euthydemus.

HUGH TREDENNICK (1970)

PART V

PHYSICIANS, ORATORS, PHILOSOPHERS

THE HIPPOCRATICS

HIPPOCRATES was a physician of Cos, and reputedly the founder of scientific medicine, active in the second half of the fifth century B.C. Most of the works attributed to him were written by his pupils and successors.

*

ENVIRONMENT AND CHARACTER[1]

We have now discussed the organic and structural differences between the populations of Asia and Europe, but we have still to consider the problem why the Asiatics are of a less warlike and a more tame disposition than the Europeans. The deficiency of spirit and courage observable in the human inhabitants of Asia has for its principal cause the low margin of seasonal variability in the temperature of that continent, which is approximately stable throughout the year. Such a climate does not produce those mental shocks and violent bodily dislocations which would naturally render the temperament ferocious and introduce a stronger current of irrationality and passion than would be the case under stable conditions. It is invariably changes that stimulate the human mind and that prevent it from remaining passive. These, in my view, are the reasons why the Asiatic race is unmilitary, but I must not omit the factor of institutions. The greater part of Asia is under monarchical government; and wherever men are not their own masters and not free agents, but are under despotic rule, they are not concerned to make themselves militarily efficient but, on the contrary, to avoid being regarded as good military material – the reason being that they are not playing for equal stakes. It is theirs, presumably, to serve and struggle and die under compulsion from their masters and far from the sight of their wives and children

1. This work *On Airs, Waters and Places* (*On Environment*) is an authentic product of the latter half of the fifth century B.C., though it cannot be attributed with certainty to Hippocrates himself.

and friends. Whenever they acquit themselves like men, it is their masters who are exalted and aggrandized by their achievements, while their own share of the profits is the risking and the losing of their lives. And not only this, but, in the case of people so circumstanced, it is also inevitable that the inactivity consequent upon the absence of war should have a taming effect upon the temperament, so that even a naturally courageous and spirited individual would be inhibited on the intellectual side by the prevailing institutions. A strong argument in favour of my contention is furnished by the fact that all the Hellenes and non-Hellenes in Asia who are not under despotic rule, but are free agents and struggle for their own benefit, are as warlike as any populations in the world – the reason being that they stake their lives in their own cause and reap the rewards of their own valour (and the penalties of their own cowardice, into the bargain). You will also find that the Asiatics differ among one another, some being finer and others poorer in quality, and these differences also have their cause in the seasonal climatic variations, as I have stated above.

ARNOLD TOYNBEE (1952)

A DISEASE IN SOUTH RUSSIA

The natives attribute the causation of this disease to God, and they revere and worship its victims, in fear of being stricken by it themselves. I, too, take the view that these phenomena come from God; but I take the same view in regard to all phenomena and look upon no given phenomenon as more divine or more human than any other. All, in my view, are uniform and all are divine; but each phenomenon obeys its own law, and Natural Law knows no exceptions ...

The victims of this disease are not the lowest class among the Nomads, but the members of the best families who possess the strongest physical constitutions. They contract it by riding, and the poor are comparatively immune because they do not ride. On the assumption, however, that this disease is in some sense more divine than others, it ought not exclusively to attack the best connected and the wealthiest Nomads, but all classes alike, or, if there were dis-crimination, it ought to tell against those with narrow means – that is, if the Gods really take pleasure in being honoured and admired by human beings and requite such attentions with their favours. Presumably it is the wealthy, with the ample funds at their command, who make frequent sacrifices to the Gods and dedicate votive offer-ings and pay honours, while the poor are less active in the matter, partly through lack of means and in a secondary degree through their resentment against the Gods for not endowing them with worldly goods. On this showing, those with narrow means ought to incur the penalties for such lapses, rather than the wealthy. In reality, however, as I have stated already, this phenomenon is only divine in the same sense as every other, and every phenomenon obeys Natural Law.

ARNOLD TOYNBEE (1952)

LYSIAS

Athenian orator; son of a Syracusan settler in Athens. Lived *c.* 459–
c. 380 B.C.

*

THERAMENES[1]

In the first place, he was the prime cause of the first oligarchy, when
his influence caused the election of the Four Hundred. His father was
one of the Commissioners, and furthered the same movement,
while he himself was held to be one of its firmest supporters, which
led to his own election as Strategus.[2] So long as his stock was high he
maintained good faith with Athens. But when he found that Peisander,
Callaeschrus and others were gaining ground on him, while the
citizen body were no longer in their favour, he yielded to his jealousy
of them and his fears of the populace, and joined the faction of Aristo-
crates. He wanted to appear to be in with the popular party still, so
he accused and secured the death of his great friends, Antiphon and
Archeptolemus.[3] His dastardly conduct allowed him to sacrifice both
the freedom of Athens for his adherence to the oligarchs, and the
life of his friends for his adherence to the populace of Athens.

But when he was in a position of the highest honour and estimation,
he announced his intention to save Athens, and then promptly caused
its destruction, on the specious claim that he had devised a scheme of

1. A clever but changeable Athenian politician who helped both to establish
and remove the oligarchic Four Hundred (411) and after the disaster of Aegospotami (405) was sent to negotiate with the Spartan Lysander. He was appointed
one of the oligarchic Thirty Tyrants (404) but quarrelled with the extremists,
especially Critias, who had him executed.
2. i.e. one of the ten annually elected generals.
3. These were politicians who played varying roles in the revolution of the
Four Hundred.

great importance and enormous value. He promised to secure peace without the surrender of hostages, the destruction of the walls or forfeiture of the navy. He refused to reveal his scheme, urging that he should be trusted. The Council of the Areopagus[1] was in charge of measures for the protection of Athens, and there was much opposition to Theramenes. They knew that normally secrets are preserved in dealing with an enemy, whereas Theramenes in the presence of his own people refused to reveal what he intended to tell the enemy. And yet the people trusted him with the safety of their wives and children and themselves. He broke all his promises. So obsessed was he with the need to make Athens small and weak that he led her to a proceeding as far removed from the proposals of the enemy as from the expectation of Athens. He was under no compulsion from Sparta. It was he himself who put forward the proposal to pull down the walls of the Peiraeus and abolish the existing constitution. This was because he fully realized that unless every hope Athens had was speedily removed, instant retaliation would be taken upon himself. Finally, gentlemen of the jury, he did not allow a meeting of the Assembly until the moment laid down by Sparta had been faithfully observed by him, and he had summoned Lysander's fleet and the enemy force had taken up its position in the country. Then, with this position established, with Lysander, Philochares and Miltiades on the spot, they held an assembly, to forestall opposition or threats from any speaker, and to prevent a right choice by Athenian citizens, who were compelled to vote for the measures they had decided on. Theramenes now rose and ordered the city to be put into the hands of thirty individuals, and the constitution in preparation by Dracontides to be adopted. Even as things were, there was a violent outburst in refusal. It was realized that the issue of the meeting was slavery or freedom. Theramenes, as members of the jury can themselves testify, declared that he cared nothing for this outburst, as he knew that a large number of Athenians were in favour of the same measures as himself, and he was voicing the decisions approved by Sparta and Lysander. After him Lysander spoke, and among other statements pronounced that he held Athens under penalty for failing to carry out

1. The ancient council of Athens, deprived of political functions since 462 B.C.

the terms of the truce, and that the question would not be one of her constitution, but of her continued existence, if Theramenes' orders were disobeyed. True and loyal members of the Assembly realized the degree to which the position had been prepared and compulsion laid on them, and either stood still in silence or left, with their conscience clear at any rate of having voted the ruin of Athens. A few despicable characters whose deliberate intentions were traitorous held up their hands to vote as they were told. Instructions had been given to elect ten men secretly nominated by Theramenes, ten laid down by the established Ephors[1] and ten from the company present. They saw the weakness of the Athenian position and their own strength so well that they realized beforehand what would happen in the Assembly. You need not take this from me, but from Theramenes. All I have said he himself included in his Defence in the Council,[2] with his reproach to the exiles that they owed their return to him while Sparta had never thought of them, and to his associates in power that everything that happened, as I have described, had been due to him, and this was his reward for it – when in fact he had given every sort of pledge and exacted oaths of fidelity from them. All this and more, great and small, late and soon, stands to his name in defiance of morality and right. And yet people are brazen enough to call themselves his friends, though it was not for the welfare of Athens that he met his death, but for his own outrageous conduct. It was a penalty that would have been as just under the oligarchy he had dissolved as under democracy. He had twice enslaved Athens in his contempt for her existing régime and his desire for revolution. He made constant claim to the finest of titles, when he had instigated the foulest treason.

A. N. W. SAUNDERS (1970)

1. The principal Spartan officials, five in number, elected annually.
2. i.e. the Boule of 500 members, temporarily suspended during the oligarchic revolutions.

ISOCRATES

Athenian orator, rhetorician and educationalist, 436–338 B.C.

*

WHAT IT MEANS TO BE GREEK

Philosophy took a part in the discovery and development of all these, and gave us education in the field of affairs and civilized relations with each other, drawing the distinction between misfortunes due to ignorance and others due to necessity, and teaching us to guard against the former and bear the latter bravely. Our city showed the way to it, and also gave honour to skill in words, which is the desire and the envy of all. She realized that this alone is the particular and natural possession of man, and that its development has led to all other superiorities as well. She saw that other activities showed such confusion in practice that wisdom was often the way to failure in them, and folly to success, while good and skilled powers of speech were outside the scope of the ordinary people, but were the province of the well-ordered mind: and that in this respect wisdom and ignorance are furthest apart, and the birthright of a liberal education is marked not by courage, wealth and similar distinctions, but most clearly of all by speech, the sign which presents the most reliable proof of education, so that a fine use of words gives not merely ability at home, but honour abroad. Athens has so far outrun the rest of mankind in thought and speech that her disciples are the masters of the rest, and it is due to her that the word 'Greek' is not so much a term of birth as of mentality, and is applied to a common culture rather than a common descent.

A. N. W. SAUNDERS (1970)

SPARTA HAS LET PERSIA HAVE TOO MUCH POWER[1]

It will be clear that it used to be ourselves who laid down the boundaries of Persian territory, and in some cases stated tribute to be paid, and barred her from access to the sea. Now it is the King of Persia who directs the affairs of the Greek world, gives orders for individual states, and almost establishes a governor in each city. There is little else lacking. It was he who took control of the war and presided over the peace, and he who remains as a supervisor of the present political situation. He is a despot to whose court we sail to accuse each other. We call him the Great King, as though we were subject prisoners of war, and if we engage in war with each other, it is on him that our hopes are set, though he would destroy both sides without compunction.

We should be ready to reflect on this, to resent the present position, and to desire to regain our place as leaders. We should cast blame on Sparta for beginning the war with the aim of liberating the Greeks and in the end reducing so many of them to subjection, for causing the revolt of the Ionian states from Athens – which had been the source of their foundation and, so often, their salvation – and putting them at the mercy of Persia, the enemy of their very existence and their unceasing opponent in war. At that time they were incensed at our perfectly legal claim to control some of the cities, but now that these have been reduced to such slavery they feel no more concern for them. For these unfortunate cities it is not enough that they should be subject to tribute and see their strong places in the grip of their enemies; their communal troubles are intensified by personal suffering greater than under the tax collectors of Athens. No Athenian inflicts such cruelty on his slaves as the Persian punishment of free men. But the greatest misery of their subjects is the compulsion to join in the fight for slavery against the cause of freedom, and to endure the prospect of defeat which will cause their instant destruction or a success which will plunge them further into slavery in the future.

At whose doors but Sparta's can we lay the blame for this? Despite

1. This passage is from the *Panegyricus*, published in 380 B.C. after ten years of composition.

their great power they stand aside and watch the pitiable plight of people once their allies, and the construction of a Persian empire out of the strength of Greece. In the past their habit was to expel tyrants and to give their support to the people, but now they have so changed as to make war on free states and throw in their lot with despotism. The city of Mantinea, at any rate, is an instance. After peace had been made, the Spartans razed it to the ground. They captured the Cadmeia at Thebes.[1] They have now laid siege to Olynthus and Phlius,[2] and they are giving assistance to Amyntas king of Macedon, Dionysius tyrant of Syracuse, and the Persian power in Asia, to help them to supremacy. Indeed, it is surely a paradox that the leading power in Greece should make one man master of such countless numbers, and not allow the greatest of cities to be autonomous, but drive it to an alternative of slavery or utter disaster. The final degradation is to see the claimants to the leadership of Greece at war day after day with Greek states and in permanent alliance with a non-Greek people.

Let it not be supposed to be due to ill will that I make a somewhat brusque reference to these subjects after a prelude promising reconciliation. My intention in speaking in this way is not to defame Sparta in the eyes of others so much as to put a check on her, in so far as my discourse is able, and to put an end to her present attitude. It is impossible to prevent wrong aims or inspire better without strong denunciation of the old ones. But one should put down damaging attacks as accusation, but beneficent criticism as admonition. The same words should be taken in different ways according to the intention. A further criticism could be made of the Spartans, that they reduce their neighbours to serfdom for the benefit of their own country, but they refuse to do the same in dealing with the common interests of the allied states, when they could settle differences with us and make the whole non-Greek world subsidiary to the Greek. Yet for men whose pride springs from nature rather than circumstances this is much more the right pursuit than collecting tribute from islanders who deserve our pity, when we see them farming the rocky hills for lack

1. The Cadmeia was the citadel of Thebes.
2. These towns, in the Chalcidice (Macedonia) and north-east Peloponnese respectively, were both reduced by Sparta in 379 B.C.

of good soil, while the mainland is so productive that most of the land can be left idle and great wealth comes from the only part which is cultivated.

It seems to me that an outside observer of the present political situation would condemn it as utter insanity on both sides that we risk disaster on such slender grounds, when we might enrich our-selves in a moment: we tear our own land to pieces and neglect the harvest we could reap in Asia. Nothing is more profitable for Persia than to ensure our continuing to fight each other for ever.

A. N. W. SAUNDERS (1970)

IS IT POSSIBLE TO ADVISE PHILIP OF MACEDON?[1]

I shall not hesitate to mention the trouble I have been given by some of my pupils, because I think it may be useful to hear it. When I revealed to them my intention to address a discourse to you, not for the purpose of display or as an encomium on your military successes, which will be done by others, but in an attempt to urge you to a more fitting, noble and valuable course of action than that on which you have lately been engaged, they were so terrified that old age might have driven me out of my wits, as to give me an unprecedented reproof: it would be an intolerable folly to contem-plate a message of advice to Philip, who might in the past have thought himself less of a diplomat than some, but after his recent noteworthy achievements must think himself more so than most. 'Furthermore,' I was told, 'his entourage includes the keenest intelligences in Mace-donia, who, even if they are inexperienced in most other matters, know better than you do where his advantage lies. You will find a number of Greeks who have settled there, men who are by no means without distinction or ability, and his association with them has not at all dimmed the greatness of Macedon. The position he has achieved is ideal. There are no weak points in it. Why, the previous controllers of Macedonia, Thessaly, have been brought to such close

1. Written in 346 B.C. Isocrates sees Philip II as the potential leader of a united Greece against the Persians.

relations with him that any section of them feels greater confidence in Philip than in other groups of their own fellow-citizens. The states in that district he has either brought into his own orbit by the benefits he has conferred, or liquidated the really troublesome. He has reduced Magnesia, Perrhaebia and Paeonia and made them subject states. He has secured his power, official as well as actual, over the great bulk of Illyria, except for the Adriatic coast.[1] With all this behind him do you not suppose he will think it pure stupidity to address discourses to him, and conclude that you have a very distorted idea of the power of words and of his own intelligence?' I will omit my initial dismay on hearing this, and my subsequent recovery and reply to it in detail, for fear of appearing complacent at making a neat defence. But having, I thought, given a moderate rebuff to the critics who had ventured to attack me, I ended with an undertaking that they should be the only people in Athens to whom I would disclose the discourse, and that I would accept their decision what to do about it. What their frame of mind was when they left, I cannot tell. But after a few days, when the text was completed and I showed it to them, they changed their attitude enough to feel ashamed of their outspoken tone, to regret what they had said and own that they had never made a greater mistake. They showed more enthusiasm than my own for sending the speech to you, and added their hopes that I should be received with gratitude for it not only by yourself and by Athens, but by the Greek states in general.

A. N. W. SAUNDERS (1970)

1. These are all territories bordering on Macedonia.

DEMOSTHENES

THE greatest Athenian orator, 384–322 B.C.; instigated the Greek city-states to unite unsuccessfully against Philip II of Macedonia (338).

*

THE NEED FOR NATIONAL DEFENCE

Were it a new question, gentlemen, which lay before us, I should wait until most of the regular speakers had made their contribution, and if I were satisfied with the views expressed, I should add nothing; if not, I should try to voice my own. But as it is the reconsideration of a subject frequently discussed by speakers before, I hope I may be pardoned for speaking first. Had my opponents urged the right policy in the past, this discussion would be superfluous.

First, then, we must not be downhearted at the present situation, however regrettable it seems. The worst feature of it in the past is the best hope for the future. What feature? The fact that it is plain dereliction of duty on our part which has brought us to this position. If it followed on a period of exemplary conduct by the people of Athens, there would be no hope of improvement. Next we should reflect upon what history or our own memory can tell us of the greatness of Sparta not so long ago, and of the glorious and honourable part played by Athens in maintaining the war against them in the cause of right.[1] Why mention this? To set this fact firmly before your minds, gentlemen, that if you are awake, you have nothing to fear, if you close your eyes, nothing to hope for. To prove this I point to two things, the past power of Sparta, which we defeated by sheer attention to business, and the present aggression of Macedon,[2] which alarms us because our attitude is wrong. If the belief is held that Philip is an

1. i.e. in the Corinthian War, 394–387 B.C.
2. After the defeat of the Phocian Onomarchus in the Third Sacred War (352 B.C.).

enemy hard to face in view of the extent of his present strength and the loss to Athens of strategic points, it is a correct belief. But it must be remembered that at one time we had Pydna, Potidaea, Methone and the whole surrounding district on friendly terms, and that a number of communities now on his side were then autonomous and unfettered, and would have preferred our friendship to his. If Philip had then adopted this belief in the invincibility of Athens in view of her control of points commanding Macedonian territory, while he himself lacked support, he could not have achieved any of his present successes nor acquired the strength he has. As it was, he observed with insight that these strategic points were the prizes of war, that they were open to the contestants, and it is a natural law that ownership passes from the absentee to the first comer, from the negligent to the energetic and enterprising. This is the spirit which has won him the control of what he holds, in some cases by the methods of military conquest, in others by those of friendship and alliance. Indeed alliance and universal attention are the rewards to be won by obvious preparedness and the will to take action. If, then, this country is prepared to adopt a similar outlook and to break with the past, if every man is ready to take the post which his duty and his abilities demand in service to the state, and set pretences aside, if financial contribution is forthcoming from the well-to-do, and personal service from the appropriate group, in a word if we are prepared to be ourselves, to abandon the hope to evade our duty and get it done by our neighbours, we shall recover what is our own with God's will, we shall regain what inertia has lost us, and we shall inflict retribution upon Philip. You must not imagine that he is a super-human being whose success is unalterably fixed. He has enemies to hate, fear and envy him, even in places very friendly to him. His associates, one must suppose, have the same human feelings as anyone else. But now all this is beneath the surface. It has nowhere to turn because of the slowness, the inactivity of Athens. It is this that I urge you to lay aside. Consider the facts, gentlemen, consider the outrageous lengths to which Philip has gone. He does not offer us a choice between action and inaction. He utters threats, according to my information, in overbearing terms. He is not content to rest on his laurels, but is continually adding to the haul he collects in the net in which he ensnares our hesitant, inactive country. When are we to act? What is to be the signal? When compulsion drives, I suppose. Then what are we to say of the present? In my view the greatest compulsion that can be laid upon free men is their shame at the circumstances in which they find themselves. Do you need to go round and ask each other whether there is any startling news? What could be more startling than a Macedonian fighting a successful war against Athens, and dictating the affairs of Greece? 'Philip is dead', comes one report.[1] 'No, he is only ill', from another. What difference does it make? Should anything happen to Philip, Athens, in her present frame of mind, will soon create another Philip. This one's rise was due less to his own power than to Athenian apathy.

A. N. W. SAUNDERS (1970)

PHILIP OF MACEDON

Do not imagine for a moment that one and the same set of circumstances brings satisfaction both to Philip and to his subjects. His aim and ambition is glory. His way is the way of action and accepted risk, his role the greatest renown in the history of the kings of Macedon. He prefers that to safety. But they do not share these ambitions. They are torn by marching from end to end of the country, and reduced to misery and continuous hardship. They are kept from their own pursuits, their personal affairs, and even what opportunities chance allows cannot be organized, because ports in the country are closed by the war. This affords clear indication of the relation of most of Macedonia towards Philip.

As to his paid soldiers and his *corps d'élite*, who have the reputation of being a superbly welded military force, I have it from an irreproachable informant, who has been in that country, that they are no more than ordinary. Men of military experience, I was told, are discarded by a selfish leader who wants all the credit himself, because his ambition is as outstanding as anything else about him. On the other hand men of restraint and integrity in other fields, who cannot

1. This report of Philip's death was current in 352 B.C.

endure a life of drunkenness and debauchery and indecent dancing, are rejected and passed over by a man like Philip. The rest of his *entourage* are bandits and flatterers, capable of taking part in drunken revelry which I hesitate to describe. This is clearly true, because the outcasts of our society, who were thought lower than mere street-entertainers, creatures like the slave, Callias, who do comic performances and write low songs at the expense of others to get a laugh, these are the people he likes and keeps around him. This may seem little, but it is in fact a great proof of this contemptible character on a right estimate. At present, no doubt, this is obscured by success. There is nothing like success to conceal dishonour. But at any moment of failure it will be put to the test. And it will not be long, in my view, granted the consent of heaven and the determination of this country, before it begins to show signs. In physical health a man who is strong may go for a time without noticing anything amiss, but in time of illness troubles extend everywhere, to any past fracture or strain or underlying weakness. It is the same with a state, whether democratic or monarchical. In time of external war weaknesses are not commonly apparent. But war on its frontier brings them to light.

If anyone here observes Philip's prosperity and supposes him a formidable opponent, it is the view of good sense. Fortune is a powerful force, indeed it is everything, in all human affairs. None the less, given the choice, I would prefer the fortune of Athens, granted her will to follow the call of duty in detail, to that of Philip. There are many more ways open to her than to him to command the favour of heaven. Yet here we sit inactive. He could not remain inactive and still demand the assistance of his own friends, let alone the good will of heaven. No wonder that with his expeditions, his energy, his personal control of detail, his opportunism at every juncture, he gets the better of democratic hesitation, deliberation and inquiry. I am not surprised. The opposite would be surprising, if neglect of our duty in war brought success against his complete fulfilment of it. What does surprise me is this. In the past, against Sparta, this country went to war for the rights of Greek states, declined numerous opportunities of self-seeking and for the rights of others sacrificed her wealth in war expense and her security in war service. Now she is slow to offer money and slow to serve in defence of her own possessions. We saved others on many occasions collectively and singly, but the loss of our own possessions is something we do not stir a finger to prevent. This is what surprises me, this and one other fact, that there is not a man capable of reckoning the length of the war against Philip, and asking what this country has been doing in all this length of time. You know the answer. She has passed it in procrastination, in optimism, in recrimination, condemnation and yet more optimism.

A. N. W. SAUNDERS (1970)

THE ATHENIANS MUST LIVE UP TO THEIR ANCESTORS (349 B.C.)

I do not speak from an irresponsible desire to give offence. I am not so senseless or ineffectual as to seek offence without benefit. But I think the true citizen must put the reality of survival above the gratification of rhetoric. This was the method, this was the character of political dealing, I understand, as perhaps you all do, practised by the speakers of the past, who are extolled by members of this assembly, but not imitated by them; the method of the great Aristides, of Nicias, of my namesake and of Pericles.[1] Since the appearance of our modern speakers, who ask 'What are your wishes? What proposal would you like? What can I do for your gratification?', Athenian strength has been squandered for immediate popularity. This is what happens, and as their stock rises, that of the nation sinks. Think, gentlemen, what summary could be given of affairs in the past and in your own time. The account will be short. You know it well enough. The examples which could lead us in the path of success are not taken from foreign history, but your own. Your predecessors had no flattery from speakers, and no love from them, as you do. But for forty-five years they were the accepted leaders of the Greek states. They amassed over ten thousand talents on the Acropolis. The king of this district of Thrace was their subordinate, and stood in the right relation for a non-Greek to a Greek state. Many and great were the

1. Aristides the Just (died after 467), Nicias (c. 470–413 B.C.), Demosthenes who commanded in north-east Greece in the Peloponnesian War and was executed by the Syracusans (413 B.C.), and Pericles (c. 495–429 B.C.).

victories they won by land and sea as citizen fighters, and they were alone of mankind in leaving by their achievements a reputation high above carping envy. Such they proved in the sphere of Hellenic affairs. Look now at the character they bore in our city itself, in public and private relations alike. In the first the architectural beauty they created in sacred buildings and their adornment was of a quality and an extent unsurpassable by later generations. Their private lives were of such restraint, and so well in keeping with the character of the community, that if the type of house lived in by Aristides or Miltiades[1] or any of the great men of that day is known nowadays, it can be seen to be no grander than its neighbours. No one then made capital out of public affairs. It was felt that the community should be the gainer. But their integrity in the conduct of Hellenic affairs, their devotion in that of religion, their equity in that of private concerns, gained them the highest happiness. So stood the state in the past under the leaders I have mentioned. What is the position now under our present splendid administrators? Is there any similarity, any comparison with the past? I cut short a long list of instances. You can all see the degree of helplessness to which we have come. Sparta is finished. Thebes is fully occupied. No other state is strong enough to bid for the supremacy. We could retain our position in safety and hold the scales of justice for the rest of the Hellenic world. And yet we have lost territory of our own, we have spent over fifteen hundred talents to no purpose, the allies we made in the war have brought us down in the peace, and we have brought an adversary of such magnitude on the stage against us. I invite any man present to tell me here and now, what other source there is of Philip's power than ourselves. 'Well,' I am told, 'that may be very unfortunate, but at home, at least, we are better off.' What is the evidence of this? Plaster on the battlements, new streets, water supplies. These are trivialities. Turn your eyes on the pursuers of these political ends. They have risen from beggary to riches, from obscurity to prominence, and in some cases have houses which outshine the public buildings themselves, while their consequence rises with the decline of the nation.

What is the reason for all this? Why was Athenian history then so glorious? And now why is so much amiss? Because then the people

1. The victor of Marathon (490 B.C.).

of Athens had the courage to act and to serve in person, the people were the master of the politicians and the controller of all its assets. Then it was a matter of satisfaction to every man elsewhere to be admitted by the people to share its honour, its power and some of its benefits. Now the reverse is true. It is the politicians who control assets, and through whose agency all action is taken. We, the people, are enervated and our revenues and our allies whittled away.

A. N. W. SAUNDERS (1970)

PLATO

Athenian philosopher, *c.* 429–347 B.C. Founded the Academy. His publications, which purport to report the teaching of Socrates (469–399 B.C.), consist of twenty-five dialogues, the *Apology*, a number of philosophical letters, and some pieces of elegiac poetry.

*

SOCRATES ON THE CHARGES AGAINST HIM[1]

Be it so, then; I must defend myself, and endeavour to expel from your minds, in so short a time, the calumny which has had so long a time to fix itself there. I should be glad (if it be for your good and my own) that this were possible; but I think it is difficult; I do not conceal from myself the weightiness of the task. The event, however, must be as the god pleases. I must obey the law, and make my defence.

Let us go back, then, to the beginning, and see upon what accusation has been founded that prejudice against me, in reliance on which Meletus has brought the present impeachment. What, then, did my assailants allege? for we must consider them as accusers, and read the words of their indictment. 'Socrates is guilty of occupying himself with frivolous and criminal pursuits; exploring the things which are under the earth and in the sky; and making the worse appear the better reason; and teaching others to do the same.' Something of this sort is what they impute to me; and you have yourselves seen, in the comedy of Aristophanes, a certain Socrates, who professes to walk the air, with much other trifling, about which I do not understand one jot. And I do not speak in disparagement of such knowledge,

1. In 399 B.C. Socrates was brought to trial on the charges of introducing strange gods and corrupting the youth, and was condemned to death. See also above, p. 209.

if there be any one who is wise in these matters; but I have no concern with them. And I call most of yourselves to witness, and beg you to inform and to ask each other (those of you who have ever heard me converse), and there are many of them among you: tell to one another, if any of you has ever heard in my conversation anything, great or small, on such subjects; and by this you will know that all the other things which are vulgarly said about me are of the same value. Again, if you have heard any one say that I undertake to instruct people, and receive money for it, neither is this true. I think it a fine thing, no doubt, if any one is capable of instructing people, as Gorgias of Leontini does, and Prodicus of Ceos, and Hippias of Elis.[1] Each of these, going to one city after another, is able to draw round him the young men, who, though they are at liberty to converse gratis with whomsoever they please of their own citizens, are persuaded to quit the society of these, and, resorting to the newcomers, converse with them, not only paying them money, but rendering gratitude to them besides. There is now in this very town a wise man from Paros, whose arrival I happened to hear of; for I was accidentally in company with a man who has paid more money to sophists than all other men put together, Callias, the son of Hipponicus. I said to him (for he has two sons), 'O Callias, if your sons had been colts or steers, we could have found and hired a proper superintendent of their education, who could have formed them to all the good qualities befitting their nature; but now, since they are men, what superintendent have you in view for them? Who is there that is knowing in the good qualities of a man and a citizen? for I suppose that you must have considered the matter, having sons to bring up. Is there such a person,' said I, 'or not?' 'There is,' he answered. 'Who,' asked I, 'and of what country, and for what price does he teach?' 'Euenus of Paros,' replied he; 'and his price is five minae.' And I felicitated Euenus, if he in reality possesses this art, and is so zealous in the practice of it. I, too, therefore, should be proud, and make much of myself, if I knew these matters; but I do not know them, O Athenians.

Some of you may, perhaps, answer, 'But, O Socrates, what, then, is your affair? and whence did these accusations arise? for you would

1. Three eminent sophists (popular philosophers and rhetoricians).

not have been so much heard of or talked about, if you had done nothing strange, or different from other people: tell us, therefore, what it is, that we may not be left to conjecture.' This appears to me a very fair question; and I will try to explain to you what it is which has made me so talked about, and so calumniated. Listen, then: and perhaps some of you may think I am in jest; be well persuaded, however, that I am telling you the whole truth. I, O Athenians, have acquired this reputation, from no other cause than a certain wisdom. What kind of wisdom? That which, perhaps, is the true *human* wisdom; and the fact seems to be that I possess this wisdom: they whom I have just spoken of have, perhaps, a wisdom greater than that of man; but I certainly do not possess it, and whoever says so speaks falsely, and wishes to slander me. And do not clamour, O Athenians, even if I seem to speak boastfully; for what I am about to say does not come from myself, but from a source worthy of your attention. I shall produce the Delphic god as a witness to you respecting my wisdom, whether I have any, and of what sort. You knew Chaerephon, doubtless. He was my associate from youth, and was also an associate of the Athenian Many; he quitted his country with you, and returned with you.[1] And you know what kind of a man was Chaerephon, how energetic in whatsoever he engaged in. He once, going to Delphi, had the boldness to put this question to the oracle (do not clamour, O Athenians); he asked whether there existed any person wiser than I? And the oracle answered that there was no person wiser. And to this, since Chaerephon himself is dead, his brother will bear witness before you.

Observe now why I mention this; for I am now going to show you how the prejudice against me arose. Hearing the response of the oracle, I considered with myself. What can it mean? what is its hidden significance? for I am not conscious to myself of being wise in any thing, great or small; what, then, can the god mean by calling me the wisest of men? for his words cannot be falsehoods. And for a long time I was puzzled, but at last, with much difficulty, I hit upon a way of examining the matter. I went to one of those who are esteemed wise, thinking that here, if anywhere, I should prove the oracle to be

1. i.e. he left when the oligarchic revolution of the Thirty Tyrants took place in 404 B.C., and returned when they were deposed in 403.

wrong, and be able to say to it, 'Here is a man wiser than I.' After examining this man (I need not mention his name, but he was one of the politicians) and conversing with him, it was my opinion that this man *seemed* to many others, and especially to himself, to be wise, but *was* not so. Thereupon I tried to convince him that he thought himself wise, and was not. By this means, I offended him, and many of the bystanders. When I went away, I said to myself, 'I am wiser than this man: for neither of us, it would seem, knows any thing valuable; but he, not knowing, fancies he does know: I, as I really do not know, so I do not think I know. I seem, therefore, to be, in one small matter, wiser than he, viz., in not thinking that I know what in truth I know not.' After this I went to another, who was esteemed still wiser than he, and came to the same result; and by this I affronted him too, and many others. I went on in the same manner, perceiving, with sorrow and fear, that I was making enemies; but it seemed necessary to postpone all other considerations to the service of the god; and, therefore, to seek for the meaning of the oracle, by going to all who appeared to know any thing. And, O Athenians (for I must speak the truth), the impression made on me was this: The persons of most reputation seemed to me to be nearly the most deficient of all; other persons, of much smaller account, seemed much more rational people.

I must relate to you my wanderings, and the labours I underwent, that the truth of the oracle might be fairly tested. When I had done with the politicians, I went to the poets, tragic, dithyrambic, and others, thinking that I should surely find myself less knowing than they. Taking up those of their poems which appeared to me the most laboured, I asked them (that I might at the same time learn something from them) what these poems meant? I am ashamed, O Athenians, to say the truth, but I must say it; there was scarcely a person present who could not have spoken better than they, concerning their own poems. I soon found that what the poets do, they accomplish, not by wisdom, but by a kind of natural turn, and an enthusiasm like that of prophets and those who utter oracles; for these, too, speak many fine things, but do not know one particle of what they speak. The poets seemed to me to be in a similar case. And I perceived, at the same time, that, on account of their poetry, they fancied themselves the wisest of mankind in other things, in which they were not so. I left them, therefore, thinking myself to have the same superiority over them which I had over the politicians. Lastly, I resorted to the artificers; for I was conscious that I myself knew, in a manner, nothing at all, but I was aware that I should find them knowing many valuable things. And in this was I not mistaken; they knew things which I knew not, and were so far wiser than I. But they appeared to me to fall into the same error as the poets; each, because he was skilled in his own art, insisted upon being the wisest man in other and the greatest things; and this mistake of theirs overshadowed what they possessed of wisdom. So that when I asked myself, by way of verifying the oracle, whether I would be as I now am, equally without their wisdom and their ignorance, or take the one with the other, I answered that it was better for me to be as I am.

From this search, O Athenians, the consequences to me have been, on the one hand, many enmities, and of the most formidable kind, which have brought upon me many false imputations; but, on the other hand, the name and general repute of a wise man.

JOHN STUART MILL (1832-4)

ALCIBIADES (c. 450-404 B.C.) ON SOCRATES[1]

I propose to praise Socrates, gentlemen, by using similes. He will perhaps think that I mean to make fun of him, but my object in employing them is truth, not ridicule. I declare that he bears a strong resemblance to those figures of Silenus[2] in statuaries' shops, represented holding pipes or flutes; they are hollow inside, and when they are taken apart you see that they contain little figures of gods. I declare also that he is like Marsyas the satyr.[3] You can't deny yourself, Socrates, that you have a striking physical likeness to both of these,

1. For Alcibiades, see also pp. 207 and 412 (Xenophon and Plutarch).
2. Silenus, represented as a bald and dissipated old man, was the companion of Dionysus. He was also regarded as an inspired prophet.
3. Marsyas, a satyr or silenus, was sometimes credited with the invention of the flute. He challenged Apollo to a trial of skill in flute-playing and after being defeated was flayed alive.

and you shall hear in a moment how you resemble them in other respects. For one thing you're a bully, aren't you? I can bring evidence of this if you don't admit it. But you don't play the flute, you will say. No, indeed; the performance you give is far more remarkable. Marsyas needed an instrument in order to charm men by the power which proceeded out of his mouth, a power which is still exercised by those who perform his melodies (I reckon the tunes ascribed to Olympus to belong to Marsyas, who taught him); his productions alone, whether executed by a skilled male performer or by a wretched flute-girl, are capable, by reason of their divine origin, of throwing men into a trance and thus distinguishing those who yearn to enter by initiation into union with the gods. But you, Socrates, are so far superior to Marsyas that you produce the same effect by mere words without any instrument. At any rate, whereas we most of us pay little or no attention to the words of any other speaker, however accomplished, a speech by you or even a very indifferent report of what you have said stirs us to the depths and casts a spell over us, men and women and young lads alike. I myself, gentlemen, were it not that you would think me absolutely drunk, would have stated on oath the effect which his words have had on me, an effect which persists to the present time. Whenever I listen to him my heart beats faster than if I were in a religious frenzy, and tears run down my face, and I observe that numbers of other people have the same experience. Nothing of this kind ever used to happen to me when I listened to Pericles and other good speakers; I recognized that they spoke well, but my soul was not thrown into confusion and dismay by the thought that my life was no better than a slave's. That is the condition to which I have often been reduced by our modern Marsyas, with the result that it seems impossible to go on living in my present state. You can't say that this isn't true, Socrates. And even at this moment, I know quite well that, if I were prepared to give ear to him, I should not be able to hold out, but the same thing would happen again. He compels me to realize that I am still a mass of imperfections and yet persistently neglect my own true interests by engaging in public life. So against my real inclination I stop up my ears and take refuge in flight, as Odysseus did from the Sirens;[1]

1. The Sirens lured men to destruction by their singing, but Odysseus

otherwise I should sit here beside him till I was an old man. He is the only person in whose presence I experience a sensation of which I might be thought incapable, a sensation of shame; he, and he alone, positively makes me ashamed of myself. The reason is that I am conscious that there is no arguing against the conclusion that one should do as he bids, and yet that, whenever I am away from him, I succumb to the temptations of popularity. So I behave like a runaway slave and take to my heels, and when I see him the conclusions which he has forced upon me make me ashamed. Many a time I should be glad for him to vanish from the face of the earth, but I know that, if that were to happen, my sorrow would far outweigh my relief. In fact, I simply do not know what to do about him.

This is the effect which the 'piping' of this satyr has had on me and on many other people.

WALTER HAMILTON (1951)

THE DENUDATION OF ATTICA

Contemporary Attica may accurately be described as a mere relic of the original country, as I shall proceed to explain. In configuration, Attica consists entirely of a long peninsula protruding from the mass of the continent into the sea, and the surrounding marine basin is known to shelve steeply round the whole coastline. In consequence of the successive violent deluges which have occurred within the past 9,000 years, there has been a constant movement of soil away from the high altitudes; and, owing to the shelving relief of the coast, this soil instead of laying down alluvium, as it does elsewhere, to any appreciable extent, has been perpetually deposited in the deep sea round the periphery of the country or, in other words, lost; so that Attica has undergone the process observable in small islands, and what remains of her substance is like the skeleton of a body emaciated by disease, as compared with her original relief. All the rich, soft soil has melted away, leaving a country of skin and bones. At the period,

stopped his sailors' ears with wax and had himself bound to the mast so as to escape this fate.

however, with which we are dealing, when Attica was still intact, what are now her mountains were lofty, soil-clad hills; her so-called shingle-plains of the present day were full of rich soil; and her mountains were heavily forested – a fact of which there are still visible traces. There are mountains in Attica which can now keep nothing but bees, but which were clothed, not so very long ago, with fine trees producing timber suitable for roofing the largest buildings; and roofs hewn from this timber are still in existence. There were also many lofty cultivated trees, while the country produced boundless pasture for cattle. The annual supply of rainfall was not lost, as it is at present, through being allowed to flow over the denuded surface into the sea, but was received by the country, in all its abundance, into her bosom, where she stored it in her impervious potter's earth, and so was able to discharge the drainage of the heights into the hollows in the form of springs and rivers with an abundant volume and a wide territorial distribution. The shrines that survive to the present day on the sites of extinct water supplies are evidence for the correctness of my present hypothesis.

ARNOLD TOYNBEE (1952)

SOCRATES ON THE PURSUIT OF TRUTH

'Here are some more questions, Simmias. Do we recognize such a thing as absolute uprightness?'

'Indeed we do.'

'And absolute beauty and goodness too?'

'Of course.'

'Have you ever seen any of these things with your eyes?'

'Certainly not,' said he.

'Well, have you ever apprehended them with any other bodily sense? By "them" I mean not only absolute tallness or health or strength, but the real nature of any given thing – what it actually is. Is it through the body that we get the truest perception of them? Isn't it true that in any inquiry you are likely to attain more nearly to knowledge of your object in proportion to the care and accuracy with which you have prepared yourself to understand that object in itself?'

'Certainly.'

'Don't you think that the person who is likely to succeed in this attempt most perfectly is the one who approaches each object, as far as possible, with the unaided intellect, without taking account of any sense of sight in his thinking, or dragging any other sense into his reckoning – the man who pursues the truth by applying his pure and unadulterated thought to the pure and unadulterated object, cutting himself off as much as possible from his eyes and ears and virtually all the rest of his body, as an impediment which by its presence prevents the soul from attaining to truth and clear thinking? Is not this the person, Simmias, who will reach the goal of reality, if anybody can?'

'What you say is absolutely true, Socrates,' said Simmias.

'All these considerations,' said Socrates, 'must surely prompt serious philosophers to review the position in some such way as this. "It looks as though this were a bypath leading to the right track. So long as we keep to the body and our soul is contaminated with this imperfection, there is no chance of our ever attaining satisfactorily to our object, which we assert to be Truth. In the first place, the body provides us with innumerable distractions in the pursuit of our necessary sustenance; and any diseases which attack us hinder our quest for reality. Besides, the body fills us with loves and desires and fears and all sorts of fancies and a great deal of nonsense, with the result that we literally never get an opportunity to think at all about anything. Wars and revolutions and battles are due simply and solely to the body and its desires. All wars are undertaken for the acquisition of wealth; and the reason why we have to acquire wealth is the body, because we are slaves in its service. That is why, on all these accounts, we have so little time for philosophy. Worst of all, if we do obtain any leisure from the body's claims and turn to some line of inquiry, the body intrudes once more into our investigations, interrupting, disturbing, distracting, and preventing us from getting a glimpse of the truth. We are in fact convinced that if we are ever to have pure knowledge of anything, we must get rid of the body and contemplate things by themselves with the soul by itself. It seems, to judge from the argument, that the wisdom which we desire and upon which we profess to have set our hearts will be attainable only when we are dead, and not in our lifetime. If no pure knowledge is possible in the company of the body, then either it is totally impossible to acquire knowledge, or it is only possible after death, because it is only then that the soul will be separate and independent of the body. It seems that so long as we are alive, we shall continue closest to knowledge if we avoid as much as we can all contact and association with the body, except when they are absolutely necessary; and instead of allowing ourselves to become infected with its nature, purify ourselves from it until God himself gives us deliverance. In this way, by keeping ourselves uncontaminated by the follies of the body, we shall probably reach the company of others like ourselves and gain direct knowledge of all that is pure and uncontaminated – that is, presumably, of Truth."'

HUGH TREDENNICK (1954)

THE DEATH OF SOCRATES

At this Crito made a sign to his servant, who was standing near by. The servant went out and after spending a considerable time returned with the man who was to administer the poison; he was carrying it ready prepared in a cup. When Socrates saw him he said 'Well, my good fellow, you understand these things; what ought I to do?'

'Just drink it,' he said, 'and then walk about until you feel a weight in your legs, and then lie down. Then it will act of its own accord.'

As he spoke he handed the cup to Socrates, who received it quite cheerfully, Echecrates, without a tremor, without any change of colour or expression, and said, looking up under his brows with his usual steady gaze, 'What do you say about pouring a libation from this drink? Is it permitted, or not?'

'We only prepare what we regard as the normal dose, Socrates,' he replied.

'I see,' said Socrates. 'But I suppose I am allowed, or rather bound, to pray the gods that my removal from this world to the other may be prosperous. This is my prayer, then; and I hope that it may be granted.' With these words, quite calmly and with no sign of distaste, he drained the cup in one breath.

Up till this time most of us had been fairly successful in keeping back our tears; but when we saw that he was drinking, that he had actually drunk it, we could do so no longer; in spite of myself the tears came pouring out, so that I covered my face and wept broken-heartedly – not for him, but for my own calamity in losing such a friend. Crito had given up even before me, and had gone out when he could not restrain his tears. But Apollodorus, who had never stopped crying even before, now broke out into such a storm of passion-ate weeping that he made everyone in the room break down, except Socrates himself, who said:

'Really, my friends, what a way to behave! Why, that was my main reason for sending away the women, to prevent this sort of disturbance; because I am told that one should make one's end in a tranquil frame of mind. Calm yourselves and try to be brave.'

This made us feel ashamed, and we controlled our tears. Socrates walked about, and presently, saying that his legs were heavy, lay down on his back – that was what the man recommended. The man (he was the same one who had administered the poison) kept his hand upon Socrates, and after a little while examined his feet and legs; then pinched his foot hard and asked if he felt it. Socrates said no. Then he did the same to his legs; and moving gradually upwards in this way let us see that he was getting cold and numb. Presently he felt him again and said that when it reached the heart, Socrates would be gone.

The coldness was spreading about as far as his waist when Socrates uncovered his face – for he had covered it up – and said (they were his last words): 'Crito, we ought to offer a cock to Asclepius.[1] See to it, and don't forget.'

'No, it shall be done,' said Crito. 'Are you sure that there is nothing else?'

Socrates made no reply to this question, but after a little while he stirred; and when the man uncovered him, his eyes were fixed. When Crito saw this, he closed the mouth and eyes.

---

1. The god of healing. The cock is probably a thank-offering (or a prelimin-ary offering before spending the night in his precinct). Death, indicates Socrates, is the cure for life.

Such, Echecrates, was the end of our comrade, who was, we may fairly say, of all those whom we knew in our time, the bravest and also the wisest and most upright man.

HUGH TREDENNICK (1954)

SOCRATES DEFENDS HIMSELF AT HIS TRIAL

I spend all my time going about trying to persuade you, young and old, to make your first and chief concern not for your bodies nor for your possessions, but for the highest welfare of your souls, proclaiming as I go 'Wealth does not bring goodness, but goodness brings wealth and every other blessing, both to the individual and to the State.' Now if I corrupt the young by this message, the message would seem to be harmful; but if anyone says that my message is different from this, he is talking nonsense. And so, gentlemen, I would say, 'You can please yourselves whether you listen to Anytus[1] or not, and whether you acquit me or not; you know that I am not going to alter my conduct, not even if I have to die a hundred deaths.'

Order, please, gentlemen! Remember my request to give me a hearing without interruption; besides, I believe that it will be to your advantage to listen. I am going to tell you something else, which may provoke a storm of protest; but please restrain yourselves. I assure you that if I am what I claim to be, and you put me to death, you will harm yourselves more than me. Neither Meletus nor Anytus can do me any harm at all; they would not have the power, because I do not believe that the law of God permits a better man to be harmed by a worse. No doubt my accuser might put me to death or have me banished or deprived of civic rights; but even if he thinks, as he probably does (and others too, I dare say), that these are great calamities, I do not think so; I believe that it is far worse to do what he is doing now, trying to put an innocent man to death. For this reason, gentlemen, so far from pleading on my own behalf, as might be supposed, I am really pleading on yours, to save you from misusing the gift of God by condemning me. If you put me to death, you will

1. Anytus and Meletus were Socrates' prosecutors. cf. p. 237.

not easily find anyone to take my place. It is literally true (even if it sounds rather comical) that God has specially appointed me to this city, as though it were a large thoroughbred horse which because of its great size is inclined to be lazy and needs the stimulation of some stinging fly. It seems to me that God has attached me to this city to perform the office of such a fly; and all day long I never cease to settle here, there, and everywhere, rousing, persuading, reproving every one of you. You will not easily find another like me, gentlemen, and if you take my advice you will spare my life. I suspect, however, that before long you will awake from your drowsing, and in your annoyance you will take Anytus' advice and finish me off with a single slap; and then you will go on sleeping till the end of your days, unless God in his care for you sends someone to take my place.

HUGH TREDENNICK (1954)

THE NEED FOR RULERS TO BE PHILOSOPHERS

'Then how,' he asked, 'can you possibly say that society's troubles will never cease until it is ruled by philosophers, if you agree that they're useless members of society?'

'To answer that question,' I said, 'I must give you an illustration.'

'A thing which, of course, you never normally do!'

'There you go,' I said, 'pulling my leg when you've landed me with such a difficult point to prove. But just you listen to my illustration, and you'll see what a jam I'm in. For there's really no single thing one can use to illustrate the plight of the better type of philosopher in contemporary society; one must draw on several sources for one's illustrations in defence of him, like a painter combining two or more animals in one.

'Suppose the following to be the state of affairs on board a ship or ships. The captain is larger and stronger than any of the crew, but a bit deaf and short-sighted, and doesn't know much about navigation. The crew are all quarrelling with each other about how to navigate the ship, each thinking he ought to be at the helm; they know no navigation and cannot say that anyone ever taught it them, or that they spent any time studying it; indeed they say it can't be taught and are ready to murder anyone who says it can. They spend all their time milling round the captain and trying to get him to give them the wheel. If one faction is more successful than another, their rivals may kill them and throw them overboard, lay out the honest captain with drugs or drink, take control of the ship, help themselves to what's on board, and behave as if they were on a drunken pleasure-cruise. Finally, they reserve their admiration for the man who knows how to lend a hand in controlling the captain by force or fraud; they praise his seamanship and navigation and knowledge of the sea and condemn everyone else as useless. They have no idea that the true navigator must study the seasons of the year, the sky, the stars, the wind and other professional subjects, if he is to be really fit to control a ship; and they think that it's quite impossible to acquire professional skill in navigation (quite apart from whether they want it exercised) and that there's no such thing as an art of navigation. In these circumstances aren't the sailors on any such ship bound to regard the true navigator as a gossip and a star-gazer, of no use to them at all?'

'Yes, they are,' Adeimantus agreed.

'I think you probably understand, without any explanation, that my illustration is intended to show the present attitude of society towards the true philosopher.'

H. P. D. LEE (1955)

THE IDEAL CITY-STATE

'So let us first consider how our citizens, so equipped, will live. They will produce corn, wine, clothes, and shoes, and will build themselves houses. In the summer they will for the most part work unclothed and unshod, in the winter they will be clothed and shod suitably. For food they will prepare wheat-meal or barley-meal for baking or kneading. They will serve splendid cakes and loaves on rushes or fresh leaves, and will sit down to feast with their children on couches of myrtle and bryony; and afterwards they will drink wine and pray to the gods with garlands on their heads, and enjoy each other's company. And fear of poverty and war will make them keep the numbers of their families within their means.'

'I say,' interrupted Glaucon, 'that's pretty plain fare for a feast, isn't it?'

'You're quite right,' said I. 'I had forgotten; they will have a few luxuries. Salt, of course, and olive oil and cheese, and different kinds of vegetables from which to make various country dishes. And we must give them some dessert, figs and peas and beans, and myrtle-berries and acorns to roast at the fire as they sip their wine. So they will lead a peaceful and healthy life, and expect to die at a ripe old age, leaving their children to do the same in their turn.'

'Really, Socrates,' Glaucon commented, 'you might be catering for a community of pigs!'

'And how would you do it, Glaucon?' I asked.

'Give them the ordinary comforts,' he replied. 'Let them sit on chairs and eat off tables, and have normal civilized food.'

'All right,' I said, 'I understand. We are to study not only the origins of society, but also society when it enjoys the luxuries of civilization. Not a bad idea, perhaps, for in the process we may discover how justice and injustice are bred in a community. For though the society we have described seems to me to be the true norm, just as a man in health is the norm, there's nothing to prevent us, if you wish, studying one whose temperature luxury has raised. Such a society will not be satisfied with the standard of living we have described. It will want chairs and tables and other furniture, and a variety of delicacies, scents, cosmetics, sweets, and mistresses. And we must no longer confine ourselves to the bare necessities of our earlier description, houses, clothing, and shoes, but must add the fine arts of painting and embroidery, and introduce materials like gold and ivory. Do you agree?'

'Yes,' he said.

'We shall have to enlarge our state again. Our healthy state is no longer big enough, its size must be enlarged to make room for a multitude of occupations none of which is concerned with necessaries. There will be hunters and fishermen, and there will be artists, sculptors, painters, and musicians; there will be poets and playwrights with their following of reciters, actors, chorus-trainers, and producers; there will be manufacturers of domestic furniture of all sorts, and fashion-experts for the women. And we shall need a lot more servants – tutors, nurses, ladies' maids, barbers, confectioners, and cooks. And we shall need swineherds too: there were none in our former state, as we had no need of them, but now we need pigs, and cattle in quantities too, if we are to eat meat. Agreed?'

'There's no denying it.'

'We shall need doctors too, far more than we did before.'

'With our new luxuries we certainly shall.'

'And the territory which was formerly enough to support us will now be too small. If we are to have enough for pasture and plough, we shall have to cut a slice off our neighbours' territory. And if they too are no longer confining themselves to necessities and have embarked on the pursuit of unlimited material possessions, they will want a slice of ours too.'

'The consequence is inevitable!'

'And that will lead to war, Glaucon, will it not?'

'It will.'

H. P. D. LEE (1955)

ARTISTIC EDUCATION AND CENSORSHIP

'It is not only to the poets therefore that we must issue orders requiring them to represent good character in their poems or not to write at all; we must issue similar orders to all artists and prevent them portraying bad character, ill-discipline, meanness, or ugliness in painting, sculpture, architecture, or any work of art, and if they are unable to comply they must be forbidden to practise their art. We shall thus prevent our guardians being brought up among representations of what is evil, and so day by day and little by little, by feeding as it were in an unhealthy pasture, insensibly doing themselves grave psychological damage. Our artists and craftsmen must be capable of perceiving the real nature of what is beautiful, and then our young men, living as it were in a good climate, will benefit because all the works of art they see and hear influence them for good, like the breezes from some healthy country, insensibly moulding them into sympathy and conformity with what is rational and right.'

'That would indeed be the best way to bring them up.'

'And that, my dear Glaucon,' I said, 'is why this stage of education is crucial. For rhythm and harmony penetrate deeply into the mind and have a most powerful effect on it, and if education is good, bring balance and fairness, if it is bad, the reverse. And moreover the proper training we propose to give will make a man quick to perceive the shortcomings of works of art or nature, whose ugliness he will rightly dislike; anything beautiful he will welcome, and will accept and assimilate it for his own good, anything ugly he will rightly condemn and dislike, even when he is still young and cannot understand the reason for so doing, while when reason comes he will recognize and welcome her as a familiar friend because of his education.'

H. P. D. LEE (1955)

THE PSYCHOLOGY OF EDUCATION

'But anyone with any sense,' I said, 'will remember that the eyes may be unsighted in two ways, by a transition either from light to darkness or from darkness to light, and that the same distinction applies to the mind. So when he sees a mind confused and unable to see clearly he will not laugh without thinking, but will ask himself whether it has come from a clearer world and is confused by the unaccustomed darkness, or whether it is dazzled by the stronger light of the clearer world to which it has escaped from its previous ignorance. The first state is a reason for congratulation, the second for sympathy, though if one wants to laugh at it one can do so with less absurdity than at the mind that has descended from the daylight of the upper world.'

'You put it very reasonably.'

'If this is true,' I continued, 'we must reject the conception of education professed by those who say that they can put into the mind knowledge that was not there before – rather as if they could put sight into blind eyes.'

'It is a claim that is certainly made,' he said.

'But our argument indicates that this is a capacity which is innate in each man's mind, and that the faculty by which he learns is like an eye which cannot be turned from darkness to light unless the whole body is turned; in the same way the mind as a whole must be turned away from the world of change until its eye can bear to look straight at reality, and at the brightest of all realities which is what we call the Good. Isn't that so?'

'Yes.'

'Then this business of turning the mind round might be made a subject of professional skill, which would effect the conversion as easily and effectively as possible. It would not be concerned to implant sight, but to ensure that some one who had it already was turned in the right direction and looking the right way.'

H. P. D. LEE (1955)

THE DELINQUENT SON

'What a lucky thing it is,' I said, 'to have a tyrant for a son!'

'A real bit of luck,' he agreed.

'And I suppose that when he comes to the end of his father's and mother's resources, having by now a pretty considerable swarm of pleasures collected in himself, he'll start by burgling a house or holding someone up at night, and go on to clean out a temple. Meanwhile the old, accepted beliefs about right and wrong, on which he was brought up, will be overcome by others, once held in restraint but now freed to become the bodyguard of his master-passion. When he was still democratically minded and under the influence of the laws and his father, they only appeared in his dreams; but under the tyranny of the master-passion he becomes in reality what he was once only occasionally in his dreams, and there's nothing, no taboo, no murder, however terrible, from which he will shrink. His passion tyrannizes over him, a despot without restraint or law, and drives him (as a tyrant drives a state) into any venture that will profit itself and its gang, a gang collected partly from the evil company he keeps and partly from the impulses which these evil practices have freed within himself. Do you think that's the sort of life he will lead?'

'Yes, I think so.'

'And if there are only a few characters of this kind in a state and the bulk of the people are law-abiding, they will emigrate and take service with a tyrant elsewhere, or else fight as mercenaries in any war there is going on. In times of complete peace, they stay at home and commit a lot of minor crimes.'

'Such as?'

'They become thieves, burglars, pick-pockets, footpads, temple robbers, and kidnappers; or, if they have a ready tongue, they turn informers and false witnesses or take bribes.'

'I suppose you call all these minor crimes so long as the criminals are few.'

'Minor is a relative term,' I replied, 'and so far as the welfare or wickedness of the community goes, crimes like these don't come within miles of tyranny. But when the criminals and their followers increase in numbers and become aware of their strength, the folly of the people helps them to produce a tyrant, and they pick the man in whose heart passion is most tyrannical.'

'Yes, that is what best fits a man to be a tyrant.'

'And if the people submit to him, well and good. If not, he'll punish his country, if he can, just as he punished his parents, and the land which has borne and bred him, his motherland as the Cretans call it, will have to slave to maintain his upstart gang of followers. Which was the object of all his ambitions, was it not?'

'Yes, it was.'

'Men of his kind behave the same sort of way in private life, before they have gained power. Their companions are subservient parasites, and they are themselves always prepared to give way and put on the most extravagant act of friendship if it suits their purpose, though once that purpose is achieved their tune changes.'

'It does indeed.'

'So they pass their lives without a friend in the world; for tyrannical characters must always be either master or slave, and never taste true friendship or freedom.'

'True.'

'So we shall be right to call them untrustworthy and, if our definition of justice was correct, the perfect specimen of injustice.'

'Quite right.'

'We can sum it all up by saying that the worst type of man behaves as badly in real life as we said some men do in their dreams; which is just what happens when a natural tyrant gains absolute power, and the longer he holds it the greater his corruption.'

H. P. D. LEE (1955)

IS GOVERNMENT UNTEACHABLE?

I hold that the Athenians, like the rest of the Hellenes, are sensible people. Now when we meet in the Assembly, then if the State is faced with some building project, I observe that the architects are sent for and consulted about the proposed structures, and when it is a matter of shipbuilding, the naval designers, and so on with everything which the Assembly regards as a subject for learning and teaching. If anyone else tries to give advice, whom they do not consider an expert, however handsome or wealthy or nobly-born he may be, it makes no difference: the members reject him noisily and with contempt, until either he is shouted down and desists, or else he is dragged off or ejected by the police on the orders of the presiding magistrates. That is how they behave over subjects they consider technical. But when it is something to do with the government of the country that is to be debated, the man who gets up to advise them may be a builder or equally well a blacksmith or a shoemaker, merchant or shipowner, rich or poor, of good family or none. No one brings it up against any of these, as against those I have just mentioned, that here is a man who without any technical qualifications, unable to point to anybody as his teacher, is yet trying to give advice. The reason must be that they do not think this is a subject that can be taught.

W. K. C. GUTHRIE (1956)

THE UNFAIR METHODS OF SOCRATES

SOCRATES: Then go back to the beginning and answer my question. What do you and your friend say that virtue is?

MENO:[1] Socrates, even before I met you they told me that in plain truth you are a perplexed man yourself and reduce others to perplexity. At this moment I feel you are exercising magic and witchcraft upon me and positively laying me under your spell until I am just a mass of helplessness. If I may be flippant, I think that not only in outward appearance but in other respects as well you are exactly like the flat sting-ray that one meets in the sea. Whenever anyone comes into contact with it, it numbs him, and that is the sort of thing that you seem to be doing to me now. My mind and my lips are literally numb, and I have nothing to reply to you. Yet I have spoken about virtue hundreds of times, held forth often on the subject in front of large audiences, and very well too, or so I thought. Now I can't even say what it is. In my opinion you are well advised not to leave Athens and live abroad. If you behaved like this as a foreigner in another country, you would most likely be arrested as a wizard.

SOCRATES: You're a real rascal, Meno. You nearly took me in.

MENO: Just what do you mean?

SOCRATES: I see why you used a simile about me.

MENO: Why, do you think?

SOCRATES: To be compared to something in return. All good-looking people, I know perfectly well, enjoy a game of comparisons. They get the best of it, for naturally handsome folk provoke handsome similes. But I'm not going to oblige you. As for myself, if the sting-ray paralyses others only through being paralysed itself, then the comparison is just, but not otherwise. It isn't that, knowing the answers myself, I perplex other people. The truth is rather that I infect them also with the perplexity I feel myself. So with virtue now. I don't know what it is. You may have known before you came into contact with me, but now you look as if you don't. Nevertheless I am

1. Meno was a wealthy young Thessalian who joined the Greek expedition to the east (Xenophon's *Anabasis*) in 403 B.C.

ready to carry out, together with you, a joint investigation and inquiry into what it is.

W. K. C. GUTHRIE (1956)

THE MOTIVE FOR THE CREATION

TIMAEUS: Let us therefore state the reason why the framer of this universe of change framed it at all. He was good, and what is good has no particle of envy in it; being therefore without envy he wished all things to be as like himself as possible. This is as valid a principle for the origin of the world of change as we shall discover from the wisdom of men, and we should accept it. God therefore, wishing that all things should be good, and so far as possible nothing be imperfect, and finding the visible universe in a state not of rest but of inharmonious and disorderly motion, reduced it to order from disorder, as he judged that order was in every way better. It is impossible for the best to produce anything but the highest. When he considered, therefore, that in all the realm of visible nature, taking each thing as a whole, nothing without intelligence is to be found that is superior to anything with it, and that intelligence is impossible without soul, in fashioning the universe he implanted reason in soul and soul in body, and so ensured that his work should be by nature highest and best. And so that most likely account must say that this world came to be in very truth, through god's providence, a living being with soul and intelligence.

On this basis we must proceed to the next question: What was the living being in the likeness of which the creator constructed it? We cannot suppose that it was any creature that is part of a larger whole, for nothing can be good that is modelled on something incomplete. So let us assume that it resembles as nearly as possible that of which all other beings individually and generically are parts, and which comprises in itself all intelligible beings, just as this world contains ourselves and all visible creatures. For god's purpose was to use as his model the highest and most completely perfect of intelligible things, and so he created a single visible living being, containing within itself all living beings of the same natural order. Are we then right to speak of one universe, or would it be more correct to speak of a plurality or infinity? ONE is right, if it was manufactured according to its pattern; for that which comprises all intelligible beings cannot have a double. There would have to be another being comprising them both, of which both were parts, and it would be correct to call our world a copy not of them but of the being which comprised them. In order therefore that our universe should resemble the perfect living creature in being unique, the maker did not make two universes or an infinite number, but our universe was and is and will continue to be his only creation.

H. D. P. LEE (1956)

THE MYTH OF ATLANTIS[1]

CRITIAS:[2] Listen then, Socrates. The story is a strange one, but Solon,[3] the wisest of the seven wise men, once vouched for its truth. He was a relation and close friend of Dropides, my great-grandfather, as he often says himself in his poems, and told the story to my grandfather Critias, who in turn repeated it to us when he was an old man. It relates the many notable achievements of our city long ago, which have been lost sight of because of the lapse of time and destruction of human life. Of these the greatest is one that we could well recall now to repay our debt to you and to offer the goddess on her festival day a just and truthful hymn of praise.

SOCRATES: Good. And what is this unrecorded yet authentic achievement of our city that Critias heard from Solon and recounted to you?

CRITIAS: I will tell you; though the story was old when I heard it and the man who told it me was no longer young. For Critias was at

1. Atlantis was a large mythical island off the Straits of Gibraltar. Plato may have worked up the myth from reports of Atlantic islands or memories of the great volcanic eruption at Thera (Santorin) in the second millennium B.C. (though that lay in the other direction).

2. Critias (c. 460–403 B.C.) was a poet, associate of the sophists, and one of the Thirty Tyrants who took over Athens in 404–403.

3. The Athenian statesman, archon in 494–493 B.C. For a specimen of his poetry, see p. 91.

the time, so he said, nearly ninety, and I was about ten. It was Children's Day in the festival of Apatouria,[1] and there were the customary ceremonies for the boys, including prizes given by the fathers for reciting. There were recitations of many poems by different authors, but many of the competitors chose Solon's poems, which were in those days quite new. And one of the clansmen, either because he thought so or out of politeness to Critias, said that he thought that Solon was not only the wisest of men but also the most outspoken of poets. And the old man – I remember it well – was extremely pleased, and said with a smile, 'I wish, Amynander, that he hadn't treated poetry as a spare-time occupation but had taken it seriously like others; if he had finished the story he brought back from Egypt, and hadn't been compelled to neglect it because of the class struggles and other evils he found here on his return, I don't think any poet, even Homer or Hesiod, would have been more famous.' 'And what was the story, Critias?' asked Amynander. 'It was about what may fairly be called the greatest and most noteworthy of all this city's achievements, but because of the lapse of time and the death of those who took part in it the story has not lasted till our day.' 'Tell us from the beginning,' came the reply; 'how and from whom did Solon hear the tale which he told you as true?'

'There is in Egypt,' said Critias, 'at the head of the delta, where the Nile divides, a district called the Saïtic. The chief city of the district, from which King Amasis[2] came, is called Saïs. The chief goddess of the inhabitants is called in Egyptian Neïth,[3] in Greek (according to them) Athena; and they are very friendly to the Athenians and claim some relationship to them. Solon came there on his travels and was highly honoured by them, and in the course of making inquiries from those priests who were most knowledgeable on the subject found that both he and all his countrymen were almost entirely ignorant about antiquity. And wishing to lead them on to talk about early times, he embarked on an account of the earliest events known here, telling them about Phoroneus,[4] said to be the first man, and

1. A festival celebrated by the Ionians in October or November.
2. Amasis II, pharaoh of Egypt, c. 569–526 B.C.
3. Neïth was a goddess of weapons whose worship originated in Saïs.
4. An ancient mythical figure and divinity of Argos.

Niobe,[1] and how Deucalion and Pyrrha[2] survived the flood and who were their descendants, and trying by reckoning up the generations to calculate how long ago the events in question had taken place. And a very old priest said to him, 'Oh Solon, Solon, you Greeks are all children, and there's no such thing as an old Greek.'

'What do you mean by that?' inquired Solon.

'You are all young in mind,' came the reply: 'you have no belief rooted in old tradition and no knowledge hoary with age. And the reason is this. There have been and will be many different calamities to destroy mankind, the greatest of them by fire and water, lesser ones by countless other means. Your own story of how Phaëthon, child of the sun, harnessed his father's chariot, but was unable to guide it along his father's course and so burnt up things on the earth and was himself destroyed by a thunderbolt, is a mythical version of the truth that there is at long intervals a variation in the course of the heavenly bodies and a consequent widespread destruction by fire of things on the earth. On such occasions those who live in the mountains or in high and dry places suffer more than those living by rivers or by the sea; as for us, the Nile, our own regular saviour, is freed[3] to preserve us in this emergency. When on the other hand the gods purge the earth with a deluge, the herdsmen and shepherds in the mountains escape, but those living in the cities in your part of the world are swept into the sea by the rivers; here water never falls on the land from above either then or at any other time, but rises up naturally from below. This is the reason why our traditions here are the oldest preserved; though it is true that in all places where excessive cold or heat does not prevent it human beings are always to be found in larger or smaller numbers. But in our temples we have preserved from earliest times a written record of any great or splendid achievement or notable event which has come to our ears whether it occurred in your part of the world or here or anywhere else; whereas with you and others, writing and the other necessities of

1. Niobe boasted that she was the equal of Apollo's mother Leto, who then killed all her children.

2. By the advice of Prometheus, Pyrrha's uncle, she and her husband Deucalion built an ark and survived.

3. There may be reference to Egyptian irrigation systems.

civilization have only just been developed when the periodic scourge of the deluge descends, and spares none but the unlettered and uncultured, so that you have to begin again like children, in complete ignorance of what happened in our part of the world or in yours in early times. So these genealogies of your own people which you were just recounting are little more than children's stories. You remember only one deluge, though there have been many, and you do not know that the finest and best race of men that ever existed live in your country; you and your fellow citizens are descended from the few survivors that remained, but you know nothing about it because so many succeeding generations left no record in writing. For before the greatest of all destructions by water, Solon, the city that is now Athens was pre-eminent in war and conspicuously the best governed in every way, its achievements and constitution being the finest of any in the world of which we have heard tell.'

Solon was astonished at what he heard and eagerly begged the priests to describe to him in detail the doings of these citizens of the past. 'I will gladly do so, Solon,' replied the priest, 'both for your sake and your city's, but chiefly in gratitude to the Goddess to whom it has fallen to bring up and educate both your country and ours – yours first, when she took over your seed from Earth and Hephaestus, ours a thousand years later. The age of our institutions is given in our sacred records as eight thousand years, and the citizens whose laws and whose finest achievement I will now briefly describe to you therefore lived nine thousand years ago; we will go through their history in detail later on at leisure, when we can consult the records.

'Consider their laws compared with ours; for you will find today among us many parallels to your institutions in those days. First, our priestly class is kept distinct from the others, as is also our artisan class; next, each class of craftsmen – shepherds, hunters, farmers – performs its function in isolation from others. And of course you will have noticed that our soldier-class is kept separate from all others, being forbidden by the law to undertake any duties other than military: moreover their armament consists of shield and spear, which we were the first people in Asia to adopt, under the instruction of the Goddess, as you were in your part of the world. And again you see what great attention our law devotes from the beginning to

learning, deriving from the divine principles of cosmology everything needed for human life down to divination and medicine for our
health, and acquiring all other related branches of knowledge. The
Goddess founded this whole order and system when she framed your
society. She chose the place in which you were born with an eye to its
temperate climate, which would produce men of high intelligence;
for being herself a lover of war and wisdom she picked a place for her
first foundation that would produce men most like herself in
character. So you lived there under the laws I have described, and
even better ones, and excelled all men in every kind of accomplishment, as one would expect of children and offspring of the gods. And
among all the wonderful achievements recorded here of your city,
one great act of courage is outstanding. Our records tell how your
city checked a great power which arrogantly advanced from its base
in the Atlantic ocean to attack the cities of Europe and Asia. For in
those days the Atlantic was navigable. There was an island opposite
the strait which you call (so you say) the pillars of Heracles,[1] an island
larger than Libya and Asia combined; from it travellers could in those
days reach the other islands, and from them the whole opposite
continent which surrounds what can truly be called the ocean. For the
sea within the strait we were talking about is like a lake with a narrow
entrance; the outer ocean is the real ocean and the land which
entirely surrounds it is properly termed continent. On this island of
Atlantis had arisen a powerful and remarkable dynasty of kings, who
ruled the whole island, and many other islands as well and parts of the
continent; in addition it controlled, within the strait, Libya up to the
borders of Egypt and Europe as far as Tyrrhenia.[2] This dynasty,
gathering its whole power together, attempted to enslave, at a single
stroke, your country and ours and all the territory within the strait.
It was then, Solon, that the power and courage and strength of your
city became clear for all men to see. Her bravery and military skill
were outstanding; she led an alliance of the Greeks, and then when
they deserted her and she was forced to fight alone, after running
into direst peril, she overcame the invaders and celebrated a victory;
she rescued those not yet enslaved from the slavery threatening them,

1. The Straits of Gibraltar.
2. Etruria.

and she generously freed all others living within the Pillars of Heracles. At a later time there were earthquakes and floods of extraordinary violence and in a single dreadful day and night all your fighting men were swallowed up by the earth, and the island of Atlantis was similarly swallowed up by the sea and vanished; this is why the sea in that area is to this day impassable to navigation, which is hindered by mud just below the surface, the remains of the sunken island.'

H. D. P. LEE (1956)

PERSIA AND ATHENS: HOW MUCH FREEDOM OUGHT THERE TO BE?

ATHENIAN: Then let's listen to the story. Under Cyrus,[1] the life of the Persians was a judicious blend of liberty and subjection, and after gaining their own freedom they became the masters of a great number of other people. As rulers, they granted a degree of liberty to their subjects and put them on the same footing as themselves, with the result that soldiers felt more affection for their commanders and displayed greater zeal in the face of danger. The king felt no jealousy if any of his subjects was intelligent and had some advice to offer; on the contrary, he allowed free speech and valued those who could contribute to the formulation of policy; a sensible man could use his influence to help the common cause. Thanks to freedom, friendship, and the practice of pooling their ideas, during that period the Persians made progress all along the line.

CLEINIAS: It does rather look as if that was the situation in the period you describe.

ATHENIAN: So how are we to explain the disaster under Cambyses, and the virtually complete recovery under Darius? To help our reconstruction of events, shall we have a shot at some inspired guessing?

CLEINIAS: Yes, because this topic we've embarked on will certainly help our inquiry.

1. The successive kings of Persia mentioned here were Cyrus I (c. 559–529 B.C.), Cambyses (529–522), Darius I (522–486) and Xerxes I (486–465).

ATHENIAN: My guess, then, about Cyrus, is that although he was doubtless a good commander and a loyal patriot, he never considered, even superficially, the problem of correct education; and as for running a household, I'd say he never paid any attention to it at all.

CLEINIAS: And what interpretation are we to put on a remark like that?

ATHENIAN: I mean that he probably spent his entire life after infancy on campaign, and handed over his children to the women to bring up. These women reared them from their earliest years as though they were already Heaven's special favourites and darlings, endowed with all the blessings that implies. They wouldn't allow anyone to thwart 'their Beatitudes' in anything, and they forced everybody to rhapsodize about what the children said or did. You can imagine the sort of person they produced.

CLEINIAS: And a fine old education it must have been, to judge from your account.

ATHENIAN: It was a womanish education, conducted by the royal harem. The teachers of the children had recently come into considerable wealth, but they were left all on their own, without men, because the army was preoccupied by wars and constant dangers.

CLEINIAS: That makes sense.

ATHENIAN: The children's father, for his part, went on accumulating herds and flocks for their benefit – and many a herd of human beings too, quite apart from every other sort of animal; but he didn't know that his intended heirs were not being instructed in the traditional Persian discipline. This discipline (the Persians being shepherds, and sons of a stony soil) was a tough one, capable of producing hardy shepherds who could camp out and keep awake on watch and turn soldier if necessary. He just didn't notice that women and eunuchs had given his sons the education of a Mede,[1] and that it had been debased by their so-called 'blessed' status. That is why Cyrus' children turned out as children naturally do when their teachers have never corrected them. So, when they succeeded to their inheritance on the death of Cyrus, they were living in a riot of unrestrained debauchery. First, unwilling to tolerate an equal, one of them killed the other;

1. i.e. an education of extreme luxury.

next, he himself, driven out of his senses by liquor and lack of self-control, was deprived of his dominions by the Medes and 'the Eunuch' (as he was then called), to whom the idiot Cambyses was an object of contempt.[1]

CLEINIAS: So the story goes, and it seems probable enough.

ATHENIAN: And it goes on, I think, to say that the empire was regained for the Persians by Darius and 'the Seven'.

CLEINIAS: Certainly.

ATHENIAN: Now let's carry on with this story of ours and see what happened. Darius was no royal prince, and his upbringing had not encouraged him to self-indulgence. When he came and seized the empire with the aid of the other six, he split it up into seven divisions, of which some faint outlines still survive today. He thought the best policy was to govern it by new laws of his own which introduced a certain degree of equality for all; and he also included in his code regulations about the tribute promised to the people by Cyrus. His generosity in money and gifts rallied all the Persians to his side, and stimulated a feeling of community and friendship among them; consequently his armies regarded him with such affection that they added to the territory Cyrus had bequeathed at least as much again. But Darius was succeeded by Xerxes, whose education had reverted to the royal pampering of old. ('Darius' – as perhaps we'd be entitled to say to him – 'you haven't learnt from Cyrus' mistake, so you've brought up Xerxes in the same habits as Cyrus brought up Cambyses.') So Xerxes, being a product of the same type of education, naturally had a career that closely reproduced the pattern of Cambyses' misfortunes. Ever since then, hardly any king of the Persians has been genuinely 'great', except in style and title. I maintain that the reason for this is not just bad luck, but the shocking life that the children of dictators and fantastically rich parents almost always lead: no man, you see, however old or however young, will ever excel in virtue if he has had this sort of upbringing. We repeat that this is the point the legislator must look out for, and so must we here and now. And in all fairness, my Spartan friends, one must give your state credit for at least this much: rich man, poor man, commoner and king are held in

1. Gomates impersonated Cambyses' dead brother in order to seize the kingdom.

honour to the same degree and are educated in the same way, without privilege, except as determined by the supernatural instructions you received from some god when your state was founded. A man's exceptional wealth is no more reason for a state to confer specially exalted office on him than his ability to run, his good looks, or his physical strength, in the absence of some virtue – or even if he *has* some virtue, if it excludes self-control.

MEGILLUS: What do you mean by that, sir?

ATHENIAN: Courage, I take it, is one part of virtue.

MEGILLUS: Of course.

ATHENIAN: So now that you've heard the story, use your own judgement: would you be glad to have as a resident in your house or as a neighbour a man who in spite of considerable courage was immoderate and licentious?

MEGILLUS: Heaven forbid!

ATHENIAN: Well then, what about a skilled workman, knowledgeable in his own field, but unjust?

MEGILLUS: No, I'd never welcome him.

ATHENIAN: But surely, in the absence of self-control, justice will never spring up.

MEGILLUS: Of course not.

ATHENIAN: Nor indeed will the 'wise' man we put forward just now, who keeps his feelings of pleasure and pain in tune with right reason and obedient to it.

MEGILLUS: No, he certainly won't.

ATHENIAN: Now here's another point for us to consider, which will help us to decide whether civic distinctions are, on a given occasion, conferred correctly or incorrectly.

MEGILLUS: And what is that?

ATHENIAN: If we found self-control existing in the soul in isolation from all other virtue, should we be justified in admiring it? Or not?

MEGILLUS: I really couldn't say.

ATHENIAN: A very proper reply. If you had opted for either alternative it would have struck an odd note, I think.

MEGILLUS: So my reply was all right, then.

ATHENIAN: Yes. But if you have something which in itself

deserves to be admired or execrated, a mere additional element isn't worth talking about: much better pass it over and say nothing.

MEGILLUS: Self-control is the element you mean, I suppose.

ATHENIAN: It is. And in general, whatever benefits us most, when this element is added, deserves the highest honour, the second most beneficial thing deserves the second highest honour, and so on: as we go down the list, everything will get in due order the honour it deserves.

MEGILLUS: True.

ATHENIAN: Well then, shan't we insist again that the distribution of these honours is the business of the legislator?

MEGILLUS: Of course.

ATHENIAN: Would you prefer us to leave the entire distribution to his discretion and let him deal with the details of each individual case? But as we too have something of a taste for legislation, perhaps you'd like us to try our hands at a three-fold division and distinguish the most important class, then the second and the third.

MEGILLUS: Certainly.

ATHENIAN: We maintain that if a state is going to survive to enjoy all the happiness that mankind can achieve, it is vitally necessary for it to distribute honours and marks of disgrace on a proper basis. And the proper basis is to put spiritual goods at the top of the list and hold them – provided the soul exercises self-control – in the highest esteem; bodily goods and advantages should come second, and third those said to be provided by property and wealth. If a legislator or a state ever ignores these guide-lines by valuing riches above all or by promoting one of the other inferior goods to a more exalted position, it will be an act of political and religious folly. Shall we take this line, or not?

MEGILLUS: Yes, emphatically and unambiguously.

ATHENIAN: It was our scrutiny of the political system of the Persians that made us go into this business at such length. Our verdict was that their corruption increased year by year; and the reason we assign for this is that they were too strict in depriving the people of liberty and too energetic in introducing authoritarian government, so that they destroyed all friendship and community of spirit in the state. And with that gone, the policy of rulers is framed not in the interests of their subjects the people, but to support their own authority: let them only think that a situation offers them the prospect of some profit, even a small one, and they wreck cities and ruin friendly nations by fire and sword; they hate, and are hated in return, with savage and pitiless loathing. When they come to need the common people to fight on their behalf, they discover the army has no loyalty, no eagerness to face danger and fight. They have millions and millions of soldiers – all useless for fighting a war, so that just as if manpower were in short supply, they have to hire it, imagining that mercenaries and foreigners will ensure their safety. Not only this, they inevitably become so stupid that they proclaim by their very actions that as compared with gold and silver everything society regards as good and valuable is in their eyes so much trash.

MEGILLUS: Exactly.

ATHENIAN: So let's have done with the Persians. Our conclusion is that the empire is badly run at the moment because the people are kept in undue subjection and the rulers excessively authoritarian.

MEGILLUS: Precisely.

ATHENIAN: Next we come to the political system of Attica. We have to demonstrate, on the same lines as before, that complete freedom from all authority is infinitely worse than submitting to a moderate degree of control.

At the time of the Persian attack on the Greeks – on virtually everyone living in Europe, is perhaps a better way of putting it – we Athenians had a constitution, inherited from the distant past, in which a number of public offices were held on the basis of four property-classes. Lady Modesty was the mistress of our hearts, a despot who made us live in willing subjection to the laws then in force. Moreover, the enormous size of the army that was coming at us by land and sea made us desperately afraid, and served to increase our obedience to the authorities and the law. For all these reasons we displayed a tremendous spirit of cooperation. You see, about ten years before the battle of Salamis, Datis had arrived at the head of a Persian army;[1] he had been sent by Darius against the Athenians and the Eretrians with explicit instructions to make slaves of them and bring

1. In 490 B.C.

them home, and he had been warned that failure would mean death.
With his vast numbers of soldiers, Datis made short work of the
Eretrians, whom he completely overpowered and captured. He then
sent to Athens a blood-curdling report that not a single Eretrian had
got away – propaganda which asked us to believe that Datis' soldiers,
hand in hand in a long line, had combed over every inch of Eretria.
Well, whatever the truth or otherwise of this tale, it terrified the
Greeks; the Athenians were particularly scared, and they sent off
envoys in all directions, but no one was prepared to help them except
the Spartans – who were, however, prevented by the Messenian war,[1]
which was going on at that time, or perhaps by some other distraction
(I'm not aware of any information being given on the point). However that may be, the Spartans arrived at Marathon one day too late
for the battle. After this, reports of vast preparations and endless
threats on the part of the king came thick and fast. The years went by,
and then we were told that Darius was dead, but that his son, young
and impetuous, had inherited the kingdom and was determined not to
give up the invasion. The Athenians reckoned that all these preparations were directed against themselves, because of what had
happened at Marathon; and when they heard of the canal that had
been dug through Athos, the bridging of the Hellespont and the huge
number of Xerxes' ships, they calculated that neither land nor sea
offered any prospects of safety. No one, they thought, would come
to help them. They remembered the previous attack and the success
of the Persians in Eretria: no one had assisted the Athenians then, no
one had faced the danger by fighting at their side. On land they
expected the same thing to happen this time; and as for the sea, they
realized that escape by this route was out of the question, in view of
the thousand or more ships coming to the attack. They could think of
only one hope, and a thin, desperate hope it was; but there was simply
no other. Their minds went back to the previous occasion, and they
reflected how the victory they won in battle had been gained in
equally desperate circumstances. Sustained by this hope, they began to
recognize that no one but they themselves and their gods could
provide a way out of their difficulties. All this inspired them with a
spirit of solidarity. One cause was the actual fear they felt at the time,

1. The Messenians were Sparta's subjects in the south-western Peloponnese.

but there was another kind too, encouraged by the traditional laws of the state. I mean the 'fear' they had learned to experience as a result of being subject to an ancient code of laws. In the course of our earlier discussion we have called this fear 'modesty' often enough, and we said that people who aspire to be good must be its slave. A coward, on the other hand, is free of this particular kind of fear and never experiences it. And if 'ordinary' fear had not overtaken the cowards on that occasion, they would never have combined to defend themselves or protected temples, tombs, fatherland, and friends and relatives as well, in the way they did. We would all have been split up and scattered over the face of the earth.

MEGILLUS: Yes, sir, you are quite right, and your remarks reflect credit both on your country and yourself.

ATHENIAN: No doubt, Megillus; and it is only right and proper to tell you of the history of that period, seeing that you've been blessed with your ancestors' character. Now then, you and Cleinias, consider: have these remarks of ours any relevance at all to legislation? After all, this is the object of the exercise – I'm not going through all this simply for the story. Look: in a way, we Athenians have had the same experience as the Persians. They, of course, reduced the people to a state of complete subjection, and we encouraged the masses to the opposite extreme of unfettered liberty, but the discussion we have had serves well enough as a pointer to the next step in the argument, and shows us the method to follow.

MEGILLUS: Splendid! But do try to be even more explicit about what you mean.

ATHENIAN: Very well. When the old laws applied, my friends, the people were not in control: on the contrary, they lived in a kind of 'voluntary slavery' to the laws.

MEGILLUS: Which laws have you in mind?

ATHENIAN: I'm thinking primarily of the regulations about the music of that period (music being the proper place to start a description of how life became progressively freer of controls). In those days Athenian music comprised various categories and forms. One type of song consisted of prayers to the gods, which were termed 'hymns'; and there was another quite different type, which you might well have called 'laments'. 'Paeans'[1] made up a third category, and there was also a fourth, called a 'dithyramb' (whose theme was, I think, the birth of Dionysus). There existed another kind of song too, which they thought of as a separate class, and the name they gave it was this very word that is so often on our lips: 'nomes'[2] ('for the lyre', as they always added). Once these categories and a number of others had been fixed, no one was allowed to pervert them by using one sort of tune in a composition belonging to another category. And what was the authority which had to know these standards and use its knowledge in reaching its verdicts, and crack down on the disobedient? Well, certainly no notice was taken of the catcalls and uncouth yelling of the audience, as it is nowadays, nor yet of the applause that indicates approval. People of taste and education made it a rule to listen to the performance with silent attention right through to the end; children and their attendants and the general public could always be disciplined and controlled by a stick. Such was the rigour with which the mass of the people was prepared to be controlled in the theatre, and to refrain from passing judgement by shouting. Later, as time went on, composers arose who started to set a fashion of breaking the rules and offending good taste. They did have a natural artistic talent, but they were ignorant of the correct and legitimate standards laid down by the Muse. Gripped by a frenzied and excessive lust for pleasure, they jumbled together laments and hymns, mixed paeans and dithyrambs, and even imitated pipe tunes on the lyre. The result was a total confusion of styles. Unintentionally, in their idiotic way, they misrepresented their art, claiming that in music there are no standards of right and wrong at all, but that the most 'correct' criterion is the pleasure of a man who enjoyed the performance, whether he is a good man or not. On these principles they based their compositions, and they accompanied them with propaganda to the same effect. Consequently they gave the ordinary man not only a taste for breaking the laws of music but the arrogance to set himself up as a capable judge. The audiences, once silent, began to use their tongues; they claimed to know what was good and bad in music, and instead of a

1. Hymns in praise of Apollo.
2. The Greek word is *nomoi*, which also means 'laws'.

'musical meritocracy', a sort of vicious 'theatrocracy' arose. But if this democracy had been limited to gentlemen and had applied only to music, no great harm would have been done; in the event, however, music proved to be the starting-point of everyone's conviction that he was an authority on everything, and of a general disregard for the law. Complete licence was not far behind. The conviction that they *knew* made them unafraid, and assurance engendered effrontery. You see, a reckless lack of respect for one's betters is effrontery of peculiar viciousness, which springs from a freedom from inhibitions that has gone much too far.

MEGILLUS: You're absolutely right.

ATHENIAN: This freedom will then take other forms. First people grow unwilling to submit to the authorities, then they refuse to obey the admonitions of their fathers and mothers and elders. As they hurtle along towards the end of this primrose path, they try to escape the authority of the laws; and the very end of the road comes when they cease to care about oaths and promises and religion in general. They reveal, reincarnated in themselves, the character of the ancient Titans[1] of the story, and thanks to getting into the same position as the Titans did, they live a wretched life of endless misery.

T. J. SAUNDERS (1970)

THE NEED FOR LAW TO RULE SUPREME

ATHENIAN: You realize that some people maintain that there are as many different kinds of laws as there are of political systems? (And of course we've just run through the many types of political systems there are popularly supposed to be.) Don't think the question at issue is a triviality: it's supremely important, because in effect we've got back to arguing about the criteria of justice and injustice. These people take the line that legislation should be directed not to waging war or attaining complete virtue, but to safeguarding the interests of the established political system, whatever that is, so that it is never over-

1. Children of Heaven and Earth, and long-standing enemies of the Olympian gods.

thrown and remains permanently in force. They say that the definition of justice that measures up to the facts is best formulated like this.

CLEINIAS: How?

ATHENIAN: It runs: 'Whatever serves the interest of the stronger'.

CLEINIAS: Be a little more explicit, will you?

ATHENIAN: The point is this: according to them, the element in control at any given moment lays down the law of the land. Right?

CLEINIAS: True enough.

ATHENIAN: 'So do you imagine,' they say, 'that when a democracy has won its way to power, or some other constitution has been established (such as dictatorship), it will ever pass any laws, unless under pressure, except those designed to further its own interests and ensure that it remains permanently in power? That'll be its main preoccupation, won't it?'

CLEINIAS: Naturally.

ATHENIAN: So the author of these rules will call them 'just' and claim that anyone who breaks them is acting 'unjustly', and punish him?

CLEINIAS: Quite likely.

ATHENIAN: So this is why such rules will always add up to 'justice'.

CLEINIAS: Certainly, on the present argument.

ATHENIAN: We are, you see, dealing with one of those 'claims to authority'.

CLEINIAS: What claims?

ATHENIAN: The ones we examined before, when we asked who should rule whom. It seemed that parents should rule children, the elder the younger, and the noble those of low birth; and there was a large number of other titles to authority, if you remember, some of which conflicted with others. The claim we're talking about now was certainly one of these: we said, I think, that Pindar turned it into a law of nature – which meant that he 'justified the use of force extreme', to quote his actual words.[1]

CLEINIAS: Yes, those are the points that were made.

ATHENIAN: Now look: to which side in the dispute should we

---

1. i.e. that the stronger should rule the weaker.

entrust our state? In some cities, you see, this is the sort of thing that has happened thousands of times.

CLEINIAS: What?

ATHENIAN: When offices are filled competitively, the winners take over the affairs of state so completely that they totally deny the losers and the losers' descendants any share of power. Each side passes its time in a narrow scrutiny of the other, apprehensive lest someone with memories of past injustices should gain some office and lead a revolution. Of course, our position is that this kind of arrangement is very far from being a genuine political system; we maintain that laws which are not established for the good of the whole state are bogus laws, and when they favour particular sections of the community, their authors are not citizens but party-men; and people who say those laws have a claim to be obeyed are wasting their breath. We've said all this because in your new state we aren't going to appoint a man to office because of his wealth or some other claim like that, say strength or stature or birth. We insist that the highest office in the service of gods must be allocated to the man who is best at obeying the established laws and wins *that* sort of victory in the state; the man who wins the second prize must be given second rank in that service, and so on, the remaining posts being allocated in order on the same system. Such people are usually referred to as 'rulers', and if I have called them 'servants of the laws' it's not because I want to mint a new expression but because I believe that the success or failure of a state hinges on this point more than on anything else. Where the law is subject to some other authority and has none of its own, the collapse of the state, in my view, is not far off; but if law is the master of the government and the government is its slave, then the situation is full of promise and men enjoy all the blessings that the gods shower on a state. That's the way I see it.

CLEINIAS: By heaven, sir, you're quite right. You've the sharp eye of an old man for these things.

ATHENIAN: Yes, when we're young, we're all pretty blind to them; old age is the best time to see them clearly.

CLEINIAS: Very true.

T. J. SAUNDERS (1970)

ARTISTIC TRADITIONALISM IN EGYPT

ATHENIAN: So, in a society where the laws relating to culture, education and recreation are, or will be in future, properly established, do we imagine that authors will be given a free hand? The choruses will be composed of the young children of law-abiding citizens: will the composer be free to teach them *anything* by way of rhythm, tune and words that amuses him when he composes, without bothering what effect he may have on them as regards virtue and vice?[1]

CLEINIAS: That's certainly not sensible; how could it be?

ATHENIAN: But it is precisely this that they are allowed to do in virtually all states – except in Egypt.

CLEINIAS: Egypt! Well then, you'd better tell us what legislation has been enacted there.

ATHENIAN: Merely to hear about it is startling enough. Long ago, apparently, they realized the truth of the principle we are putting forward only now, that the movements and tunes which the children of the state are to practise in their rehearsals must be good ones. They compiled a list of them according to style, and displayed it in their temples. Painters and everyone else who represent movements of the body of any kind were restricted to these forms; modification and innovation outside this traditional framework were prohibited, and are prohibited even today, both in this field and the arts in general. If you examine their art on the spot, you will find that ten thousand years ago (and I'm not speaking loosely: I mean literally ten thousand years ago), paintings and reliefs were produced that are no better and no worse than those of today, because the same artistic rules were applied in making them.

CLEINIAS: Fantastic!

ATHENIAN: No: simply a supreme achievement of legislators and statesmen. You might, even so, find some other things to criticize there, but in the matter of music this inescapable fact deserves our attention: it has in fact proved feasible to take the kind of music that shows a natural correctness and put it on a firm footing by legislation. But it is the task of a god, or a man of god-like stature; in fact, the

1. cf. above, p. 271.

Egyptians do say that the tunes that have been preserved for so long are compositions of Isis. Consequently, as I said, if one could get even a rough idea of what constitutes 'correctness' in matters musical, one ought to have no qualms about giving the whole subject systematic expression in the form of a law. It is true that the craving for pleasure and the desire to avoid tedium lead us to a constant search for novelty in music, and choral performances that have been thus consecrated may be stigmatized as out of date; but this does not have very much power to corrupt them. In Egypt, at any rate, it does not seem to have had a corrupting effect at all: quite the contrary.

CLEINIAS: So it would seem, to judge from your account.

T. J. SAUNDERS (1970)

EPITAPHS BY PLATO

THE STAR

Thou wert the morning star among the living,
    Ere thy fair light had fled; –
Now, having died, thou art as Hesperus, giving
    New splendour to the dead.

PERCY BYSSHE SHELLEY (died 1822)

SHIPWRECKED [1]
God by land and sea defend you,
    Sailors all, who pass my grave;
Safe from wreck his mercy send you, –
    I am one he did not save.

T. F. HIGHAM (1938)

1. Authorship doubtful.

ARISTOTLE

ATHENIAN philosopher, scientist and polymath, 384–322 B.C. Founder
of the Peripatetic school.

*

THE SUPREME GOOD IS HAPPINESS

In our actions we aim at more ends than one – that seems to be certain
– but, since we choose some (wealth, for example, or flutes and tools
or instruments generally) as means to something else, it is clear that
not all of them are ends in the full sense of the word, whereas the good,
that is the supreme good, is surely such an end. Assuming then that
there is some one thing which alone is an end beyond which there are
no further ends, we may call *that* the good of which we are in search.
If there be more than one such final end, the good will be that end
which has the highest degree of finality. An object pursued for its own
sake possesses a higher degree of finality than one pursued with an eye
to something else. A corollary to that is that a thing which is never
chosen as a means to some remoter object has a higher degree of
finality than things which are chosen both as ends in themselves and
as means to such ends. We may conclude, then, that something which
is always chosen for its own sake and never for the sake of something
else is without qualification a final end.

Now happiness more than anything else appears to be just such an
end, for we always choose it for its own sake and never for the sake of
some other thing. It is different with honour, pleasure, intelligence
and good qualities generally. We choose them indeed for their own
sake in the sense that we should be glad to have them irrespective of
any advantage which might accrue from them. But we also choose
them for the sake of our happiness in the belief that they will be
instrumental in promoting that. On the other hand nobody chooses

happiness as a means of achieving them or anything else whatsoever than just happiness.

J. A. K. THOMSON (1953)

GOOD AND BAD ACTION IS NOT INVOLUNTARY

Since then it is the end that is the object of our wishing, and the means to the end that is the object of our deliberating and choosing, the actions which deal with means must be done by choice and must be voluntary. Now when the virtues are exercised it is upon means. So virtue also is attainable by our own exertions. And so is vice. For what it lies in our power to do, it lies in our power not to do; when we can say 'no', we can say 'yes'. If, then, it is in our power to perform an action when it is right, it will be equally in our power to refrain from performing it when it is wrong; and if it lies with us to refrain from doing a thing when that is right, it will also lie with us to do it when that is wrong. But if it is in our power to do the right or the wrong thing, and equally in our power to refrain from doing so; and if doing right or wrong is, as we saw, the same as being good or bad ourselves, we must conclude that it depends upon ourselves whether we are to be virtuous or vicious. The words

> To sin and suffer – that offends us still:
> But who is ever blest against his will?

must be regarded as a half-truth. It is true that no one is blest against his will, but untrue that wickedness is involuntary.

J. A. K. THOMSON (1953)

EQUITY: FAIRNESS

We must next say something about equity, and about the fair and equitable. What is the relation of equity to justice, and of the equitable to the just? When we look into the matter we find that justice and equity are not absolutely identical, yet cannot be classified as different. Actually we sometimes commend the equitable and the equitable man to the extent of applying the epithet as a term of approbation to other things as if it were equivalent to 'good' and saying that a thing is 'more equitable' when all we mean is that it is better. At other times, however, when we follow the train of our reflections, it does seem odd that the equitable, if it differs from justice, should yet be thought worthy of commendation. If this difference exists, then of two things, one: either the just or the equitable is not good. Conversely, if both are good the difference does not exist, and justice and equity are identical. That is roughly the difficulty which presents itself when we consider the equitable from this point of view. Yet, sound as the objections are, there is no real inconsistency. Equity, though a higher thing than one form of justice, is itself just and is not generically different from justice. Thus, so far as both are good, they coincide, though equity is to be preferred. What puzzles people is the fact that equity, though just, is not the justice of the law courts but a method of restoring the balance of justice when it has been tilted by the law. The need for such a rectification arises from the circumstance that law can do no more than generalize, and there are cases which cannot be settled by a general statement. So in matters where it is necessary to make a general statement, and yet that statement cannot exclude the possibility of error, the law takes no account of particular cases, though well aware that this is not a strictly correct proceeding. Yet that does not make it a bad law, the error lying not in the law or the lawgiver but in the nature of the case; the *data* of human behaviour simply will not be reduced to uniformity.

J. A. K. THOMSON (1953)

FRIENDSHIP

The ability of grim and elderly persons to make friends is limited by the fact that they tend to be cross-grained and take small pleasure in society; for it is qualities just the opposite of these that are most amiable and most apt to win friendship. Hence the young strike up friendships quickly, but not the old, for one does not make friends with people whose company gives us no satisfaction. And much the same may be said of morose persons. True, the old and the morose may be inclined to like each other, since they may wish one another well, or even supply each other's needs. But friends in the full sense they are not, as they do not seek to remain in the society of each other or find pleasure in that, although these are regarded as the best evidences of the love between friends.

But to have many friends in the way of perfect friendship is no more possible than to be in love with many at the same time. It is not even easy for a man to have at the same time a large circle of agreeable acquaintances, and indeed it may be doubted if good men are so common. When you do find such a man you must become intimate with him and learn to know him before you make him your friend, and nothing is harder than that. On the other hand it is perfectly possible to have a *liking* for quite a number of people at the same time for the pleasure and profit one gets out of them. There are plenty of people capable of providing us with either, and it does not take long to furnish ourselves with the advantages they offer.

Of the secondary forms of friendship that which has pleasure for its object is nearer than the other to true friendship, for in it the con-tribution of both friends is the same. That is to say, they have common tastes and like to be together. The friendships of the young are like that. In them one finds a more generous spirit than in utilitarian friendships, such as are affected by the vulgar. Then the well-to-do have no need of useful friends, but do need agreeable ones. Some associates they must have, and these must be such as they find to their taste. For, although they may put up with what is disagree-able for a time, they cannot any more than other people stand it for ever – even the absolute good would be too much for us at last, if it got to be a bore. So the rich look out for friends who shall be agree-able. Of course they should require them to be good as well – good in themselves and good for them – since in that case their friendship will be everything a true friendship ought to be. But princes and potentates, it would seem, prefer to have their friends specialized for different services; some are useful to them, others agreeable, hardly any are both. For what these great personages seek are not pleasant companions who are also good, nor profitable friends to serve some high purpose, but witty talkers when they want amusement and, when they want value for the connexion, practical men of business – characters rarely combined in one man. We have said that the good man is also both useful and agreeable, but he does not become the *friend* of a superior in rank who is not his superior in goodness as well. If it happen otherwise, the inferior in rank is not in a position to make up for the difference by giving more than he gets. But how many important people possess this moral superiority?

J. A. K. THOMSON (1953)

THE 'SLAVE BY NATURE'

But whether anyone does in fact by nature answer to this description, and whether or not it is a good and a right thing for one to be a slave to another, and whether we should not regard all slavery as contrary to nature – these are questions which must next be considered.

Neither theoretical discussion nor empirical observation presents any difficulty. There can be no objection in principle to the mere fact that one should command and another obey; that is both necessary and expedient. Indeed some things are so divided right from birth, some to rule, some to be ruled. There are many different forms of this ruler-ruled relationship and they are to be found everywhere. Wherever there is a combination of elements, continuous or discontinuous, and a common unity is the result, in all such cases the ruler-ruled relationship appears. It appears notably in living creatures as a consequence of their whole nature; the living creature consists in the first place of mind and body, and of these the former by nature is ruler, the latter ruled. Now in dealing with any phenomena dependent on natural growth we must always look to nature's own norm and not base our observations on degenerate forms. We must therefore in this connexion consider the man who is in good condition mentally and physically, one in whom the rule of mind over body is conspicuous. The opposite state, where body rules over mind, being in itself a bad thing and contrary to nature, would be found to exist in bad men or in men in bad condition. However, as I say, it is within living creatures that we first see the exercise of ruling or commanding power, both the absolute rule of a master and the non-absolute or constitutional. The rule of mind over body is absolute, the rule of intelligence over desire is constitutional and royal. In all these it is clear that it is both natural and expedient for the body to be ruled by the mind, and for the emotional part of our natures to be ruled by that part which possesses reason, our intelligence. The reverse, or even parity, would be fatal all round. This is also true as between man and other animals; for tame animals are by nature better than wild, and it is better for them to be ruled by men; for one thing, it secures their safety. Again, as between male and female the former is by nature superior and ruler, the latter inferior and subject. And this must hold good of mankind in general. We may therefore say that wherever there is the same wide discrepancy between two sets of human beings as there is between mind and body or between man and beast, then the inferior of the two sets, those whose condition is such that their function is the use of their bodies and nothing better can be expected of them, those, I say, are slaves by nature. It is better for them, just as in the analogous cases mentioned, to be thus ruled and subject.

The 'slave by nature' then is he that can and therefore does belong to another, and he that participates in the reasoning faculty so far as to understand but not so as to possess it. For the other animals serve their owner not by exercise of reason but passively. The use, too, of slaves hardly differs at all from that of domestic animals; from both we derive that which is essential for our bodily needs. It is then part of nature's intention to make the bodies of free men to differ from those of slaves, the latter strong enough for the necessary menial tasks, the former erect and useless for that kind of work, but well suited for the life of a citizen of a state, a life divided between war and peace. But though that may have been nature's intention, the opposite often happens. We see men who have the right kind of bodily physique for a free man but not the mind, others who have the right mind but not the body. This much is clear: suppose that there were men whose bodily physique alone showed the same superiority as is shown by the super-human size of statues of gods, then all would agree that the rest of mankind would deserve to be their slaves. And if this is true in relation to physical superiority, the distinction would be even more legitimately made in respect of superiority of mind. But it is much more difficult to see quality of mind than it is to see quality of body. It is clear then that by nature some are free, others slaves, and that for these it is both right and expedient that they should serve as slaves.

T. A. SINCLAIR (1962)

THE OWNERSHIP OF PROPERTY

What are the best arrangements to make about property, if a state is to be as well constituted as it is possible to make it? Is property to be held in common or not? It will be observed that the answer to this question may well be different from the answer as to children and wives. A possible answer is that while there should be separate households, as is the universal practice, it would be better that property, both in respect of ownership and usufruct, should be held communally. Or ownership and usufruct might be separated; then either the land is held in common and its produce pooled for general use (as is done by some peoples) or the land is communally held and communally worked but its produce is distributed according to individual requirements. This is a form of communal ownership which is said to exist among certain non-Greek peoples. There is also the alternative already mentioned – that both the land and its produce be communally owned. As to its cultivation – any system of communal ownership will run more smoothly if the land is worked by persons other than the citizens; because, if they themselves work the land for their own benefit, there will be greater ill-feeling about the common ownership. For if the work done and the benefit accrued are equal, well and good; but if not, there will inevitably be ill-feeling between those who get a good income without doing much work and those who work harder but get no corresponding extra benefit. Communal life and communal ownership are hard enough to achieve at the best of times and such a state of affairs makes it doubly hard. The same kind of trouble is evident when a number of people club together for the purpose of travel. How often have we not seen such partnerships break down over quarrels arising out of trivial and unimportant matters! In a household also we are most likely to get annoyed with those servants whom we employ to perform the routine tasks.

These then are some of the difficulties inherent in the joint ownership of property. Far better is the present system of private ownership provided that it has a moral basis in sound laws. It will then have the advantages of both systems, both the communal and the private. For, while property should up to a point be held in common, the general principle should be that of private ownership. If the responsibility for looking after property is distributed over many individuals, this will not lead to mutual recriminations; on the contrary, with every man busy with his own, there will be increased production all round. 'All things in common among friends' the saying goes, but it is the personal qualities of individuals that ensure their common use. And politically such an arrangement is by no means impossible; it exists, even if only in outline, in some countries, and in well-governed ones too, either in operation or soon to be. Briefly it would work thus: each man has his own possessions; part of these he makes available for his own immediate circle, part he uses in common with others. For example, in Sparta they use each others' slaves practically as if they were their own, and horses and dogs too; and if they need food on a journey, they get it in the country as they go. Clearly then it is better for property to remain in private hands, but we should make the right to use it communal.

T. A. SINCLAIR (1962)

THE SITING OF THE PERFECT CITY-STATE

We have already noted that a city should have easy access both to the sea and to the interior, and, so far as conditions allow, be equally accessible to the whole of its territory. The land upon which the city itself is to be sited should be sloping. That is something that we must just hope to find, but we should keep four considerations in mind. First and most essential the situation must be a healthy one. A slope facing east, with winds blowing from the direction of sunrise, gives a healthy site, rather better than one on the lee side of north though this gives good weather. Next, it should be well situated for carrying out all its civil and military activities. For the purposes of defence the site should be one from which defenders can easily make a sally but which attackers will find difficult to approach and difficult to surround. Water, and especially spring water, should be abundant and if possible under immediate control in time of war; alternatively a way has been discovered of catching rain water in large quantities in vessels numerous enough to ensure a supply when fighting prevents the defenders from going far afield.

Since consideration must be given to the health of the inhabitants, which is partly a matter of siting in the best place and facing the right way, partly also dependent on a supply of pure water, this too must receive careful attention. I mention situation and water supply in particular because air and water, being just those things that we make most frequent and constant use of, have the greatest effect on our bodily condition. Hence, in a state which has welfare at heart, water for human consumption should be separated from water for all other purposes, unless of course all the water is alike and there are plenty of springs that are drinkable.

In the matter of defensive positions it should be remembered that what is best for one type of government is not so good for another. A lofty central citadel suits both oligarchy and monarchy, a level plain democracy; neither suits an aristocracy, which prefers a series of strongly held points. In laying out areas for private dwelling houses, the modern or Hippodamean method[1] has the advantage of regularity; it is also more attractive and for all purposes save one, more practical. For ease of defence, the old-fashioned irregular siting of houses was better, hard for foreign mercenaries to get out of and for attackers to penetrate. It follows that both methods should be used and this is quite possible: arrange the buildings in the same pattern as is used for planting vines, not in rows but in *quincunx*,[2] and do not lay out the whole city with geometric regularity but only certain parts. This will meet the needs both of safety and good appearance.

As for walls, it is quite out of date to say, as some do, that cities that

---

1. Hippodamus of Miletus (fifth century B.C.) was the most famous Greek town-planner.
2. cf. arrangement of five pellets on dice.

lay claim to valour have no need of walls; we have only to look at what in fact has happened to cities that made that boast. Doubtless there is something not quite honourable in seeking safety behind solid walls, at any rate against an enemy equal in numbers or only very slightly superior. But it may happen, and does happen, that the numerical superiority of the attackers is too much for the courage of the defenders, both of the average man and of a chosen few. If then we are to save our city and avoid the miseries of cruelty and oppression, we must concede that the greatest degree of protection that walls can afford is also the best military measure. The truth of this is emphasized by all the modern improvements in missiles and artillery for attacking a besieged town. Deliberately to give cities no walls at all is like choosing an easily attacked position and clearing away the surrounding high ground. It is as if we were to refrain from putting walls round private property for fear of rendering the inhabitants unmanly. Another thing that should not be lost sight of is that those who have provided their city with a wall are in a position to regard that city in both ways, to treat it either as a fortified or an unfortified city. Those who have no walls have no such choice. And if this is so, then it is a duty not only to build walls but also to maintain them in a manner suitable both for the city's appearance and for its defensive needs, which in these days are very numerous. Just as the attacking side is always on the look-out for methods which will give them an advantage, so too the defenders must seek additional means of defence by the aid of scientific inquiry. An enemy will not even attempt an attack on those who are really well prepared to meet it.

T. A. SINCLAIR (1962)

POETICAL AND HISTORICAL TRUTH

It will be clear from what I have said that it is not the poet's function to describe what has actually happened, but the kinds of thing that might happen, that is, that could happen because they are, in the circumstances, either probable or necessary. The difference between the historian and the poet is not that the one writes in prose and the other in verse; the work of Herodotus might be put into verse, and in this metrical form it would be no less a kind of history than it is without metre. The difference is that the one tells of what has happened, the other of the kinds of things that might happen. For this reason poetry is something more philosophical and more worthy of serious attention than history; for while poetry is concerned with universal truths, history treats of particular facts.

By universal truths are to be understood the kinds of thing a certain type of person will probably or necessarily say or do in a given situation; and this is the aim of poetry, although it gives individual names to its characters. The particular facts of the historian are what, say, Alcibiades did, or what happened to him. By now this distinction has become clear where comedy is concerned, for comic poets build up their plots out of probable occurrences, and then add any names that occur to them; they do not, like the iambic poets, write about actual people.[1] In tragedy, on the other hand, the authors keep to the names of real people, the reason being that what is possible is credible. Whereas we cannot be certain of the possibility of something that has not happened, what has happened is obviously possible, for it would not have happened if this had not been so. Nevertheless, even in some tragedies only one or two of the names are well known, and the rest are fictitious; and indeed there are some in which nothing is familiar, Agathon's *Antheus*,[2] for example, in which both the incidents and the names are fictitious, and the play is none the less well liked for that. It is not necessary, therefore, to keep entirely to the traditional stories which form the subjects of our tragedies. Indeed it would be absurd to do so, since even the familiar stories are familiar only to a few, and yet they please everybody.

What I have said makes it obvious that the poet must be a maker of plots rather than of verses, since he is a poet by virtue of his representation, and what he represents is actions. And even if he writes about things that have actually happened, that does not make him any the less a poet, for there is nothing to prevent some of the things that have happened from being in accordance with the laws of possibility and probability, and thus he will be a poet in writing about them.

1. Notably Archilochus; see above, p. 75.
2. For Agathon, see above, p. 168.

Of simple plots and actions those that are episodic are the worst. By an episodic plot I mean one in which the sequence of the episodes is neither probable nor necessary. Plays of this kind are written by bad poets because they cannot help it, and by good poets because of the actors; writing for the dramatic competitions, they often strain a plot beyond the bounds of possibility, and are thus obliged to dislocate the continuity of events.

However, tragedy is the representation not only of a complete action, but also of incidents that awaken fear and pity, and effects of this kind are heightened when things happen unexpectedly as well as logically, for then they will be more remarkable than if they seem merely mechanical or accidental. Indeed, even chance occurrences seem most remarkable when they have the appearance of having been brought about by design – when, for example, the statue of Mitys at Argos killed the man who had caused Mitys's death by falling down on him at a public entertainment. Things like this do not seem mere chance occurrences. Thus plots of this type are necessarily better than others.

T. S. DORSCH (1965)

TRAGIC DRAMA

Following upon the points I have already made, I must go on to say what is to be aimed at and what guarded against in the construction of plots, and what are the sources of the tragic effect.

We saw that the structure of tragedy at its best should be complex, not simple, and that it should represent actions capable of awakening fear and pity – for this is a characteristic function of representations of this type. It follows in the first place that good men should not be shown passing from prosperity to misery, for this does not inspire fear or pity, it merely disgusts us. Nor should evil men be shown progressing from misery to prosperity. This is the most untragic of all plots, for it has none of the requisites of tragedy; it does not appeal to our humanity, or awaken pity or fear in us. Nor again should an utterly worthless man be seen falling from prosperity into misery. Such a course might indeed play upon our humane feelings, but it would not arouse either pity or fear; for our pity is awakened by undeserved misfortune, and our fear by that of someone just like ourselves – pity for the undeserving sufferer and fear for the man like ourselves – so that the situation in question would have nothing in it either pitiful or fearful.

There remains a mean between these extremes. This is the sort of man who is not conspicuous for virtue and justice, and whose fall into misery is not due to vice and depravity, but rather to some error, a man who enjoys prosperity and a high reputation, like Oedipus and Thyestes and other famous members of families like theirs.

Inevitably, then, the well-conceived plot will have a single interest, and not, as some say, a double. The change in fortune will be, not from misery to prosperity, but the reverse, from prosperity to misery, and it will be due, not to depravity, but to some great error either in such a man as I have described or in one better than this, but not worse. This is borne out by existing practice. For at first the poets treated any stories that came to hand, but nowadays the best tragedies are written about a handful of families, those of Alcmaeon, for example, and Oedipus and Orestes and Meleager and Thyestes and Telephus, and others whom it has befallen to suffer or inflict terrible experiences.

The best tragedies in the technical sense are constructed in this way. Those critics are on the wrong tack, therefore, who criticize Euripides for following such a procedure in his tragedies, and complain that many of them end in misfortune; for, as I have said, this is the right end. The strongest evidence of this is that on the stage and in the dramatic competitions plays of this kind, when properly worked out, are the most tragic of all, and Euripides, faulty as is his management of other points, is nevertheless regarded as the most tragic of our poets.

The next best type of structure, ranked first by some critics, is that which has a double thread of plot, and ends in opposite ways for the good and the bad characters.[1] It is considered the best only because of the feeble judgement of the audience, for the poets pander to the taste of the spectators. But this is not the pleasure that is proper to tragedy. It belongs rather to comedy, where those who have been the

1. Aristotle cites the *Odyssey* in comparison.

bitterest of enemies in the original story, Orestes and Aegisthus, for example, go off at the end as friends, and nobody is killed by anybody.

Fear and pity may be excited by means of spectacle; but they can also take their rise from the very structure of the action, which is the preferable method and the mark of a better dramatic poet. For the plot should be so ordered that even without seeing it performed anyone merely hearing what is afoot will shudder with fear and pity as a result of what is happening – as indeed would be the experience of anyone hearing the story of Oedipus. To produce this effect by means of stage-spectacle is less artistic, and requires the cooperation of the producer. Those who employ spectacle to produce an effect, not of fear, but of something merely monstrous, have nothing to do with tragedy, for not every kind of pleasure should be demanded of tragedy, but only that which is proper to it; and since the dramatic poet has by means of his representation to produce the tragic pleasure that is associated with pity and fear, it is obvious that this effect is bound up with the events of the plot.

Let us now consider what kinds of incident are to be regarded as fearful or pitiable. Deeds that fit this description must of course involve people who are either friends to one another, or enemies, or neither. Now if a man injures his enemy, there is nothing pitiable either in his act or in his intention, except in so far as suffering is inflicted; nor is there if they are indifferent to each other. But when the sufferings involve those who are near and dear to one another, when for example brother kills brother, son father, mother son, or son mother, or if such a deed is contemplated, or something else of the kind is actually done, then we have a situation of the kind to be aimed at. Thus it will not do to tamper with the traditional stories, the murder of Clytemnestra by Orestes, for instance, and that of Eriphyle by Alcmaeon;[1] on the other hand, the poet must use his imagination and handle the traditional material effectively.

I must explain more clearly what I mean by 'effectively'. The deed may be done by characters acting consciously and in full knowledge of the facts, as was the way of the early dramatic poets, when for

1. Alcmaeon, son of Amphiaraus, avenged his father's death on his mother Eriphyle.

instance Euripides made Medea kill her children. Or they may do it without realizing the horror of the deed until later, when they discover the truth; this is what Sophocles did with Oedipus. Here indeed the relevant incident occurs outside the action of the play; but it may be a part of the tragedy, as with Alcmaeon in Astydamas's play, or Telegonus in *The Wounded Odysseus*.[1] A third alternative is for someone who is about to do a terrible deed in ignorance of the relationship to discover the truth before he does it. These are the only possibilities, for the deed must either be done or not done, and by someone either with or without knowledge of the facts.

The least acceptable of these alternatives is when someone in possession of the facts is on the point of acting but fails to do so, for this merely shocks us, and, since no suffering is involved, it is not tragic. Hence nobody is allowed to behave like this, or only seldom, as when Haemon fails to kill Creon in the *Antigone*. Next in order of effectiveness is when the deed is actually done, and here it is better that the character should act in ignorance and only learn the truth afterwards, for there is nothing in this to outrage our feelings, and the revelation comes as a surprise. However, the best method is the last, when, for example, in the *Cresphontes* Merope intends to kill her son, but recognizes him and does not do so; or when the same thing happens with brother and sister in *Iphigenia in Tauris*; or when, in the *Helle*, the son recognizes his mother when he is just about to betray her.[2]

This then is the reason why, as I said before, our tragedies keep to a few families. For in their search for dramatic material it was by chance rather than by technical knowledge that the poets discovered how to gain tragic effects in their plots. And they are still obliged to have recourse to those families in which sufferings of the kind I have described have been experienced.

I have said enough now about the arrangement of the incidents in a tragedy and the type of plot it ought to have.

T. S. DORSCH (1965)

1. Astydamas was a tragic poet of *c.* 340 B.C., the son of another such writer of the same name. Telegonus, the son of Odysseus by Circe, killed his father.

2. The first two of these plays were by Euripides. The sons of Merope and Helle were Aeypytus and Paeon (or Edonus) respectively.

THEOPHRASTUS

PHILOSOPHER, scientist and psychologist, *c.* 370–288/5 B.C., from Eresus on the island of Lesbos. Succeeded Aristotle as head of the Peripatetic school at Athens.

*

FIVE CHARACTERS

Abominable behaviour is not hard to define: it is blatant and offensive levity.

The abominable man is one who on meeting respectable women will lift his clothing and display his private parts. In the theatre he claps when the rest have stopped; and hisses players whom everyone else is enjoying; and when there is a silence he will lift his head and belch, to make the audience turn round. Just when the market is most crowded he goes to the stalls where they sell nuts, or myrtle-berries, or fruit, and stands there nibbling away while he chats to the stall-keeper. In company he will address by name someone with whom he is not acquainted. If he sees that people are in a hurry, he insists on their stopping a little. If you have just lost an important lawsuit he comes up as you leave the court and congratulates you. He goes out to do his own shopping, hires a couple of flute-girls, and then if you meet him shows you what he has got and invites you to come and share them. He will stand talking outside the barber's or the myrrh-shop, and announce that he intends to get drunk. When his mother has just come in from visiting the fortune-teller he deliberately uses unlucky words. When prayers or libations are going on, he drops his cup and then laughs as if he had done something funny. When he is being played to on the flute, he will be the one person to tap the tune with his fingers and to whistle an accompaniment, and then severely ask the flute-girl why she didn't stop at once. When he wants to spit, he spits across the table at the slave who is pouring wine.

Unseasonableness is an annoying faculty for choosing the wrong moment.

The unseasonable man is the kind who comes up to you when you have no time to spare and asks your advice. He sings a serenade to his sweetheart when she has influenza. Just after you have gone bail for somebody and had to pay up, he approaches you with a request that you will go bail for him. If he is going to give evidence he turns up when judgement has just been pronounced. When he is a guest at a wedding he makes derogatory remarks about the female sex. When you have just reached home after a long journey he invites you to come for a stroll. He is certain to bring along a buyer who offers more, when you have just sold your house. When people have heard a matter and know it by heart, he stands up and explains the whole thing from the beginning. He eagerly undertakes a service for you which you don't want performed but which you have not the face to decline. When people are sacrificing and spending money, he arrives to ask for his interest on a loan. When a friend's slave is being beaten he will stand there and tell how he once had a slave who hanged himself after a similar beating. If he takes part in an arbitration, he will set everyone at blows again just when both sides are ready to cry quits. And after dancing once he will seize as partner another man who is not yet drunk.

The presumptuous man is one who makes the kind of promise he will not be able to keep. When a matter is generally admitted to be just, he raises objections, and is then overruled. He insists on his slave mixing more wine than the company can finish. He tries to separate two men fighting, even when he doesn't know them. He begins to show you a short cut, and presently has no idea where he is going. He will walk up to the colonel and ask him when he intends to put the troops in battle-formation, and what will be his orders for the day after tomorrow. He will go to his father and tell him that his mother is still fast asleep in their bedroom. When the doctor has forbidden an invalid to be given wine, he says he wants to try an experiment, and makes the patient tipsy. When a woman relative has died, he inscribes on her tombstone her husband's name, and her father's and her mother's, as well as her own name and her place of birth, and adds, that 'they were all estimable people'. And when about to take an oath he remarks to those standing round, 'I've done this scores of times.'

Late learning would seem to be a love of difficult tasks which is excessive in view of one's age.

The late learner is the sort of man who, at sixty, learns by heart speeches from the tragedies, and when reciting them over the wine forgets them. He gets his son to instruct him how to do a 'right wheel' or 'left wheel' or 'about turn'. At heroes' festivals he competes with boys in the torch-race. And of course, if he is invited somewhere to a feast of Heracles and asked to choose a victim, he throws off his cloak and chooses the bull, so that he can bend back its neck for slaughter. He goes into the wrestling-schools and submits to training. At a variety show he will sit through three or four performances, learning the songs by heart. When undergoing initiation in the mysteries of Sabazios,[1] he is determined to acquit himself the best in the eyes of the priest. He falls in love with a girl of the town, and when caught by a rival client in the act of forcing her door with a crowbar, and given a beating, he then brings an action for assault. He rides out to the country on a borrowed horse, practises horsemanship on the way, falls off, and breaks his head. At a tenth-day festival he collects a group to sing with him. He plays at 'Long John' with his own slave. He competes at archery and javelin-throwing with his children's tutor, whom he advises to learn from *him* – as if the tutor too knew nothing about it. When wrestling at the baths he wriggles his bottom rapidly, so that people may think he has been properly trained: and when there's a performance of women's dancing, he too practises the steps, whistling the tune for himself.

By 'love of evil' I mean a partiality for the criminal character.

The 'lover of evil' is the sort of man who contacts those who have lost lawsuits or been found guilty in criminal cases, and reckons that by associating with them he will become more experienced and more

1. A non-Greek god worshipped chiefly in Phrygia and Lydia; but private associations devoted to his worship had also existed at Athens since the later fifth century B.C.

formidable. If someone is referred to as honest, he adds, 'To all appearance', and goes on to say that there is no such thing as an honest man; that all men are alike; indeed he uses the phrase 'What a good man' as a joke. A criminal type he will describe as 'Independent-minded, if you look at him fairly. Many of the things people say of him,' he admits, 'are true; but there are some things they don't know. He's naturally talented; he sticks to his friends; and he's no fool.' He insists emphatically that he has never met a more capable person. He will take the side of a man who is making his defence in the Assembly, or on trial in a law-court; and he will probably tell the jury that 'They must judge the case and not the man.' He will describe the defendant as a 'watchdog of the people, one who keeps his eye on wrong-doers. Unless we value such men,' he says, 'we shall have no one left who cares what goes wrong in public life.' He can't resist championing worthless men; on a jury he organizes a pressure-group in a bad cause; when judging a case he takes the statements of the opposed parties in the worst sense.

PHILIP VELLACOTT (1967)

EPICURUS

PHILOSOPHER from Samos, 341–270 B.C.; migrated to Athens. Founder of the Epicurean school.

*

THE DOCTRINES OF EPICURUS

Accustom thyself to believe that death is nothing to us, for good and evil imply sentience, and death is the privation of all sentience; therefore a right understanding that death is nothing to us makes the mortality of life enjoyable, not by adding to life an illimitable time, but by taking away the yearning after immortality. For life has no terrors for him who has thoroughly apprehended that there are no terrors for him in ceasing to live. Foolish, therefore, is the man who says that he fears death, not because it will pain when it comes, but because it pains in the prospect. Whatsoever causes no annoyance when it is present, causes only a groundless pain in the expectation. Death, therefore, the most awful of evils, is nothing to us, seeing that, when we are, death is not come, and, when death is come, we are not. It is nothing, then, either to the living or to the dead, for with the living it is not and the dead exist no longer. But in the world, at one time men shun death as the greatest of all evils, and at another time choose it as a respite from the evils in life. The wise man does not deprecate life nor does he fear the cessation of life. The thought of life is no offence to him, nor is the cessation of life regarded as an evil. And even as men choose of food not merely and simply the larger portion, but the more pleasant, so the wise seek to enjoy the time which is most pleasant and not merely that which is longest. And he who admonishes the young to live well and the old to make a good end speaks foolishly, not merely because of the desirableness of life, but because the same exercise at once teaches to live well and die well. Much worse is he who says that it were good not to be born, but when once one is born to pass with all speed through the gates of Hades.[1] For if he truly believes this, why does he not depart from life? It were easy for him to do so, if once he were firmly convinced. If he speaks only in mockery, his words are foolishness, for those who hear believe him not.

We must remember that the future is neither wholly ours nor wholly not ours, so that neither must we count upon it as quite certain to come nor despair of it as quite certain not to come.

We must also reflect that of desires some are natural, others are groundless; and that of the natural some are necessary as well as natural, and some natural only. And of the necessary desires some are necessary if we are to be happy, some if the body is to be rid of uneasiness, some if we are even to live. He who has a clear and certain understanding of these things will direct every preference and aversion toward securing health of body and tranquillity of mind, seeing that this is the sum and end of a blessed life. For the end of all our actions is to be free from pain and fear, and, when once we have attained all this, the tempest of the soul is laid; seeing that the living creature has no need to go in search of something that is lacking, nor to look for anything else by which the good of the soul and of the body will be fulfilled. When we are pained because of the absence of pleasure, then, and then only, do we feel the need of pleasure. Wherefore we call pleasure the alpha and omega of a blessed life. Pleasure is our first and kindred good. It is the starting point of every choice and of every aversion, and to it we come back, in as much as we make feeling the rule by which to judge of every good thing. And since pleasure is our first and native good, for that reason we do not choose every pleasure whatsoever, but oft-times pass over many pleasures when a greater annoyance ensues from them. And oft-times we consider pains superior to pleasures when submission to the pains for a long time brings us as a consequence a greater pleasure. While therefore all pleasure because it is naturally akin to us is good, not all pleasure is choice-worthy, just as all pain is an evil and yet not all pain is to be shunned. It is, however, by measuring one against another, and by looking at the conveniences and inconveniences, that all these matters must be judged. Sometimes we treat the good as an evil, and the evil,

1. See above, pp. 92, 127f., 186.

on the contrary, as a good. Again, we regard independence of outward things as a great good, not so as in all cases to use little, but so as
to be contented with little if we have not much, being honestly
persuaded that they have the sweetest enjoyment of luxury who stand
least in need of it, and that whatever is natural is easily procured and
only the vain and worthless hard to win. Plain fare gives as much
pleasure as a costly diet, when once the pain of want has been removed, while bread and water confer the highest possible pleasure
when they are brought to hungry lips. To habituate one's self, therefore, to simple and inexpensive diet supplies all that is needful for
health, and enables a man to meet the necessary requirements of life
without shrinking, and it places us in a better condition when we
approach at intervals a costly fare, and renders us fearless of fortune.

JASON L. SAUNDERS (1966)

PART VI

HELLENISTIC POETRY[1]

<hr />

1. The fluctuating term 'Hellenistic' is used here to denote the period of Greek literature between Alexander the Great (died 323 B.C.) and the Roman conquest of the last great Greek kingdom, Egypt (30 B.C.).

MENANDER

Poet and dramatist of the Athenian New Comedy, 342/1–293/89 B.C.

*

CHANGES OF FORTUNE

If, when your mother bore you, you were born
Alone of men, young sir, always to do
Your pleasure and live always happily, –
If some god promised you such privilege,
Then rightly are you angry. He has lied
And done you singular wrong. But if one law
Of Nature holds, and you breathed common air –
So let me phrase it in the tragic style –
Put on a better grace and use your reason.
To sum up what I mean, you are a man,
Than whom no creature suffers change more quickly,
Climbing up high, then falling back to the depths, –
It's logic. He, whom Nature made so weak,
Plays manager to all that is most great,
And when he falls, shatters so much that's good.

C. M. BOWRA (1938)

THE COMMON LOT

If you with your true self would be acquainted,
look at the grave-stones as you travel past.
Bones lie beneath and the light-drifting dust
of kings and despots, of the skilled and wise,
of men who gloried in their birth or riches
or reputation won or beauty of body –

then all was gone before the assault of Time.
One place of death men share, and share alike.
Look to the graves – and make your own acquaintance.

T. F. HIGHAM (1938)

THE RIGHT ATTITUDE TO LIFE

I'll tell you, Parmenon,
Who seems to me to have the happiest life: the man
Who takes a steady look at the majestic sights
Our world offers – the common sun, stars, water, clouds,
Fire; and having seen them, and lived free from pain, at
    once
Goes back to where he came from. These same sights
    will be,
If you live to a hundred, always there, always the same;
And equally if you die young; but you will never
See more majestic sights than these. Think of this time
I speak of as a people's festival, or as
A visit to some city, where you stand and watch
The crowds, the streets, the thieves, the gamblers, and
    the way
People amuse themselves. If you go back early
To your lodging, you'll have money in your pocket, and
No enemies. The man who stays too long grows tired,
Loses what he once had, gets old, wretched, and poor,
Wanders about, makes enemies, or falls a prey
To plotters; till at last an ignominious death
Sends him off home.

PHILIP VELLACOTT (1967)

CHANCE

Stop talking about 'mind'; the mind of man can do
Nothing. It is Chance (has Chance a 'mind' or a 'holy
    spirit'?)

– Whatever you call it, Chance steers, governs, and
  preserves
Everything. Human forethought is all smoke, all bilge.
It's true – you take my word; you'll never say I'm
  wrong.
Each single thought, each word, each act of ours is just
Chance. All you and I can do is sign on the dotted line.

PHILIP VELLACOTT (1967)

THE LIMITS OF DIVINE INTERVENTION

SMICRINES: Oh! You immortal gods!
ONESIMOS: Smicrines, do you imagine the immortal gods
  Have so little to do that they can spend their days
  Dealing out good and bad to individuals?
SMICRINES: What do you mean?
ONESIMOS: I'll put it simply for you. How many
  Cities are there in the whole world? Let's say a thousand.
  In each of them three hundred thousand people live.
  Do the gods punish or reward each one of them
  Separately? That's not how the gods live! The gods
  Are at peace. A life like that would be one endless headache!
  You'll ask me, Don't the gods then care about us at all?
  They do. They assign to each man his appropriate
  Character, to command the garrison of his soul.
  This inner force drives one man straight to ruin, if ever
  He has abused it; leads another to happiness.
  Character is our god, which apportions to each man
  Good luck or bad. Propitiate this god, by acting
  Kindly and decently; and deserve a happy life.
SMICRINES: You snivelling scab! Don't I act decently?
    What's wrong
With *my* character, then?

PHILIP VELLACOTT (1967)

SUSPICION

DEMEAS: I'd just gone in
To hurry on preparations for my son's wedding.
I was telling them all, 'Moschion's to be married today;
So just get everything ready, clean the whole place up,
Make cakes, and fill the basket for the ceremony.'
Well, things were going smoothly enough; though naturally
The sudden hurry put them all in a bit of a stew; –
And there, lying on a bed, just shoved down out of the
    way,
Was the baby, howling. The maids were shouting, 'Where's
    the flour?
Fetch in some water; hand me the oil; put on more coal!'
Well, I was issuing stores, and helping; and I'd just
Gone into the store-room, where I was busy choosing out
Still more stuff, keeping an eye on everything; and so
I didn't come out at once; and while I was still in there
A woman came down the stairs into the room that's just
Opposite the store-room door. It's a sort of weaving-room;
The way upstairs is through it; and I go through it too
To get to the store-room. Now, this woman was once nurse
To Moschion; she's free now, but I keep her on
As a servant; she's quite elderly. Well, she saw the baby
Left there alone and crying. She had no idea
I was in the store-room; for all she knew, she was safe in
    saying
Whatever she pleased. She went up to the kid, and began
The usual baby-talk – 'Duckie, sweetie-pie,' says she,
And 'Aren't you a beautiful boy?' and 'Where's your
    mummy gone?'
She kissed it, carried it up and down; and when it stopped
Crying, 'Oh, dear,' says she, 'it seems only yesterday
I was nursing Moschion, a darling little mite like this.
Now Moschion's got a son of his own; and someone else
Will nurse it, and in turn . . .'

Some little maid came running in, and the old woman
Called to her, 'Give the baby his bath, lazybones!
This is a fine way to go on,' says she, 'to leave
The baby uncared-for on his father's wedding-day!'
Then straight away the little maid said, 'Hush, you fool –
Talking like that! Master's in the house.' – 'No! Is he?
  'Where?'
– 'He's in the store-room.' Then she changed her voice a
  bit;
'Nurse, the mistress is calling you; go on, be quick.
– He hasn't heard a thing; that's a bit of luck.' So then
The old woman went off, muttering, 'Dear, oh dear,
My tongue again!' – and disappeared. Then I stepped
  out,
Quite quiet and calm – the way I came out here just now,
Exactly as if I'd seen nothing, heard nothing; – and there
I saw Chrysis herself in the courtyard holding the child,
And as I went past she was putting it to her breast.
So this at least is certain, that the baby's hers;
But who's the father? Me? Or . . .? Friends, I'd rather not
Say anything, or even guess; but I put to you
The plain facts, and the words I heard with my own ears.
No, I'm not angry – yet.

PHILIP VELLACOTT (1967)

FAMILY

Family? I'm fed up with this talk of 'family'.
Mother, don't – if you love me – every time I mention
A man, start talking about his family. People who
Haven't a single good quality to call their own –
They are the ones who talk like that of family,
Or titles, or decorations; reel off grandfathers
One after the other, and that's all they've got. Can you
Tell me of a man who hasn't got grandfathers? or how
A man could be born without them? People who, for one

Reason or another – living abroad, or losing friends –
Can't name their grandfathers – are they any worse born
    than those
Who can? Mother, if a man has a noble character
Which prompts him to a good life, then he's of noble
    birth,
Even if he's a black African.

PHILIP VELLACOTT (1967)

FAMILY DINNER-PARTY

It's no joke, to plunge into a family dinner-party, where
First papa leads off the speeches, cup in hand, and gives them all
Pointed good advice; mama comes second; then a grandmother
Rambles on a little; then great-uncle, in a growling bass;
Then comes some old lady who alludes to you as 'dearest boy'.
All the time you nod your head and beam at them . . .

PHILIP VELLACOTT (1967)

DIFFERENT TASTES IN FOOD

This dinner is for entertaining a visitor.
What visitor? Where's he from? That makes a difference
To a Cook, you know. Now, take these fancy visitors
From the islands, reared on fresh-caught fish from far and near –
They don't find sea-food all that wonderful; to them
It's just a side-dish. Seasoned stuffing, savoury sauce –
That's what those gentry go for. Now, an Arcadian –
He's different; doesn't live by the sea; what fetches him
Is limpets. Then there's your Ionian: rich and coarse.
Thick soup I give him; Lydian hot-pot; tasty stews
Flavoured with Aphrodisiac herbs.

PHILIP VELLACOTT (1967)

CLEANTHES

Philosopher from Assos near Troy; migrated to Athens. Lived 331–232 B.C. Successor of Zeno, founder of the Stoic school, which emerged as the principal rival of the Epicureans (see p. 297).

*

HYMN TO ZEUS

O God most glorious, called by many a name,
Nature's great King, through endless years the same;
Omnipotence, who by thy just decree
Controllest all, hail, Zeus, for unto thee
Behoves thy creatures in all lands to call.
We are thy children, we alone, of all
On earth's broad ways that wander to and fro,
Bearing thine image wheresoe'er we go . . .
Chaos to thee is order: in thine eyes
The unloved is lovely, who didst harmonize
Things evil with things good, that there should be
One Word through all things everlastingly.
One Word – whose voice alas! the wicked spurn;
Insatiate for the good their spirits yearn:
Yet seeing see not, neither hearing hear
God's universal law, which those revere,
By reason guided, happiness who win.
The rest, unreasoning, diverse shapes of sin
Self-prompted follow: for an idle name
Vainly they wrestle in the lists of fame:
Others inordinately riches woo,
Or dissolute, the joys of flesh pursue.
Now here, now there they wander, fruitless still,
For ever seeking good and finding ill.
Zeus the all-bountiful, whom darkness shrouds,

Whose lightning lightens in the thunder-clouds,
Thy children save from error's deadly sway:
Turn thou the darkness from their souls away.

JAMES ADAM (1940)

ASCLEPIADES

POET from Samos, also known as Sicelidas. Writing in *c.* 290 B.C. Perhaps the chief epigrammatist of the Alexandrian Age.

*

VIOLENT GIRL

Voracious Philainion bit me. The bite doesn't show
yet pain crawls in me, creeps to my very fingertips.
Love, I am drained, done in, dead! I fell half-dazed
on a viperous whore, and her embrace was death.

WILLIS BARNSTONE (1962)

BLACK BUT BEAUTIFUL

Didyme waved her wand at me.
I am utterly enchanted.
The sight of her beauty makes me
Melt like wax before the fire. What
Is the difference if she is black?
So is coal, but alight, it shines like roses.

KENNETH REXROTH (1962)

SHE KNOWS WHAT TO DO

Although she's a girl, Dorkion
Is wise to the ways of the boys.
Like a chubby kid, she knows how
To throw over her shoulder, from

Under her broadbrimmed hat, the quick
Glance of Public Love, and let her
Cape show a glimpse of her bare butt.

KENNETH REXROTH (1962)

THEOCRITUS

A SYRACUSAN who went to live at Cos and Alexandria. *C.* 300–*c.* 260(?)
B.C. He made pastoral (bucolic) poetry into a literary form and wrote
mimes.

*

SEDUCTION

GIRL: What do you mean (uncivil as you are)
To touch my breasts, and leave my bosom bare?

DAPHNIS: These pretty bubbies first I make my own.

GIRL: Pull out your hand, I swear, or I shall swoon.

DAPHNIS: Why does thy ebbing blood forsake thy face?

GIRL: Throw me at least upon a cleaner place:
My linen ruffled, and my waistcoat soiling,
What, do you think new clothes were made for spoiling?

DAPHNIS: I'll lay my lambskins underneath thy back.

GIRL: My head-gear's off. What filthy work you make.

DAPHNIS: To Venus first I lay these offerings by.

GIRL: Nay first look round, that nobody be nigh:
Methinks I hear a whispering in the grove.

DAPHNIS: The cypress trees are telling tales of love.

GIRL: You tear off all behind me, and before me;
And I'm naked as my mother bore me.

DAPHNIS: I'll buy thee better clothes than these I tear,
And lie so close I'll cover thee from air.

GIRL: Y'are liberal now; but when your turn is sped,
You'll wish me choked with every crust of bread.

DAPHNIS: I'll give thee more, much more than I have told;
Would I could coin my very heart to gold.

GIRL: Forgive thy handmaid, Huntress of the wood –
I see there's no resisting flesh and blood!

313

DAPHNIS: The noble deed is done; my herds I'll cull;
      Cupid, be thine a calf; and Venus, thine a bull.
GIRL: A maid I came, in an unlucky hour,
      But thence return without my virgin flower.
DAPHNIS: A maid is but a barren name at best;
      If thou canst hold, I bid for twins at least.

Thus did this happy pair their love dispense
With mutual joys, and gratified their sense;
The God of Love was there a bidden guest;
And present at his own mysterious Feast.
His azure mantle underneath he spread,
And scattered roses on the nuptial bed;
While folded in each other's arms they lay,
He blew the flames, and furnished out the play,
And from their foreheads wiped the balmy sweat away.
First rose the maid, and with a glowing face
Her downcast eyes beheld her print upon the grass;
Thence to her herd she sped herself in haste:
The bridegroom started from his trance at last,
And piping homeward jocundly he passed.

JOHN DRYDEN (1685)

POLYPHEMUS WOOS GALATEA

Fair one, I know why you avoid me thus:
It is because one rugged eyebrow spreads
Across my forehead, solitary and huge,
Shading a single eye: – my nose too presses
Flat towards my lip; and yet, such as I am,
I feed a thousand sheep, and from them drink
Excellent milk; and never want for cheese
In summer, nor in autumn, nor dead winter,
My dairies are so full. I too know how
To play the pipe, so as no Cyclops can,
Singing, sweet apple mine, of you and me,

314

Often till midnight; and I keep for you
Eleven fawns with collars round their necks.
Come to me then, for you shall have no less;
And leave the sea to strain on the dull shore.
Much sweeter nights here in my cave with me
You shall enjoy; for here the laurel grows,
Slim cypresses, brown ivy, and the vine
Sweet-fruited; and here too is water cold,
A heavenly draught, which from its pure white snows
The many-wooded Aetna sends me down. –
Who, with this choice, would live in the salt waves?
And yet, if in your eyes I seem still rougher
Than my own trees, they furnish me with wood,
And fire is on my hearth, and I could burn
My being rather than be without you,
Or my sole eye, though nothing else is dearer.
Ah me, that I was born a finless body,
And cannot dive to you, and kiss your hand;
Or if you grudged me that, bring you white lilies,
Or the young poppy with its thin red leaves.
And yet not so; for poppies grow in summer,
Lilies in spring; and so I could not both.
But should a visitor, sweetest, in his ship
Come here to see me, I would learn to swim;
And then I might find out, what joy there is
In living, as you do, in the dark deeps.

O Galatea, that you would come forth,
And having come, forget, as I do now
Here where I sat me, to go home again!
You should keep flocks with me, and draw the milk,
And press the cheese from the sharp-tasted curd.
It is my mother that's to blame. She never
Tells you one kind endearing thing of me,
Though you might see me wasting, day by day.
My very head and my two feet, for wretchedness,
Throb; – and so let them, for I too am wretched.

315

O Cyclops, Cyclops, where are thy poor senses!
Go, make thee pails for milk, and pluck their food
For the young lambs; – 'twere wiser for thee far.
Milk where thou canst. Why hunt for what is fled?
Perhaps thou'lt find another Galatea,
Another and a lovelier; for at night
Many girls call to me to come and sport,
And when I listen to them, they all giggle:
So that even I seem something in the world.

'Twas thus the Cyclops quieted his love
With pipe and song; and passed an easier life,
Than if he had had gold to give for one.

LEIGH HUNT (1818)

THE CYCLOPS POLYPHEMUS WOOS GALATEA[1]

White Galatea, why disdain thy love?
White as a pressed cheese, delicate as the lamb,
Wild as the heifer, soft as summer grapes!
If sweet sleep chain me, here thou walk'st at large;
If sweet sleep loose me, straightway thou art gone,
Scared like a sheep that sees the grey wolf near.
I loved thee, maiden, when thou cam'st long since,
To pluck thy hyacinth-blossom on the fell,
Thou and my mother, piloted by me.
I saw thee, see thee still, from that day forth
For ever; but 'tis naught, ay naught, to thee.
I know, sweet maiden, why thou art so coy:
Shaggy and huge, a single eyebrow spans
From ear to ear my forehead, whence one eye
Gleams, and an o'erbroad nostril tops my lip.
Yet I, this monster, feed a thousand sheep
That yield me sweetest draughts at milking-tide:
In summer, autumn, or midwinter, still

1. Part of the same piece again, rendered fifty-one years later.

Fails not my cheese; my milkpail aye o'erflows.
Then I can pipe as ne'er did Giant yet,
Singing our loves – ours, honey, thine and mine –
At dead of night: and hinds I rear eleven
(Each with her fawn) and bearcubs four, for thee.
Oh come to me – thou shalt not rue the day –
And let the mad seas beat against the shore!
'Twere sweet to haunt my cave the livelong night:
Laurel, and cypress tall, and ivy dun,
And vines of sumptuous fruitage, all are there:
And a cold spring that pine-clad Aetna flings
Down from the white snow's midst, a draught for gods!
Who would not change for this the ocean-waves?

C. S. CALVERLEY (1869)

AT THE FESTIVAL OF ADONIS

GORGO: Is Praxinoa in?

PRAXINOA: Of course she is.
Dear Gorgo, what a long time since I saw you,
I thought we were quite forgotten. A chair, Eunoa,
And throw a cushion on it.

GORGO: O, no thank you,
It's quite nice as it is.

PRAXINOA: Then do sit down.

GORGO: It really was a madness to come out –
I don't know how I'm here alive, my dear!
There's such a crush, and horses everywhere:
Nothing but boots and men in uniform –
The street went on for ever: I never knew
How far away your house was built before.

PRAXINOA: O, all my idiot's fault! He would come here,
Right at the world's end, and a den at that,
Not a human habitation: all for spite!
To get me as far away as he could from you –
He's made up of pure jealousy: always the same –

317

GORGO: My dear, don't talk so harshly of your Dinon
   Before the baby. How's he staring at you!
   Lullaby little Zopyros, honey-pet –
   It's not your daddy that she's speaking of.
PRAXINOA: O, by our Lady, the child understands.
GORGO: Pretty daddy!
PRAXINOA: Yes, that pretty fellow
   The other day – I said to him – the other day –
   'Dad, please buy mother here some soap and rouge,'
   And, would you credit it? the great big boob
   Came back and handed me a packet of salt.
GORGO: O, men are all the same, my Diocleidas
   Simply flings money away. He paid seven shillings,
   Just yesterday, for what's nothing but dog's combings,
   Five fleeces, he said! the shreddings of old bags,
   All utter trash – O, trouble upon trouble.

JACK LINDSAY (1929)

SERENADE

I am off to serenade Amaryllis, and my goats
Are cropping the high grass, Tityrus is minding them;
Tityrus, be a good fellow, let the goats graze,
Then drive them to the springs, Tityrus; but the he-goat,
The big buff Libyan, careful, or he'll butt you!

Sweet Amaryllis, why do you not await me,
Looking from your cave to call me? Do you hate me?
Or when you look at me close, is my nose so squat,
And bristly my beard? I shall hang myself, that's what!
But look, here are ten apples, I found a store
Just where you said, and tomorrow shall bring more.

O, do look out! Heartsick, I wish I were the bee
That, blundering, buzzes its way into your cave
Past the ivy, the fern that hide you from me!

Who Love is, now I know, harsh god, by sorrow:
Suckled by a lioness, bred in a forest shade:
His fire once kindled burns me to the marrow.

O bright and stony glancer from brows of night,
But once, to kiss me, come once to your goatherd's arms:
For even mere vain kisses hold delight.

You will make me tear my garland all to shreds –
The ivy-crown I wear for you, cruel lady,
Where rose-leaves twine with savoury parsley-threads.

(Alas, but what'll befall me? You do not listen at all.)

I will shed my shaggy jerkin and plunge beneath
The waves where the fishermen watch for the tunny-shoals;
And, if you want to, plume yourself on my death!

G. S. FRASER (1955)

APPEAL TO PRIAPUS, THE GOD OF SEX

Goatherd, when you turn the corner by the oaks
you'll see a freshly carved statue in fig wood.
The bark is not peeled off. It is legless, earless,
but strongly equipped with a dynamic phallus
to perform the labour of Aphrodite.
                    A holy hedge
runs around the precinct where a perennial brook
spills down from upper rocks and feeds a luxuriance
of bay, myrtle and fragrant cypress trees.

A grape vine pours its tendrils along a branch,
and spring blackbirds echo in pure transparency
of sound to high nightingales who echo back
with pungent honey.
                    Come, sit down, and beg Priapus

319

to end my love for Daphnis. Butcher a young goat
in sacrifice. If he will not, I make three vows:
I will slay a young cow, a shaggy goat and a darling
lamb I am raising. May God hear you and assent.

WILLIS BARNSTONE (1962)

LATE SUMMER

Many poplars and many elms shook overhead,
and close by, holy water swashed down noisily
from a cave of the nymphs. Brown grasshoppers
whistled busily through the dark foliage. Far
treetoads gobbled in the heavy thornbrake.

Larks and goldfinch sang, turtledoves were moaning,
and bumblebees whizzed over the plashing brook.

The earth smelled of rich summer and autumn fruit:
we were ankle-deep in pears, and apples rolled
all about our toes. With dark damson plums
the young sapling branches trailed on the ground.

WILLIS BARNSTONE (1962)

THYRSIS AND THE GOATHERD[1]

THYRSIS:
Listen. The pine
　　　　is whispering. You
with the goats, listen –
　　　　how the pine's
dim whisper over the pebbled
　　　　spring

1. An adaptation or imitation rather than a translation.

320

runs in stealth
        beside the current of your pipe,
the running notes
        that Pan only
can send it with lither
        motion: in skill
second to Pan
        you'll win, if his prize
is a goat bold-horned,
        a kid.

GOATHERD:
And you, shepherd –
        your song
is woven with more grace
        than that stream's braided fall
from rock ledge to rock
        basin:
you may take – after the Muses –
        what pleases you,
sheep or lamb.

THYRSIS:
        Go, sit
there on the hillside, there
        by the tamarisks
and play for me.
        Play, I will not let
your goats wander.

GOATHERD:
        I cannot
play. No –
        it is noon
I cannot play, I am afraid
        of Pan

the hunter coming at noon
           tired
out of the hills,
           anger corroding thin
patience.
           No, I cannot play,
but you, Thyrsis
           you know the song
of Daphnis
           his lament
and sing it best of shepherds.
           Let us sit
there under the elm by Priapus'
           water, there
under the oaks.
           And
if you sing
           as on that day
you sang against Chromis of Libya
           I shall give you
a goat (dam of twins) to milk
           three times,
two pails to each milking –
           a goat
and a cup
           of wood
lathe-smoothe
           rubbed with beeswax
rimmed top & bottom
           with ivy & gold honeysuckle:
between the two borders
           figured
in snood and full gown
           a woman –
beauty to startle gods' eyes
           – and each side
a man

322

fair-headed
wrangling to catch her ear
       & heart,
but no word
       nothing
holds her, she bends
       now toward one
laughing
       and now, laughing, bends
a brief glance
       on the other,
while they
       shadow-eyed
and taut under Love's hand
       live in barren
pain.
       And elsewhere
an old man on a scaly
       rock, an old fisherman
scoured to the bone by the grey sea
       casts his net, working
as hard, though an old
       man, as a man
could:
       the veins
swell on his neck,
       the muscles bunch, his strength
though an old man's
       worthy of youth.
And
       nearby
a small boy sits on the drystone wall
       that circles a vineyard,
his chore
       to guard the heavy
reddening grapes.
       Two

foxes have crept in, one trots
        up & down
the rows, eating its fill,
        the other starts in
on the boy's lunch
        but he
plaiting a cricket-cage out of reeds
        and the stalks of asphodel
is unaware
        of grapes or lunch
in boy's absorption.
        This cup
craft to bewilder eye & mind
        for which I gave
the ferryman (working the straits
        at Calydon)
a goat & a huge cheese,
        this cup
whose lip my
        lips have never touched
I shall give
        to you
if you sing the song I want.
        Remember
friend – you will remember
        no songs
when you are dead.

ANDREW MILLER (1969)

LEONIDAS

FROM Taras (Tarentum), early third century B.C.; a leading epi-grammatist of the Alexandrian era.

*

WATER

Traveller in the wilds, do not
Drink this roiled, muddy, warm water,
But go on over the hill where
The cows are grazing, and by the
Shepherds' pine you will find a
Murmuring spring, flowing from the
Rock, cold as snow on the North Wind.

KENNETH REXROTH (1962)

ANYTE

Arcadian poetess from Tegea, early third century B.C.

*

THE FOUNTAIN

I, Hermes, by the grey sea-shore
    Set where the three roads meet,
Outside the wind-swept garden,
    Give rest to weary feet;
    The waters of my fountain
    Are clear, and cool and sweet.

RENNELL RODD (1916)

DIOTIMUS

EPIGRAMMATIST, third century B.C.

*

DEATH BY LIGHTNING

The cattle in the evening found their way
Home through the snow themselves and reached the byre.
Therimachus, alas, touched by heaven's fire,
Remains by the oak on the hill for a longer day.

WILLIAM J. PHILBIN (1971)

CALLIMACHUS

MIGRATED from Cyrene to become the most famous poet of the Alexandrian school. *C.* 305–*c.* 240 B.C.

*

HERACLITUS

They told me, Heraclitus, they told me you were dead,
They brought me bitter news to hear and bitter tears to shed.
I wept as I remembered how often you and I
Had tired the sun with talking and sent him down the sky.

And now that thou art lying, my dear old Carian guest,
A handful of grey ashes, long, long ago at rest,
Still are thy pleasant voices, thy nightingales, awake;
For Death, he taketh all away, but them he cannot take.

WILLIAM CORY (1858)

HERACLITUS[1]

The brief words, Heraclitus, fell –
    Your death; and with them drew
Tears to my eyes; old memories thronged –
    How many times we two

Had sunk the tired-out sun beneath
    Our talk! – Dear friend of old,
And you there now in Caria – dust,
    A charred ash, ages cold.

But thy sweet voices are not dead,
    Those nightingales yet wake;

1. The same piece again: a less famous version, but a more faithful one.

328

Death with his clutch takes all away,
    But those he shall not take.

WALTER HEADLAM (1910)

I DETEST COMMON THINGS

I hate your hackneyed epic; have no taste
For roads where crowds hither and thither haste;
Loathe vagrant loves; and from the public springs
I drink not; I detest all common things.

R. A. FURNESS (1931)

APPEAL TO ZEUS

Hate him O Zeus if he hates me –
Theokritos, my Theokritos, deliciously bronzed –
Hate the boy four times as much as he hates me.

Heavenly Zeus, by Ganymede[1] I swear,
The goldenhaired,
You in your time have loved.

                I say no more.

DUDLEY FITTS (1957)

SHIPWRECKED SAILOR

Who are you, O shipwrecked stranger?
Leontichos found your corpse on the beach,
buried you in this grave
and cried thinking of his own hazardous life.
For he knows no rest:
he too roams over the sea like a gull.

WILLIS BARNSTONE (1962)

1. The beautiful cup-bearer of Zeus.

APOLLONIUS RHODIUS

So called because of his retirement to Rhodes from Egypt, where his *Argonautica* adapted the epic tradition to Alexandrian poetry. Born *c.* 295 B.C.

*

MEDEA AND JASON

Meanwhile the maid her secret thoughts enjoyed
And one dear object all her soul employed:
Her train's gay sports no pleasure can restore,
Vain was the dance, and music charmed no more;
She hates each object, every face offends,
In every wish her soul to Jason sends;
With sharpened eyes the distant lawn explores
To find the hero whom her soul adores;
At every whisper of the passing air,
She starts, she turns, and hopes her Jason there;
Again she fondly looks, nor looks in vain,
He comes, her Jason shines along the plain.
As when, emerging from the watery way,
Resurgent Sirius¹ lifts his golden ray,
He shines terrific! for his burning breath
Taints the red air with fevers, plagues and death;
Such to the nymph approaching Jason shows,
Bright author of unutterable woes;
Before her eyes a swimming darkness spread,
Her flushed cheeks glowed, her very heart was dead:
No more her knees their wonted office knew,
Fixed, without motion, as to earth they grew.
Her train recedes – the meeting lovers gaze

1. The dog star, described as the brightest star in the heavens.

In silent wonder, and in still amaze.
As two fair cedars on the mountain's brow,
Pride of the groves! with roots adjoining grow;
Erect and motionless the stately trees
Short time remain, while sleeps each fanning breeze,
Till from the Aeolian caves[1] a blast unbound
Bends their proud tops, and bids their boughs resound:
Thus gazing they; till by the breath of love,
Strongly at last inspired, they speak, they move;
With smiles the love-sick virgin he surveyed,
And fondly thus addressed the blooming maid:
   'Dismiss, my fair, my love, thy virgin fear;
'Tis Jason speaks, no enemy is here!
Dread not in me a haughty heart to find,
In Greece I bore no proud inhuman mind.
Whom would'st thou fly? Stay, lovely virgin, stay!
Speak every thought! far hence be fears away!
Speak! and be truth in every accent found!
Scorn to deceive! we tread on hallowed ground.
By the stern power who guards this sacred place,
By the famed authors of thy royal race;
By Jove, to whom the stranger's cause belongs,
To whom the suppliant, and who feels their wrongs;
O guard me, save me, in the needful hour!
Without thy aid thy Jason is no more.
To thee a suppliant, in distress I bend,
To thee a stranger, one who wants a friend!
Then, when between us seas and mountains rise,
Medea's name shall sound in distant skies;
All Greece to thee shall owe her heroes' fates,
And bless Medea through her hundred states.
The mother and the wife, who now in vain
Roll their sad eyes fast-streaming o'er the main,
Shall stay their tears: the mother, and the wife,
Shall bless thee for a son's or husband's life!'

FRANCIS FAWKES (1750)
1. This phrase is not in the original.

THE GOLDEN FLEECE

Along the path the sacred grove they sought,
Where towered the beech, with fleecy treasure fraught,
They see the plant its giant arms unfold,
And bright between appears the pendant gold,
Like flaming clouds, with curling radiance bright,
That blush illumined by the dawning light.
The watchful dragon, that the fleece defends,
A length immense his waving neck extends.
Onward the lovers move; his eyeballs flame,
And direful hissings their advance proclaim.
Baleful and shrill was that ill-omened sound;
The extended shores re-echoed all around.
They heard, who, far from Titanian strand,
Plough the wide limits of the Colchian land;[1]
Where Lycus from Araxes loud divides,
And joys, with Phasis mixed, to roll his sacred tides.[2]
Scared by the noise, the mothers start from rest,
And press their new-born infants to the breast.
From burning woods ascending to the pole,
As globes of smoke in fiery volumes roll,
Cloud urges cloud, the incessant vapours rise,
Enormous wreaths, and whirl along the skies;
The monster huge impelled his countless spires,
O'erlaid with scales, that shone like distant fires.
Onward he laboured with tremendous sway;
The maid advanced, and stood athwart his way.
With softest sweetest notes she called a power,
Bland, but sufficient in that dangerous hour;
With warbled strain she called the god of sleep,
In Lethe's dew those watchful eyes to steep:
Yet more she summons from beneath the ground,
The queen revered in shades of night profound.

1. 'From Titanian Aea' in the original, Aea being a city of Colchis (north-east corner of the Black Sea), the home of Medea.
2. These are rivers of the area.

'Rise, awful Hecate,[1] propitious power,
Aid the bold purpose of this fatal hour!'
Brave as he was, and oft in perils tried,
With faltering steps the youth pursued his guide.
   Now wrought the mystic charm with potent sway.
Entranced, dissolved, the dreadful monster lay,
With spine relaxed, extended o'er the plain,
In orbs diffuse uncoiled his scaly train.
When breezes fill the expansive sail no more,
And not a wave is heard to lash the shore,
In placid silence thus the billows sleep,
And languid curls are spread along the deep.
Yet still aloft his horrid head he reared,
And still in act to close his jaws appeared
With dreadful menace. But the nymph displayed
A mystic bough, cut from the sacred shade,
A branch of juniper in drugs bedewed,
With potency by magic spell imbued.
Melodious charm her tuneful voice applies;
She waves her opiate o'er the monster's eyes.
Diffused around narcotic vapour flows;
The dragon sinks subdued in deep repose,
Unmoving, harmless as the silent dead;
His gaping jaws were fixed, he hung his head;
And spreading like some vast meandering flood,
His powerless volumes stretched along the wood.
Exhorted by the maid, without delay,
The youth approached the tree to seize the prey;
While, near the dragon fixed, the intrepid maid
O'er his dire head the flattering unction laid.
She waited thus unmoved and unappalled,
Till to the ship the youth her steps recalled,
When now departing from the sacred grove,
He gave the sign of safety and of love.
   As when, exulting in reflected light,
The full-orbed moon displays the torch of night;

1. Goddess of the underworld.

Some maid delighted sees the splendour fall
On the high ceiling, or the chamber wall;
Around she sees the circling lustre dance,
And spreads her veil to catch the illusive glance;
So joyed the youthful hero to behold
The light reflected from the fleece of gold;
While as he bore the glorious prize on high,
The ruddy splendours lightened to the sky.
O'er his fresh cheek the fiery lustre beams,
The radiance on his front of ivory streams.
That fleece was ample as an heifer's hide,
Or skin of hinds, that in Achaia bide;
So large it spread with the metallic freight,
Of golden locks that curled, enormous weight.
The rays were darted round so bright and strong,
The path seemed gilded as he strode along.
O'er his broad shoulders now the treasure flung,
Descending ponderous to his footsteps hung;
Now in his hands the precious fleece he holds,
And turns with anxious care the shining folds;
While round his eyes are glanced with jealous fear,
Lest god or mortal should the conquest bear.

W. PRESTON (1803)

THE SAILING OF THE ARGO

As boys begin their dancing to Apollo
At Pytho or Quail Island or the fount
Ismenus;[1] there to the sound
Of lyre's concent around his hearth they follow
Their rapid measure, the feet stamping the ground;
So now to Orpheus' lute the oarsmen urge
The rushing water with oars, until the surge
Covers their blades awash.

1. Delphi, Delos or Boeotia.

All ways the dark salt sea boils in an eddy
Of roaring foam that oarsmen's strength pulls steady.
Like flames their weapons in the sunshine flash
As the ship moves, her wake a long bright line
As white as path seen cutting the greensward.
This day the gods in heaven all regard
The ship and strength of heroes half divine,
Men in their time the best that sailed the sea.
And there upon the mountain tops amazed
The nymphs of Pelion gazed
At this, Athene's work in Thessaly,
The ship, the heroes plying hand to oar;
And Chiron son of Philyra[1] descends
From his high peak to where the sea inshore
Breaks in white foam; he wades in it, and tarries
Often waving his sturdy hand, invoking
Godspeed and good returning for his friends.

GEORGE ALLEN (1938)

MEDEA'S PASSION FOR JASON (cf. p. 330)

... With torment, the heart in her was tossed.
As round a room the sunlight flickers from the face
Of water in pail or cauldron poured – in endless chase
Headlong hither and thither its sparkles wheel and whirl;
So leapt her heart, and quivered, in the bosom of the girl.
With pitying tears her eyes grew wet; and all her frame
Shuddered with inward anguish as with a smouldering flame.
Through each fine nerve, through the meeting of head and nape, it
    pressed
(For there the ache is keenest, when the Loves that know not rest,
Let loose upon men's hearts the arrows of their pain).
Now she resolved to reveal him her magic – now again

1. The only Centaur who was wise and kind. His father was Cronos, and
he was the teacher of Achilles.

Resolved she would not give it; but die herself as well –
Then vowed she would neither perish nor yet bestow the spell,
But still endure to the end, dumb though infatuate.
So down she sat and said, her soul torn with debate:
'Ah, wretch! To what choice of evils must I turn me in my grief?
Whatever I do, my spirit fails, nor finds relief.
Nothing can quench its fever. Ah, would that Artemis
With the swiftness of her arrows had struck me down ere this! –
Or ever I looked on Jason, or the sons of Chalciope[1]
Set foot on the coasts of Achaea! To bring us misery
Some God, or some Erinys,[2] has sent them here again.
Nay then, let Jason perish, if destiny ordain
His death in the field of Ares! If I fashion him the spell,
How hide it from my parents? What story can I tell?
What stratagem can save him from being overthrown?
Can I meet him without his comrades? – can I go to him alone?
Ah bitter, although he perish, e'en then what hope have I
Of respite from unhappiness? – though he should die,
His memory will haunt me still. Nay now, have done
With shame, have done with honour! Once that my hand has won
His life, let him sail in safety – wherever he would be!
And then, his quest accomplished, let *that* day bring to me
Death! – no matter whether from a beam of the roof I sway,
Throat in a noose; or swallow some poison swift to slay.
And yet, although I perish so, they will heap my name
With insults – ay, every city shall shout aloud my shame,
Through many a land! And here, from tongue to taunting tongue
Of all the Colchian women, shall my ill fame be flung –
"A girl that in her passion for a stranger's foreign face
Died covering her parents and her home with black disgrace,
A lewd and blinded wanton!" What scorn must I not bear!
Ay me for this infatuate heart! Better it were
This night in my maiden chamber should make an end of me,

1. The half-sister of Medea. Her four sons, shipwrecked, were rescued by Jason and the Argonauts.
2. Fury.

Dead none knows how, delivered from all their calumny,
Rather than such dishonour – too foul for lips to say.'
With that she sought, arising, a casket wherein lay
Her many drugs – some healing, and some of deadly bane,
And on her knees she set it down, while in her pain
For the fate now came upon her, her tears streamed on unstayed,
Till wet grew all her bosom.

F. L. LUCAS (1951)

WRITER of poetic, literary mimes; third century B.C.

*

MOTHER TO SCHOOLMASTER

METROTIME:

As you desire the Muses to be friendly,
Lampriscos, as you hope to savour life,
please hoist this wicked boy and thrash away
until his soul (god curse it) 's but one thread
of feeble breath between his lips. This boy
has knocked the roof clean off my wretched head
with playing pitch- &-toss! for knucklebones,
Lampriscos, wouldn't satisfy his whim,
but every day he's getting worse and worse.
He couldn't tell me how to find the way
to where his writing-master lives; and yet,
pat on the cruel thirtieth of the month,
in comes the bill. The only road he knows
is that which leads him to the gambling den,
the bolthole of deserting slaves and touts . . .
yes, well enough he knows it to lead others
the same bad way. His slighted writing-tablet,
which every month I take such care to wax,
is left to lie forgotten against the wall
under his bed . . . unless he scowls in rage
as though it were his death and scrapes it bare
instead of writing on it; but his satchel
always holds knucklebones far glossier
than even the oilflask which we use each day.
Why, the first letter of the alphabet's

a blank to him, unless you've shouted it
some half-a-dozen times. Two days ago
his father tried him with some easy spelling . . .
Maron he said; and this fine fellow here
wrote Simon down. O how I felt a fool
that I'd not had him set to feeding asses
rather than learning letters in the hope
I'd have a good support for my old age.
And when he's asked, like any other scholar,
by me, or by his father (who, I may mention,
is slightly old, and dim in eye and ear)
well, when we merely ask him to oblige us
with some choice piece of tragic recitation,
then he lets dribble out in stuttering phrases
from his sieved mind, O *Phoibos*[1] . . . *Lord* . . . *of Hunting* . . .
What's this? say I, you hopeless ignoramus,
why, your own grandmama could tell you that,
though she has never had an education,
or any Phrygian slave you chanced to meet.
And if we lift our voices in reproof,
either he won't come home for three whole days,
goes gallivanting to his grandma's cottage
and eats the poor old lady, who's so poor,
out of her house and home; or else he squats
perched on our rooftree, jiggling out his legs,
and peers down, like a monkey, while we plead.
Can you imagine how I feel inside,
poor me! when I stand there below and watch him;
and yet it is not only that he hurts me,
he smashes up the tiles like brittle biscuits;
and when the winter comes I have to pay
three good hemaitha[2] for each broken tile,
despite my tears . . . since the whole tenement
says: It was Cottalos that broke the tiles,
the son of Metrotime. And it's true;

1. Apollo.
2. A currency denomination: half an obol.

and so we're hardly able to buy food
to save our teeth from rotting with no use.
Just look now at the grime upon his clothes!
he got like that from wandering in the woods.
You'd think he was some Delian fisherlad
dragging a weary life out on the sea;
and yet he knows when holidays are near,
the sevenths and the twentieths of the month,
better than any old astronomer.

JACK LINDSAY (1929)

THE MATCH-MAKER

GYLLIS:
No, child. It's time to wonder:
how much longer are you going to be a widow,
all alone, wearing out a lonely bed?
Ten months ago your fellow sailed to Egypt,
and he hasn't sent you a word since.
No. He's forgotten. He's drunk from a new jug.

It's the House of Aphrodite, Egypt is,
what with everything there and more to follow.
Wealth, sports, power, peace, fame,
shows, philosophers, gold, boys,
the Holy Royal Grounds, a good king,
the Museum, wine, all the good things,
all you could want;
more women, I swear, than the stars
the sky claims to carry,
and for looks like the goddesses
that once upon a time ran to Paris to have him judge their beauty.
I hope They don't hear me.

Poor dear! What's wrong with you?
Why be a bench-warmer?

You'll get old before you know it,
and ashes will swallow your bloom.
Look around. Three days or two can change your view.
Cheer up. Look for another man.
A ship with one cable is anchored unstable.
If Death comes, there's no one to raise us up again,
far from it!
Winter is wild, it swoops down and blows terrible,
and none of us knows the future.
Wretched humanity lives in uncertainty.
But . . .
is anyone around?

METRICHE:

No one.

GYLLIS:

Then listen. Here's what I came to tell you:
Gryllas, son of Pataikios and Matakine,
winner in five events,
one at the Pythians in the Junior Class,
twice in Corinth in the Youth Class,
and at Pisa twice in the Men's Boxing,[1]
by knockouts;
nice and rich;
so gentle a stepper he doesn't jiggle a twig;
and as for love, a seal intact!

RICHARD BRAUN (1963)

1. i.e. in the Pythian, Isthmian and Olympic Games.

MOSCHUS

BORN at Syracuse; wrote *c.* 150 B.C. Pastoral and erotic poet.

*

SEA AND LAND

When a smooth wind runs on the far green sea,
This coward thought of mine feels pleasantly,
And lost to poetry itself, can lie
Wrapt in a wistful quietness of eye.
But when the deeps are moved, and the waves come
Shuddering along, and tumbling into foam,
I turn to earth, which trusty seems, and staid,
And love to get into a green wood shade;
In which the pines, although the winds be strong,
Can turn the bluster to a sylvan song.
A wretched life a fisherman's must be,
His home a ship, his labour in the sea,
And fish, the slippery object of his gain: –
I love a sleep under a leafy plane,
And a low fountain coiling in mine ear,
Which fills the soul with smiling, not with fear.

LEIGH HUNT (1816)

SEA AND LAND[1]

When winds that move not its calm surface sweep
The azure sea, I love the land no more;
The smiles of the serene and tranquil deep
Tempt my unquiet mind. – But when the roar

1. The same piece.

342

Of Ocean's grey abyss resounds, and foam
Gathers upon the sea, and vast waves burst,
I turn from the drear aspect to the home
Of Earth and its deep woods, where, interspersed,
When winds blow loud, pines make sweet melody.
Whose house is some lone bark, whose toil the sea,
Whose prey the wandering fish, an evil lot
Has chosen. – But I my languid limbs will fling
Beneath the plane, where the brook's murmuring
Moves the calm spirit, but disturbs it not.

PERCY BYSSHE SHELLEY (1816)

BION

BORN at Phlossa, near Smyrna; wrote *c.* 100 B.C. Writer of erotic and moralizing poems, sometimes with a pastoral note. The *Lament for Adonis* is conjecturally attributed to him.

*

LAMENT FOR ADONIS[1]

I mourn Adonis. *Lovely Adonis is dead,*
lovely Adonis . . . dead the Loves respond in mourning.

Sleep no more, Cypris, in crimson blankets –
wake up in sadness, dark-robed,
beat your breasts, tell everyone *lovely Adonis is dead* –
I mourn Adonis,
        the Loves respond in mourning.

Adonis the lovely lies in the mountains,
his thigh tusk-gored,
        the white tusk piercing the white,
wounding Cypris with the light
breathing-out of his life.
        The dark blood drips
over his skin of snow,
his eyeballs stiffen, the rose
fades from his lips,
        and on them also the kiss
which Cypris cannot recover dies.
To kiss him even when dead
humours her now, though he remains
unconscious of that dying kiss.

1. The son of Cinyras; beloved of Aphrodite (Cypris, Cytherea); an eastern divinity of fertility and vegetation.

I mourn Adonis,
        the Loves respond in mourning.

Brutal, brutal the wound in his thigh, but
worse the wound Cytherea holds in her heart.
His faithful pack stand baying around him,
the mountain nymphs are weeping.
                Desolate, barefoot
Aphrodite wanders the woods,
hair unbraided, dishevelled.
            As she runs, brambles
cut her so that she bleeds; screaming
she crosses the glens,
        calling out
for her Syrian husband, her lover.

The blood spouts over his navel,
Purples his chest, his nipples
                  (snow-white before).
Alas Cytherea the Loves respond in mourning.
Her lover – lost. And her beauty,
so perfect while he was alive
              – dead with him.
Cypris alas the mountains all say
and *ah* the oaktrees *Adonis*.
Rivers grieve for Aphrodite's affliction,
mountain springs weep for Adonis,
flowers blush in distress. Cytherea
sings piteously over her slopes and glens
alas Cytherea,
        lovely Adonis is dead
and Echo returns *lovely Adonis is dead*.
Who'd not have wept *alas*
            for Cypris's pitiful love?

Seeing his incurable wound, the deathly
blood round his wasting thigh,
she spread her arms, weeping

345

'Wait, Adonis, poor darling,
              wait till I'm with you
'holding you for the last time,
              our lips together . . .
'Wake up a while, Adonis,
              kiss me once
'more, for the last
              lifetime of a kiss . . .
'till you expire in my mouth
              and your spirit
'flows into my heart,
              and I have milked your sweet
'charms and drained your love . . .
              and oh I will treasure
'that kiss as your very self,
              Adonis, now that
'you're leaving me, poor thing,
              leaving for so
'long, my Adonis,
              plunged towards Acheron
'to the brutal & merciless king,
              while I remain
'a goddess trapped miserably in life,
              unable to follow.
'Take him, Persephone, take
              my husband. – Since you are
'stronger than me by far,
              and everything lovely
'slips to you.
              Inexhaustible anguish and pain
' & fear of you make me cry
              to my Adonis, my dead one . . .
'Dying, my most longed-for love,
              my longing, gone like a dream,
'Cytherea a widow, the Loves
              useless in her home,
'her charmed girdle destroyed?

Hunting . . . you went . . .
'oh why?
So lovely, yet mad enough
'to taunt . . . beasts?'

So Cypris moaned. The Loves respond in mourning
alas Cytherea, lovely Adonis is dead.

She weeps, Adonis bleeds,
drop matching drop.
On the ground both blood and tears
turn into flowers –
the blood bears a rose,
teardrops the anemone.
I mourn Adonis. *Lovely Adonis is dead*.

Stop mourning him in the woods, Cypris.
Leaves make a poor death-bed for Adonis.
Lend him your bed, Cytherea, even in death –
even dead he is lovely,
lovely in death
as if he was sleeping.
Wrap him in soft blankets on the gold bed
where he spent his nights sleeping with you –
the lack of his presence is felt there.
Throw garlands and flowers on him. Let them all,
let all the flowers die his death.
Pour Syrian oils and perfumes over him. –
Let all fragrance perish –
Adonis your balm is dead.

There he lies in crimson shrouds,
fragile Adonis.
Around him, locks clipped for his sake,
the Loves raise their lament.
One threw his arrows,
another a bow, one a feather, a quiver on him.

One took off Adonis's shoes; others fetch water
in a gold basin,
        another washes his thighs –
one fans Adonis behind with his wings.
Alas Cytherea the Loves respond in mourning.

Hymenaeus has put out the torches.
Darkness at every door
        and the wedding garlands dismantled.
Hymen is his refrain no more,
        he is chanting
alas and *Adonis* in place of the wedding-song.
Among themselves the Graces lament
        with *dead, lovely Adonis*
– mourning Cinyras' son with cries
        sharper than any Paean.
Even the Fates call Adonis,
        call him back with their spells;
but there is no answer,
        no reprieve,
not from his lack of will
        but the Maiden's.

Leave off your mourning, Cypris,
stop hurting yourself for today.

You face another year yet of weeping.

PETER JAY (1970)

ANTIPATER OF SIDON

EPIGRAMMATIST, wrote *c.* 120 B.C.

*

EPITAPH FOR ANACREON

Let the four-leaved ivy spread
Where Anacreon[1] may lie,
Let flowers raise their purple head,
Let milk foam to the sky,
Let wine spill from his ashy bed
To show joy cannot die,
To show delight can touch the dead –
Or must it pass them by?

ANDREW SINCLAIR (1967)

1. See above, p. 79.

MELEAGER

POET and philosopher, *c.* 100 B.C. Born at Gadara in Syria, lived in Tyre, retired to Cos. His *Garland* was the first large critical selection of poetic epigrams.[1]

FLOWERS FOR HELIODORA

White violets I'll bring
And soft narcissus
And myrtle and laughing lilies
The innocent crocus
Dark hyacinth also
And roses heavy with love

And these I'll twine for Heliodora
And scatter the bright petals on her hair.

DUDLEY FITTS (1957)

*

ON THE LAKE OF LOVE

Asklepias adores making love. She gazes at a man,
her aquamarine eyes calm like the summer seas,
and persuades him to go boating on the lake of love.

WILLIS BARNSTONE (1962)

1. Another talented Gadarene poet, writing in the middle of the first century B.C., was Philodemus; cf. Michael Grant, *Cities of Vesuvius*, Weidenfeld & Nicolson, London, 1971, pp. 109, 125, 138, 208 and 210.

ANONYMOUS[1]

THE UNGENTLE GUEST

Cupid abroad was lated in the night;
His wings were wet with ranging in the rain:
Harbour he sought, to me he took his flight,
To dry his plumes: I heard the boy complain;
    I oped the door, and granted his desire;
    I rose myself, and made the wag a fire.

Prying more narrow by the fire's flame,
I spied his quiver hanging at his back:
Doubting the boy might my misfortune frame,
I would have gone for fear of further wrack;
    But what I fear'd, did me, poor wretch, betide,
    For forth he drew an arrow from his side.

He pierced the quick, and I began to start;
A pleasing wound, but that it was too high:
His shaft procured a sharp, yet sugar'd smart:
Away he flew, for now his wings were dry;
    But left the arrow sticking in my breast,
    That sore I grieve I welcomed such a guest.

ROBERT GREENE (1589)

TO THE SWALLOW

Gentle Swallow, thou we know
Every year dost come and go,

1. The next five poems are traditionally classified as 'Anacreontea', but were written centuries after Anacreon (p. 79). These early versions by Greene, Stanley and Cowley are imitations rather than translations.

In the Spring thy nest thou mak'st;
In the Winter it forsak'st,
And divert'st thy self awhile
Near the Memphian Towers, or Nile;
But Love in my suffering breast
Builds, and never quits his nest;
First one Love's hatched; when that flies,
In the shell another lies;
Then a third is half exposed;
Then a whole brood is disclosed,
Which for meat still peeping cry,
Whilst the others that can fly
Do their callow brethren feed,
And grown up, they young ones breed.
What then will become of me,
Bound to pain incessantly,
Whilst so many loves conspire
On my heart by turns to tire!

THOMAS STANLEY (1651)

THIRST

Fruitful earth drinks up the rain;
Trees from earth drink that again;
The sea drinks the air, the sun
Drinks the sea, and him the moon –
Is it reason then, d'ye think,
I should thirst when all else drink?

THOMAS STANLEY (1651)

THE PLEASURES OF WINE

When my sense in wine I steep,
All my cares are lulled asleep:

Rich in thought, I then despise
Croesus, and his royalties;
Whilst with ivy twines I wreathe me
And sing all the world beneath me.
Others run to martial fights,
I to Bacchus's delights;
Fill the cup then, boy, for I
Drunk than dead had rather lie.

THOMAS STANLEY (1651)

POOR ANACREON

Oft am I by the women told,
'Poor Anacreon, thou grow'st old,
Look how hairs are falling all;
Poor Anacreon, how they fall.'
Whether I grow old or no,
By the effects I do not know:
This I know, without being told,
'Tis time to live if I grow old;
'Tis time short pleasures now to take,
Of little life the best to make,
And manage wisely the last stake.

ABRAHAM COWLEY (1683)

LOVERS OF BOYS

Brainsick boy-lovers, rid your fruitless pain
And stay your toil; we rave, we hope in vain.
To drain the sea to dryness, or in our hands
To number the molecules of the Libyan sands –
That's love of boys; though man and God they cheat
With their vainglorious beauty seeming-sweet.

Look all of you on me, how my long toil
Is idly scattered on a barren soil.

R. A. FURNESS (1931)

THE DETERMINED SERENADER

Boy, hold my wreath for me.
The night is black,
                    the path is long,
And I am completely and beautifully drunk.
Nevertheless I will go
To Themison's house and sing beneath his window.
You need not come with me:
                    Though I may stumble,
He is a steady lamp for the feet of love.

DUDLEY FITTS (1957)

PART VII

HISTORY AND CRITICISM IN HELLENISTIC AND ROMAN IMPERIAL TIMES

POLYBIUS

BORN at Megalopolis in Arcadia; *c.* 200 – after 118 B.C. The first important universal historian: chronicler of the rise of Rome to world power.

*

ATTACK ON THE HISTORIAN
PHYLARCHUS[1]

Since, among those writers who were contemporary with Aratus,[2] Phylarchus is accepted as trustworthy by some, and the opinions of the two authors are opposed in many points and their statements contradictory, and since I follow Aratus in my account of the Cleomenic war,[3] it will be advantageous, or rather necessary, for me to go into the question, and not by any neglect on my part to suffer misstatements in historical writings to enjoy an authority equal to that of truth. The fact is that Phylarchus has, throughout the whole of his history, made statements at random and without discrimination. It is not, however, necessary for me to criticize him on other points on the present occasion, or to call him to strict account concerning them; but such of his statements as relate to the period which I have now in hand, that is the Cleomenic war – these I must thoroughly sift. They will be quite sufficient to enable us to form a judgement on the general spirit and character of his historical writing. It was his object to bring into prominence the cruelty of Antigonus and the Macedonians, as well as

1. Phylarchus of Athens was the most important historian of the middle period of the third century B.C.
2. Aratus of Sicyon (271–213 B.C.), the principal spokesman of the Achaean League (based on Achaea, northern Peloponnese).
3. Cleomenes III of Sparta (*c.* 260–219 B.C.) provoked the Achaean League into war (228) and captured Mantinea in Arcadia.

that of Aratus and the Achaeans; and he accordingly asserts that, when Mantinea fell into their hands, it was cruelly treated, and that the most ancient and important of all the Arcadian towns was involved in calamities so terrible as to move all Greece to horror and tears. And, being eager to stir the hearts of his readers to pity, and to enlist their sympathies by his story, he talks of women embracing, tearing their hair, and exposing their breasts, and again of the tears and lamentations of men and women led off into captivity along with their children and aged parents. And this he does again and again throughout his whole history, by way of bringing the terrible scene vividly before his readers.

I say nothing of the unworthiness and unmanliness of the course Phylarchus has adopted; let us only inquire what is essential and to the purpose in history. Surely a historian's object should not be to amaze his readers by a series of thrilling anecdotes; nor should he seek after men's probable speeches, nor enumerate the possible consequences of the events under consideration, like a writer of tragedy; but his function is above all to record with fidelity what was actually said or done, however commonplace it may be. For the purposes of history and tragedy are not the same, but widely opposed to each other. In the latter the object is to thrill and delight the audience for the moment by words true to nature, in the former to instruct and convince serious students for all time by genuine words and deeds. In the latter, again, the power of beguiling an audience is the chief excellence, because the object is to create illusion; but in the former the thing of primary importance is truth, because the object is to benefit the learner.

And apart from these considerations, Phylarchus, in most of the catastrophes which he relates, omits to suggest the causes which give rise to them, or the course of events which led up to them; and without knowing these it is impossible to feel the due indignation or pity at anything which occurs. For instance, everybody looks upon it as an outrage that the free should be beaten; still, if a man provokes it by an act of violence, he is considered to have got no more than he deserved, and, where it is done for correction and discipline, those who strike free men are deemed worthy of honour and gratitude. Again, the killing of a citizen is regarded as a most heinous crime, deserving the highest penalty; and yet it is notorious that the man who kills a thief or adulterer is held guiltless, while he who kills a traitor or tyrant in every country receives honours and pre-eminence. And so in everything our final judgement does not depend upon the mere things done, but upon their causes and the views of the actors, according as these differ.

E. S. SHUCKBURGH (1889)

THE NOVELTY OF UNIVERSAL HISTORY

Had the praise of history been passed over by former chroniclers it would perhaps have been incumbent upon me to urge the choice and special study of histories of this sort, as knowledge of the past is the readiest means men can have of correcting their conduct. But my predecessors have not been sparing in this respect. They have all begun and ended, so to speak, by enlarging on this theme: asserting again and again that the study of history is in the truest sense an education, and a training for political life; and that the most instructive, or rather the only, method of learning to bear with dignity the vicissitudes of Fortune is to recall the catastrophes of others. It is evident, therefore, that no one need think it his duty to repeat what has been said by many, and said well. Least of all myself, for the surprising nature of the events which I have undertaken to relate is in itself sufficient to challenge and stimulate the attention of everyone, old or young, to the study of my work. Can anyone be so indifferent or idle as not to care to know by what means, and under what kind of polity, almost the whole inhabited world was conquered and brought under the single dominion of the Romans, and that too within a period of not quite fifty-three years? Or who again can be so completely absorbed in other subjects of contemplation or study as to think any of them superior in importance to the accurate understanding of an event for which the past offers no precedent?

We shall best show how marvellous and vast our subject is by comparing the most famous empires which preceded and which have been the favourite themes of historians, and measuring them with the superior greatness of Rome. Those that deserve to be so compared and measured are the following. The Persians for a certain length of time were possessed of a great empire and dominion. But every time they ventured beyond the limits of Asia, they found not only their empire but their own existence also in danger. The Lacedaemonians,[1] after contending for supremacy in Greece for many generations, when they did get it, held it without dispute for barely twelve years. The Macedonians obtained dominion in Europe from the lands bordering on the Adriatic to the Danube – which after all is but a small fraction of this continent – and, by the destruction of the Persian Empire,[2] they afterwards added to that the dominion of Asia. And yet, though they had the credit of having made themselves masters of a larger number of countries and states than any people had ever done, they still left the greater half of the inhabited world in the hands of others. They never so much as thought of attempting Sicily, Sardinia or Libya; and as to Europe, to speak the plain truth, they never even knew of the most warlike tribes of the West. The Roman conquest, on the other hand, was not partial. Nearly the whole inhabited world was reduced by them to obedience, and they left behind them an empire not to be paralleled in the past or rivalled in the future. Students will gain from my narrative a clearer view of the whole story, and of the numerous and important advantages which such exact record of events offers.

My *History* begins in the 140th Olympiad (220–217 B.C.). The events from which it starts are these. In Greece, what is called the Social War: the first waged by Philip,[3] son of Demetrius and father of Perseus, in league with the Achaeans against the Aetolians. In Asia, the war for the possession of Coele Syria which Antiochus and Ptolemy Philopator carried on against each other.[4] In Italy, Libya and their neighbourhood, the conflict between Rome and Carthage, generally called the Hannibalic War.[5] My work thus begins where that of Aratus of Sicyon leaves off. Now up to this time the world's history had been, so to speak, a series of disconnected transactions, as widely

1. The Spartans.
2. By Alexander the Great (334–330 B.C.).
3. Philip V of Macedon (238–179 B.C.).
4. Southern Syria was contested by the Seleucid Antiochus III (c. 242–178 B.C.) and the Lagid Ptolemy IV (c. 244–205 B.C.).
5. The Second Punic War (218–201 B.C.).

History of Timaeus left off;[1] and it falls in the 129th Olympiad (264–261 B.C.). I shall accordingly have to describe what the state of their affairs in Italy was, how long that settlement had lasted, and on what resources they reckoned when they resolved to invade Sicily. For this was the first place outside Italy in which they set foot. The precise cause of their thus crossing I must state without comment; for if I let one cause lead me back to another, my point of departure will always elude my grasp, and I shall never arrive at the view of the subject which I wish to present. As to dates, then, I must fix on some era agreed upon and recognized by all; and as to events, one that is self-evident, even though I may be obliged to go back some short way in point of time, and take a summary review of the inter- mediate transactions. For if the facts with which one starts are un- known, or even open to controversy, all that comes after will fail of approval and belief. But opinion being once formed on that point, and a general assent obtained, all the succeeding narrative becomes acceptable.

E. S. SHUCKBURGH (1889)

ROMAN RELIGION AND MORALITY

But the most important difference for the better which the Roman commonwealth appears to me to display is in their religious beliefs.[2] For I conceive that what in other nations is looked upon as a reproach, I mean superstition, is the very thing which keeps the Roman commonwealth together. To such an extraordinary height is this carried among them, both in private and public business, that nothing could exceed it. Many people might think this unaccountable, but in my opinion their object is to use it as a check upon the common people. If it were possible to form a state wholly of philosophers, such a custom would perhaps be unnecessary. But seeing that every multitude is fickle, and full of lawless desires, unreasoning anger and

1. Timaeus of Tauromenium (*c.* 356–260 B.C.) wrote primarily about his native Sicily.

2. Polybius has been favourably comparing the institutions of the Romans with those of the Carthaginians.

violent passion, the only resource is to keep them in check by mysterious terrors and scenic effects of this sort. Wherefore, to my mind, the ancients were not acting without purpose or at random when they brought in among the vulgar those opinions about the gods and the belief in the punishments in Hades; much rather do I think that men nowadays are acting rashly and foolishly in rejecting them. This is the reason why, apart from anything else, Greek statesmen if entrusted with a single talent, though protected by ten checking-clerks, as many seals, and twice as many witnesses, yet cannot be induced to keep faith; whereas among the Romans, in their magistracies and embassies, men have the handling of a great amount of money, and yet from pure respect of their oath keep their faith intact. And again in other nations it is a rare thing to find a man who keeps his hands out of the public purse and is entirely pure in such matters, but among the Romans it is a rare thing to detect a man in the act of committing such a crime. ...

E. S. SHUCKBURGH (1889)

THE CONSTITUTIONS OF GREEK CITY-STATES

Nearly all historians have recorded as constitutions of eminent excellence those of Lacedaemon [Sparta], Crete, Mantinea and Carthage. Some have also mentioned those of Athens and Thebes. The former I may allow to pass, but I am convinced that little need be said of the Athenian and Theban constitutions: their growth was abnormal, the period of their zenith brief, and the changes they experienced unusually violent. Their glory was a sudden and fortuitous flash, so to speak; and while they still thought themselves prosperous, and likely to remain so, they found themselves involved in circumstances completely the reverse. The Thebans got their reputation for valour among the Greeks by taking advantage of the senseless policy of the Lacedaemonians and the hatred of the allies towards them, owing to the valour of their leaders which gave the Thebans their success. For the great power of Thebes notoriously took its rise, attained its zenith, and fell to the ground with the lives of Epaminondas and

Pelopidas.[1] We must therefore conclude that it was not its constitution but its men that caused the high fortune which it then enjoyed.

A somewhat similar remark applies to the Athenians' constitution also. For though it perhaps had more frequent interludes of excellence, yet its highest perfection was attained during the brilliant career of Themistocles,[2] and having reached that point it quickly declined, owing to their essential instability. For the Athenian people is always in the position of a ship without a commander. In such a ship, if fear of the waves or the occurrence of a storm induce the crew to be of one mind and to obey the helmsman, they do their duty; but if they recover from this fear, and begin to treat their officers with contempt, and to quarrel with each other because they are no longer all of one mind – one party wishing to continue the voyage, and the other urging the steersman to bring the ship to anchor, some letting out the sheets, and others hauling them in and ordering the sails to be furled – their discord and quarrels make a sorry show to lookers-on; and the position of affairs is full of risk to those on board engaged on the same voyage; the result has often been that, after escaping the dangers of the widest seas and the most violent storms, they wreck their ship in harbour and close to shore. And this is what has often happened to the Athenian state. For, after repelling on various occasions the greatest and most formidable dangers by the valour of the people and their leaders, there have been times when, in periods of secure tranquillity, it has gratuitously and recklessly encountered disaster. Therefore I need say no more about either it or the Theban constitution, in both of which a mob manages everything on its own unfettered impulse – a mob in the one city distinguished for headlong outbursts of fiery temper, in the other trained in long habits of violence and ferocity.

Passing to the Cretan polity, there are two points which deserve our consideration. The first is how such writers as Ephorus, Xenophon, Callisthenes and Plato[3] – who are the most learned of the ancients –

1. These heroes of the short-lived supremacy of Thebes died in 362 and 364 B.C. respectively.

2. Themistocles (c. 528–462 B.C.) defeated the Persians at Salamis (p. 194).

3. Ephorus of Cyme (c. 405–330 B.C.) wrote a universal history, and Callis-

assert that it was like that of Sparta, and secondly how they came to assert that it was all admirable. I can agree with neither assertion; and I will explain why I say so. And first as to its dissimilarity with the Spartan constitution. The peculiar merit of the latter is said to be its land laws, by which no one possesses more than another, but all citizens have an equal share in the public land. The next distinctive feature regards the acquisition of money: for as it is utterly discredited among them, the jealous competition which arises from inequality of wealth is entirely removed from the city. A third peculiarity of the Lacedaemonian polity is that, of the officials by whose hands and with whose advice the whole government is conducted, the kings hold an hereditary office, while the members of the Gerusia[1] are elected for life.

Among the Cretans the exact reverse of all these arrangements obtains. The laws allow them to possess as much land as they can get with no limitation whatever. Money is so highly valued among them that its possession is thought not only to be necessary but in the highest degree creditable. And in fact greed and avarice are so native to the soil in Crete that they are the only people in the world among whom no stigma attaches to any sort of gain whatever. Again, all their offices are annual and on a democratic footing. I have therefore often felt at a loss to account for these writers speaking of the two constitutions, which are radically different, as though they were closely united and allied. But, besides overlooking these important differences, these writers have gone out of their way to comment at length on the legislation of Lycurgus: 'He was the only legislator,' they say, 'who saw the important points. For, there being two things on which the safety of a commonwealth depends – courage in the face of the enemy and concord at home – by abolishing covetousness he with it removed all motive for civil broil and contest, whence it has been brought about that the Lacedaemonians are the best governed and most united people in Greece.' Yet while giving utterance to these sentiments, and though they see that, in contrast to this, the Cretans by their ingrained avarice are engaged in countless

thenes of Olynthus, a nephew of Aristotle, accompanied Alexander's expedition as a historian.

1. The Spartan Council of Elders.

public and private seditions, murders, and civil wars, yet they regard these facts as not affecting their contention, but are bold enough to speak of the two constitutions as alike.

E. S. SHUCKBURGH (1889)

JOSEPHUS

THE greatest Jewish historian; A.D. 37/8 – after 94/5. His four works include *The Jewish War* and *Jewish Antiquities*. The former, relating to the First Jewish Rebellion or First Roman War (66–73), was written in Aramaic for the Mesopotamian Jews before appearing in Greek.

*

HEROD (DIED 4 B.C.) AND HERODIUM

If ever a man was full of family affection, that man was Herod. In memory of his father he founded a city, choosing a site in the loveliest plain in his kingdom with an abundance of rivers and trees, and naming it Antipatris; and the fortress overlooking Jericho he re-fortified, making it oustandingly strong and beautiful, and dedicated it to his mother under the name Cypros. To his brother Phasael he erected the tower in Jerusalem that took his name; its design and tremendous size we shall describe later. He also founded another city in the valley running north from Jericho and called it Phasaelis.

Having immortalized his family and friends he did not neglect to make his own memory secure. He built a fortress in the hills facing Arabia and called it Herodium after himself, and seven miles from Jerusalem he gave the same name to an artificial hill, the shape of a woman's breast, adorning it more elaborately than the other. He en-circled the top with round towers, filling the enclosed space with a palace so magnificent that in addition to the splendid appearance of the interior of the apartments the outer walls, copings, and roofs had wealth lavished on them without stint. At very heavy cost he brought in an unlimited supply of water from a distance, and furnished the ascent with 200 steps of the whitest marble; the mound was of con-siderable height, though entirely artificial. Round the base he built other royal apartments to accommodate his furniture and his friends, so that in its completeness the stronghold was a town, in its compactness a palace.

G. A. WILLIAMSON (1959)

KING AGRIPPA II ADVISES HIS FELLOW-JEWS NOT TO REVOLT (A.D. 66)

'If I had found you all eager for war with the Romans, whereas in fact the most honest and sincere section of the people are bent on keeping the peace, I should not have come forward to address you or ventured to give advice, for it is a waste of breath to say anything in favour of a wise course when the audience is unanimously in favour of a foolish one. But some of you are young men with no experience of the horrors of war, others are too sanguine about the prospects of independence, others are led on by selfish ambition and the profit to be made out of weaker men if the explosion occurs. So in the hope that these men may learn sense and change their ways, and that the folly of a few may not be visited on good citizens, I felt obliged to call you all together and tell you what I think is best. Please do not interrupt me if you disapprove of what I say; for those who have absolutely made up their mind to revolt will be free to feel the same after hearing my views, but my words will be lost even on those who want to listen unless everyone keeps quiet.

'Now I am aware that many orate against the insolence of the procurators and rhapsodize about the wonders of liberty; but before I go into the question of who you are and whom you are planning to fight, I must first sort out your jumble of pretexts. If you are trying to avenge your wrongs, why do you prate about liberty? If on the other hand slavery seems unbearable, it is a waste of time to blame your rulers; if they were the mildest of men, it would still be disgraceful to be slaves.

'Consider these pretexts one at a time, and see how feeble are your grounds for war. First, the charges against the procurators. You should flatter, not provoke, the authorities; when for trifling errors you pile on reproaches, it is yourselves you hurt by your denunciation of the offenders; instead of injuring you secretly and shamefacedly they plunder you openly. Nothing damps an aggressor like patient submission, and the meekness of the persecuted puts the persecutor to shame. I grant that the ministers of Rome are unbearably harsh; does it follow that all the Romans are persecuting you, including Caesar? Yet it is on them that you are going to make war! It is not by their wish that an unscrupulous governor comes from Rome, nor can western eyes see the goings-on in the east; it is not easy in Rome even to get up-to-date news of what happens here. It would be absurd because of the trifling misdemeanours of one man to go to war with a whole nation and such a nation – a nation that does not even know what it is all about! Our grievances can be quickly put right; the same procurator will not be here for ever, and his successors are almost sure to be more reasonable. But once set on foot, war cannot easily be either broken off or fought to a conclusion without disaster.

'As for your new passion for liberty, it comes too late; you ought to have made a supreme effort to retain it long ago. For the experience of slavery is a painful one, and to escape it altogether any effort is justified; but the man who has once submitted and then revolts is a refractory slave, not a lover of liberty.'

G. A. WILLIAMSON (1959)

THE FIRST JEWISH WAR AGAINST ROME (A.D. 66–73)

The war of the Jews against the Romans was the greatest of our time; greater too, perhaps, than any recorded struggle whether between cities or nations. Yet persons with no first-hand knowledge, accepting baseless and inconsistent stories on hearsay, have written garbled accounts of it; while those of eyewitnesses have been falsified either to flatter the Romans or to vilify the Jews, eulogy or abuse being substituted for factual record. So for the benefit of the Emperor's subjects I have decided to translate into Greek the books which I wrote some time ago in my native language, for circulation in the Middle East. I myself (Josephus, son of Matthias) am a Hebrew by race, and a priest from Jerusalem; in the early stages I fought against the Romans, and of the later events I was an unwilling witness.

This upheaval, as I said, was the greatest of all time; and when it occurred Rome herself was in a most unsettled state. Jewish revolutionaries took advantage of the general disturbance; they had vast resources of men and money; and so widespread was the ferment that some were filled with hope of gain, others with fear of loss, by the state of affairs in the East; for the Jews expected all their Mesopotamian brethren to join their insurrection. From another side Roman supremacy was being challenged by the Gauls on their borders, and the Celts were restive – in fact after Nero's death disorder reigned everywhere. Presented with this opportunity many aspired to the imperial throne, while the soldiery were eager for a transference of power as a means of enriching themselves.

G. A. WILLIAMSON (1959)

THE CAPTURE OF JERUSALEM BY TITUS (A.D. 70)

All the prisoners taken from beginning to end of the war totalled 97,000; those who perished in the long siege 1,100,000. Of these the majority were Jews by race but not Jerusalem citizens: they had come together from the whole country for the Feast of Unleavened Bread and had suddenly been caught up in the war, so that first the overcrowding meant death by pestilence, and later hunger took a heavier toll. That so many could crowd into the City was shown by the census held in Cestius' time. He, wishing to bring home the strength of the city to Nero, who despised the nation, instructed the chief priests to hold a census of the population if it was possible to do so. They chose the time of the Passover Feast, at which sacrifice is offered from three to five in the afternoon, and as it is not permissible to feast alone a sort of fraternal group is formed round each victim, consisting of at least ten adult males, while many groups have twenty members. The count showed that there were 255,600 victims; the men, reckoning ten diners to each victim, totalled 2,700,000, all ceremonially clean; for persons suffering from leprosy, venereal disease, monthly periods, or any form of defilement were debarred from participation, as were the foreigners who came from abroad in large numbers to be present at the ceremonies.

But now fate had decreed that one prison should confine the whole nation and that a city solid with men should be held fast in war's embrace. No destruction ever wrought by God or man approached the wholesale carnage of this war. Every man who showed himself was either killed or captured by the Romans, and then those in the sewers were ferreted out, the ground was torn up, and all who were trapped were killed. There too were found the bodies of more than 2,000, some killed by their own hand, some by one another's, but most by starvation. So foul a stench of human flesh greeted those who charged in that many turned back at once. Others were so avaricious that they pushed on, climbing over the piles of corpses; for many valuables were found in the passages and all scruples were silenced by the prospect of gain. Many prisoners of the party chiefs were brought up; for not even at their last gasp had they abandoned their brutality. But God rewarded them both as they deserved: John, starving to death with his brothers in the sewers, after so many scornful refusals at last appealed to the Romans for mercy, while Simon after battling long against the inevitable, as will be described later, gave himself up. John was sentenced to life-imprisonment, but Simon was kept for the triumphal procession and ultimate execution. The Romans now fired the outlying districts of the town and demolished the walls.

So fell Jerusalem in the second year of Vespasian's reign ... captured five times before and now for the second time laid utterly waste.

G. A. WILLIAMSON (1959)

JOSEPHUS CRITICIZES GREEK HISTORIANS

On the other hand criticism may fairly be levelled at those Greek scholars who, knowing that the wars of the past fade into insignificance beside the astonishing events of their own times, sit in judgement upon the latter and severely censure those who make an effort to record them. For though their own flow of words is greater, their historical sense is inferior. They write histories themselves about the Assyrians and Medes, implying that the earlier writers did not do the work properly. Yet they are no more a match for them as writers than as thinkers. For the old historians were all eager to set down the events of their own lifetime, and their participation in these events gave vitality to their account, while it was impossible to depart from the truth without being detected. Surely to leave a permanent record of contemporary events for the benefit of posterity is worthy of the highest praise; and the real worker is not the man who merely changes the order and arrangement of another man's work, but the one who has something new to say and constructs a historical edifice of his own. I myself have gone to great trouble and expense, though an alien, so that I may offer to the Greeks and Romans a permanent record of their triumphs: native writers on the other hand, though the chance of profit from litigation finds them possessed of ready tongue and an unlimited flow of words, when they turn to history (which requires them to speak the truth after laboriously collecting the facts) appear to be gagged, and pass over to inferior writers unaware of the facts the task of recording the achievements of the great. I am determined therefore to respect the truth of history, though it has been neglected by the Greeks.

G. A. WILLIAMSON (1959)

GREEK IGNORANCE OF THE JEWS

Most excellent Epaphroditus:[1]

In my work on Ancient History, I conceive that I have sufficiently demonstrated to anyone who may be good enough to be my reader the extreme antiquity of our Jewish race, the pureness of its original stock and the circumstances in which it first settled in the country which still remains our home. This story, which extends over a period of five thousand years, I have taken from our sacred books and rewritten in Greek. Nevertheless, I find that a considerable portion of the public is sufficiently impressed by the malicious misrepresentations

1. This may be a learned Greek ex-slave and grammarian, Marcus Mettius Epaphroditus of Chaeronea. This pamphlet is known to us by the title *Against Apion* (a long-dead Greco-Egyptian grammarian attacked in the second book), but Josephus is refuting more recent critics of the Jews as well.

of certain of our enemies to be sceptical of my account of our ancient history, and to find evidence of the recent origin of our race in the fact that its existence is ignored by the most celebrated of the Hellenic historians. I have therefore felt myself obliged to make a brief contribution to this controversy, in order to expose the malicious intent and deliberate mendacity of our detractors, to correct the ignorance of their dupes, and to enlighten all who are genuinely concerned to know the truth in regard to our origins. In support of my own contentions, I shall cite the evidence of writers who are regarded by the Hellenes as the highest authorities in the whole field of ancient history, while I shall show how the writers who have slandered and misrepresented us may be confuted out of their own mouths. I shall attempt to explain the reasons why comparatively few members of our race have been mentioned by the Hellenes in their historical works, and I shall further point out the cases in which our history has not been ignored, to those readers who either are or profess to be unaware of them.

My first impulse is to express my astonishment at those who regard the Hellenes as the only trustworthy authorities from whom the truth regarding antiquity can be learned, while they consider us and all others to be unworthy of credence. As I see it, this is an exact inversion of the facts, if we are not to be ruled by empty speculations but are to allow the facts to speak for themselves. In reality, you will find that the whole of Hellenic civilization is so recent that it might be described as a growth of yesterday or the day before. I refer to the foundation of the Hellenic states, to their material inventions, and to the codification of their law, but the activity with which they have concerned themselves almost last of all in Hellas is the writing of history. On the other hand, the Hellenes admit themselves (and they will not contradict me) that Egypt, Chaldaea and Phoenicia – to omit Judaea from the list for the time being – possess the most ancient and permanent historical records. All these nations inhabit regions singularly exempt from destructive atmospheric effects, and they have taken extreme pains to leave none of their transactions unrecorded, but to have them constantly enshrined by experts in public registers. On the contrary, the region in which Hellas lies has been exposed to innumerable ravages of nature which have obliterated the record of the past; her inhabitants have been constantly under the necessity of starting life afresh, on each of which occasions they have regarded their own epoch as the beginning of all things; and their acquisition of the art of writing was a belated and a painful process. Even those who claim the highest antiquity for its introduction boast that they acquired it from Cadmus and the Phoenicians.[1]

ARNOLD TOYNBEE (1952)

1. The Greeks acquired the art of writing from the Phoenicians. Cadmus was a mythical king of Tyre in Phoenicia who came to Greece and founded Thebes.

'LONGINUS'

The author of the famous treatise *On the Sublime*, who was ascribed this name without good reason by the medieval tradition, is now believed to have written during the first century A.D.

*

THE TRUE SUBLIME

It must be understood, my dear friend, that, as in everyday life nothing is great which it is considered great to despise, so is it with the sublime. Thus riches, honours, reputation, sovereignty, and all the other things which possess in marked degree the external trappings of a showy splendour, would not seem to a sensible man to be great blessings, since contempt for them is itself regarded as a considerable virtue; and indeed people admire those who possess them less than those who could have them but are high-minded enough to despise them. In the same way we must consider, with regard to the grand style in poetry and literature generally, whether certain passages do not simply give an impression of grandeur by means of much adornment indiscriminately applied, being shown up as mere bombast when these are stripped away – passages which it would be more noble to despise than to admire. For by some innate power the true sublime uplifts our souls; we are filled with a proud exaltation and a sense of vaunting joy, just as though we had ourselves produced what we had heard.

If an intelligent and well-read man can hear a passage several times, and it does not either touch his spirit with a sense of grandeur or leave more food for reflection in his mind than the mere words convey, but with long and careful examination loses more and more of its effectiveness, then it cannot be an example of true sublimity – certainly not unless it can outlive a single hearing. For a piece is truly great only if it can stand up to repeated examination, and if it is difficult, or, rather, impossible to resist its appeal, and it remains firmly and ineffaceably in the memory. As a generalization, you may take it that sublimity in all its truth and beauty exists in such works as please all men at all times. For when men who differ in their pursuits, their ways of life, their ambitions, their ages, and their languages all think in one and the same way about the same works, then the unanimous judgement, as it were, of men who have so little in common induces a strong and unshakeable faith in the object of admiration.

T. S. DORSCH (1965)

SOME PRACTICAL ADVICE

It is well, then, that we too, when we are working at something that demands grandeur both of conception and of expression, should carefully consider how perhaps Homer might have said this very thing, or how Plato, or Demosthenes, or Thucydides in his History, might have given it sublimity. For conjured up before our eyes, as it were, by our spirit of emulation, these great men will raise our minds to the standards we have laid down for ourselves.

Still more will this be so if we put to ourselves the further query, 'How would Homer or Demosthenes, if he had been present, have listened to this passage of mine, and how would it have affected him?' For indeed it would be a severe ordeal to bring our own utterances before such a court of justice and such a theatre as this, to make a pretence of submitting our writings to the scrutiny of such semi-divine judges and witnesses.

It would be even more stimulating if you added the question, 'What kind of hearing should I get from all future ages if I wrote this?' But if anyone shrinks from the expression of anything beyond the comprehension of his own time and age, the conceptions of his mind are obviously obscure and incomplete, and are bound to come to nothing, since they are by no means brought to such perfection as to ensure their fame in later ages.

T. S. DORSCH (1965)

SUBLIMITY AND LITERARY FAME

Now with regard to authors of genius, whose grandeur always has some bearing on questions of utility and profit, it must be observed at the outset that, while writers of this quality are far from being faultless, yet they all rise above the human level. All other attributes prove their possessors to be men, but sublimity carries one up to where one is close to the majestic mind of God. Freedom from error escapes censure, but the grand style excites admiration as well. It need scarcely be added that each of these outstanding authors time and again redeems all his failures by a single happy stroke of sublimity; and, most decisive of all, that if we were to pick out all the blunders of Homer, Demosthenes, Plato, and the greatest of all our other authors, and were to put them all together, it would be found that they amounted to a very small part, say rather an infinitesimal fraction, of the triumphs achieved by these demigods on every page. That is why the judgement of all ages, which envy itself cannot convict of perversity, has awarded them the palm of victory, guarding it as their inalienable right, and likely so to preserve it 'as long as rivers run and tall trees flourish'.[1]

As for the writer who maintains that the faulty Colossus is not superior to Polycleitus's spearman, one obvious retort, among many others, is to point out that meticulous accuracy is admired in art, grandeur in the works of nature, and that it is by nature that man is endowed with the power of speech. Moreover, in statues we look for the likeness of a man, whereas in literature, as I have said, we look for something transcending the human. However, to revert to the doctrine with which I began my commentary, since freedom from faults is usually the result of art, and distinction of style, however unevenly sustained, is due to genius, it is right that art should everywhere be employed as a supplement to nature, for in cooperation the two may bring about perfection.

So much it has been necessary to say in order to resolve the problems before us. But everyone is welcome to his own taste.

T. S. DORSCH (1965)

1. Author unknown.

378

PART VIII

GREEK EPIGRAMS IN ROMAN
IMPERIAL TIMES

LOLLIUS BASSUS

EPIGRAMMATIST of the time of Tiberius (A.D. 14–37).

*

HUMAN SHAPE IS QUITE CONVENIENT

I refuse to become a shower of gold,
A bull or a swan as in days of old.
Let Zeus do tricks. Corinna's more willing,
If I remain human and give her a shilling.[1]

ANDREW SINCLAIR (1967)

1. A curious example of how translations date: the shilling has been abolished.

MARCUS ARGENTARIUS

Epigrammatist, early first century A.D.

*

NOTHING BETWEEN US

'Take a hard look at scrawny Diokleia.
She's a skinny Aphrodite
but sweet.'

'Then nothing will stand between us;
when I lie on her skinny breasts
I'll be pressing right against her heart.'

WILLIS BARNSTONE (1962)

LUCILLIUS

EPIGRAMMATIST of the time of Nero (A.D. 54–68).

*

THE FORTUNE-TELLERS

Firmly, as with one voice,
The entire Faculty of the College of Applied Astrology
Foretold a healthy old age for my father's brother.

Hermokleides alone
Maintained that he would die young:
                  but he made this statement
At the funeral service we held for my father's brother.

DUDLEY FITTS (1957)

STRATO

Epigrammatist from Sardis in Lydia. Wrote on homosexual themes in the time of Hadrian (A.D. 117–38).

*

UNDESIRABLE BOYS

Those pampered boys in purple-edged attire,
To whom we, Diphilus, do not aspire,
Are like ripe figs that on the crag-tops grow,
Food for a vulture or a carrion-crow.

R. A. Furness (1931)

RUFINUS

EPIGRAMMATIST; perhaps second century A.D.

*

THE GOLDEN MEAN

Do not put your arms about
Girl too thin, or girl too stout,
But choose the middle term between
The two extremes of fat and lean.

One has redundant fleshy stuff,
The other has not flesh enough;
Make it your practice to select
Neither excess nor yet defect.

R. A. FURNESS (1931)

PTOLEMY

Claudius Ptolemaeus, astronomer, mathematician and geographer in Alexandria during the second quarter of the second century A.D.

*

THE UNIVERSE

Mortal though I be, yea ephemeral, if but a moment
    I gaze up to the night's starry domain of heaven,
Then no longer on earth I stand; I touch the Creator,
    And my lively spirit drinketh immortality.

ROBERT BRIDGES (1916)

LUCIAN

He wrote mainly in prose; see also pp. 433-41.

He wrote mainly in prose; see also pp. 433-41.

*

A DEAD CHILD

The frowning fates have taken hence
    Callimachus, a child
Five years of age: ah well is he
    From cruel care exiled.
What though he lived but little time,
    Wail nought for that at all:
For as his years not many were,
    So were his troubles small.

TIMOTHY KENDALL (1577)

A DEAD CHILD[1]

Little Callimachus harsh Death bore hence
In his fifth summer's heedless innocence.
Yet do not weep for me. Of life I knew
Little; but little of life's sorrows too.

F. L. LUCAS (1951)

---

1. The same piece: translated nearly four centuries later.

PART IX

PHILOSOPHY, BIOGRAPHY, SATIRE AND MEDICINE IN ROMAN IMPERIAL TIMES

PLUTARCH

Lucius (?) Mestrius Plutarchus of Chaeronea. Born before
A.D. 50, died after 120. Philosopher and biographer.

*

INTELLIGENT ELEPHANTS

At Rome not very long ago, there were many Elephants that were
taught many dangerous Postures, many Windings and Turnings, and
circular Screwings of their bulky Bodies, hard to be exprest; among
which there was one, which being duller than the rest, and therefore
often rated and chastized for his Stupidity, was seen in the Night-
time, by Moon-light, without being forced to it, to practise over his
Lessons, with all the Industry imaginable.

Agno tells a Story of an Elephant in Syria, that was bred up in a
certain House, who observed that his Keeper took away and de-
frauded him every Day of half the Measure of his Barley, only that
once the Master being present and looking on, the Keeper poured out
the whole Measure; which was no sooner done, but the Elephant
extending his Proboscis, separated the Barley, and divided it into two
equal Parts, thereby ingeniously discovering, as much as in him lay,
the Injustice of his Keeper.

Another in revenge that his Keeper mixed Stones and Dirt with
his Barley, as the Keeper's Meat was boiling upon the Fire, took up
the Ashes, and flung them into the Pot.

Another being vexed and provoked by the Boys in Rome, that
pricked his Proboscis with the sharp Ends of their Writing-steels,
caught one of them in his Proboscis, and mounted him up into the
Air, as if he intended to have squashed out his Guts; but upon the
loud Outcries of the Spectators, set him gently down again upon his
Feet, and so went on, believing he had sufficiently punished the Boy
in scaring him. Many other Things are reported of the wild Elephants

that feed without Control, as being under their own Jurisdiction; but
nothing more to be admired than their passing of great Rivers. For
first of all the youngest and the least flounces into the Stream; whom
the rest beholding from the Shore, if they see that the less bulky
Leader keeps steady footing with his Back above Water, they are then
assured and confident that they may boldly adventure without any
Danger.

JOHN PHILLIPS (1718)

ANTONY AND CLEOPATRA

Antony . . . was simply ignorant of most things that were done in his
name; not that he was so indolent, as he was prone to trust frankly in
all about him. For there was much simplicity in his character; he was
slow to see his faults, but when he did see them, was extremely
repentant, and ready to ask pardon of those he had injured; prodigal
in his acts of reparation, and severe in his punishments, but his
generosity was much more extravagant than his severity; his raillery
was sharp and insulting, but the edge of it was taken off by his
readiness to submit to any kind of repartee; for he was as well contented to be rallied, as he was pleased to rally others. And this
freedom of speech was, indeed, the cause of many of his disasters. He
never imagined those who used so much liberty in their mirth would
flatter or deceive him in business of consequence, not knowing how
common it is with parasites to mix their flattery with boldness, as
confectioners do their sweetmeats with something biting, to prevent
the sense of satiety. Their freedoms and impertinences at table were
designed expressly to give to their obsequiousness in council the air
of being not complaisance, but conviction.

Such being his temper, the last and crowning mischief that could
befall him came in the love of Cleopatra, to awaken and kindle to fury
passions that as yet lay still and dormant in his nature, and to stifle
and finally corrupt any elements that yet made resistance in him of
goodness and a sound judgement. He fell into the snare thus. When
making preparation for the Parthian war, he sent to command her to
make her personal appearance in Cilicia, to answer an accusation that

she had given great assistance, in the late wars, to Cassius.[1] Dellius, who was sent on this message, had no sooner seen her face, and remarked her adroitness and subtlety in speech, but he felt convinced that Antony would not so much as think of giving any molestation to a woman like this; on the contrary, she would be the first in favour with him. So he set himself at once to pay his court to the Egyptian, and gave her his advice, 'to go', in the Homeric style, to Cilicia, 'in her best attire', and bade her fear nothing from Antony, the gentlest and kindest of soldiers. She had some faith in the words of Dellius, but more in her own attractions; which, having formerly recommended her to Caesar and the young Cnaeus Pompey,[2] she did not doubt might prove yet more successful with Antony. Their acquaintance was with her when a girl, young and ignorant of the world, but she was to meet Antony in the time of life when women's beauty is most splendid, and their intellects are in full maturity. She made great preparation for her journey, of money, gifts, and ornaments of value, such as so wealthy a kingdom might afford, but she brought with her her surest hopes in her own magic arts and charms.

She received several letters, both from Antony and from his friends, to summon her, but she took no account of these orders; and at last, as if in mockery of them, she came sailing up the river Cydnus, in a barge with gilded stern and outspread sails of purple, while oars of silver beat time to the music of flutes and fifes and harps. She herself lay all along under a canopy of cloth of gold, dressed as Venus in a picture, and beautiful young boys, like painted Cupids, stood on each side to fan her. Her maids were dressed like sea nymphs and graces, some steering at the rudder, some working at the ropes. The perfumes diffused themselves from the vessel to the shore, which was covered with multitudes, part following the galley up the river on either bank, part running out of the city to see the sight. The market-place was quite emptied, and Antony at last was left alone sitting upon the tribunal; while the word went through all the

1. She was summoned to Tarsus in 41 B.C. to answer the unfounded charge that she had helped Cassius and Brutus, the assassins of Julius Caesar, before their defeat by Marcus Antonius (Antony) and Octavian (the future Augustus) at Philippi (42 B.C.).

2. Cnaeus, son of Pompey the Great, had visited Egypt in 49 B.C., and it was rumoured that he had been struck by Cleopatra's beauty.

multitude, that Venus was come to feast with Bacchus,[1] for the common good of Asia. On her arrival, Antony sent to invite her to supper. She thought it fitter he should come to her; so, willing to show his good-humour and courtesy, he complied, and went. He found the preparations to receive him magnificent beyond expression, but nothing so admirable as the great number of lights; for on a sudden there was let down altogether so great a number of branches with lights in them so ingeniously disposed, some in squares, and some in circles, that the whole thing was a spectacle that has seldom been equalled for beauty.

The next day, Antony invited her to supper, and was very desirous to outdo her as well in magnificence as contrivance; but he found he was altogether beaten in both, and was so well convinced of it that he was himself the first to jest and mock at his poverty of wit and his rustic awkwardness. She, perceiving that his raillery was broad and gross, and savoured more of the soldier than the courtier, rejoined in the same taste, and fell into it at once, without any sort of reluctance or reserve. For her actual beauty, it is said, was not in itself so remarkable that none could be compared with her, or that no one could see her without being struck by it, but the contact of her presence, if you lived with her, was irresistible; the attraction of her person, joining with the charm of her conversation, and the character that attended all she said or did, was something bewitching. It was a pleasure merely to hear the sound of her voice, with which, like an instrument of many strings, she could pass from one language to another; so that there were few of the barbarian nations that she answered by an interpreter; to most of them she spoke herself, as to the Aethiopians, Troglodytes, Hebrews, Arabians, Syrians, Medes, Parthians, and many others, whose language she had learnt; which was all the more surprising because most of the kings, her predecessors, scarcely gave themselves the trouble to acquire the Egyptian tongue, and several of them quite abandoned the Macedonian.

Antony was so captivated by her that, while Fulvia his wife maintained his quarrels in Rome against Caesar[2] by actual force of arms,

1. i.e. Aphrodite and Dionysus.
2. i.e. Octavian. Fulvia and Anthony's brother Lucius fought the Perusine War against him in 41–40 B.C.

and the Parthian troops, commanded by Labienus (the king's generals having made him commander-in-chief), were assembled in Mesopotamia, and ready to enter Syria, he could yet suffer himself to be carried away by her to Alexandria, there to keep holiday, like a boy, in play and diversion, squandering and fooling away in enjoyments that most costly, as Antiphon says, of all valuables, time. They had a sort of company, to which they gave a particular name, calling it that of the Inimitable Livers. The members entertained one another daily in turn, with an extravagance of expenditure beyond measure or belief. Philotas, a physician of Amphissa, who was at that time a student of medicine in Alexandria, used to tell my grandfather Lamprias that, having some acquaintance with one of the royal cooks, he was invited by him, being a young man, to come and see the sumptuous preparations for supper. So he was taken into the kitchen, where he admired the prodigious variety of all things; but particularly, seeing eight wild boars roasting whole, says he, 'Surely you have a great number of guests.' The cook laughed at his simplicity, and told him there were not above twelve to sup, but that every dish was to be served up just roasted to a turn, and if anything was but one minute ill-timed, it was spoiled; 'And,' said he, 'maybe Antony will sup just now, maybe not this hour, maybe he will call for wine, or begin to talk, and will put it off. So that,' he continued, 'it is not one, but many suppers must be had in readiness, as it is impossible to guess at his hour.' This was Philotas's story; who related besides, that he afterwards came to be one of the medical attendants of Antony's eldest son by Fulvia, and used to be invited pretty often, among other companions, to his table, when he was not supping with his father. One day another physician had talked loudly, and given great disturbance to the company, whose mouth Philotas stopped with this sophistical syllogism: 'In some states of fever the patient should take cold water; every one who has a fever is in some state of fever; therefore in a fever cold water should always be taken.' The man was quite struck dumb, and Antony's son, very much pleased, laughed aloud, and said, 'Philotas, I make you a present of all you see there,' pointing to a sideboard covered with plate. Philotas thanked him much, but was far enough from ever imagining that a boy of his age could dispose of things of that value. Soon after, however, the plate was all brought to him, and he was desired to set his mark upon it; and when he put it away from him, and was afraid to accept the present, 'What ails the man?' said he that brought it; 'do you know that he who gives you this is Antony's son, who is free to give it, if it were all gold? but if you will be advised by me, I would counsel you to accept of the value in money from us; for there may be amongst the rest some antique or famous piece of workmanship, which Antony would be sorry to part with.' These anecdotes, my grandfather told us, Philotas used frequently to relate.

To return to Cleopatra; Plato admits four sorts of flattery, but she had a thousand. Were Antony serious or disposed to mirth, she had at any moment some new delight or charm to meet his wishes; at every turn she was upon him, and let him escape her neither by day nor by night. She played at dice with him, drank with him, hunted with him; and when he exercised in arms, she was there to see. At night she would go rambling with him to disturb and torment people at their doors and windows, dressed like a servant-woman, for Antony also went in servant's disguise, and from these expeditions he often came home very scurvily answered, and sometimes even beaten severely, though most people guessed who they were. However, the Alexandrians in general liked it all well enough, and joined good-humouredly and kindly in his frolic and play, saying they were much obliged to Antony for acting his tragic parts at Rome, and keeping his comedy for them.

A. H. CLOUGH (1864)

THE BIOGRAPHER'S TASK

It being my purpose to write the lives of Alexander the king, and of Caesar, by whom Pompey was destroyed,[1] the multitude of their great actions affords so large a field that I were to blame if I should not by way of apology forewarn my reader that I have chosen rather to epitomize the most celebrated parts of their story, than to insist at large on every particular circumstance of it. It must be borne in mind

1. Pompey the Great was killed by the Egyptians in 48 B.C. after his defeat by Julius Caesar at Pharsalus.

that my design is not to write histories, but lives. And the most glorious exploits do not always furnish us with the clearest discoveries of virtue or vice in men; sometimes a matter of less moment, an expression or a jest, informs us better of their characters and inclinations, than the most famous sieges, the greatest armaments, or the bloodiest battles whatsoever. Therefore as portrait-painters are more exact in the lines and features of the face, in which the character is seen, than in the other parts of the body, I must be allowed to give my more particular attention to the marks and indications of the souls of men, and while I endeavour by these to portray their lives, may be free to leave more weighty matters and great battles to be treated of by others.

A. H. CLOUGH (1864)

SULLA'S CAPTURE OF ATHENS[1]

For there was something terrible and quite inexorable about Sulla's lust to capture Athens. Perhaps it was some spirit of envious emulation which drove him to fight as it were with the shadow of the city's former greatness; perhaps he had been made angry by the insults and vulgar abuse which were constantly hurled at him and at Metella from the walls by the tyrant Aristion, who would accompany his foul language with the most obscene gestures.

Aristion had a character which was compounded of cruelty and licentiousness. He was like a sink into which had run all the worst of the vicious and diseased qualities of Mithridates, and now, like some fatal malady, he had fastened himself on Athens in these last days of hers – a city which in the past had survived innumerable wars and many periods of dictatorship and civil strife. This man, at a time when a bushel of wheat was being sold in the city at 1,000 drachmas, when people were subsisting on the feverfew which grew on the Acropolis and were boiling down shoes and leather oil flasks to eat, was himself spending his time in continual drinking parties and revels in broad daylight, or showing off his steps in a war dance, or making jokes

1. During the first war against Mithridates of Pontus, Sulla sacked the Piraeus (the port of Athens) and, in part, Athens (86 B.C.).

about the enemy. Meanwhile he allowed the sacred lamp of the goddess to go out for want of oil; and when the chief priestess asked him for a twelfth of a bushel of wheat, he sent her pepper instead. When the members of the Council and the priests came to him as suppliants and begged him to take pity on the city and come to terms with Sulla, he drove them off with a volley of arrows. Finally, when things had already gone too far, with much ado he sent out two or three of his drinking companions to negotiate a peace. These men made no proposals that could be of any help to Athens, but instead went off into long dissertations about Theseus and Eumolpus[1] and the Persian wars. They were interrupted by Sulla who said: 'My friends, you can pack up your speeches and be off. Rome did not send me to Athens to study ancient history. My task is to subdue rebels.'

Meanwhile Sulla received news from some soldiers of his who had overheard in the Cerameicus[2] some old men talking together and abusing the tyrant for not guarding the approach to the wall at the Heptachalcum, at which point alone it was not only possible but easy for the enemy to force an entry. Sulla took this information seriously. He came down to the place by night, satisfied himself that it would be taken and went into action immediately. He says himself in his *Memoirs* that the first man to scale the wall was Marcus Ateius, who was opposed by one of the enemy, and cutting downwards at him with his sword broke the sword on the man's helmet; nevertheless he stood firm and held his ground without giving way. Certainly it was at this point that the city was taken, as used to be reported by the oldest of the Athenians.

Sulla himself entered the city at midnight, after having thrown down and levelled with the ground the fortifications between the Piraeic and the Sacred Gate. It was a moment made the more terrible by the blowing of trumpets, the blasts of bugles, and the shouting and yelling of his troops who were now let loose by him to pillage and to slaughter and who poured down the narrow alley-ways with drawn swords in their hands. There was thus no counting of the slain; to this day their numbers are estimated simply by the area of ground that was covered with blood. The blood shed in the market-place

1. Mythical ancestors of the Athenians.
2. A north-western suburb of Athens.

alone (without counting the slaughter that took place in the rest of the city) spread all through the Cerameicus inside the Double Gate; in fact many people say that it flowed out through the Gate and washed right over the suburb outside. And yet though many indeed perished in this way, equally numerous were those who, out of pity and love for their native city, took their own lives. They thought that their city was doomed to extinction, and this it was that made the best of them give up all hope and fear the prospect of survival, since they expected from Sulla neither generosity nor ordinary humanity. Finally, however, partly because of the exiles Midias and Calliphon, who threw themselves at his feet and begged him to have mercy, partly because of the Roman senators with the army who also interceded for the city, Sulla, who was himself by this time sated with vengeance, made a few remarks in praise of the ancient Athenians and then announced, 'I forgive a few for the sake of the many, the living for the sake of the dead.'

REX WARNER (1958)

AN APPROACH TO MYTHOLOGY

You know, Sosius Senecio,[1] how geographers, when they come to deal with those parts of the earth which they know nothing about, crowd them into the margins of their maps with the explanation, 'Beyond this lie sandy, waterless deserts full of wild beasts', or 'trackless swamps', or 'Scythian snows', or 'ice-locked sea'. Now that in writing my *Parallel Lives* I have reached the end of those periods in which theories can be tested by argument or where history can find a solid foundation in fact, I might very well follow their example and say of those remoter ages, 'All that lies beyond are prodigies and fables, the province of poets and romancers, where nothing is certain or credible.'

However, after I had published my account of Lycurgus the lawgiver and Numa the king, there seemed to be nothing unreasonable in going back a step further to Romulus, since my history had brought

1. Quintus Sosius Senecio (consul A.D. 98 and 107) was one of Plutarch's most influential Roman friends.

me so close to his times. Then, when I asked myself, as Aeschylus puts it:

> With such a champion who will dare to engage?
> Who shall I match against him? Who can face the challenge?

it seemed clear that I could find no more fitting counterpart for the father of glorious and unconquerable Rome than Theseus, the founder of the lovely and far-famed city of Athens. Let us hope, then, that I shall succeed in purifying fable, and make her submit to reason and take on the appearance of history. But when she obstinately defies probability and refuses to admit any element of the credible, I shall throw myself on the indulgence of my readers and of those who can listen with forbearance to the tales of antiquity.

IAN SCOTT-KILVERT (1960)

THE ACHIEVEMENT OF SOLON

However, once the disturbances concerning Cylon[1] were past and those involved in the blood-guilt had been banished, as I have described, the Athenians relapsed into their perennial squabbles about the form their government should take. The city was divided into as many parties as there were geographical features in its territory. The party of the Hill supported an extreme democracy, the Plain an extreme oligarchy, while the Shore formed a third party, which wanted a mixed form of government somewhere in between, opposed the other two and prevented either of them from getting the upper hand. At this point, too, the inequalities between rich and poor had, as it were, come to a head. The city stood on the brink of revolution, and it seemed as if the only way to put a stop to its perpetual disorders and achieve stability was to set up a tyranny. All the common people were weighed down with the debts they owed to a few rich men. They either cultivated their lands for them and paid them a sixth of the produce ... or else they pledged their own persons to raise money

1. An Athenian nobleman who attempted a *coup* by seizing the Acropolis in c. 632 B.C.

and could be seized by their creditors, some of them being enslaved at home, and others being sold to foreigners abroad. Many parents were even forced to sell their own children (for there was no law to prevent this), or to go into exile because of the harshness of their creditors. However, the majority, which included the men of most spirit, began to make common cause together and encourage one another not to resign themselves to these injustices, but to choose a man they could trust to lead them. Having done this, they proposed to set all enslaved debtors free, redistribute the land and make a complete reform of the constitution.

At this point the most level-headed of the Athenians began to look towards Solon. They saw that he, more than anyone else, stood apart from the injustices of the time and was involved neither in the extortions of the rich nor the privations of the poor, and so finally they appealed to him to come forward and settle their differences. Phanias of Lesbos, however, maintains that Solon of his own accord went behind the backs of both parties in order to save the city, and secretly promised the poor that he would redistribute the land, and the rich that he would guarantee the pledges which were their security. Solon's own version is that he only engaged in politics very unwillingly, because he was afraid of the grasping nature of the one party and the arrogance of the other. However, he was chosen archon[1] in succession to Philombrotus to act both as arbitrator and as legislator, for the rich were ready to accept him as a man of wealth and the poor as a man of principle. It is also said that a remark of his to the effect that 'equality breeds no strife' was widely repeated before his election and pleased property-owners and paupers alike; the first assumed that he meant an equality based on merit and achievement, and the second a quantitative equality based on the counting of heads. Consequently, both sides' hopes were raised and both sets of leaders repeatedly pressed upon Solon the idea of establishing a tyranny: they sought to persuade him that he could seize control of the city with all the greater confidence now that he had it in his power. There were many people, besides, who were not attached to either party and who saw

1. 594 B.C. (until 487 the nine archons were still the most important officials in Athens). But it is nowadays believed that many of his reforms should be dated to the 570s. See p. 91.

that it would be a weary and laborious process to bring about any radical change by means of debate and legislation, and they were by no means unwilling to have a single man, the justest and wisest in the state, placed at the head of affairs. There are some who say that Solon received an oracle from Delphi, which ran as follows:

Seat yourself now amidships, for you are the pilot of Athens.
Grasp the helm fast in your hands; you have many allies in your city.

His intimate friends reproached him most of all for turning his back upon absolute power merely because he shrank from the name of tyrant, without allowing for the fact that the virtues of the man who assumed such authority could transform it at once into a lawful sovereignty. They quoted the earlier precedent of Tynnondas in Euboea and the contemporary one of Pittacus, whom the people of Mytilene had chosen to be their tyrant.

None of these arguments could shake Solon's resolution. His reply to his friends, we are told, was that tyranny is a fine place in itself, but there is no way down from it, and in one of his poems he writes to Phocus:

> And if I spared my country
> Refrained from ruthless violence and tyranny
> And chose to keep my name free from all taint
> I feel no shame at this; instead, I believe
> It will be my greatest glory.

From this it seems clear that he enjoyed a great reputation, even before he became the lawgiver of Athens. As for the taunts that were hurled at him for refusing the tyranny, he has written as follows:

Solon was no deep thinker, not even a man of sound judgement;
When the gods showered good fortune upon him, he only refused it.
When his nets swarmed with fish, he could not pull them in for
   amazement.
Give me the chance to be tyrant, with such power and infinite
   riches
I should not turn it down, though I ruled but a day over Athens;
Then I could bear to be flayed and my name cast into oblivion.

This is how he makes the unscrupulous elements and, indeed, the people in general speak of him. But in spite of his refusal to become a tyrant, he was by no means over-indulgent in his handling of affairs and there was nothing feeble about his legislation. It did not make concessions to the strong, nor did it humour the whims of the voters. Wherever he approved of the existing arrangement, he made no attempt to remedy or meddle with it, for he feared that if he turned everything upside down and thoroughly disorganized the state, he might not have power enough to restore order and reconstitute it for the best. He only introduced changes where he believed he could get his way by persuasion or enforce it by authority, and, in this fashion, as he puts it, he

Made force and justice work in harmony.

And so, when at a later date he was asked whether he had provided the best laws for the Athenians, his reply was, 'The best that they would accept.'

IAN SCOTT-KILVERT (1960)

ARISTIDES THE JUST

Of all Aristides' virtues it was his justice which most impressed itself on the masses, since it was this which he practised most consistently and which affected most people. For this reason, although he was poor and had no standing but that of a popular leader, he won that most royal and godlike title of The Just. That is an epithet which was never sought after by kings or tyrants: some of them delighted in being styled The Besieger of Cities, The Thunderbolt, or The Conqueror, and others The Eagle or The Hawk, but all of them, apparently, preferred a renown which was founded on power or violence rather than on virtue. And yet the divine nature, with which these men strive to be associated and to resemble, is believed to be distinguished by three superior attributes, immortality, power and virtue, and of these the noblest and the most truly divine is virtue. The void and the elements are, in a sense, immortal, and earthquakes, thunderbolts, floods and hurricanes can overwhelm by their power, but

GREEK LITERATURE IN TRANSLATION

justice belongs only to those beings who are capable of reason and the knowledge of the divine.

So when we consider the three sentiments, admiration, fear and reverence, which divinity inspires among mankind, we find that men appear to admire the gods and think them blessed because they are immortal and unchangeable; to stand in fear and awe of them because of their power and authority; and to love, honour and reverence them because of their justice. At the same time men long for immortality, to which no flesh can attain, and for power, which remains for the most part in the hands of fortune, while they give virtue, the only divine excellence of which we are capable, the last place in their scheme of values. But here they show themselves fools, since a life that is spent in the midst of power and great fortune and authority still needs justice to make it divine, for injustice renders it merely brutish.

But to return to Aristides. It was his fate first of all to be loved because of this surname, but afterwards to be envied and hated, especially when Themistocles put about the story that, by the fact of his acting as arbitrator and judging all cases referred to him in private, Aristides had abolished the public courts, and that without anybody noticing it, he had made himself virtually the ruler of Athens, and only lacked an armed bodyguard. By this time, too, the people had become so exultant because of their victory over the Persians that they thought themselves capable of anything and were offended at anybody whose name and reputation rose above the common level. So they flocked into the city from all over Attica and proceeded to ostracize Aristides,[1] disguising their jealousy of his fame under the pretext that they were afraid of a tyranny.

This sentence of ostracism was not in itself a punishment for wrongdoing. It was described for the sake of appearances as a measure to curtail and humble a man's power and prestige in cases where these had grown oppressive; but in reality it was a humane device for appeasing the people's jealousy, which could thus vent its desire to do harm, not by inflicting some irreparable injury, but by a sentence of ten years' banishment. Later on the penalty came to be inflicted on various ignoble creatures, the scum of the political world, and it was

1. 482 B.C. He had been a general in 490–89 B.C. and archon in 489–8.

then abandoned, the last man to be ostracized being Hyperbolus.[1] Hyperbolus's banishment is said to have been brought about in this way. Alcibiades and Nicias, the two most powerful men in the state, were the leaders of the two opposing parties. So when the people were on the point of carrying out an ostracism and were obviously going to vote against one or the other, the two men came to terms, combined their rival factions and so arranged matters that Hyperbolus was ostracized. The people were enraged at this and felt that the institution of ostracism had been abused and degraded, and so they not only ceased to resort to it but formally abolished the practice.

The procedure, to give a general account of it, was as follows. Each voter took an *ostrakon*, or piece of earthenware, wrote on it the name of the citizen he wished to be banished and carried it to a part of the market-place which was fenced off with a circular paling. Then the archons first counted the total number of votes cast, for if there were less than six thousand, the ostracism was void. After this they sorted the votes and the man who had the most recorded against his name was proclaimed to be exiled for ten years, with the right, however, to receive the income from his estate.

The story goes that on this occasion, while the votes were being written down, an illiterate and uncouth rustic handed his piece of earthenware to Aristides and asked him to write the name Aristides on it. The latter was astonished and asked the man what harm Aristides had ever done him. 'None whatever,' was the reply, 'I do not even know the fellow, but I am sick of hearing him called The Just everywhere!' When he heard this, Aristides said nothing, but wrote his name on the *ostrakon* and handed it back. At the last, as he was leaving the city, he lifted his hands to heaven and uttered a prayer, which, it appears, took the opposite form to the prayer of Achilles:[2] in it he begged that no crisis might befall the Athenians which would force them to remember Aristides.

IAN SCOTT-KILVERT (1960)

1. In about 417 B.C. Conservative politicians regarded Hyperbolus as a demagogue.

2. Achilles had prayed that Agamemnon might come to see his blindness in not honouring him – by bitter experience.

PERICLES[1]

Pericles had an unbounded admiration for Anaxagoras,[2] and his mind became steeped in the so-called higher philosophy and abstract speculation. From it he derived not only a dignity of spirit and a nobility of utterance which was entirely free from the vulgar and unscrupulous buffooneries of mob-oratory, but also a composure of countenance that never dissolved into laughter, a serenity in his movements and in the graceful arrangement of his dress which nothing could disturb while he was speaking, a firm and evenly modulated voice, and other characteristics of the same kind which deeply impressed his audience. It is a fact, at any rate, that once in the market-place, where he had urgent business to transact, he allowed himself to be abused and reviled for an entire day by some idle hooligan without uttering a word in reply. Towards evening he returned home unperturbed, while the man followed close behind, still heaping every kind of insult upon him. When Pericles was about to go indoors, as it was now dark, he ordered one of his servants to take a torch and escort the man all the way to his own house.

The poet Ion,[3] however, says that Pericles had a rather disdainful and arrogant manner of address, and that his pride had in it a good deal of superciliousness and contempt for others. By contrast, he praises the ease, good humour, and polished manner which Cimon[4] showed in his dealings with the world. But we need not pay much attention to Ion, who apparently expects that virtue, like a complete dramatic tetralogy, must include an element of low comedy. Against this, Zeno used to urge all those who derided Pericles' austere manner as nothing more than pride and a craving for popularity to go

1. Pericles (c. 495–429 B.C.) guided the destiny of Athens during the last twenty-five years of his life, with a brief intermission shortly before his death.

2. Anaxagoras of Clazomenae (c. 500–428 B.C.) was the first philosopher to reside in Athens.

3. Ion of Chios (484–424 B.C.) was a leading tragic poet, historian and philosopher.

4. Cimon (died 450 B.C.), leader of the aristocratic party, had been the most prominent Athenian statesman before Pericles.

and affect something like it themselves; his idea was that the mere imitation of these noble qualities might, after a time, cause them to be adopted unconsciously as a habit and even admired.

These were not the only advantages that Pericles gained from his association with Anaxagoras. He seems also to have learned from his teaching to rise above the superstitious terror which springs from an ignorant wonder at the common phenomena of the heavens. It affects those who know nothing of the causes of such things, who fear the gods to the point of madness and are easily confused through their lack of experience. A knowledge of natural causes, on the other hand, banishes these fears and replaces morbid superstition with a piety which rests on a sure foundation supported by rational hopes.

There is a story that Pericles was once sent from his country estate the head of a one-horned ram. Thereupon Lampon,[1] the soothsayer, when he saw how the horn grew strong and solid out of the middle of the creature's forehead, declared that the mastery of the two dominant parties in the city – which at that time were led by Thucydides[2] and Pericles respectively – would be concentrated in the hands of one man, and that he would be the one to whom this sign had been given. Anaxagoras, on the other hand, had the skull dissected and proceeded to demonstrate that the brain had not filled its natural space, but had contracted into a point like an egg at that place in the cavity from which the horn grew. On that occasion, so the story goes, it was Anaxagoras who won the admiration of the onlookers, but not long after Lampon came into his own, for Thucydides was overthrown and the entire control of affairs fell into Pericles' hands.

In my opinion, however, there was nothing to prevent both the scientist and the prophet from being right, since the one correctly diagnosed the cause and the other the meaning of the prodigy. It was the business of the first to observe why something happens and how it becomes what it is, and of the second to foretell the purpose of an event and its significance. Those who say that to discover the cause of a phenomenon disposes of its meaning fail to notice that the same reasoning which explains away divine portents would also dispense

1. A famous soothsayer and interpreter of oracles.
2. Thucydides the son of Melesias (not the historian), ostracized in 443 B.C.

with the artificial symbols created by mankind. The beating of gongs, the blaze of beacons, and the shadows on sundials all have their particular causes, but have also been contrived to signify something else. However, this is perhaps a subject for a separate essay.

As a young man Pericles was inclined to shrink from facing the people. One reason for this was that he was considered to bear a distinct resemblance to the tyrant Pisistratus,[1] and when men who were well on in years remarked on the charm of Pericles' voice and the smoothness and fluency of his speech, they were astonished at the resemblance between the two. The fact that he was rich and that he came of a distinguished family and possessed exceedingly powerful friends made the fear of ostracism very real to him, and at the beginning of his career he took no part in politics but devoted himself to soldiering, in which he showed great daring and enterprise. However, the time came when Aristides was dead, Themistocles in exile, and Cimon frequently absent on distant campaigns. Then at last Pericles decided to attach himself to the people's party and to take up the cause of the poor and the many instead of that of the rich and the few, in spite of the fact that this was quite contrary to his own temperament, which was thoroughly aristocratic. He was afraid, apparently, of being suspected of aiming at a dictatorship; so when he saw that Cimon's sympathies were strongly with the nobles and that he was the idol of the aristocratic party, he began to ingratiate himself with the people, partly for self-preservation and partly by way of securing power against his rival.

He now entered upon a new mode of life. He was never to be seen walking in any street except the one which led to the market-place and the Council-chamber. He refused not only invitations to dinner but every kind of friendly or familiar intercourse, so that through all the years of his political career, he never visited one of his friends to dine. The only exception was an occasion when his great-uncle Euryptolemus gave a wedding-feast. Pericles sat at table until the libations were poured at the end of the meal, and then at once rose and took his leave. Convivial occasions have a way of breaking down the most majestic demeanour, and in familiar relationships it is hard to keep up an imposing exterior which is assumed for appearances'

1. Autocratic ruler of Athens 546–527 B.C.

sake. On the other hand, genuine virtue can only be more impressive the more it is seen, and the daily life of a really good man is never so much admired by the outside world as it is by his intimate friends.

Pericles, however, took care not to make himself too familiar a figure, even to the people, and he only addressed them at long intervals. He did not choose to speak on every question, but reserved himself, as Critolaus says, like the state galley, the *Salaminia*, for great occasions, and allowed his friends and other public speakers to deal with less important matters.

IAN SCOTT-KILVERT (1960)

NICIAS[1]

The ceremonies which Nicias organized at Delos[2] have gone down in history both as acts of devotion to the god and as demonstrations of lavish public generosity. In earlier years the choirs which other cities sent for the worship of Apollo had been accustomed to put in at the island in a very haphazard style: the multitude of worshippers would run down to the ship and call on them to sing, not in any properly conducted ceremony, but as they scrambled off the ship in a disorderly crowd and were in the act of huddling on their robes and garlands. When Nicias took charge of the sacred company, he first put the choir ashore on the neighbouring islet of Rheneia, together with the sacrificial victims and everything else that was needed for the ritual. Before leaving Athens he had had a bridge of boats made to the required size, magnificently gilded, painted and hung with garlands and tapestries. During the night this was placed in position across the channel between Rheneia and Delos, which is quite narrow, and at dawn he led over the procession in honour of the god, splendidly dressed and chanting their hymn as they marched. After the sacrifices and the choral contests and the banquets were over, he dedicated to Apollo the well-known palm-tree of bronze and also a small estate, which he had bought for 10,000 drachmae. The revenue from this was to be devoted by the islanders to offering sacrifices and

1. Athenian statesman and general, *c.* 487–413 B.C. See above, p. 199, for his capitulation in Sicily in 413.

2. Nicias reorganized these ceremonies in 428 B.C.

providing themselves with a banquet, at which they would pray for blessings for Nicias from the gods. These instructions were engraved on a column which he set up on Delos, as it were to guard his benefaction. The bronze palm-tree was later overturned by a storm, fell against the colossal statue of the god presented by the people of Naxos, and threw it to the ground.

In all this there are signs of a certain vulgarity and ostentation aimed at increasing Nicias's prestige and satisfying his ambition. But to judge from his other qualities and his general character, it seems likely that his love of display was the outcome of his religious piety, and that the winning of popularity and hence of influence over the masses was quite a secondary object. He was one of those who stood in great awe of the supernatural and he was particularly subject, as Thucydides tells us, to the influence of divination. It is mentioned in one of Pasiphon's dialogues that he offered sacrifice to the gods every day and always kept a diviner at his house. Nicias gave out that he was constantly taking the omens for guidance on matters of public policy, but, in fact, most of his questions concerned his personal affairs, especially his silver mines. He was the owner of large concessions from the state in the mining district of Laurium, where the diggings were extremely lucrative, but also dangerous to operate. He kept a large labour force of slaves there and most of his wealth consisted of the silver which they produced.[1] For this reason he was constantly surrounded by hangers-on, who not only pressed him for money but got it out of him. It was his practice to make presents not only to those who had deserved well of him, but also to those he believed could do him harm, so that his fears were as much a source of income to scoundrels as his generosity was to honest men.

We can find evidence of this in the comic playwrights. Telecleides, for example, wrote these verses on one of the public informers:

> Charicles gave him a mina[2] to stop him telling
> How he was his mother's first child, born in a purse.
> But Nicias, Niceratus's son, gave him four.

1. Nicias held a concession on permanent lease from the state, and sublet both his mines and his slaves.
2. A currency denomination.

> I know the reason, too, but I'm not telling;
> For Nicias is my friend and a man I trust.

And the subject of Eupolis's[1] comedy, *Maricas*, brings on some poor inoffensive man in front of the audience and says:

MARICAS: How long is it since you met Nicias?
PAUPER: Not till this moment, in the market-place.
MARICAS: You see, he admits he *has* seen Nicias!
         But what for, unless he was up to no good?
CHORUS: You hear, my friends, Nicias was caught in the act!
PAUPER: You half-wits, do you suppose a man like Nicias
         Would ever be caught in any dirty work?

In Aristophanes' *Knights* Cleon utters the threat:

> I'll shout down every orator and put the wind up Nicias!

and Phrynichus[2] gives us a hint of his lack of courage and of how easy it was to intimidate him in these verses.

> He was an upright citizen, as well I know,
> Not one to cringe and creep about like Nicias.

Nicias was so much on his guard against informers that he would never dine out with another Athenian or take part in an exchange of opinions or any of the normal social occasions, indeed, he would not even allow himself the time for amusements of this kind. When he served on the board of generals, he made it his practice to stay at the War Department till nightfall, and as a member of the Council he was the first to enter the Council-chamber and the last to leave it. Even when he had no public business on his hands, he made himself inaccessible by staying at home and locking his doors. Then his friends would go up to whoever might be waiting outside and beg them to excuse him, explaining that even at that hour Nicias was engaged on affairs of state and was not at leisure.

The person who helped him most to act out this part and invested

---

1. Eupolis was a comic poet like his contemporary Aristophanes.
2. This was Phrynichus the comic poet – a contemporary of Aristophanes and Eupolis – not the tragic poet (who was of an earlier generation).

him with an air of solemnity and importance was Hiero, a man who had been well educated in music and letters in Nicias's family. He claimed to be the son of Dionysius, surnamed Chalcus, a poet whose work is still extant and who had led the well-known expedition of Greek colonists to Italy and founded Thurii.[1] Hiero handled all the secrets which Nicias entrusted to the diviners and he was constantly putting out to the Athenians stories of the onerous and care-worn existence which Nicias led for his country's sake.

'He can scarcely get a moment's peace at meal-times, or even in the bath,' Hiero would tell people, 'without his privacy being interrupted by some urgent public matter. He is so much concerned with the people's interests and so little with his own that he hardly ever goes to bed until most people are waking up. The result is that his health suffers and he cannot even be cheerful or at ease with his friends. He loses them as well as his own money through his devotion to Athens, while other men exploit their public activities to win friends and pick up fortunes, so that they can live in luxury and make politics their pastime.'

IAN SCOTT-KILVERT (1960)

ALCIBIADES

No man is so surrounded and lapped about by fortune with the so-called good things of life that he is completely out of reach of philosophy, or cannot be stung by its mordant and outspoken questions, and so it proved with Alcibiades. Even though he was pampered from the very beginning by companions who would say nothing but what they thought would please him, and hindered from listening to anybody who would advise or discipline him, yet because of his innate virtues, he recognized Socrates' worth, attached himself to him, and rejected his rich and famous lovers. Soon, as he came to know Socrates and listened to the words of a lover who neither pursued unmanly pleasures nor asked for kisses and embraces, but constantly sought to point out his weaknesses and put down his empty and foolish conceit:

1. This was a Pan-Hellenic foundation on the site of the former Sybaris in south Italy, sponsored by Pericles.

> The cock crouched down like a slave
> And let its feathers droop.

And he came to the conclusion that the role Socrates played was really part of a divine dispensation to watch over and rescue the young. In this way by disparaging himself, admiring his friend, loving that friend's kindness towards him and revering his virtues, he unconsciously formed what Plato calls 'an image of love to match love'. Everyone was amazed to see him taking his meals and his exercise with Socrates and sharing his tent, while he remained harsh and unaccommodating towards the rest of his lovers. Some of them, in fact, he treated with the greatest insolence, as happened in the case of Anytus, the son of Anthemion.

This man, who was one of Alcibiades' admirers, was entertaining some guests to dinner and invited Alcibiades among them. Alcibiades refused the invitation, but that night he got drunk at home with a number of his friends and led a riotous procession to Anytus's house. He stood at the door of the room in which the guests were being entertained, and there he noticed a great many gold and silver cups on the tables. He told his slaves to take half of these and carry them home for him; then he went off to his own house, without even deigning to enter the room. The guests were furious and declared that he had insulted Anytus outrageously. 'On the contrary, I think he has behaved quite reasonably, you might even say considerately,' was Anytus's comment. 'He could have taken everything; but at least he has left us half.'

IAN SCOTT-KILVERT (1960)

THE SURRENDER OF ATHENS TO LYSANDER THE SPARTAN (404 B.C.)[1]

So Lysander received the surrender of the entire fleet, except for twelve ships, and also of the walls of Athens. Then on the sixteenth day of the month Munychion [September] which was also the anniversary of the victory over the barbarians at Salamis, he set about changing the form of government. When the Athenians showed their

1. See above, pp. 208, 223.

bitter resentment and opposed his measures, he informed the people that he had caught the city violating the terms of its capitulation, since the walls were still standing, although the time within which they should have been pulled down had expired. He declared that as they had broken the articles of the treaty, he would submit their case to the allies to be completely reconsidered. Indeed, some people say that a proposal was actually laid before the congress of the allies to sell the whole Athenian people into slavery, and that on this occasion Erianthus the Theban went so far as to move that Athens should be razed to the ground and the country around it made a pasture for sheep. But later, so the story goes, when the principal delegates met for a banquet, a man from Phocis sang the opening chorus from Euripides' *Electra*, which begins with the lines:

> Daughter of Agamemnon
> I have come, Electra, to your rustic court.

At this the whole company was moved to pity and felt that it would be an outrage to destroy so glorious a city which had produced such great men.

After the Athenians had finally given way to all Lysander's demands, he sent for a great company of flute girls from the city and collected all those who were in his camp. Then to the sound of their music, he pulled down the walls and burned the ships, while the allies garlanded themselves with flowers, rejoiced together, and hailed that day as the beginning of freedom for Greece. Next, without any delay, Lysander set about making changes in the constitution, and established a council of thirty in Athens and ten in the Piraeus. He also posted a garrison in the Acropolis and appointed Callibius, a Spartan, to be its military governor.

IAN SCOTT-KILVERT (1960)

THE DEATH OF THE ORATOR DEMOSTHENES
(322 B.C.)[1]

Demosthenes did not have long to enjoy his return to his native land, for in the month of Metageitnion in the following year the Greek cause went down to defeat at the battle of Crannon.[2] In the following month of Boedromion a Macedonian garrison was installed in Athens, and in the next, Pyanepsion, Demosthenes met his death in the following way.

When reports came in that Antipater and Craterus were marching upon Athens, Demosthenes and his supporters escaped secretly from the city, and the people condemned them to death on the motion of Demades. Meanwhile they had split up and fled in different directions, and Antipater sent out troops to scour the country and arrest them: these detachments were under the command of one Archias, who was known as 'the exile-hunter'. This man was a citizen of the colony of Thurii in Italy: it was said that he had once been a tragic actor and that Polus of Aegina, the finest actor of his time, had been a pupil of his. According to Hermippus, however, Archias had studied rhetoric under Lacritus, while Demetrius of Phaleron says that he was a pupil of Anaximenes the historian.[3] At any rate Archias discovered that Hyperides the orator, Aristonicus of Marathon, and Himeraeus, the brother of Demetrius of Phaleron, had all taken refuge in the sanctuary of Aeacus on Aegina.[4] He then had them dragged out by force and sent to Antipater at Cleonae.[5] There they were put to death, and it is said that Hyperides also had his tongue cut out.

When Archias learned that Demosthenes had taken sanctuary in the

1. For Demosthenes, see above, p. 230.

2. In August 322 B.C. The Greeks were decisively defeated at Crannon in Thessaly by the Macedonian generals Antipater and Craterus.

3. Demetrius of Phaleron was made governor of his native Athens by the Macedonian Cassander; later he became librarian at Alexandria (297 B.C.).

4. Aeacus was the mythical son of Zeus and Aegina (daughter of the river-god Asopus).

5. A small town between Corinth and Argos.

temple of Poseidon at Calauria,[1] he crossed over in some small boats with a detachment of Thracian spearmen: he then tried to persuade Demosthenes to leave the sanctuary and go with him to Antipater, assuring him that he would not be harshly treated. It so happened that the night before Demosthenes had experienced a strange dream, in which he had seen himself acting in a tragedy and competing against Archias. But although he acted well and won the applause of the audience, the verdict went against him because of the lack of stage decorations and costumes and the poverty of the production. So when Archias offered him this string of assurances, Demosthenes remained seated where he was, looked him full in the face and said, 'Archias, I was never convinced by your acting, and I am no more convinced now by your promises.' Then, when Archias became angry and began to threaten him, he remarked, 'Ah, before this you were acting a part. Now you are speaking like the genuine Macedonian oracle. Give me a few moments to write a letter to my family.' With those words he retired into the inner part of the temple. There he picked up his tablets, as if he were about to write, put his pen to his mouth, and bit it, as was his habit when he was thinking out what to say. He kept the reed between his lips for some while, then covered his head with his cloak, and bent down. The soldiers who stood at the door jeered at him, because they supposed that he was afraid to die and called him a coward and weakling. Then Archias came near, urged him to get up, and began to repeat his assurances about reconciling him to Antipater. By this time Demosthenes recognized from his sensations that the poison was beginning to work upon him and overcome him. So he uncovered his head, looked steadfastly at Archias, and said, 'Now you can play the part of Creon as soon as you wish, and throw out my body without burying it.[2] But I, good Poseidon, will leave your sanctuary while still alive, although Antipater and his Macedonians would have been ready to defile it with murder.' With these words, he asked to be supported, since by now he was trembling and could scarcely stand. Then as they were help-

1. An island near Troezen: the temple was famous as a supposedly inviolable sanctuary for the persecuted.

2. The allusion is to Sophocles' *Antigone*, in which Creon decrees that the body of Polyneices, Antigone's brother, is to be left unburied.

ing him to walk past the altar, he fell, and with a groan gave up the ghost.

IAN SCOTT-KILVERT (1972)

THE SENSIBLE ADVICE OF CINEAS TO KING PYRRHUS OF EPIRUS (319–272 B.C.)

In Pyrrhus' entourage there was a Thessalian named Cineas whose judgement was greatly respected. He had been a pupil of Demosthenes and was considered to be the only public speaker of his time who could revive in his audience's minds, as a statue might do, the memory of the Athenian's power and eloquence. He was in Pyrrhus' service and was often sent as his representative to various cities, where he proved the truth of Euripides' saying,

> Words can achieve
> All that an enemy's sword can hope to win.[1]

At any rate Pyrrhus used to say that Cineas had conquered more cities by his oratory than he himself by force of arms, and he continued to pay him exceptional honours and to employ his services. This man noticed that Pyrrhus was eagerly preparing for his expedition to Italy[2] and, finding him at leisure for the moment, he started the following conversation.

'Pyrrhus,' he began, 'everybody tells me that the Romans are excellent soldiers and that they rule over many warlike nations. Now if the gods allow us to defeat them, how shall we use our victory?' 'The answer is obvious,' Pyrrhus replied. 'If we can conquer the Romans, no other city, Greek or barbarian, can be a match for us. We shall straightaway become the masters of the whole of Italy, and nobody knows the size and the strength and the resources of the country better than yourself.' There was a moment's pause before Cineas went on, 'Then, sire, after we have conquered Italy, what shall we do next?' Pyrrhus did not yet see where the argument was leading. 'After Italy, Sicily, of course,' he said. 'The place positively

1. Euripides, *Phoenician Women*, lines 517–18.
2. Pyrrhus invaded Italy in 280 B.C., and then Sicily.

beckons to us. It is rich, well-populated and easy to capture. Now that Agathocles is dead, the whole island is torn by factions, there is no stable government in the cities, and the demagogues have it all their own way.' 'No doubt what you say is true,' Cineas answered, 'but is our campaign to end with the capture of Sicily?' 'If the gods grant us victory and success in this campaign,' Pyrrhus told him, 'we can make it the spring-board for far greater enterprises. How could we resist making an attempt upon Libya and Carthage once we came within reach of them? Even Agathocles very nearly succeeded in capturing them when he slipped out of Syracuse with only a handful of ships. And when we have conquered these countries, none of our enemies, who are so insolent to us now, will be able to stand up to us. I do not have to emphasize that.' 'Certainly not,' replied Cineas. 'There is no doubt that once we have achieved that position of strength, we shall be able to recover Macedonia and we shall have the rest of Greece at our feet. But after all these countries are in our power, what shall we do then?' Pyrrhus smiled benevolently and replied, 'Why then we shall relax. We shall drink, my dear fellow, every day, and talk and amuse one another to our hearts' content.' Now that he had brought Pyrrhus to this point, Cineas had only to ask him, 'Then what prevents us from relaxing and drinking and enter-taining one another *now*? We have the means to do that all around us. So the very prizes which we propose to win with all this toil and danger and bloodshed and all the suffering inflicted on other people and ourselves, we could enjoy without taking another step!'

These arguments disturbed Pyrrhus, but they did not convert him. He could see clearly enough the contentment that he was leaving behind, but he could not give up the hopes he had set his heart on.

IAN SCOTT-KILVERT (1972)

THE RIGHT AND WRONG KIND OF FRIENDS

In the houses of rich men and rulers, the people see a noisy throng of visitors offering their greetings and shaking hands and playing the part of armed retainers, and they think that those who have so many friends must be happy. Yet they can see a far greater number of flies in those persons' kitchens. But the flies do not stay on after the good food is gone, nor the retainers after their patron's usefulness is gone. But true friendship seeks after three things above all else: virtue as a good thing, intimacy as a pleasant thing, and usefulness as a necessary thing, for a man ought to use judgement before accepting a friend, and to enjoy being with him and to use him when in need of him, and all these things stand in the way of one's having many friends; but most in the way is the first (which is the most important) – the approval through judgement. Therefore we must, in the first place, consider whether it is possible in a brief period of time to test dancers who are to dance together, or rowers who are to pull together, or servants who are to be guardians of property, or attendants of children, let alone the testing of a multitude of friends who are to strip for a general contest with every kind of fortune, each one of whom

> Put his successes with the common store,
> And shares in bad luck, too, without distress.[1]

For no ship is launched upon the sea to meet so many storms, nor do men, when they erect protecting walls for strongholds, and dams and moles for harbours, anticipate perils so numerous and so great as those from which friendship, rightly and surely tried, promises a refuge and protection. But when some thrust their friendship upon us without being tried, and are found to be like bad coins when put to the test,

> Those who are bereft rejoice,
> And those who have them pray for some escape.[2]

But here is the difficulty – that it is not easy to escape or to put aside an unsatisfactory friendship; but as harmful and disquieting food can neither be retained without causing pain and injury, nor ejected in the form in which it was taken in, but only as a disgusting and repulsive mess, so an unprincipled friend either causes pain and intense discomfort by his continued association, or else with accompanying enmity and hostility is forcibly ejected like bile.

1. Author unknown.   2. From an unknown play of Sophocles.

We ought therefore not to accept readily chance acquaintances, or attach ourselves to them, nor ought we to make friends of those who seek after us, but rather we should seek after those who are worthy of friendship. For one should by no means take what can be easily taken. In fact we step over or thrust aside bramble and brier, which seize hold upon us, and make our way onward to the olive and the vine. Thus it is always an excellent thing not to make an intimate acquaintance of the man who is ready with his embraces, but rather, of our own motion, to embrace those of whom we approve as worthy of our attention and useful to us.

F. C. BABBITT (1928)

KEEP SELF-PRAISE WITHIN LIMITS

It remains to state how we may each avoid unseasonable self-praise. Boasting has in self-love a powerful base of operations, and we can often detect its assaults even against those who are held to take but a modest interest in glory. For as one of the rules of health is either to avoid unwholesome places altogether, or being in them to take the greater care, so with self-love: there are certain treacherous situations and themes that make us blunder into it on the slightest occasion.

First, when others are praised, our rivalry erupts, as we said, into praise of self; it is seized with a certain barely controllable yearning and urge for glory that stings and tickles like an itch, especially when the other is praised for something in which he is our equal or inferior. For just as in the hungry the sight of others eating makes the appetite sharper and keener, so the praise of others not far removed inflames with jealousy those who are intemperate in seeking glory.

Second, in telling of exploits that have been lucky and have turned out according to plan, many are so pleased with themselves that before they know it they have drifted into vainglorious boasting. For once they come to talk of some victory or political success or act or word of theirs that found favour with leading men, they get out of hand and go too far. To this sort of self-glorification one may observe that courtiers and the military most readily succumb. But it may also attack those who have returned from a governor's banquet or from handling affairs of state. For with the mention of illustrious and royal personages they interweave certain gracious remarks that these personages have addressed to them, and fancy that they are not praising themselves but recounting praise received from others. Some even suppose that the self-praise is quite unobserved by their audience when they report the greetings, salutations, and attentions of kings and generals, feeling that what they recite is not their own praise but proofs of the courtesy and affability of others. We must therefore look warily to ourselves when we recount praise received from others and see that we do not allow any taint or suggestion of self-love and self-praise to appear, lest we be thought to make Patroclus our excuse, while we are really singing our own praise.

P. H. de Lacy and B. Einarson (1959)

LOVE

Love is not born suddenly and all at once as anger is, nor does it pass away quickly, for all that it is said to have wings. It takes fire gently, almost melting its way in, as it were; and when it has taken hold of the soul it long endures – in some men it does not sleep even when they grow old, but remains in its prime, still fresh and vigorous when their hairs are grey. But if it does abate and dissolve, either drying away with the passage of time or being extinguished by some rational consideration, it does not remove itself finally and completely from the soul, but leaves charred matter and a hot trail there behind it, smouldering as thunderbolts do when they have fallen. When grief has gone or savage anger subsided no trace of them remains lodging in the soul; the inflammation of desire, too, subsides, sharp though the disturbance may be that it causes. But the bites inflicted by love do not rid themselves of his venom, even if the brute leaves go; no, the internal lacerations swell, and no one knows what the trouble is, how it arose or from where it came to attack the victim's soul.

F. H. Sandbach (1969)

THE MYSTERY OF DEATH

At its time of dying the soul's feelings are like those of initiates into the Great Mysteries; that is why our words for 'dying', *teleutan*, and 'initiation', *teleisthai*, are alike, because they mean almost the same thing. Lost at first. Exhaustion. Whirling race. Frightening, aimless ways in darkness. Just before the end itself, all terror; cold shuddering, trembling, sweat, bewilderment. After that there is astounding light. The soul is welcomed by clear places. Here are deep fields, and in them voices and dancing, majesty of pure sounds and holy sights, which enfold the dead man and make his initiation perfect. He is free, there are no more chains. Part of the Mystery now, he wears his garland and walks among men who are sacred, clean of wickedness. A vision under his feet: the mass of men who were not initiated, not cleaned during life. These were afraid of death, not believing what happens there, and so took the evil side. They are trampled and compacted under him in a blur of mud and mist.

Friend, this might help you to see that the soul's entanglement, its imprisonment in the body, is no true part of nature.

C. J. HERINGTON (1969)

EPICTETUS

Stoic philosopher from Hierapolis (Pamukkale) in Phrygia (Asia Minor). A slave by birth. His lectures were collected and published by his pupil Arrian of Bithynia.

*

THE ESSENTIAL THINGS ARE IN OUR OWN POWER

Of Things, some are in our Power, and others not. In our Power are Opinion, Pursuit, Desire, Aversion, and in one Word, whatever are our own Actions. Not in our Power, are Body, Property, Reputation, Command, and, in one Word, whatever are not our own Actions.

Now, the things in our Power are, by Nature, free, unrestrained, unhindered: but those not in our Power, weak, slavish, restrained, belonging to others. Remember then, that, if you suppose things by Nature slavish, to be free; and what belongs to others, your own; you will be hindered; you will lament; you will be disturbed; you will find faults both with gods and Men. But, if you suppose that only to be your own, which is your own; and what belongs to others, such as it really is; no one will ever compel you; no one will restrain you: you will find fault with no one; you will accuse no one, you will do no one thing against your Will: no one will hurt you: you will not have an Enemy; for you will suffer no Harm.

Aiming therefore at such great things, remember, that you must not allow yourself to be carried, even with a slight tendency, towards the Attainment of the others: but that you must entirely quit some of them, and for the present postpone the rest. But if you would both have these, and Command, and Riches, at once, perhaps you will not gain so much as the latter; because you aim at the former too: but you will absolutely fail of the former; by which alone Happiness and Freedom are procured.

Study, therefore, to be able to say to every harsh Appearance, 'You are but an Appearance, and not absolutely the Thing you appear to be.' And then examine it by those Rules which you have: and first, and chiefly, by this: Whether it concerns the Things which are in our own Power, or those which are not; and, if it concerns any Thing not in our Power, be prepared to say, that it is nothing to *you*.

ELIZABETH CARTER (1758)

BODY IS UNIMPORTANT

You ought to possess your whole *Body* as a paltry Ass, with a Pack-saddle on, as long as may be, as long as it is allowed you. But, if there should come a Press, and a Soldier should lay hold on it, let it go. Do not resist, or murmur: otherwise you will be first beat, and lose the Ass after all. And, since you are to consider the Body itself in this manner, think what remains to do concerning those things which are provided for the Sake of the Body. If *that* be an Ass, the rest are Bridles, Pack-saddles, Shoes, Oats, Hay, for the Ass. Let these go too. Quit them more easily and expeditiously than the Ass. And when you are thus prepared, and thus exercised, to distinguish what belongs to others from your own; what is liable to Restraint, from what is not; to esteem the one your own Property, the other not; to keep your Desire, to keep your Aversion, carefully turned to this Point; whom have you any longer to fear? – 'No one.' – For about what should you be afraid? About what is your own, in which consists the Essence of Good and Evil? And who hath any Power over *this*? Who can take it away? Who can hinder you? No more than God can be hindered. But are you afraid for Body, for Possessions, for what belongs to others, for what is nothing to you? And what have you been studying all this while, but to distinguish between your own, and not your own; what is in your Power, and what is not in your Power; what is liable to Restraint, and what is not? And for what Purpose have you applied to the Philosophers?

ELIZABETH CARTER (1758)

DO NOT FEAR DEATH

But what, if I should be sick?
You will be sick as you ought.
Who will take care of me?
God: your Friends.
I shall lie in a hard Bed.
But like a Man.
I shall not have a convenient Room.
You will be sick in an inconvenient one then.
Who will provide Victuals for me?
They who provide for others too: you will be sick like Manes.[1]
But, besides, what will be the Conclusion of my
    Sickness? Any other than Death?
Why, do not you know, then, that the Origins of all human Evils,
and of Meanspiritedness, and Cowardice, is not *Death*, but rather the
Fear of Death? Fortify yourself therefore against this. Hither let all
your Discourses, Readings, Exercises, tend. And then you will know,
that thus alone are Men made free.

ELIZABETH CARTER (1758)

NO TYRANT CAN REALLY HARM ME

When a Tyrant threatens, and sends for me; I say, Against what is
your Threatening pointed? If he says, 'I will chain you'; I answer, It is
my *Hands* and *Feet* that you threaten. If he says, 'I will cut off your
Head'; I answer, it is my *Head* that you threaten. If he says, 'I will
throw you into Prison'; I answer, It is the Whole of this paltry *Body*
that you threaten: and, if he threatens Banishment, just the same.

Doth not he threaten *you*, then?

If I am persuaded, that these things are nothing to me, he doth not:
but if I fear any of them, it is *me* that he threatens. Whom, after all, is
it that I fear? The Master of what? Of Things in my own Power? Of

1. The name of a slave who had once belonged to Diogenes the Cynic. The
story to which Epictetus refers is unknown.

425

these no one is the Master. Of Things not in my Power? And what are these to *me*?

What then, do you Philosophers teach us a Contempt of Kings?

By no means. Who of us teaches anyone to contend with them, about things of which they have the Command? Take my Body; take my Possessions; take my Reputation; take those who are about me. If I persuade any one to contend for these things, as his own, accuse me, with Justice. – 'Aye: but I would command your "*Principles*" too.' – And who hath given you that Power? How can you conquer the Principle of another? – By applying Terror, I will conquer it. – Do not you see, that what conquers itself, is not conquered by another? And nothing but itself can conquer the Choice.

ELIZABETH CARTER (1758)

MARCUS AURELIUS

ROMAN emperor (A.D. 161–80) and author of twelve books of Stoic *Meditations*, written in Greek.

*

MEDITATIONS

Hour by hour resolve firmly, like a Roman and a man, to do what comes to hand with correct and natural dignity, and with humanity, independence and justice. Allow your mind freedom from all other considerations. This you can do, if you will approach each action as though it were your last, dismissing the wayward thought, the emotional recoil from the commands of reason, the desire to create an impression, the admiration of self, the discontent with your lot. See how little a man needs to master, for his days to flow on in quietness and piety: he has but to observe these few counsels, and the gods will ask nothing more.

*

In the life of a man, his time is but a moment, his being an incessant flux, his senses a dim rushlight, his body a prey of worms, his soul an unquiet eddy, his fortune dark, and his fame doubtful. In short, all that is of the body is as coursing waters, all that is of the soul as dreams and vapours; life a warfare, a brief sojourning in an alien land; and after repute, oblivion. Where, then, can man find the power to guide and guard his steps? In one thing and one alone: Philosophy. To be a philosopher is to keep unsullied and unscathed the divine spirit within him, so that it may transcend all pleasure and all pain, take nothing in hand without purpose and nothing falsely or with dissimulation, depend not on another's actions or inactions, accept each and every dispensation as coming from the same Source as itself –

and last and chief, wait with a good grace for death, as no more than a simple dissolving of the elements whereof each living thing is composed. If those elements themselves take no harm from their ceaseless forming and re-forming, why look with mistrust upon the change and dissolution of the whole? It is but Nature's way; and in the ways of Nature there is no evil to be found.

*

In your actions let there be a willing promptitude, yet a regard for the common interest; due deliberation, yet no irresolution; and in your sentiments no pretentious over-refinement. Avoid talkativeness, avoid officiousness. The god within you should preside over a being who is virile and mature, a statesman, a Roman, and a ruler; one who has held his ground, like a soldier waiting for the signal to retire from life's battlefield and ready to welcome his relief; a man whose credit need neither be sworn to by himself nor avouched by others. Therein is the secret of cheerfulness, of depending on no help from without and needing to crave from no man the boon of tranquillity. We have to stand upright ourselves, not be set up.

*

If you do the task before you, always adhering to strict reason with zeal and energy and yet with humanity, disregarding all lesser ends and keeping the divinity within you pure and upright, as though you were even now faced with its recall – if you hold steadily to this, staying for nothing and shrinking from nothing, only seeking in each passing action a conformity with nature and in each word and utterance a fearless truthfulness, then shall the good life be yours. And from this course no man has the power to hold you back.

*

Men seek for seclusion in the wilderness, by the seashore or in the mountains – a dream you have cherished only too fondly yourself. But such fancies are wholly unworthy of a philosopher, since at any moment you choose you can retire within yourself. Nowhere can man find a quieter or more untroubled retreat than in his own soul; above all, he who possesses resources in himself, which he need only contemplate to secure immediate ease of mind – the ease that is but another word for a well-ordered spirit. Avail yourself often, then, of this retirement, and so continually renew yourself. Make your rules of life brief, yet so as to embrace the fundamentals; recurrence to them will then suffice to remove all vexation, and send you back without fretting to the duties to which you must return.

After all, what is it that frets you? The vices of humanity? Remember the doctrine that all rational beings are created for one another; that toleration is a part of justice; and that men are not intentional evildoers. Think of the myriad enmities, suspicions, animosities, and conflicts that are now vanished with the dust and ashes of the men who knew them; and fret no more.

Or is it your allotted portion in the universe that chafes you? Recall once again the dilemma, 'if not a wise Providence, then a mere jumble of atoms', and consider the profusion of evidence that this world is as it were a city.[1] Do the ills of the body afflict you? Reflect that the mind has but to detach itself and apprehend its own powers, to be no longer involved with the movements of the breath, whether they be smooth or rough. In short, recollect all you have learnt and accepted regarding pain and pleasure.

Or does the bubble reputation distract you? Keep before your eyes the swift onset of oblivion, and the abysses of eternity before us and behind; mark how hollow are the echoes of applause, how fickle and undiscerning the judgements of professed admirers, and how puny the arena of human fame. For the entire earth is but a point, and the place of our own habitation but a minute corner in it; and how many are therein who will praise you, and what sort of men are they?

Remember then to withdraw into the little field of self. Above all, never struggle or strain; but be master of yourself, and view life as a man, as a human being, as a citizen, and as a mortal. Among the truths you will do well to contemplate most frequently are these two: first, that things can never touch the soul, but stand inert outside it, so that disquiet can arise only from fancies within; and secondly, that all visible objects change in a moment, and will be no more. Think of the countless changes in which you yourself have had a part. The

1. See below, p. 430.

whole universe is change, and life itself is but what you deem it.[1]

*

If the power of thought is universal among mankind, so likewise is the possession of reason, making us rational creatures. It follows, therefore, that this reason speaks no less universally to us all with its 'thou shalt' or 'thou shalt not'. So then there is a world-law; which in turn means that we are all fellow-citizens and share a common citizenship, and that the world is a single city. Is there any other common citizenship that can be claimed by all humanity? And it is from this world-polity that mind, reason, and law themselves derive. If not, whence else? As the earthy portion of me has its origin from earth, the watery from a different element, my breath from one source and my hot and fiery parts from another of their own elsewhere (for nothing comes from nothing, or can return to nothing), so too there must be an origin for the mind.

*

Remind yourself constantly of all the physicians, now dead, who used to knit their brows over their ailing patients; of all the astrologers who so solemnly predicted their clients' doom; the philosophers who expatiated so endlessly on death or immortality; the great commanders who slew their thousands; the despots who wielded powers of life and death with such terrible arrogance, as if themselves were gods who could never die; the whole cities which have perished completely, Helice, Pompeii, Herculaneum, and others without number. After that, recall one by one each of your own acquaintances; how one buried another, only to be laid low himself and buried in turn by a third, and all in so brief a space of time. Observe, in short, how transient and trivial is all mortal life; yesterday a drop of semen, tomorrow a handful of spice or ashes. Spend, therefore, these fleeting moments on earth as Nature would have you spend them, and then go to your rest with a good grace, as an olive falls in its season, with a blessing for the earth that bore it and a thanksgiving to the tree that gave it life.

*

1. cf. *Hamlet*, Act II, scene 2: 'There's nothing either good or bad but thinking makes it so.'

When meat and other dainties are before you, you reflect: This is dead fish, or fowl, or pig; or: This Falernian[1] is some of the juice from a bunch of grapes; my purple robe is sheep's wool stained with a little gore from a shellfish; copulation is friction of the members and an ejaculatory discharge. Reflections of this kind go to the bottom of things, penetrating into them and exposing their real nature. The same process should be applied to the whole of life. When a thing's credentials look most plausible, lay it bare, observe its triviality, and strip it of the cloak of verbiage that dignifies it. Pretentiousness is the arch deceiver, and never more delusive than when you imagine your work is most meritorious.

*

An empty pageant; a stage play; flocks of sheep, herds of cattle; a tussle of spearmen; a bone flung among a pack of curs; a crumb tossed into a pond of fish; ants, loaded and labouring; mice, scared and scampering; puppets, jerking on their strings – that is life. In the midst of all you must take your stand, good-temperedly and without disdain, yet always aware that a man's worth is no greater than the worth of his ambitions.

*

What do the baths bring to your mind? Oil, sweat, dirt, greasy water, and everything that is disgusting. Such, then, is life in all its parts, and such is every material thing in it.

*

In the interruption of an activity, or the discontinuance and, as it were, death of an impulse, or an opinion, there is no evil. Look back at the phases of your own growth: childhood, boyhood, youth, age: each change itself a kind of death. Was this so frightening? Or take the lives you lived under your grandfather and then under your mother and then your father; trace the numerous differences and changes and discontinuances there were in those days, and ask yourself, 'Were they so frightening?' No more so, then, is the cessation, the interruption, the change from life itself.

MAXWELL STANIFORTH (1964)

1. A celebrated wine from northern Campania, south-east of Rome.

GALEN

PHYSICIAN of Pergamum (Bergama) in Asia Minor who became the court doctor of Marcus Aurelius (A.D. 161–80). Writer of voluminous philosophical, scientific and especially medical treatises.

THE HUMILITY OF A SCHOLAR

I am not, however, unaware that I shall achieve either nothing at all or else very little. For I find that a great many things which have been conclusively demonstrated by the Ancients are unintelligible to the bulk of the Moderns owing to their ignorance – nay, that, by reason of their laziness, they will not even make an attempt to comprehend them; and even if any of them have understood them, they have not given them impartial examination.

The fact is that he whose purpose is to know anything better than the multitude do must far surpass all others both as regards his nature and his early training. And when he reaches early adolescence he must become possessed with an ardent love for truth, like one inspired; neither day nor night may he cease to urge and strain himself in order to learn thoroughly all that has been said by the most illustrious of the Ancients. And when he has learnt this, then for a prolonged period he must test and prove it, observing what part of it is in agreement, and what in disagreement with obvious fact; thus he will choose this and turn away from that. To such an one my hope has been that my treatise would prove of the very greatest assistance.

A. J. BROCK (1916)

LUCIAN

POPULAR philosopher and satirist from Samosata (Samsat on Turkey's Syrian border); *c.* A.D. 120 – after 180.

*

THRASYCLES AND TIMON[1]

But who comes now? is it not Thrasycles the Philosopher? it can be no other: see how he strokes his beard at length, lifts up his eyebrows, and comes muttering somewhat to himself, looking like a Titan, and the hair of his forehead cast back like some Boreas or Triton pictured by Zeuxis:[2] this man that hath such a grave countenance, such a sober gait: and is so succinct in his apparel: he that in a morning will deliver you a thousand precepts for virtue, cry out upon them that are addicted to pleasure, and speak in praise of frugality, as soon as he hath bathed and come in to supper, and his boy filled him one full bowl (for he loves a cup of good wine with all his heart) as if he drunk of the water of Lethe, will pleasantly give an instance contrary to his forenoon speeches, strike at the meat like a kite at his prey, jostle his next neighbour out of his place, slabber all his beard over with sauce and cram in like any cur dog, hanging his head perpetually over the platters, as if he meant to find out virtue in the bottom of the dishes, and wipes them every one with his fore-finger as clean as a cup, because he would not leave a drop of sauce behind him: he is as sure a card at his cup as at his meat, and will be as drunk as any ape, not only to the height of singing, and dancing, but till it make him brabble, and fall out: then will he pass many speeches over the pot, and talk of nothing else but temperance and sobriety, when he is all-to-pieces himself, and brings out his words so scurvily, that all the company

1. A semi-legendary Athenian misanthrope, first mentioned by Aristophanes (fifth century B.C.).
2. Zeuxis of Heraclea in Lucania (south-west Italy) was an eminent painter of the later fifth and early fourth century B.C.

laughs him to scorn: then falls he to spewing, until at the last some take him away, and carry him out of the room, though he catch hold upon some of the wenches as strongly as he can: but when he is at the best, he shall subscribe to no man for lying, and audaciousness, and covetousness: he is the prime of all parasites, and the easiest drawn to commit perjury: imposture leads the way with him, and impudency follows after: yet would he seem to be wholly made of wisdom, and every way forth absolute and perfect. I will make him smoke for it, as soon as he comes, for his goodness' sake. What's the reason that Thrasycles hath been so slow in coming to visit me?

THRASYCLES: I come not, Timon, with the same intent as other men do, which aim at thy riches, and run themselves out of breath in hope to get silver, gold and good cheer by thee, expressing a great deal of flattery towards a man so honest and plain as thou art, and so ready to impart of any thing that is within thy power: as for me, you know a piece of barley bread will serve me to supper sufficiently, and no better victuals with it than a salad of thyme, and cresses, or if I list to exceed, a bit or two of powdered meat: my drink is no other but clear fountain water, and this thread-bare cassock I prefer before the richest purple you can desire: but for gold I have it in no more estimation, than the rubbish that lies upon the seashore: for your sake it is that I am come hither, lest this mischievous and most deceitful possession of riches should corrupt you, which hath often-times been the cause of incurable mischiefs to many men: wherefore if you will be ruled by me, take it and cast it all into the sea as an unnecessary clog to a good man that is able to discern the riches of Philosophy: I mean not into the main sea, good Sir, but that you would go into it as far as a man is forked before the going forth of the tide, and suffer no man to see you but my self: or if you like not well of this take another course, which perhaps may do better: disburden your self of it so soon as you can, leave not one half-penny, but distribute it to all that stand in need: to one man, five drachmas, to another, a pound, to a third a talent: but if any Philosopher come in your way, you cannot upon your conscience, but give him twice or thrice as much as any other: for my part I crave nothing for my self: but to bestow upon my friends that are in want, and I shall hold myself well satisfied, if you will but fill me this satchel, which doth not altogether contain two bushels of Aegina measures: for a Philosopher ought to be content with a little, and observe the mean, and never stretch his thoughts wider than his scrip.

TIMON: I commend thee, Thrasycles, for this in faith: but before I deal with thy scrip, let me try whether I can fill thy head with blows and measure them out with my mattock.

THRASYCLES: O Democracy and laws: I am beaten by a rebellious wretch in a free city.

TIMON: Why dost thou complain, my honest Thrasycles? have I deceived thee in thy measure? I am sure I put in four quarts more than was thy due.

FRANCIS HICKS (1634)

LUCIAN PARODIES TRAVELLERS' TALES

Next morning we set sail in a very high wind, and after battling with it for a couple of days, were unlucky enough to run into some pirates. They were savages from one of the neighbouring islands, who evidently made a practice of attacking all the shipping in their area. Their own ships were made of enormous dried pumpkins, about ninety feet in diameter, hollowed out and fitted with bamboo masts and pumpkin-leaves for sails.

Two of these vessels came bearing down on us and started bombarding us with pumpkin-pips, which wounded many of us severely. However, we managed to give as good as we got, and towards midday we sighted several other vessels coming up behind them, which apparently belonged to some enemies of theirs, for as soon as they saw them they lost all interest in us and prepared to fight them instead. We seized this opportunity to sail away at full speed, leaving them hard at it. It was fairly obvious who was going to win, for the new arrivals outnumbered their opponents by five to two, and their ships were much stronger, consisting as they did of hollowed-out nutshells, which were also about ninety feet in diameter.

As soon as we had got well away from them, we dressed our casualties' wounds, and from then on went fully armed day and night, for we never knew when we might not be attacked. Sure enough, just before sunset twenty more pirates suddenly darted out at us from an apparently uninhabited island. They were mounted on large dolphins, which neighed like horses as they bounded across the waves. The pirates quickly surrounded our ship and started pelting us at close range with dried squids and crabs' eyes, but as soon as we let fly with our arrows and javelins, so many of them were wounded that the whole lot turned tail and fled back to the island.

About midnight, when the sea was very calm, we inadvertently ran aground on a halcyon's nest. It was nearly seven miles in circumference, and the bird that was sitting on it was not much smaller. We interrupted her in the process of incubating her eggs, and she flew up into the air with a melancholy cry, creating such a draught with her wings that she practically sank our ship. As soon as it was light we disembarked and went for a walk round the nest, which consisted of a vast number of trees plaited together to form a sort of raft. On it were five hundred eggs, each about the size of a barrel, from which impatient chirpings could already be heard.

So we broke one open with an axe, and hatched out a chick approximately twenty times as big as a vulture.

A few miles further on we were startled by some most unusual phenomena. The goose-shaped projection at the stern of the ship suddenly started flapping its wings and quacking. Simultaneously Scintharus, who had been bald for years, developed a fine head of hair, and most surprising of all, the mast began putting out branches, and some figs and some black grapes appeared at the top of it – though unfortunately they were not quite ripe. Naturally we were rather taken aback, having no idea what disasters these portents were meant to portend; so we just prayed to the gods to avert them, whatever they were.

We sailed another fifty miles and sighted a huge thick forest of pines and cypresses. They were growing, not on dry land as we thought at first, but in the middle of the bottomless deep – so of course they had no roots. In spite of this disadvantage, they somehow contrived to keep vertical and stay absolutely still: presumably they were floating. When we got nearer and began to realize what we were up against, we felt completely baffled, for the trees grew too close together for us to sail between them, and by that time it seemed equally impossible to turn back.

I climbed to the top of the tallest tree I could find, to see what happened the other side of the forest, and discovered that after about five miles of it there was open sea again. In the circumstances we decided that our only hope was to get the ship up on top of the trees, where the foliage looked quite thick enough to support it, and somehow carry it across to the other side. So that is what we did. We tied a good strong rope round the prow, then climbed to the top of the trees, and with some difficulty hauled the ship up after us. Once we had got it there, things were easier than we had expected. All we had to do was spread our sails, and the wind pushed us along across the branches – in fact it was just like sailing through the water, only of course rather slower. It reminded me of a striking line in a poem by Antimachus:[1]

> They voyaged onward o'er a sea of leaves.

Having thus solved the problem of the forest, we lowered our ship into the water again, and continued our journey through a clear and sparkling sea until we came to a deep cleft in the ocean, rather like one of those fissures that sometimes develop on land as a result of earthquakes. We hastily took in sail, but our momentum carried us right up to the edge, and we very nearly went over. Peeping down, we saw to our surprise and horror that there was a sheer drop of approximately 600,000 feet, as if the sea had been sliced in half from top to bottom.

PAUL TURNER (1958)

ZEUS IS INDISPOSED

POSEIDON: Oh, Hermes, could I have a word with Zeus, do you think?

HERMES: Out of the question, I'm afraid, Poseidon.

POSEIDON: All the same, just let him know I'm here.

HERMES: He mustn't be disturbed, I tell you. You've chosen a very awkward moment – you simply can't see him just now.

[1]. A poet of the fifth century B.C., from Colophon in Ionia.

POSEIDON: Why, is he in bed with Hera?

HERMES: No, it's something quite different.

POSEIDON: Oh, I see what you mean. He's got Ganymede in there.

HERMES: No, it's not that either. The fact is, he's feeling rather unwell.

POSEIDON: Why, Hermes, what a terrible thing! What's the matter with him?

HERMES: Well, I hardly like to tell you.

POSEIDON: Oh, come on, I'm your uncle – you can tell *me*.

HERMES: All right, then – he's just had a baby.

POSEIDON [*roaring with laughter*]: Had a baby? Him? Whoever by? Do you mean to say he's been a hermaphrodite all these years without our realizing? But there wasn't any sign of pregnancy – his stomach looked perfectly normal.

HERMES: You're quite right. That wasn't where he had it.

POSEIDON: Oh, I see. He produced it like Athena, out of his head. It's a very prolific organ.

HERMES: No, he's been carrying this child of Semele's in his thigh.

POSEIDON: What a splendid chap he is! He can produce babies from every part of his anatomy! But who, exactly, is Semele?

HERMES: A girl from Thebes, one of Cadmus's daughters. Zeus had an affair with her, and got her in the family way.

POSEIDON: What? And then had the baby instead of her?

HERMES: Strange as it may sound, yes. You see, Hera – you know how jealous she is – went and talked Semele into asking Zeus to bring his thunder and lightning with him next time he came to call. Zeus did as he was asked, and arrived complete with thunderbolt. The house went up in flames, and Semele was burnt to death. Zeus told me to cut her open and fetch him the embryo – it was only seven months old and pretty undeveloped. So I did that, and he slit open his thigh and popped the little thing inside to mature. Now, two months later, he's given birth, and is feeling rather poorly as a result.

POSEIDON: And where's the baby now?

HERMES: Oh, I've taken it off to Nysa,[1] and put it out to nurse with some Nymphs. It's called Dionysus.

1. Nysa or the Nysaean mount, the home of the nymphs who nursed Dionysus, was attributed to at least fifteen different countries.

POSEIDON: Then, strictly speaking, my brother is not only Dionysus's father, but his mother as well?

HERMES: It looks like it. Well, I must go and get some water to clean
him up, and see to all the other little things that need doing on these
occasions.

PAUL TURNER (1961)

THE RELIGIOUS IMPOSTOR
ALEXANDER OF ABONUTICHUS[1]

Just as Alexander was beginning to grow a beard, his master died and
left him without any means of support – for he couldn't live on his
looks any more. However, he now had more ambitious plans, so he
teamed up with an even lower type, a ballet-dancer from Byzantium
– I think he was called Cocconas – and the two of them went round
cheating and fleecing 'fatheads' – a technical term used by magicians
to denote people with money. While they were so engaged, they
came across a Macedonian heiress who was past her prime but still
liked to be thought attractive. They lived on her for some time, and
when she went back to Macedonia, they went too. She came from a
place called Pella, which had been very prosperous in the old days,
when the Kings of Macedonia lived there, but now had only a tiny
population.

There they saw some enormous snakes, which were so tame and
domesticated that women used to keep them as pets, and children
even took them to bed with them. They didn't mind being pinched
or trodden on, and would actually take milk from the breast like
babies. These creatures are very common in those parts – which is
doubtless the origin of that story about Olympias, the mother of
Alexander the Great. I suppose she must have been seen with a pet
snake in her bed.

Anyway, they bought a magnificent specimen for a few coppers,
and that, as Thucydides would say, was how it all started. For those
two unscrupulous adventurers put their heads together, and decided

1. Leader of a successful new religion in Asia Minor in Lucian's own day.
He claimed to possess a new manifestation of Asclepius (Aesculapius) in the
form of a snake named Glycon.

that human life is ruled by a pair of tyrants called Hope and Fear, and if you treat them right, you can make a lot of money out of them. They saw that the one thing people want, and one thing they must have, when they're oppressed by either Hope or Fear, is information about the future. That was why places like Delphi, Delos, Claros, and Branchidae[1] had become so fabulously wealthy – because the tyrants I mentioned made people keep going there and paying exorbitant prices, in cattle or in gold, for any sort of prophecy. Having turned these facts over in their minds, they finally cooked up a plan to establish an oracle of their own. If all went well, they expected it to show an immediate profit – and in fact the results surpassed their wildest dreams.

PAUL TURNER (1961)

DISCUSSION BETWEEN TWO PROSTITUTES

AMPELIS: But look here, Chrysis. Suppose he never got jealous or lost his temper – suppose he never knocked you about, or cut off your hair, or tore your clothes, would you really call that being in love with you?

CHRYSIS: Why, is that the only way you can tell?

AMPELIS: Of course it is. That shows he's really in a state about you. Things like kisses and tears and promises and constant visits are merely the first symptoms. It's only when they start getting jealous that you know they're really in love. So if Gorgias has been knocking you about as much as you say, it's a very good sign. Let's hope he goes on like that.

CHRYSIS: Goes on knocking me about, do you mean?

AMPELIS: Not necessarily, but goes on being upset if you ever look at another man. For if he weren't in love with you, why should he care how many lovers you had?

CHRYSIS: Well, actually, I haven't any. But he's got a silly idea into his head that that rich gentleman's in love with me, just because I happened to mention him the other day.

1. Claros and Branchidae (Didyma) in western Asia Minor were, like Delphi and Delos, oracles of Apollo.

AMPELIS: Oh, that's splendid, if he thinks someone rich is after you. He'll be all the more upset, and start offering you better terms. He won't want his rival to outbid him.

CHRYSIS: Well, all he's done so far is get cross and knock me about. He hasn't given me a thing.

AMPELIS: He will, don't you worry. They always do if they're jealous – especially if you make them really miserable.

CHRYSIS: Darling, I don't quite see why you're so anxious for me to be knocked about.

AMPELIS: I'm not, but the way I see it is this. If you want him to develop a real passion for you, you must pretend not to care for him. If he thinks he's got a monopoly, he'll very soon lose interest. You can take my word for it – I've had twenty years' experience in the trade, and you can't be more than eighteen, if that.

Shall I tell you what happened to me a few years ago? I was having an affair with Demophantus – you know, that money-lender who lives at the back of the Town Hall. He never gave me more than five drachmas a time, and for that he seemed to regard me as his personal property. But his feelings for me never went at all deep. There was never any question of sighing or weeping or turning up on my doorstep in the middle of the night. He merely slept with me from time to time – and at pretty long intervals too.

Then one night I refused to let him in – I'd got an artist called Callides with me, and he'd given me ten drachmas. Well, all he did at the time was go off shouting abuse, but when several days went by without his hearing from me, Demophantus began to get rather hot under the collar. When he reached boiling-point, he suddenly burst into the house one day – he'd been watching for the door to open – and started crying, and hitting me, and threatening to murder me, and tearing my clothes, and goodness knows what else. Finally he gave me a whole talent, on the strength of which I lived for eight months exclusively with him. His wife told everyone I'd given him an aphrodisiac and sent him crazy with it. But all I'd actually given him was a dose of jealousy. So I suggest you use the same prescription on Gorgias. He'll be quite a rich young man when his father dies.

PAUL TURNER (1961)

441

BABRIUS

PROBABLY a Hellenized Roman; wrote verse fables in about the second century A.D., some original, but most adapting older fables associated with the semi-legendary name of Aesop (sixth century B.C.).

*

THE HARES AND THE FROGS[1]

Once upon a time the *Hares* found themselves mightily unsatisfied with the miserable condition they lived in, and called a council to advise upon't. Here we live, says one of 'em, at the mercy of men, dogs, eagles, and I know not how many other creatures and vermin, that prey upon us at pleasure; perpetually in frights, perpetually in danger; and therefore I am absolutely of opinion that we had better die once for all, than live at this rate in a continual dread that's worse than death itself. The motion was seconded and debated, and a resolution immediately taken, *One and All*, to drown themselves. The vote was no sooner passed, but away they scudded with that determination to the next lake. Upon this hurry, there leapt a whole shoal of *Frogs* from the bank into the water, for fear of the *Hares*. Nay, then my masters, says one of the gravest of the company, pray let's have a little patience. Our condition I find is not altogether so bad as we fancied it; for there are those you see that are as much afraid of us, as we are of others.

ROGER L'ESTRANGE (1669)

1. There are some good modern renderings of the fables in verse, but the prose medium is not inappropriate here since 'Aesop's fables' seem to have been originally in prose.

THE TOWN MOUSE AND THE COUNTRY MOUSE

There goes an old story of a *Country Mouse* that invited a *City-Sister* of hers to a country collation, where she spared for nothing that the place afforded; as mouldy crusts, cheese parings, musty oatmeal, rusty bacon, and the like. Now the *City-Dame* was so well bred, as seemingly to take all in good part: but yet at last, Sister (says she, after the civillest fashion) why will you be miserable when you may be happy? Why will you lie pining, and pinching your self in such a lonesome starving course of life as this is; when 'tis but going to town along with me, to enjoy all the pleasures, and plenty that your heart can wish? This was a temptation the *Country Mouse* was not able to resist; so that away they trudged together, and about midnight got to their journey's end. The *City Mouse* shewed her friend the larder, the pantry, the kitchen, and other offices where she laid her stores; and after this, carried her into the parlour, where they found, yet upon the table, the relics of a mighty entertainment of that very night. The *City-Mouse* carved her companion of what she liked best, and so to it they fell upon a velvet couch together: The poor Bumpkin that had never seen, nor heard of such doings before, blessed herself at the change of her condition, when (as ill luck would have it) all on a sudden, the doors flew open, and in comes a crowd of roaring bullies, with their wenches, their dogs, and their bottles, and put the poor *Mice* to their wit's end, how to save their skins. The stranger especially, that had never been at this sport before; but she made a shift however for the present, to slink into a corner, where she lay trembling and panting till the company went their way. So soon as ever the house was quiet again, Well: my *Court Sister*, says she, if this be the way of your *Town-Gambols*, I'll e'en back to my cottage, and my mouldy cheese again; for I had much rather lie knabbing of crusts, without either fear or danger, in my own little hole, than be mistress of the whole world with perpetual cares and alarums.

ROGER L'ESTRANGE (1669)

PART X

THE GREEK NOVEL

HELIODORUS

NOVELIST from Emesa (Homs) in Syria. Probably third century A.D. His surviving novel is the *Aethiopica*.

*

THE BEGINNING OF THE 'ETHIOPIAN STORY'

The cheerful smile of day was just appearing, as the rays of the sun began to light up the mountain tops, when some men armed like brigands peered over the ridge that stretches alongside the outlets of the Nile and that mouth of the river which is named after Hercules.[1] They halted there for a little while, scanning with their eyes the sea that lay below them; and when they had cast their first glances over the ocean and found no craft upon it and no promise there of pirates' plunder, they bent their gaze down upon the shore near by. And what it showed was this: a merchant ship was moored there by her stern cables, bereft of her ship's company, but full laden; so much could be inferred even at a distance, for her burthen brought the water as high as the third waling-piece of her timbers. The shore was thickly strewn with newly slain bodies, some quite lifeless, and others half dead whose limbs were still aquiver, thus indicating that the conflict had only just ceased. That it had been no regular engagement was betokened by what was visible; for there lay mingled the pitiful remnants of a feast that had thus come to no happy conclusion. There were tables still laden with their victuals; some others, overturned on the ground, were held in the grasp of those of the vanquished who had used them as armour in the struggle, for it had been a fight on the spur of the moment; and underneath others were men who had crept there in the hope of concealment. Wine-bowls were upset, and some

1. The most westerly or Canopic mouth of the Nile, near the Libyan desert.

447

were slipping from the hands of their holders – either drinkers or those who had taken them up to use as missiles instead of stones. The suddenness of the clash enforced innovations in the uses of things and prompted the hurling of drinking-cups. Here lay a man wounded with an axe, there one struck by a stone that the shingle had provided on the spot, another mangled by a piece of timber and another burnt to death by a firebrand; but most had fallen victims to darts and arrows. Countless were the varieties of sights that Fate had produced upon that small area – befouling wine with blood, thrusting battle upon banquet, with conjunction of killing and swilling, libation and laceration – so strange was the scene thus displayed to the Egyptian brigands. They had taken their places on that mountain height as spectators of this scene, but could not apprehend its meaning: they had the vanquished lying there, but nowhere could they see the victors. The conquest was clear as day, but the spoils were unseized; while the vessel, deserted and void of men, yet held its cargo intact, as though protected by a strong guard, and it rocked gently at its moorings as in a time of peace. But, although at a loss to know what could have occurred, they looked to the gain to be had in the booty, and assuming the part of victors they dashed on.

When they had advanced to a little way short of the ship and the fallen, they came upon a sight more unaccountable than what they had seen before. A young girl was seated on a rock, so inconceivably beautiful as to convince one that she was a goddess. Though sorely anguished by her present plight, she yet breathed forth a high and noble spirit. Her head was crowned with laurel; a quiver was slung over her shoulder; and her left arm was propped upon her bow, beyond which the hand hung negligently down. The elbow of her other arm she supported on her right thigh, while on its palm she rested her cheek; and with downcast eyes she held her head still, gazing intently on a prostrate youth. He, cruelly wounded, seemed to be faintly awakening as from a deep slumber that was wellnigh death. Yet, for all that, he had upon him the bloom of manly beauty, and his cheek, stained red by the gushing of his blood, showed forth its whiteness all the more brightly. The sufferings of the youth were weighing down his eyes; but the sight of her drew them upward to her, compelled to see by merely seeing her. Then, collecting his

448

breath and heaving a profound sigh, in a weak undertone he said: 'My sweet one, are you truly with me, still alive? Or have you too fallen by chance a victim to the fighting, and cannot any way endure, even after death, to be parted from me, but your wraith and your soul yet show concern for my fortunes?' 'On you,' she answered, 'it rests whether I live or die. Now, do you see this?' she added, showing a sword that lay upon her knees. 'Hitherto it has been idle, withheld by your breathing.' As she spoke she sprang up from the rock: the men on the mountain, struck with wonder and alarm by the sight, as though by some fiery blast, cowered under bushes here and there, for she seemed to them to be something greater and more divine when she stood erect. Her arrows rattled with her sudden movement; the inwoven gold of her dress glistened in the beams of the sun, and her hair, tossing below the wreath like the tresses of a Bacchant, flowed widespread over her back.

W. R. M. LAMB (1961)

THE LOVERS THEAGENES AND CHARICLEA ARE CARRIED OFF TO AN EGYPTIAN LAGOON

After passing along the seashore for about two furlongs they turned and made straight for the mountain slopes, having the sea on their right. They climbed over the ridge with some difficulty, and then hastened on to a lagoon, which extended below the far side of the range and was of this nature: the whole region is named by the Egyptians 'Herdsmen's Home'; it is a low-lying tract in those parts which receives certain overflows of the Nile, so as to form a lake which is of immense depth at its centre but dwindles towards its edges into a swamp. What shores are to seas, swamps are to lakes. Here it is that Egyptians of the bandit kind have their city: one man has built himself a cabin on a patch of land that may lie above the water level; another makes his dwelling in a boat which serves at once for transport and for habitation; upon this the women spin their wool, and also bring forth their children. When a child is born, it is reared at first on its mother's milk, but thereafter on the fish taken

449

from the lagoon and broiled in the sun. When they observe the child attempting to crawl, they fasten a thong to its ankles which allows it to move to the limits of the boat or the hut, thus singularly making the tethering of their feet serve instead of leading them by the hand.

Hence many a herdsman has been born on the lagoon, and reared in this manner, and so come to regard the lagoon as his homeland; and it fully serves as a strong bastion for brigands. Into it therefore flows a stream of men in that way of life, all relying on the water as a wall, and the abundant growth of reeds in the swamp as a stockade. By cutting a number of winding paths which straggle in many twists and turns, and by contriving exits which, while easy enough for them through their familiarity, are bewildering to strangers, they have ingeniously produced a fastness of surpassing strength to ward off harm that might come upon them from an onslaught. So much for the lagoon and the herdsmen who dwell within it.

W. R. M. LAMB (1961)

CHARICLEA MOURNS FOR THE LOST THEAGENES

As she spoke these words she suddenly flung herself prone on the bed, and spreading out her arms embraced it with sobs and heavy sighs, until from the excess of her grief a misty dizziness crept upon her, overclouding her mental faculties, and insensibly drawing her into a sleep which held her until broad daylight had come. Calasiris,[1] surprised that he did not see her at the usual time, went in search of her. Coming to her room, he knocked loudly and repeatedly called her name, till he roused her from slumber. Chariclea, alarmed by this sudden call, darted to the door in the state in which she was disturbed, drew back the bolt and opened for the old man to enter. When he saw her dishevelled hair, her dress all tattered on her bosom, and her eyes still swollen and showing traces of the frenzy that held her before she fell asleep, he understood the cause. He led her back to the bed, seated her and put a cloak about her. Having her thus more suitably attired, he asked: 'What is this, Chariclea? Why such excessive, such

1. An Egyptian sage.

immoderate dismay? Why this senseless subjection to circumstances? I do not recognize you at this moment, you whom I have hitherto found so gallant always and sagacious under the strokes of Fortune. Come now, have done with this extravagant folly! Recollect that you are human, a thing unstable, wont to swerve of a sudden this way and that. Why hasten to destroy yourself, when better prospects may well be just appearing? And be considerate of us, my child; be considerate, if not of yourself yet at least of Theagenes, to whom only life with you is desirable, and existence has value only if you survive.'

W. R. M. LAMB (1961)

CREATOR of the pastoral romance; perhaps third century A.D. His surviving work, *Daphnis and Chloe*, is staged on the island of Lesbos.

*

THE GARDEN OF LESBOS

So as summer was already departing and autumn was approaching, Lamon began to prepare for his master's reception, and tried to make everything a pleasure to look at. He cleaned out the springs to ensure that the water was pure, carted the dung out of the farmyard lest the smell should cause annoyance, and tidied up the garden so that it could be seen in all its beauty.

This garden was indeed a very beautiful place even by comparison with a royal garden. It was two hundred yards long, lay on high ground, and was about a hundred yards wide. It was not unlike a long field. It contained all sorts of trees, apple-trees, myrtles, pear-trees, pomegranate-trees, fig-trees and olives. On one side there was a tall vine that grew over the apple-trees and pear-trees; its grapes were turning dark, as if ripening in competition with the apples and the pears. So much for the cultivated trees; but there were also cypresses and laurels and plane-trees and pines. All these were overgrown, not by a vine, but by ivy; and the clusters of ivy-berries, which were big and beginning to turn black, looked exactly like bunches of grapes.

The fruit-trees were in the middle, as if for protection, and the other trees stood round them, as if to wall them in; but these in their turn were encircled by a narrow fence. Each tree grew separate and distinct from all its neighbours, and there were spaces between trunk and trunk. But overhead the branches met each other and interlaced their foliage; and though it had happened naturally this too gave the impression of having been done on purpose. There were also flower-beds, in which some of the flowers were wild and some were cultivated. The cultivated ones were roses, hyacinths and lilies: the wild ones were violets, narcissi and pimpernels. And there was shade in summer, and flowers in springtime, and fruit in autumn, and delight all the year round.

From that point there was a fine view of the plain, where you could see people grazing their flocks, and a fine view of the sea, where you could watch people sailing past; and this too contributed to the charm of the garden.

In the very middle of the length and breadth of the garden were a temple and an altar sacred to Dionysus. The altar was surrounded with ivy and the temple with vine-shoots.

PAUL TURNER (1956)

THE WEDDING FEAST OF DAPHNIS AND CHLOE

And there in front of the cave, as the weather was fine, Dionysophanes had couches of green leaves heaped up, and after inviting all the villagers to lie on them he entertained them lavishly. Lamon and Myrtale were there, and Dryas and Nape, and Dorcon's relations, and Philetas and his sons, and Chromis and Lycaenion. Not even Lampis was missing, for he had been judged worthy of forgiveness.

As was only to be expected with guests like these, everything that took place was of an agricultural and rustic nature. One man sang the kind of songs that reapers sing, another cracked the sort of jokes that are heard round the wine-press. Philetas played his pipe; Lampis played a flute; Dryas and Lamon danced; Chloe and Daphnis kissed one another. Even the goats were there, grazing close by as if they too were taking part in the feast. The visitors from town did not find this altogether pleasant; but Daphnis called to some of the goats by name, fed them with green leaves, and seized them by the horns and kissed them.

And it was not only then that they behaved like this, for as long as they lived they spent most of their time in pastoral pursuits, worshipping the Nymphs and Pan and Love as their gods, possessing a great many flocks of sheep and goats, and thinking that fruit and milk made a most delicious diet.

PAUL TURNER (1956)

XENOPHON OF EPHESUS

ROMANTIC novelist; probably third century A.D. Author of the *Ephesiaca* or *Anthia and Habrocomes*.

*

THE HERO AND HEROINE, HABROCOMES AND ANTHEA, SAIL AWAY AND ARE CAPTURED BY PIRATES

Now began the Sailors to bawl aloud, the Anchors were weighed, the Pilot took his Place, the Ship gained Way, and the promiscuous Shouts, as well of those on the Shore, as of these on Board, succeeded: Those calling out, 'O! dear Children, say, Shall your tender and indulgent Parents ever behold you again?' And These 'O Parents! Shall we ever again receive the Happiness of seeing you?' Hence followed Tears, Wailings, Sighs, every one, on Shore, calling to those on board, by Name, as it were to imprint their Ideas the firmer on their Memory. MEGAMEDES, taking a Cup, pours out his Libation, and offers up his Prayers so loud as to be heard to the Ship: 'Farewell, my dear Children,' cries he, 'and may you avoid the unhappy Prediction; may the Ephesians again receive you safe and sound; and may you, once more, taste the Sweets of your native Soil. But, if the Gods have otherwise decreed, know, we shall not long survive you. We suffer you to undertake an Expedition, dangerous indeed, but necessary.' A Flood of Tears restrained him from further speaking, and all the Multitude returned into the City, exhorting him, by Turns, to be of good Courage.

ABROCOMAS and ANTHIA comforted, and embraced each other, while a thousand Thoughts occurred. They had Compassion on their Parents, a Desire for their Country; they dreaded the Oracle's Answer; they feared the Success of the Voyage, but their only

Comfort was, they were both in one Vessel. That Day, they sailed with a prosperous Gale, and reached Samos, an Island sacred to JUNO.[1] There, they Sacrifice, there they Sup, there they offer up their Prayers, and, as soon as Night approached, prosecute their Voyage. In the Second Day's sailing they had much Discourse, Whether the Fates would always suffer them to live together? ABROCOMAS fetching a deep Sigh, and remembering his past Troubles, 'O my ANTHIA,' says he, 'dearer to me than Life, how happy should I be would the Gods permit us to enjoy Health, and preserve us together, but if we are doomed to suffer, why should we be separated? Let us swear solemnly to each other, Thou, my better Part, to preserve thy self for ever chaste, and never to receive the Addresses of any Man, I, never to offer Love to any other Woman.' ANTHIA no sooner heard this, than she wept bitterly, 'O my ABROCOMAS,' says she, 'why shouldst thou suffer such Thoughts to harbour in thy Breast? If I should be torn from thee, canst thou suppose I would ever encourage the Addresses of another, when I am not able to live one Moment without thee? I call the great DIANA,[2] my Country's Goddess, to witness, and this Sea we are now passing over, as also the God who exercises his Power over us both, that were I deprived of Thee, for never so small a space of Time, I should neither enjoy Light nor Life afterwards.' ABROCOMAS took his Oath to the same Purpose, and that Circumstance of Time added no small Terror to their Oaths on both Sides. Their Ship, in the mean time, passed by Cos and Cnidos, and came within Sight of Rhodes, a large and beautiful Island. There, the Sailors pretended a Necessity of casting Anchor, as well to take in a Store of Water, as to refresh the Passengers who had already endured the Fatigues of a long Voyage.

Their Ship is accordingly brought into Rhodes, the Mariners go on Shore, ABROCOMAS also descends, handing down his beloved ANTHIA. The Rhodians assemble together to gaze on their Beauty, and whoever beheld them could not keep Silence. Some cried out, That a God and Goddess were arrived, others offered them Adoration, and begged they would be propitious to them. The Names of ABROCOMAS and ANTHIA soon reached the most distant Parts of the

1. Hera.   2. Artemis.

City; the Citizens made public Prayers to them, offered many Sacrifices, and proclaimed the Day of their Arrival, a Festival. They, having viewed the City, dedicate their Golden Armour to the SUN, hang them up in his Temple, and in Memory thereof, have this Epigram inscribed upon them.

> *Young* ABROCOMAS *and* AṄTHIA, *here*
> *Ephesian Citizens, their Strength retrieve,*
> *And to the Sun, great Ruler of the Year,*
> *These Golden Arms, a grateful Present leave.*

After the Dedication was ended, they tarried some few Days in the Island; but then, the Mariners pressing for their Departure, and their Provisions being put on Board, they unmoored, a great Multitude of the Rhodians following them. A pleasing Gale, and a prosperous Fate attended them all that Day; and, the next Night, they reached the Sea, commonly called the Egyptian Sea: But, the Day following, the Wind ceasing, they lay becalmed; hence happened a Slow sailing, a neglect of Duty in the Mariners, as also Feasting and Drunkenness.

Then begun the Predictions of the Oracle to be fulfilled. A Woman in a Purple Habit, of a terrible Aspect, and more than human Size, seemed to stand upon ABROCOMAS's ship; She denounced Death to the Crew, and assured him, that, after most of the rest were swallowed up by the Waves, or fallen by Fire, or Sword, He, with ANTHIA, should escape: He was exceedingly troubled at this Vision, but no sooner recovered himself, than he prepared for the Event, which accordingly happened.

For a huge Rhodian Pirate Galley, with three Banks of Oars, had chosen this Place for her Station. The Pirates themselves were Phoenicians, and made a Show as if their Galley had been loaden with Merchandise, whereas, in reality, she was full of stout and undaunted Sailors. They had received Intelligence, that the Ship, they lay in wait for, was freighted with Gold and Silver, besides Slaves, and other things of great Value. They resolved, therefore, to fall upon them, by Surprise; to slay all who resisted, and carry the others into Phoenicia, to be disposed of, among the rest of the Cargo, they looking upon them, as below their Rage: The Name of the Captain of those Pirates was CORYMBUS, a young Man of a fierce Aspect, piercing Eyes, and a Beard rough and deformed. No sooner had the Pirate Crew taken these Resolutions, than they came up with ABROCOMAS's Ship, and it being then near Mid-day, while all the Sailors lay wallowing in Sloth and Debauchery, part of them drowned in Sleep, and the rest half-dead; CORYMBUS approaches with his swift Galley, and when they came nigh enough, the savage Crew, completely armed, leapt into the Ship, with each his Sword in Hand. Then, some of the Mariners, in the utmost Consternation, throw themselves overboard, and perish; others, running to their Arms, to defend themselves, are suddenly slain. ABROCOMAS and ANTHIA press forward to meet CORYMBUS, and falling down before him, embraced his Knees. 'Our Treasures,' say they, 'take freely into thy Possession, and our selves we yield to thee, to remain at thy Disposal; but we adjure thee, by this Sea, and by that Right-hand of thine, to forbear to slay those who voluntarily surrender themselves into thy Power. Carry us whithersoever it shall please thee: Sell us as Slaves, only out of mere Compassion, grant that we may be both sold to one Master.' CORYMBUS listening to this Discourse, commands their Lives to be spared; and when his Crew had taken on board the most valuable part of the Lading, with ABROCOMAS and ANTHIA, and some few of the Slaves, they set Fire to the Ship, so that all the Mariners who escaped the Fury of the Sword perished in the Flames, it being thought neither easy nor safe to bring them away. A miserable Scene it was, to behold one part of the Ships' Company hurried into Slavery, and the other, still on board their flaming Vessel, wringing their Hands, and bewailing their bitter Fate. They were heard to cry out, 'Whither, O my Masters, will ye be carried? What Land will now receive you? What City will you inhabit?' And they who were going into Slavery answered, 'O thrice happy you, who are to suffer immediate Death, rather than enter into Bondage, and experience the Chains of this Piratical Crew.' In the mean while ABROCOMAS's Tutor, an old Man, of a venerable Aspect, and worthy of Compassion, on account of his grey Hairs, not able to see ABROCOMAS hurried into Slavery, cast himself headlong into the Sea, and endeavoured to gain the Pirate Galley by swimming; crying out, at the same time, 'O Abrocomas, my Son, where dost thou leave thy hoary Tutor? Whither art thou going? Do thou slay me, a miserable Wretch, with thy own Hands, and perform my Funeral Rites, who am not able to live without thee.' Having thus said, and despairing, at last, to gain the Ship, wherein Abrocomas was, he yielded himself to the Mercy of the Waves, and was drowned. No Scene could be more dreadful to Abrocomas than this, he oft stretched out his Hands to him, and entreated the Pirates to receive him on board. But they slighted his Request.

J. Rooke (1727)

PART XI

THE LAST GREAT PAGAN PHILOSOPHER

PLOTINUS

PERHAPS from Lycopolis in Egypt; A.D. 205–269/70. The latest and one of the greatest of the pagan philosophers.

*

THE ONE

What then do we mean by 'One', and how do we fit this Unity into our thought? 'One' is used in more senses than that of the unity of a numerical unit or a point: in this sense the soul, taking away magnitude and numerical plurality, arrives at the smallest possible and rests on something which is certainly without parts, but belongs to the divisible and exists in something else. But the One is not in something else or in the divisible, nor is It without parts in the sense of the smallest possible. For It is the greatest of all things, not in size but in power – that which is without magnitude can be great in power, for the things which come after It are indivisible and without parts in their powers, not in their bulk. It must be considered as infinite, not by unlimited extension of size or number but by the unboundedness of Its power.

When you think of Him as Mind or God, He is still more: and when you unify Him in your thought, the degree of unity by which He transcends your thought is still greater than you imagine it to be. For He exists in and by Himself without any attributes. One might conceive of His unity in terms of His self-sufficiency. For He must be the most sufficient of all things, the most independent, and the most without wants. Everything which is multiple and not one is defective since it is composed of many parts. Substance needs Him in order to be one: but He does not need Himself; for He is Himself. A thing which is multiple needs its full number of parts and each of its parts, since it exists with the others and not independently, is in need of the others; so a thing of this kind shows itself defective as a whole and in each individual part. If then, as is in fact true, there must be something supremely self-sufficing, it must be the One, which is the only Thing of such a kind as not to be defective either in relation to Itself or to anything else.

It seeks nothing towards Its being or Its well-being or Its establishment in Its place. It does not derive Its being from others, for It is the Cause of the others; and what from outside Itself could conduce to Its well-being? To be in a good state is not something accidental to It, for It is the Good. And it has no place: It needs no establishing as if It could not support Itself; that which has to be established is a lifeless mass which falls till it is set in place. All other things are established through It. Through It they at once exist and receive the place ordained for each. That which seeks place is defective. But a principle has no need of what comes after it; and the Principle of all things needs none of them; for that which is defective is defective because it is in quest of a principle. Then again, if the One is defective, it is clear that It is seeking not to be one; that is, It is in need of something to destroy It. But everything which is said to be in need is in need of well-being and something to preserve it: so there is nothing which is good for the One, nor does It wish for anything.

It transcends good, and is Good not for Itself, but for the others, if any of them can participate in It. It is not thought, for there is no otherness in It. It is not movement, but prior to movement and thought. For what would It think about? Itself? But then It would be ignorant before Its thought, and would need thought to know Itself, It which is self-sufficient! There is no ignorance in It because It does not know or think Itself, because ignorance is always of something else, when one of two things does not know the other. But That Which is One Alone neither knows nor has anything of which to be ignorant; being One, present to Itself, It needs no thought of Itself. We ought not in fact even to speak of 'self-presence', in order to preserve the unity. We should leave out thought and self-presence, and thinking about Itself and other things. We ought not to class It as a thinking being but rather as thought; for thought does not think, but is cause of thinking to something else; and the cause is not the same as its effect. So the Cause of all things is none of them. We should not even speak of It as Good, in the sense of the good which It gives to others. It is the Good in a different sense, transcending all other goods.

A. H. ARMSTRONG (1953)

THE MYSTIC EXPERIENCE

So we must ascend again to the Good, which every soul desires. Anyone who has seen it knows what I mean when I say that it is beautiful. It is desired as good, and the desire for it is directed to good, and the attainment of it is for those who go up to the higher world and are converted and strip off what we put on in our descent (just as for those who go up to the celebrations of sacred rites there are purifications, and strippings off of the clothes they wore before, and going up naked); until, passing in the ascent all that is alien to the God, one sees with one's self alone, That alone, simple, single and pure, from which all depends and to which all look and are and live and think; for it is cause of life and mind and being. If anyone sees it, what passion will he feel, what longing in his desire to be united with it, what a shock of delight! The man who has not seen it may desire it as good, but he who has seen it glories in its beauty and is full of wonder and delight, enduring a shock which causes no hurt, loving with true passion and piercing longing; he laughs at all other loves and despises what he thought beautiful before; it is like the experience of those who have met appearances of gods or spirits and do not any more appreciate as they did the beauty of other bodies. 'What then are we to think, if anyone contemplates the absolute beauty which exists pure by itself, uncontaminated by flesh or body, not in earth or heaven, that it may keep its purity?' All these other things are external additions and mixtures and not primary, but derived from it. If then one sees That which provides for all and remains by itself and gives to all but receives nothing into itself, if he abides in the contemplation of this kind of beauty and rejoices in being made like it, how can he need any other beauty? For this, since it is beauty most of all, and primary beauty, makes its lovers beautiful and lovable. Here the greatest, the ultimate contest is set before our souls; all our toil and trouble is for this, not to be left without a share in the best of visions.

The man who attains this is blessed in seeing that 'blessed sight', and he who fails to attain it has failed utterly. A man has not failed if he fails to win beauty of colours or bodies, or power of office or kingship even, but if he fails to win this and only this. For this he should give up the attainment of kingship and of rule over all earth and sea and sky, if only by leaving and overlooking them he can turn to That and see . . .

This is what the command given in those mysteries intends to proclaim, 'Do not reveal to the uninitiated.' Because the Divine is not to be revealed it forbids us to declare It to anyone else who has not himself had the good fortune to see. Since there were not two, but the seer himself was one with the Seen (for It was not really seen, but united to him), if he remembers who he became when he was united to That, he will have Its image in himself. He was One himself then, with no distinction in him either in relation to himself or anything else; for there was no movement in him, and he had no emotion, no desire for anything else when he had made the ascent, no reason or thought; his own self was not there for him, if we should say even this. He was as if carried away or possessed by a god, in a quiet solitude, in the stillness of his being turning away to nothing and not busy about himself, altogether at rest and having become a kind of rest.

A. H. ARMSTRONG (1953–66)

LIST OF DATES

(The dates of writers, in so far as they are known, are given in the text.)

B.C.

Later 13th cent.	Destruction of Troy, possibly by Greeks.
Later 11th cent.	Greek colonization of Ionia and other regions on the west coast of Asia.
776	Traditional date of the first Olympic Games.
Later 8th cent.	First Greek colonization of Sicily and south Italy.
7th cent.	First Greek colonization of the Black Sea and its approaches.
c. 650	Cypselus replaces aristocratic régime by dictatorial government ('tyranny') at Corinth.
594; 507	Solon and Cleisthenes direct reforms at Athens.
c. 550?	Sparta dominant in the Peloponnese.
546?	Pisistratus becomes 'Tyrant' of Athens.
c. 545	Cyrus of Persia overthrows Croesus of Lydia and conquers Ionia.

*

499–494	Ionian revolt against Persia.
490	Persian invasion of Greece. Battle of Marathon.
480	Invasion of Greece by Xerxes. Battles of Thermopylae, Artemisium and Salamis.
479	Battles of Plataea and Mycale.
478–477	Athens founds Confederacy of Delos, which later becomes empire.

*

431	Outbreak of Peloponnesian war between Athens and Sparta (with Corinth).
428–427; 416	Revolts of Mytilene and Melos against Athens.
415–413	Disastrous Athenian expedition against Syracuse.
411–410	Oligarchic revolution of the Four Hundred at Athens.
405	Dionysus I becomes 'Tyrant' of Syracuse. Final defeat of the Athenians at Aegospotami.
404	Surrender of Athens and oligarchic revolution of the Thirty.

*

401	Retreat of the Ten Thousand from Mesopotamia to the sea.
362	Death of Epaminondas at Mantinea ends brief ascendancy of Thebes.
338	Philip II of Macedonia defeats Athens and Thebes at Chaeronea.
336–323	Conquests of Alexander the Great.
Later 4th cent.	Establishment of Successor States (Diadochi) of Alexander: the Antigonids based on Macedonia; the Seleucids based on Syria and Mesopotamia; the Lagids (Ptolemies) based on Egypt. Taras (Tarentum) becomes leading city-state of south Italy.
3rd cent.	Rise of kingdoms of Pergamum and Bactria (Indo-Greeks); Rhodes becomes richest city-state. Aeolian and Achaean Leagues control much of Greece.

★

280–275	Pyrrhus of Epirus invades south Italy and Sicily.
241	Romans annex Sicily after First Punic War against Carthage.
215	Philip V of Macedon makes treaty with Hannibal during Second Punic War.
2nd cent.	Romans defeat Macedonians (197; 168) and Seleucids (189) and annex Macedonia and Achaia (sack of Corinth, 146), North Africa (after Third Punic War) and 'Asia' (Pergamum, 133).
87–86	Athens joins Mithridates of Pontus against Rome and is reduced by Sulla.
63	Pompey defeats Mithridates and annexes Seleucid Syria.
49–44	Dictatorships of Julius Caesar, who defeats Pompey (48) and his sons (46–45).

★

| 31–27 | Octavian defeats Antony and Cleopatra at Actium (31), annexes Egypt (30) and establishes principate in which Italy is predominant; assuming the name of Augustus (27). |

466

A.D.

66–73; 132–5	First and Second Jewish Revolts.
3rd and 4th cents.	Rise of Greek east to dominant position in Roman empire (Christian from 312–13), culminating in establishment of Constantinople (Byzantium) as capital (324–30).

SOURCES AND ACKNOWLEDGEMENTS

HOMER

p. 23: *Iliad*, XXIV, 503.

p. 24: *Iliad*, XVIII, 203.

p. 25: *Iliad*, XVIII, 478, 509, 561.

p. 28: *Iliad*, I, 595.

p. 29: *Iliad*, III, 203.

p. 30: *Iliad*, IV, 422.

p. 31: *Iliad*, VIII, 553.

p. 31: *Iliad*, II, 198.

p. 33: *Iliad*, II, 453.

p. 34: *Iliad*, VI, 464. (From Richmond Lattimore, *Iliad*, Routledge & Kegan Paul Ltd, London, 1951. Copyright © by Richmond Lattimore, 1951. Reprinted with the permission of Routledge & Kegan Paul and the University of Chicago Press.)

p. 36: *Iliad*, I, 101. (Translated by Peter Green, from *The Craft and Context of Translation: A Critical Symposium*, edited by W. Arrowsmith and R. Shattuck, University of Texas Press, 1961. By arrangement with the New American Library Inc., New York.)

p. 37: *Iliad*, XIV, 166. (Translated by Ian Fletcher, from ibid.)

p. 38: *Iliad*, XVI, 1, 7. (From Christopher Logue, *Patrocleia*, Scorpion Press, London. Reprinted with the permission of the Scorpion Press and the University of Michigan Press.)

p. 40: *Iliad*, XXII, 289. (From Ennis Rees, *Iliad*, Modern Library Inc., New York.)

p. 43: *Iliad*, XVII, 735. (From Edwin Morgan, in *Arion* (University of Texas), vol. VII, No. 1, 1968.)

p. 45: *Odyssey*, XXII, 1.

p. 46: *Odyssey*, IX, 437.

p. 47: *Odyssey*, VI, 110. (From Ennis Rees, *Odyssey*, Modern Library Inc., New York.)

p. 50: *Odyssey*, V, 225. (From *The Odyssey of Homer* translated by Richmond Lattimore, pp. 94–5. Copyright © 1965, 1967 by Richmond Lattimore. Reprinted by permission of Harper & Row, Publishers, Inc., New York.)

p. 52: *Odyssey*, X, 210. (From ibid., pp. 157–8.)

SOURCES AND ACKNOWLEDGEMENTS

HESIOD

    p. 54: *Works and Days*, 368. (From *Greek Poetry*, translated by F. L. Lucas, Everyman's Library edition. Published by J. M. Dent & Sons Ltd, London, and E. P. Dutton & Co. Inc., New York, and reprinted with their permission.)

    p. 54: *Works and Days*, 504, 493. (From ibid.)

    p. 55: *Works and Days*, 11 (From Richmond Lattimore, *Hesiod*, University of Michigan Press, 1959.)

    p. 56: *Works and Days*, 286. (From ibid.)

    p. 58: *Theogony*, 561. (From ibid.)

    p. 60: *Theogony*, 689. (From ibid.)

HOMERIC HYMNS

    p. 63: *Hymn*, VII, 1.

    p. 65: *Hymn*, XXX, 1.

    p. 66: *Hymn*, III, 143. (From *Greek Poetry*, translated by F. L. Lucas, Everyman's Library edition. Published by J. M. Dent & Sons Ltd, London, and E. P. Dutton & Co. Inc., New York, and reprinted with their permission.)

    p. 67: *Hymn*, XIX, 1. (From Emily Vermeule in *Arion* (University of Texas), vol. III, No. 1, 1968.)

    p. 69: *Hymn*, XIX, 1. (From Peter Jay, *Agenda*, vol. VII, No. 1, 1969.)

    p. 70: *Hymn*, VII, 1. (From Peter Jay, *Agenda*, vol. VI, Nos. 3–4, 1968.)

ARCHILOCHUS

    p. 75: E. Diehl, *Anthologia Lyrica Graeca*, 3rd edition (1949), No. 79a. (From Richmond Lattimore, *Greek Lyrics*, University of Chicago Press, 1955.)

    p. 75: F. Lasserre and A. Bonnard, *Archiloque: Fragments*, Paris, 1958, No. 13. (From ibid.)

    p. 76: ibid., No. 118. (From *Archilochus: The Fragments*, translated by Guy Davenport, University of California Press.)

    p. 76: ibid., No. 12. (From ibid.)

    p. 76: ibid., No. 249. (From ibid.)

ALCMAN

    p. 77: D. L. Page, *Poetae Melici Graeci* (1962), No. 89. (From A. E. Zimmern, *The Greek Commonwealth*, 5th edition, Clarendon Press, Oxford, 1951.)

    p. 77: ibid., No. 26. (From *Greek Lyric Poetry*, translated by Willis

Barnstone. Copyright © by Bantam Books Inc., New York, 1962.)

p. 77: ibid., No. 56. (From ibid.)

p. 78: ibid., No. 17. (From ibid.)

ANACREON

p. 79: ibid., No. 395. (Translated by T. F. Higham, from *The Oxford Book of Greek Verse in Translation*, edited by T. F. Higham and C. M. Bowra, 1938. Reprinted with the permission of the Clarendon Press, Oxford.)

p. 79: ibid., Nos. 372, 373. (From *Greek Lyric Poetry*, translated by Willis Barnstone. Copyright © by Bantam Books Inc., New York, 1962.)

ALCAEUS

p. 81: E. Lobel and D. L. Page, *Poetarum Lesbiorum Fragmenta* (1955), No. z 14 (338). (From Richmond Lattimore, *Greek Lyrics*, University of Chicago Press, 1955.)

p. 81: ibid., No. z 23a (347a). (From *Greek Lyric Poetry*, translated by Willis Barnstone. Copyright © by Bantam Books Inc., New York, 1962.)

p. 82: ibid., Nos. z 2, a 6 (326). (From ibid.)

p. 82: ibid. No. ni (283). (Translated by Andrew Meade Miller. Copyright © 1971.)

p. 83: 'Epitaph'. (Translated by William J. Philbin, *To You Simonides*. Reprinted by permission of the Dolmen Press Ltd, Dublin.)

SAPPHO

p. 84: E. Lobel and D. L. Page, *Poetarum Lesbiorum Fragmenta* (1955), No. 55. (From Richmond Lattimore, *Greek Lyrics*, University of Chicago Press, 1955.)

p. 84: ibid., No. 96. (From C. M. Bowra, *The Greek Experience*. Published by permission of George Weidenfeld & Nicolson Ltd, London, and Frederick A. Praeger Inc., New York.)

p. 85: ibid., No. 31. (From *Greek Lyric Poetry*, translated by Willis Barnstone. Copyright © by Bantam Books Inc., New York, 1962.)

p. 85: ibid., No. 130. (Translated by Suzy Q. Groden, in *Arion* (University of Texas), vol. iii, No. 3., 1964. Reprinted with the permission of The Bobbs-Merrill Co. Inc., New York.)

p. 86: ibid., No. 2. (From A. R. Burn, *A Traveller's History of Greece*, Hodder & Stoughton Ltd, London, 1965. Published as *The Pelican History of Greece*, Penguin Books, Harmondsworth, 1966.)

SIMONIDES

p. 87: D. L. Page, *Poetae Melici Graeci* (1962), No. 521. (From Richmond Lattimore, *Greek Lyrics*, University of Chicago Press, 1955.)

p. 87: E. Diehl, *Anthologia Lyrica Graeca*, 3rd edition, 1949, No. 87. (From *Greek Lyric Poetry*, translated by Willis Barnstone. Copyright © by Bantam Books Inc., New York, 1962.)

p. 87: ibid., No. 161. (From ibid.)

p. 88: ibid., No. 122. (From A. R. Burn, *A Traveller's History of Greece*, Hodder & Stoughton Ltd, London, 1965. Published as *The Pelican History of Greece*, Penguin Books, Harmondsworth, 1966.)

p. 88: ibid., No. 161. (From Andrew Sinclair, *Selections from the Greek Anthology*, George Weidenfeld & Nicolson, 1967. Reprinted by permission of Weidenfeld & Nicolson Ltd, London, and The Macmillan Co., New York.)

IBYCUS

p. 89: D. L. Page, *Poetae Melici Graeci* (1962), No. 286. (From *Greek Lyric Poetry*, translated by Willis Barnstone. Copyright © by Bantam Books Inc., New York, 1962.)

XENOPHANES

p. 90: G. S. Kirk and J. E. Raven, *The Presocratic Philosophers*, Cambridge University Press (paperback edition, 1966), p. 179, Nos. 191, 189, 190. (From ibid.)

p. 90: ibid., pp. 168f., Nos. 170, 172, 171. (From ibid.)

SOLON

p. 91: J. M. Edmonds, *Greek Elegy and Iambus* (Loeb edition), Heinemann and Harvard University Press, I (1931), p. 121, fragment 5. (From Richmond Lattimore, *Greek Lyrics*, University of Chicago Press, 1955.)

THEOGNIS

p. 92: ibid., p. 285, line 457. (From J. M. Edmonds, *Some Greek Poems of Love and Beauty*, Cambridge University Press, 1937.)

p. 92: ibid., p. 249, line 173. (From *Greek Lyric Poetry*, translated by Willis Barnstone. Copyright © by Bantam Books Inc., New York, 1962.)

p. 92: ibid., p. 281, line 425. (From ibid.)

p. 93: ibid., p. 395, line 1335. (From ibid.)

p. 93: ibid., p. 257, line 237. (Translated by Andrew Meade Miller. Copyright © 1971.)

p. 94: ibid., p. 323, line 783. (Translated by Andrew Meade Miller. Copyright © 1971.)

BACCHYLIDES

p. 96: B. Snell, *Bacchylides*, 8th edition, Teubner (1961), No. 13. (From Robert Fagles, *Bacchylides: Complete Poems*, Yale University Press. Copyright © 1961 by Robert Fagles.)

EMPEDOCLES

p. 99: G. S. Kirk and J. E. Raven, *The Presocratic Philosophers*, Cambridge University Press (paperback edition, 1966), p. 351, No. 471. (Translated by T. F. Higham, in *The Oxford Book of Greek Verse in Translation*, edited by T. F. Higham and C. M. Bowra, 1938. Reprinted with the permission of the Clarendon Press, Oxford.)

PINDAR

p. 100: *Pythian Odes*, VIII, 81. (From C. M. Bowra, *The Odes of Pindar*, Penguin Books, Harmondsworth, 1969.)

p. 101: *Olympian Odes*, I, 1 (From ibid.)

p. 102: *Olympian Odes*, X, 22 (From ibid.)

p. 103: *Isthmian Odes*, VIII, 5 (From ibid.)

p. 103: *Nemean Odes*, VII, 11 (From ibid.)

p. 104: *Nemean Odes*, VI, 1 (From ibid.)

p. 105: B. Snell, *Pindarus*, 3rd edition, Leipzig (1959–64), No. 129. (From *Greek Lyric Poetry*, translated by Willis Barnstone. Copyright © by Bantam Books Inc., New York, 1962.)

PRAXILLA

p. 106: D. L. Page, *Poetae Melici Graeci* (1962), No. 747. (From Richmond Lattimore, *Greek Lyrics*, University of Chicago Press.)

TIMOTHEUS

p. 107: ibid., No. 796. (Translated by Gilbert Highet, in *The Oxford Book of Greek Verse in Translation*, edited by T. F. Higham and

C. M. Bowra, 1938. Reprinted with the permission of the Clarendon Press, Oxford.)

ARIPHRON

p. 108: P. Maas, *Epidaurische Hymnen* (Halle, 1933), pp. 184ff. (From C. M. Bowra, *The Greek Experience*. Reprinted with the permission of George Weidenfeld & Nicolson Ltd, London, and Frederick A. Praeger Inc., New York.)

ANONYMOUS

p. 109: E. Lobel, *Sapphous Mele* (1925), incerti autoris No. 6. (Translated by Suzy Q. Groden, in *Arion* (University of Texas), vol. III, No. 3, 1964. Reprinted with the permission of The Bobbs-Merrill Co. Inc., New York.)

p. 109: D. L. Page, *Poetae Melici Graeci* (1962), No. 853. (From Kenneth Rexroth, *Poems from the Greek Anthology*. Reprinted with the permission of the University of Michigan Press.)

AESCHYLUS

p. 113: *Prometheus Bound*, 425.

p. 113: *Seven Against Thebes*, 848. ('Septem Contra Thebas' by Aeschylus, translated by A. E. Housman, in *The Collected Poems of A. E. Housman*, Jonathan Cape, London, 1939. Reproduced by permission of Jonathan Cape Ltd and the Society of Authors, London, and of Holt, Rinehart & Winston Inc., New York. Copyright © 1939, 1940 by Holt, Rinehart & Winston Inc. Copyright © 1967, 1968 by Robert E. Symons.)

p. 114: *Agamemnon*, 464. (From George Thomson, *Oresteia of Aeschylus*, Cambridge University Press, 1958.)

p. 115: *Edoni*, fragment 57, A. Nauck, *Tragicorum Graecorum Fragmenta*, 2nd edition, 1889. (Anonymous translation, in *The Oxford Book of Greek Verse in Translation*, edited by T. F. Higham and C. M. Bowra, 1938. Reprinted with the permission of the Clarendon Press, Oxford.)

p. 115: *Prometheus Bound*, 168. (From Rex Warner, *Prometheus Bound*, The Bodley Head, London, 1947.)

p. 116: *Persians*, 353. (From A. R. Burn, *A Traveller's History of Greece*, Hodder & Stoughton Ltd, London, 1965. Published as *The Pelican History of Greece*, Penguin Books, Harmondsworth, 1966.)

SOURCES AND ACKNOWLEDGEMENTS

SOPHOCLES

p. 119: *Oedipus the King*, 863.

p. 120: *Women of Trachis*, 93.

p. 121: *Ajax*, 645.

p. 122: *Oedipus the King*, 924. (From J. T. Sheppard, *Sophocles: Oedipus Tyrannus*, Cambridge University Press, 1920.)

p. 127: *Oedipus at Colonus*, 1211. (Translated by A. E. Housman, in *The Oxford Book of Greek Verse*, edited by T. F. Higham and C. M. Bowra, 1938. Reprinted with the permission of the Clarendon Press, Oxford.)

p. 128: ibid. (From 'A Young Man and an Old Man', translated by W. B. Yeats, in *The Collected Poems of W. B. Yeats*, 1950. Reproduced by permission of Mr M. B. Yeats, Macmillan & Co., London, The Macmillan Co. of Canada and The Macmillan Co., New York.)

p. 129: *Philoctetes*, 271. (Translated by C. M. Bowra, in *The Oxford Book of Greek Verse*, edited by T. F. Higham and C. M. Bowra, 1938. Reprinted with the permission of the Clarendon Press, Oxford.)

p. 130: *Tereus*, fragment 524, A. Nauck, *Tragicorum Graecorum Fragmenta*, 2nd edition, 1889. (Translated by C. M. Bowra in ibid.)

p. 130: *Oedipus at Colonus*, 693. (From Robert Fitzgerald, *Greek Tragedies*, vol. III, edited by D. Grene and R. Lattimore, University of Chicago Press, 1960.)

p. 131: *Antigone*, 332. (Translated by Gilbert Murray, from Arnold J. Toynbee, *Greek Historical Thought*. Reprinted with the permission of J. M. Dent & Sons Ltd, London, and the Beacon Press, Boston.)

p. 133: *Oedipus the King*, 774. (From Paul Roche, *The Oedipus Plays of Sophocles*. Copyright © 1958 by Paul Roche. By arrangement with the New American Library Inc., New York.)

p. 134: *Antigone*, 332. (From Richard Braun, in *Arion* (University of Texas), vol. I, No. 3, 1962.)

p. 136: *Antigone*, 223. (From T. H. Banks, *Three Theban Plays of Sophocles*, Oxford University Press Inc. Copyright © 1956 by Theodore Howard Banks.)

EURIPIDES

p. 139: *Cyclops*, 356.

p. 140: *Bellerophon*, fragment 286, A. Nauck, *Tragicorum Graecorum Fragmenta*, 2nd edition, 1889.

p. 140: *Madness of Heracles*, 359.

p. 143: *Hippolytus*, 375. (From Gilbert Murray, *Euripides and His Age*, George Allen & Unwin Ltd, London.)

p. 143: *Trojan Women*, 799. (From ibid.)

p. 144: *Phrixus*, fragment 833, A. Nauck, *Tragicorum Graecorum Fragmenta*, 2nd edition, 1889. (From ibid.)

p. 144: *Ion*, 859. (From Hilda Doolittle, *Euripides: Ion*, Chatto and Windus, London 1937.)

p. 148: *Ion*, 82. (From C. M. Bowra, *The Greek Experience*. Published by permission of George Weidenfeld & Nicolson Ltd, London, and Frederick A. Praeger Inc., New York.)

p. 149: Fragment 910, A. Nauck, *Tragicorum Graecorum Fragmenta*, 2nd edition, 1889. (From ibid.)

p. 150: *Medea*, 824. (From ibid.)

p. 150: *Medea*, 213. (From 'The Medea of Euripides', in *Three Greek Plays of Euripides*, translated by Rex Warner. Copyright © 1958 by Rex Warner. By arrangement with the New American Library Inc., New York.)

p. 152: *Helen*, 393, 503, 362. (From 'The Helen of Euripides', in ibid. Copyright © 1958 by Rex Warner. By arrangement with the New American Library Inc., New York.)

p. 152: *Iphigenia in Tauris*, 1089. (Translated by Ian Scott-Kilvert, in *Voices of the Past*, vol. 1, edited by James and Janet Maclean Todd.)

p. 154: *Madness of Heracles*, 1340. (Translated by William Arrowsmith, in *The Complete Greek Tragedies*, edited by D. Grene and R. Lattimore. Reprinted with the permission of the University of Chicago Press.)

p. 155: *The Bacchants*, 677. (Translated by William Arrowsmith, in ibid.)

ARISTOPHANES

p. 158: *Clouds*, 275, 298.

p. 159: *Birds*, 685, 708.

p. 161: *Acharnians*, 628. (From Patric Dickinson, *Aristophanes Against War*, Oxford University Press.)

p. 163: *Acharnians*, 497. (From ibid.)

p. 164: *Clouds*, 42. (From Patric Dickinson, *Plays of Aristophanes*, Oxford University Press.)

p. 164: *Birds*, 30. (From William Arrowsmith, *Aristophanes: The Birds*, University of Michigan Press.)

p. 165: *Birds*, 522. (From ibid.)

p. 166: *Lysistrata*, 506. (From Dudley Fitts, *Lysistrata of Aristophanes*. Reprinted with permission of Faber & Faber Ltd, London, and Harcourt, Brace & World Inc., New York.)

p. 167: *Thesmophoriazusae*, 384. (From ibid.)

p. 168: *Thesmophoriazusae*, 130. (Translated by Ian Fletcher, in *Arion* (University of Texas), vol. II, No. 3, 1963.)

p. 170: *Frogs*, 718. (From David Barrett, *Aristophanes: The Frogs and Other Plays*, Penguin Books, Harmondsworth, 1964.)

p. 171: *Wasps*, 1102. (From ibid.)

HERODOTUS

p. 175: II, 124.

p. 177: VII, 207.

p. 178: I, 94. (From Aubrey de Selincourt, *Herodotus: The Histories*, Penguin Books, Harmondsworth, 1954.)

p. 179: I, 8. (From ibid.)

p. 181: IV, 22. (From ibid.)

p. 182: IV, 71. (From ibid.)

p. 183: III, 115. (From ibid.)

p. 184: VI, 129. (From ibid.)

p. 185: VII, 44. (From ibid.)

p. 185: VII. (From ibid.)

THUCYDIDES

p. 187: II, 89.

p. 190: III, 82.

p. 192: VII, 70.

p. 194: I, 138. (From Rex Warner, *Thucydides: The Peloponnesian War*, Penguin Books, Harmondsworth, 1954. Reprinted with the permission of The Bodley Head.)

p. 195: I, 1 (From ibid.)

p. 196: I, 70. (From ibid.)

p. 197: II, 40. (From ibid.)

p. 198: III, 36. (From ibid.)

p. 199: VII, 84. (From ibid.)

XENOPHON

p. 201: *Anabasis*, I, 5. (From Rex Warner, *Xenophon: The Persian Expedition*, Penguin Books, Harmondsworth, 1949.)

p. 202: *Anabasis*, I, 5. (From ibid.)

p. 202: *Anabasis*, IV, 5. (From ibid.)

p. 204: *Anabasis*, IV, 6. (From ibid.)

p. 205: *Anabasis*, IV, 7. (From ibid.)

p. 206: *Anabasis*, V, 4. (From ibid.)

p. 207: *Hellenica*, II, 1. (From Rex Warner, *Xenophon: A History of My Times*, Penguin Books, Harmondsworth, 1966.)

p. 209: *Memorabilia*, I, 3. (From Hugh Tredennick, *Xenophon: Memoirs of Socrates and the Symposium*, Penguin Books, Harmondsworth, 1970.)

p. 210: *Memorabilia*, III, 6; IV, 2. (From ibid.)

THE HIPPOCRATICS

p. 219: *On Environment* (*De Aeribus*), 16. (From Arnold J. Toynbee, *Greek Historical Thought*. Reprinted with the permission of J. M. Dent & Sons, London, and the Beacon Press, Boston.)

p. 220: *On Environment* (*De Aeribus*), 22. (From ibid.)

LYSIAS

p. 222: *Against Eratosthenes*, 65. (From A. N. W. Saunders, *Greek Political Oratory*, Penguin Books, Harmondsworth, 1970.)

ISOCRATES

p. 225: *Panegyricus*, 47. (From ibid.)

p. 226: *Panegyricus*, 113. (From ibid.)

p. 228: *Philip*, 17. (From ibid.)

DEMOSTHENES

p. 230: *First Philippic*, 1. (From ibid.)

p. 232: *Second Olynthiac*, 26. (From ibid.)

p. 234: *Third Olynthiac*, 21. (From ibid.)

PLATO

p. 237: *Apology*, 19.

p. 241: *Symposium*, 215. (From Walter Hamilton, *Plato: The Symposium*, Penguin Books, Harmondsworth, 1951.)

p. 243: *Critias*, 111. (From Arnold J. Toynbee, *Greek Historical Thought*. Reprinted with the permission of J. M. Dent & Sons, London, and the Beacon Press, Boston.)

p. 244: *Phaedo*, 66. (From Hugh Tredennick, *Plato: The Last Days of Socrates*, Penguin Books, Harmondsworth, 1954.)

p. 246: *Phaedo*, 117. (From ibid.)

p. 248: *Apology*, 30. (From ibid.)

p. 249: *Republic*, 487. (From H. D. P. Lee, *Plato: The Republic*, Penguin Books, Harmondsworth, 1955.)

p. 250: *Republic*, 372. (From ibid.)

p. 252: *Republic*, 401. (From ibid.)

p. 253: *Republic*, 518. (From ibid.)

p. 254: *Republic*, 574. (From ibid.)

p. 256: *Protagoras*, 319. (From W. K. C. Guthrie, *Plato: Protagoras and Meno*, Penguin Books, Harmondsworth, 1956.)

p. 257: *Meno*, 79. (From ibid.)

p. 258: *Timaeus*, 29. (From H. D. P. Lee, *Plato: Timaeus*, Penguin Books, Harmondsworth, 1956.)

p. 259: *Timaeus*, 20. (From ibid.)

p. 264: *Laws*, 694. (From T. J. Saunders, *Plato: The Laws*, Penguin Books, Harmondsworth, 1970.)

p. 273: *Laws*, 714. (From ibid.)

p. 276: *Laws*, 656. (From ibid.)

p. 277: E. Diehl, *Anthologia Lyrica Graeca*, 3rd edition (1949), No. [30].

p. 277: ibid., No. 5. (Translated by T. F. Higham, in *The Oxford Book of Greek Verse in Translation*, edited by T. F. Higham and C. M. Bowra, 1938. Reprinted with the permission of the Clarendon Press, Oxford.)

ARISTOTLE

p. 278: *Nicomachean Ethics*, I, 7. (From J. A. K. Thomson, *Aristotle: Ethics*, Penguin Books, Harmondsworth, 1955. Adapted from J. A. K. Thomson's *The Ethics of Aristotle*. Reprinted with the permission of George Allen & Unwin Ltd, London, and Barnes & Noble Inc., New York.)

p. 279: *Nicomachean Ethics*, III, 5. (From ibid.)

p. 279: *Nicomachean Ethics*, V, 10. (From ibid.)

p. 280: *Nicomachean Ethics*, VIII, 6. (From ibid.)

p. 282: *Politics*, I, 5. (From T. A. Sinclair, *Aristotle: The Politics*, Penguin Books, Harmondsworth, 1962.)

p. 284: *Politics*, II, 5. (From ibid.)

p. 285: *Politics*, VII, 11. (From ibid.)

p. 287: *Poetics*, 9. (From T. S. Dorsch, *Classical Literary Criticism*, Penguin Books, Harmondsworth, 1965.)

p. 289: *Poetics*, 13. (From ibid.)

SOURCES AND ACKNOWLEDGEMENTS

THEOPHRASTUS

p. 293: *Characters*, 11, 12, 13, 27, 29. (From Philip Vellacott, *Menander: Plays and Fragments and Theophrastus: The Characters*, Penguin Books, Harmondsworth, 1967.)

EPICURUS

p. 297: *Letter to Menoceus* (From J. L. Saunders, *Greek and Roman Philosophy after Aristotle*, The Free Press, New York.)

MENANDER

p. 303: Fragment 531, T. Kock, *Comicorum Atticorum Fragmenta*, III, p. 155. (Translated by C. M. Bowra, in *The Oxford Book of Greek Verse in Translation*, edited by T. F. Higham and C. M. Bowra. Reprinted with the permission of the Clarendon Press, Oxford.)

p. 303: Fragment 538, ibid. (Translated by T. F. Higham, in ibid.)

p. 304: *Counterfeit Baby* or *Rustic* (*Hypobolimaeus, Agroecus*), fragment 481, ibid. (From Philip Vellacott, *Menander: Plays and Fragments and Theophrastus: The Characters*, Penguin Books, Harmondsworth, 1967.)

p. 304: Fragment 482, ibid. (From ibid.)

p. 305: *Arbitration* (*Epitrepontes*), 871. (From ibid.)

p. 306: *The Girl from Samos* (*Samia*), 4. (From ibid.)

p. 307: Fragment 533, T. Kock, *Comicorum Atticorum Fragmenta*, III, p. 155. (From ibid.)

p. 308: *The Doorkeeper* (*Thyrorus*), fragment 923, ibid. (From ibid.)

p. 308: *Trophonius*, fragment 462, ibid. (From ibid.)

CLEANTHES

p. 309: *Hymn to Zeus*. (From James Adam, *The Stoic and Epicurean Philosophers*, edited by Whitney J. Oates. Reprinted with the permission of Random House Inc., New York.)

ASCLEPIADES

p. 311: A. S. F. Gow and D. L. Page, *The Greek Anthology: Hellenistic Epigrams*, Cambridge University Press (1965), No. 8. (From *Greek Lyric Poetry*, translated by Willis Barnstone. Copyright © by Bantam Books Inc., New York, 1962.)

p. 311: ibid., No. 5. (From Kenneth Rexroth, *Poems from the Greek Anthology*. Reprinted with the permission of the University of Michigan Press.)

p. 311: ibid., No. 20. (From ibid.)

SOURCES AND ACKNOWLEDGEMENTS

THEOCRITUS
- p. 313: *Idylls*, XXVII, 49.
- p. 314: *Idylls*, XI, 30.
- p. 316: *Idylls*, XI, 30.
- p. 317: *Idylls*, XV, 1. (From Jack Lindsay, *Theocritus*, Fanfrolico Press.)
- p. 318: *Idylls*, III, 1. (Translated by G. S. Fraser, in *Voices of the Past*, vol. 1, edited by James and Janet Maclean Todd.)
- p. 319: *Epigrams*, IV, 1. (From *Greek Lyric Poetry*, translated by Willis Barnstone. Copyright © by Bantam Books Inc., New York, 1962.)
- p. 320: *Idylls*, VII (From ibid.)
- p. 320: *Idylls*, I, 1. (Translated by Andrew Meade Miller. Copyright © 1971.)

LEONIDAS OF TARENTUM
- p. 325: A. S. F. Gow and D. L. Page, *The Greek Anthology: Hellenistic Epigrams*, Cambridge University Press (1958), No. 86. (From Kenneth Rexroth, *Poems from the Greek Anthology*. Reprinted with the permission of the University of Michigan Press.)

ANYTE
- p. 326: ibid., No. 17. (Translated by Rennell Rodd, in *The Oxford Book of Greek Verse in Translation*, edited by T. F. Higham and C. M. Bowra. Reprinted with the permission of the Clarendon Press, Oxford.)

DIOTIMUS
- p. 327: ibid., No. 10. (From William J. Philbin, *To You Simonides*. Reproduced by permission of the Dolmen Press Ltd, Dublin.)

CALLIMACHUS
- p. 328: ibid., No. 34.
- p. 328: ibid.
- p. 329: ibid., No. 2. (Translated by R. A. Furness, in *Translations from the Greek Anthology*, Jonathan Cape Ltd, London.)
- p. 329: ibid., No. 6. (From Dudley Fitts, *Poems from the Greek Anthology*, Faber & Faber Ltd, London. Copyright 1938, 1941, 1956 by New Directions Publishing Corporation. Reprinted with the permission of New Directions Publishing Corporation.)
- p. 329: ibid., No. 50. (From *Greek Lyric Poetry*, translated by Willis

Barnstone. Copyright © by Bantam Books Inc., New York, 1962.)

APOLLONIUS RHODIUS

p. 330: *Argonautica*, III, 938.

p. 332: *Argonautica*, IV, 123.

p. 334: *Argonautica*, I, 536. (Translated by George Allen, in *The Oxford Book of Greek Verse in Translation*, edited by T. F. Higham and C. M. Bowra. Reproduced with the permission of the Clarendon Press, Oxford.)

p. 335: *Argonautica*, III, 755. (From *Greek Poetry*, translated by F. L. Lucas. Everyman's Library edition. Published by J. M. Dent & Sons Ltd, London, and E. P. Dutton & Co. Inc., New York, and reproduced with their permission.)

HERODAS

p. 338: *Mimes*, III. (From Jack Lindsay, *Herodas*, Fanfrolico Press.)

p. 340: *Mimes*, I. (Translated by Richard Braun, in *Arion* (University of Texas), vol. I, No. 3, 1962.)

MOSCHUS

p. 342: A. S. F. Gow, *Bucolici Graeci*, Oxford University Press 1952, p. 151.

p. 342: ibid.

BION

p. 344: ibid., p. 153. (Translated by Peter Jay.)

ANTIPATER OF SIDON

p. 349: A. S. F. Gow and D. L. Page, *The Greek Anthology: Hellenistic Epigrams*, Cambridge University Press (1958), No. 13. (From Andrew Sinclair, *Selections from the Greek Anthology*, George Weidenfeld & Nicolson, London.)

MELEAGER

p. 350: ibid., No. 46. (From Dudley Fitts, *Poems from the Greek Anthology*, Faber & Faber, Ltd, London. Copyright 1938, 1941, 1956 by New Directions Publishing Corporation. Reprinted with the permission of New Directions Publishing Corporation.)

p. 350: ibid., No. 25. (From *Greek Lyric Poetry*, translated by Willis Barnstone. Copyright © by Bantam Books Inc., New York, 1962.)

SOURCES AND ACKNOWLEDGEMENTS

ANONYMOUS

- p. 351: J. M. Edmonds, *Greek Elegy and Iambus with the Anacreontea* (Loeb edition), Heinemann and Harvard University Press, II (1931), *Anacreontea*, p. 61, No. 33.
- p. 351: ibid., p. 53, No. 25.
- p. 352: ibid., p. 49, No. 20.
- p. 352: ibid., p. 83, No. 50.
- p. 353: ibid., p. 27, No. 7.
- p. 353: A. S. F. Gow and D. L. Page, *The Greek Anthology: Hellenistic Epigrams*, Cambridge University Press (1958), p. 201, No. 8. (Translated by R. A. Furness, in *Translations from the Greek Anthology*, Jonathan Cape Ltd, London.)
- p. 354: ibid., p. 207, No. 34. (From Dudley Fitts, *Poems from the Greek Anthology*, Faber & Faber Ltd, London. Copyright 1938, 1941, 1956 by New Directions Publishing Corporation. Reprinted with the permission of New Directions Publishing Corporation.)

POLYBIUS

- p. 357: II, 56.
- p. 359: I, 1.
- p. 363: VI, 56.
- p. 364: VI, 43.

JOSEPHUS

- p. 368: *Jewish War*, I, 417. (From G. A. Williamson, *Josephus: The Jewish War*, Penguin Books, Harmondsworth, 1959, 1970.)
- p. 369: *Jewish War*, II, 345. (From ibid.)
- p. 370: *Jewish War*, I, 1. (From ibid.)
- p. 371: *Jewish War*, VI, 420. (From ibid.)
- p. 372: *Jewish War*, I, 13. (From ibid.)
- p. 373: *Against Apion*, I, 1. (From Arnold J. Toynbee, *Greek Historical Thought*. Reprinted with the permission of J. M. Dent & Sons, London, and the Beacon Press, Boston.)

'LONGINUS'

- p. 376: *On the Sublime*, 36. (From T. S. Dorsch, *Classical Literary Criticism*, Penguin Books, Harmondsworth, 1965.)
- p. 377: *On the Sublime*, 7. (From ibid.)
- p. 378: *On the Sublime*, 14. (From ibid.)

LOLLIUS BASSUS

- p. 381: A. S. F. Gow and D. L. Page, *The Greek Anthology: The*

Garland of Philip, I, p. 177, No. I. (From Andrew Sinclair, *Selections from the Greek Anthology*, George Weidenfeld & Nicolson, London.)

MARCUS ARGENTARIUS
p. 382: ibid., p. 149, No. 5. (From *Greek Lyric Poetry*, translated by Willis Barnstone. Copyright © by Bantam Books Inc., New York, 1962.)

LUCILLIUS
p. 383: *Palatine Anthology*, XI, 159. (From Dudley Fitts, *Poems from the Greek Anthology*, Faber & Faber Ltd, London. Copyright 1938, 1941, 1956 by New Directions Publishing Corporation. Reprinted with the permission of New Directions Publishing Corporation.)

STRATO
p. 384: ibid., XII, 185. (Translated by R. A. Furness, in *Translations from the Greek Anthology*, Jonathan Cape Ltd, London.)

RUFINUS
p. 385: ibid., v. (From ibid.)

PTOLEMY
p. 386: ibid., IX, 577.

LUCIAN
p. 387: ibid., VII, 308.
p. 387: ibid., VII, 308. (From *Greek Poetry*, translated by F. L. Lucas, Everyman's Library edition. Published by J. M. Dent & Sons Ltd, London, and E. P. Dutton & Co. Inc., New York, and reprinted with their permission.)

PLUTARCH
p. 391: *Moralia* ('Which are the more crafty, land or water animals?'), 968 c.
p. 392: *Life of Antony*, 24, 6.
p. 396: *Life of Alexander*, 1.
p. 397: *Life of Sulla*, 13, 1. (From Rex Warner, *Plutarch: The Fall of the Roman Empire*, Penguin Books, Harmondsworth, 1958.)
p. 399: *Life of Theseus*, 1. (From Ian Scott-Kilvert, *Plutarch: The Rise*

and Fall of Athens: Nine Greek Lives, Penguin Books, Harmondsworth, 1960.)

p. 400: *Life of Solon*, 13. (From ibid.)

p. 403: *Life of Aristides*, 6. (From ibid.)

p. 406: *Life of Pericles*, 5. (From ibid.)

p. 409: *Life of Nicias*, 4. (From ibid.)

p. 412: *Life of Alcibiades*, 4. (From ibid.)

p. 413: *Life of Lysander*, 15. (From ibid.)

p. 415: *Life of Demosthenes*, 28. (From Ian Scott-Kilvert, *Plutarch: Decline of a City State*, Penguin Books, Harmondsworth, 1972.)

p. 417: *Life of Pyrrhus*, 14. (From ibid.)

p. 418: *Moralia* ('On having many friends'), 94 B. (Translated by F. C. Babbitt, in *Plutarch: Moralia*, Loeb Classical Library, vol. II. Reprinted with the permission of William Heinemann Ltd, London, and the Harvard University Press.)

p. 420: *Moralia* ('On inoffensive self-praise'), 546 B. (Translated by P. H. de Lacy and B. Einarson, ibid., Vol. VII.)

p. 421: *Moralia* ('On love'), Loeb Classical Library, vol. XV, p. 259, No. 137. (Translated by F. H. Sandbach.)

p. 422: *Moralia* ('On the soul'), in ibid., p. 317, No. 178. (Translated by C. J. Herington as 'De Anima', in *Arion* (University of Texas), vol. VII, No. 3, 1969.)

EPICTETUS

p. 423: Arrian, *Enchiridion*, 1.

p. 424: Arrian, *Discourses*, IV, I, II.

p. 425: Arrian, *Discourses*, III, 26, 2.

p. 425: Arrian, *Discourses*, I, 29, 1.

MARCUS AURELIUS

p. 427: *Meditations*, II, 5; II, 17; III, 5; III, 12; IV, 3; IV, 4; IV, 48; VI, 13; VII, 3; VIII, 24; IX, 21. (From Maxwell Staniforth, *Marcus Aurelius: Meditations*, Penguin Books, Harmondsworth, 1964.)

GALEN

p. 432: *On the Natural Faculties*, III, 10, 179. (Translated by A. J. Brock in *Galen: On the Natural Faculties*, Loeb Classical Library, vol. XV. Reprinted with the permission of William Heinemann Ltd, London, and the Harvard University Press.)

LUCIAN

p. 433: *Timon*, 54.

p. 435: *True Story (Vera Historia)*, II, 37. (From Lucian, *True History*, translated by Paul Turner, Calder & Boyars, London, 1958. Reprinted in Paul Turner, *Lucian: Satirical Sketches*, Penguin Books, Harmondsworth, 1961, 1968.)

p. 437: *Dialogues of the Gods*, 227. (From Paul Turner, *Lucian: Satirical Sketches*, Penguin Books, Harmondsworth, 1961, 1968.)

p. 439: *Alexander, or the False Prophet*, 6. (From ibid.)

p. 440: *Dialogues of the Courtesans*, 299. (From ibid.)

BABRIUS

p. 442: Fable 25.

p. 443: Fable 108.

HELIODORUS

p. 447: *Aethiopica*, I, 1. (From Heliodorus, *Ethiopian Story*, translated by Sir Walter Lamb. Everyman's Library edition. Translation © J. M. Dent & Sons Ltd, 1961. Reprinted with the permission of J. M. Dent & Sons Ltd, London, and E. P. Dutton & Co. Inc., New York.)

p. 449: *Aethiopica*, I, 5. (From ibid.)

p. 450: *Aethiopica*, VI, 9. (From ibid.)

LONGUS

p. 452: *Daphnis and Chloe*, IV, 1. (From Paul Turner, *Longus: Daphnis and Chloe*, Penguin Books, Harmondsworth, 1956, 1968.)

p. 453: *Daphnis and Chloe*, IV, 38. (From ibid.)

XENOPHON OF EPHESUS

p. 454: *Ephesiaca*, I, 10, 8.

PLOTINUS

p. 461: VI, 9, 6. (From A. H. Armstrong, *Plotinus*, George Allen & Unwin Ltd, London.)

p. 463: I, 6, 7. (From ibid.)

*

SOME BOOKS

ANDREWES, A., *The Greeks*, Hutchinson, London, 1967.

ARNOTT, P. D., *An Introduction to the Greek World*, Macmillan, London, 1967.

BALDRY, H. C., *Ancient Greek Literature in its Living Context*, Thames & Hudson, London, 1968.

BOWRA, C. M., *The Greek Experience*, Weidenfeld & Nicolson, London, 1957; revised edition, Mentor, New York, 1969.

BURN, A. R., *The Pelican History of Greece*, Penguin Books, Harmondsworth, 1966.

CARY, M., and HAARHOFF, T. J., *Life and Thought in the Greek and Roman World*, Methuen, London, 1940; paperback, 1961.

DODDS, E. R., *The Greeks and the Irrational*, University of California Press, 1951; paperback, 1968.

FINLEY, M. I., *The Ancient Greeks*, Chatto & Windus, London, 1963.

GRANT, M., *The Ancient Mediterranean*, Weidenfeld & Nicolson, London, 1969; paperback, New American Library, New York, 1971.

GREENE, W. C., *Achievement in Greece*, Allen & Unwin, London, 1967.

HADAS, M., *A History of Greek Literature*, Columbia University Press, 1950; paperback, 1962.

HAMMOND, N. G. L., *A History of Greece to 322 B.C.*, Oxford University Press, 1959.

HIGGINBOTHAM, J., *Greek and Latin Literature: a Comparative Study*, Methuen, London, 1969.

HIGHET, G., *The Classical Tradition*, Clarendon Press, Oxford, 1949; paperback, Oxford University Press, 1967.

HOOPER, F., *Greek Realities*, Charles Scribner's Sons, New York, 1967.

KITTO, H. D. F., *The Greeks*, Penguin Books, Harmondsworth, 1951.

LESLEY, A., *A History of Greek Literature*, Methuen, London, 1966.

LIVINGSTONE, R. (ed.), *The Legacy of Greece*, Clarendon Press, Oxford, 1921; paperback, Oxford University Press, 1970.

LLOYD-JONES, H. (ed.), *The Greeks*, Watts, London, 1962.

RIDLEY, M. R., *Studies in Three Literatures*, Dent, London, 1962.

ROSE, H. J., *A Handbook of Greek Literature*, Methuen, London, 1934; paperback, 1966.

SNELL, B., *The Discovery of the Mind*, Blackwell, Oxford, 1953.

STOBART, J. C., *The Glory that was Greece*, Sidgwick & Jackson, London, 1911; reprinted, 1960.

TARN, W. W., *Hellenistic Civilization*, Edward Arnold, London, 1927; 3rd edition, revised with G. T. Griffith, 1952; paperback, Methuen, London, 1966.

ZIMMERN, A., *The Greek Commonwealth*, Clarendon Press, Oxford, 1911; paperback, Oxford University Press, 1961.

*

Among the numerous recent writings on the problems of translation, the following books and publications may be found useful:

ARROWSMITH, W., and SHATTUCK, R. (eds.), *The Craft and Context of Translation: a Critical Symposium*, University of Texas Press for the Humanities Research Center, Austin, Texas, 1961; paperback, Anchor Books, New York, 1964.

BROWER, R. A. (ed.), *On Translation*, Oxford University Press, 1959; paperback, 1966.

DAY LEWIS, C., *On Translating Poetry*, Second Jackson Knight Memorial Lecture, University of Exeter, 1970.

HOLMES, J. S. (ed.), *The Nature of Translation* (Bratislava Conference), Mouton, The Hague, 1968.

SAVORY, T. H., *The Art of Translation*, Jonathan Cape, London, 1957; revised edition, 1968; paperback, 1969.

The journals *Delos*, *Arion*, *Agenda*, and *Ariel*.

INDEX

MORE ABOUT PENGUINS

Penguinews, which appears every month, contains details of all the new books issued by Penguins as they are published. From time to time it is supplemented by *Penguins in Print*, which is a complete list of all available books published by Penguins. (There are well over four thousand of these.)

A specimen copy of *Penguinews* will be sent to you free on request, and you can become a subscriber for the price of the postage. For a year's issues (including the complete lists) please send 30p if you live in the United Kingdom, or 60p if you live elsewhere. Just write to Dept EP, Penguin Books Ltd Harmondsworth, Middlesex, enclosing a cheque or postal order, and your name will be added to the mailing list.

Note: *Penguinews* and *Penguins in Print* are not available in the U.S.A. or Canada

ROMAN LITERATURE

Michael Grant

In this book Michael Grant describes the brilliant talents of the leading ancient writers in the Latin Language, and indicates their importance for the present day. Their achievement is illustrated by passages from their works, quoted in English prose and verse translations from a wide range of different periods, and interpreted in terms of each author's own life experience, and impact on his community. Something is also said of the social, educational, and political conditions in which they worked, and of the Greek and other elements which they absorbed from their background and environment without, in many cases, sacrificing their own highly distinctive originality. Professor Grant dwells on their works which have survived rather than those which have not, and writes of the influence that these have exerted upon the literature and thought of western Europe at many epochs between then and now.

ROMAN READINGS

Edited by Michael Grant

'He is an inspirer, perhaps the greatest popularizer we have known in this century, and the English-speaking world has good reason to be everlastingly grateful for it' – *Greece and Rome*

In this collection of translations from Latin prose and verse, Michael Grant gives precedence to writers of the central classical tradition, such as Cicero, Virgil, and Ovid. He has deliberately kept to the main highway of Latin literature in an attempt to reinstate its central figures who, he feels, are at present too little admired. The translations he has chosen are comprehensible, pleasing, and illuminating, and do much to narrow the gap between Roman writers and the readers of today. The selections are prefaced by introductions to the authors and appreciations of their influence on European thought.

Michael Grant has translated the following for
The Penguin Classics

TACITUS

The Annals of Imperial Rome

and

CICERO

Halcyon . Selected Political Speeches

On the Good Life

Selected Works